Santiago Canyon College
Library

WESTERN MUSIC AND RACE

This contributory volume, the first book of its kind, provides a snapshot of the ways in which discourse about Western music and race overlapped and became intertwined during the period from Wagner's death to the rise of National Socialism and fascism elsewhere in Europe. At these two framing moments such overlapping was at its most explicit: Wagner's racially inflected 'regeneration theories' were at one end and institutionalised cultural racism at the other. The book seeks to provide insights into the key national contexts in which such discourses circulated in the interim period, as well as to reflect a range of archival, historical, critical and philosophical approaches to the topic. National contexts covered include Germany, France, Spain, Italy, Great Britain and North America. The contributors to the volume are leading scholars in the field, and the book contains many illustrative music examples and images which bring the subject-matter to life.

JULIE BROWN is Senior Lecturer in Music at Royal Holloway, University of London. She publishes on early twentieth-century music and film music, and is author of *Bartók and the Grotesque* (2007).

WESTERN MUSIC AND RACE

EDITED BY
JULIE BROWN

CAMBRIDGE UNIVERSITY PRESS
Cambridge, New York, Melbourne, Madrid, Cape Town, Singapore, São Paulo

Cambridge University Press
The Edinburgh Building, Cambridge CB2 8RU, UK

Published in the United States of America by Cambridge University Press, New York

www.cambridge.org
Information on this title: www.cambridge.org/9780521838870

© Cambridge University Press 2007

This publication is in copyright. Subject to statutory exception
and to the provisions of relevant collective licensing agreements,
no reproduction of any part may take place without
the written permission of Cambridge University Press.

First published 2007

Printed in the United Kingdom at the University Press, Cambridge

A catalogue record for this publication is available from the British Library

ISBN 978-0-521-83887-0 hardback

Cambridge University Press has no responsibility for
the persistence or accuracy of URLs for external or
third-party internet websites referred to in this publication,
and does not guarantee that any content on such
websites is, or will remain, accurate or appropriate.

For my mother

Contents

List of illustrations and music examples	*page* ix
Notes on contributors	xi
Introduction. Music, history, trauma: Western music and race, 1883–1933	xiv

PART I OVERVIEWS AND CRITICAL FRAMEWORKS — 1

1 Erasure: displacing and misplacing race in twentieth-century music historiography
   Philip V. Bohlman — 3

2 Secrets, lies and transcriptions: revisions on race, black music and culture
   Guthrie P. Ramsey, Jr — 24

3 'Gypsy violins' and 'hot rhythms': race, popular music and governmentality
   Brian Currid — 37

4 The concept of race in German musical discourse
   Pamela M. Potter — 49

PART II RACIAL IDEOLOGUES — 63

5 Strange love; or, How we learned to stop worrying and love Wagner's *Parsifal*
   John Deathridge — 65

6 Otto Weininger and musical discourse in turn-of-the-century Vienna
   Julie Brown — 84

7 Ancestral voices: anti-Semitism and Ernest Bloch's racial conception of art
   Klára Móricz — 102

8 Percy Grainger and American Nordicism
   Malcolm Gillies and David Pear — 115

9   'Persian composer-pianist baffles': Kaikhosru Sorabji
    Nalini Ghuman   125

PART III   LOCAL CONTEXTS   145

10 Race and nation: musical acclimatisation and the *chansons
    populaires* in Third Republic France
    Jann Pasler   147

11 Anti-Semitic discourse in German writing on music,
    1900–1933
    Erik Levi   168

12 Italian music and racial discourses during the Fascist period
    Roberto Illiano and Massimiliano Sala   182

13 Romanticism, technology and the masses: Honegger and the
    aesthetic allure of French fascism
    Jane F. Fulcher   201

14 Racial discourses in Spanish musical literature, 1915–1939
    Gemma Pérez-Zalduondo   216

15 Manuel de Falla, flamenco and Spanish identity
    Michael Christoforidis   230

16 'The old sweet Anglo-Saxon spell': racial discourses and the
    American reception of British music, 1895–1933
    Alain Frogley   244

17 Rethinking the *revue nègre*: black musical theatre in
    inter-war Paris
    Andy Fry   258

Index   276

Illustrations and music examples

Figure 1.1: Empress Elisabeth's wedding gift (Multiple texts from the Banat, Romanian, and Serbian border region) *page* 13

Figure 1.2: Table of contents from Wilhelm Doegen (ed.), *Unter fremden Völkern: Eine neue Völkerkunde* (Berlin: Otto Stollberg, Verlag für Politik und Wirtschaft, 1925) 16

Figure 1.3: Photographs of Southern African drummers and Africans from Doegen's *Unter fremden Völkern* (facing p. 64) 17

Figure 1.4: Photograph of Gurka prisoners dancing, 'men dressed as girls' (Doegen, bottom of page facing p. 80) 18

Figure 1.5: 'Basic forms of musical thinking within major racial areas'. (Reproduced after Fritz Metzler, 'Dur, Moll und "Kirchentöne" als musikalischer Rassenausdruck'. In Guido Waldmann (ed.), *Zur Tonalität des deutschen Volksliedes* (Wolfenbüttel: Kallmeyer, 1938), pp. 1–27 (map between pp. 24 and 25) 20

Example 1.1: 'The Gypsy Laddie' (Child Ballad no. 200) 22

Figure 3.1: 'A World Full of Music': an advertisement from 1936 42

Example 5.1: Recurring dissonance (pitch identity fixed) 78

Example 5.2: *Parsifal*, Act I, bars 325–6 78

Example 5.3: *Parsifal*, Act I, bars 528–9 78

Example 5.4: *Parsifal*, Act II, bars 994–6 78

Example 5.5: *Parsifal*, Act III, bars 1–2 sketch (Nationalarchiv der Richard-Wagner-Stiftung Bayreuth, A III m 4^1 recto) 78

Example 5.6: *Parsifal*, Act III, bars 1–2 (final version) 79

Example 5.7: *Parsifal*, Act III, bars 623–4 79

Example 9.1a: Sorabji, *Opus Clavicembalisticum*, Passacaglia with eighty-one variations: 'Quasi tambura' variation 135

Example 9.1b: Passacaglia theme 135

Example 9.2: *Chaleur*, opening 138

Example 9.3a: Theme of *Symphonic Variations*, opening phrase — 140

Example 9.3b: 'Quasi rāg indiana' — 140

Example 10.1: 'Chanson mexicaine' from J. B. Weckerlin, *Echos du temps passé* — 149

Figure 10.1: Programme of the Cercle Saint-Simon, 3 June 1885 — 153

Example 10.2: 'La Pernette, version de la Franche Comté', from Julien Tiersot, *Mélodies populaires des provinces de France* (1888) — 162

Example 10.3: 'La Pernette, version primitive and version ornée', from Vincent d'Indy, *Chansons populaires du Vivarais* (1892) — 165

Example 10.4: 'La Pernette, version ornée' under selections of an Alleluia verse from Ascension Sunday and the Bach chorale, *Jesus Christus unser Heiland* — 166

Figure 17.1: 'Mantan' and 'Sleep 'n' Eat' in Spike Lee's *Bamboozled* © MM, New Line Productions, Inc. All rights reserved. Photo by David Lee. Photo appears courtesy of New Line Productions. — 259

Figure 17.2: Newspaper cartoon of Florence Mills and Johnny Hudgins in *Blackbirds of 1926* — 262

Figure 17.3: Paul Colin's poster for *Blackbirds of 1929* — 264

Example 17.1: 'Porgy' from *Blackbirds of 1928/9* (music, Jimmy McHugh; lyrics, Dorothy Fields), sung by Aida Ward, first eight bars of chorus — 266

Example 17.2: 'Diga Diga Doo' from *Blackbirds of 1928/9* (music, Jimmy McHugh; lyrics, Dorothy Fields), sung by Adelaide Hall, first sixteen bars of chorus. — 267

Figure 17.4: Newspaper cartoon of *Blackbirds of 1929* — 268

Figure 17.5: Newspaper cartoon of three stars of *Blackbirds of 1929* — 269

Notes on contributors

Philip V. Bohlman is the Mary Werkman Professor of the Humanities and of Music at the University of Chicago. He is also currently President of the Society for Ethnomusicology. He has published extensively, and among his most recent publications are *World Music: A Very Short Introduction*; *The Music of European Nationalism*; *Jüdische Volksmusik – Eine mitteleuropäische Geistesgeschichte*; and *Jewish Music and Modernity*. He also co-edited with Ronald Radano *Music and the Racial Imagination*.

Julie Brown is Senior Lecturer in Music at Royal Holloway, University of London. She publishes on early twentieth-century music and film music, and is author of 'Schoenberg's Early Wagnerisms: Atonality and the Redemption of Ahasuerus' (*Cambridge Opera Journal*) and *Bartók and the Grotesque*. She is now preparing a book on Schoenberg provisionally entitled *Re-reading Schoenberg*.

Michael Christoforidis is a Lecturer in Music at the University of Melbourne, and formerly a research associate at the Instituto Complutense de Ciencias Musicales (Madrid) and at the Archivo Manuel de Falla (Granada). He has published extensively on aspects of twentieth-century Spanish music and is currently completing a monograph on *Constructions of Hispanic Music in Belle Epoque Paris*.

Brian Currid is a freelance translator and independent scholar in Berlin. He has taught at various institutions in Germany and the US, and published widely, including his contribution '"Aint I People?": Voicing National Fantasy' in Radano and Bohlman (eds.), *Music and the Racial Imagination*. He is author of *A National Acoustics: Music and Mass Publicity in Weimar and Nazi Germany*.

John Deathridge is King Edward Professor of Music at King's College London. His recent work includes *Dokumente und Text zu 'Lohengrin'* with Klaus Döge and 'The Invention of German Music *c.* 1800' in the volume *Unity and Diversity in European Culture*.

Alain Frogley is Professor of Music History at the University of Connecticut. He has published extensively on music of the late nineteenth and twentieth centuries, particularly that of Britain and America, and on Beethoven. His major publications include *Vaughan Williams's Ninth Symphony* and *Vaughan Williams Studies*.

Andy Fry is Lecturer in Music at King's College London. He completed his graduate studies at the University of Oxford and has published articles on Josephine Baker and jazz in inter-war Paris. His book on *African-American Music and Musicians in Paris Through the Fifties* is forthcoming.

Jane F. Fulcher is Professor of Music at Indiana University. She is an expert on French nineteenth- and twentieth-century music in its political and cultural context and author of *The Nation's Image: French Grand Opera as Politics and Politicized Art*; *French Cultural Politics and Music: From the Dreyfus Affair to the First World War*; and *The Composer as Intellectual: Music and Ideology in France 1914–1940*. She is contributing editor of *Debussy and His World* and *Music and Society from Monteverdi to Adorno*.

Nalini Ghuman is Assistant Professor of Music at Mill's College. She received her Ph.D. from the University of California at Berkeley, where she was a Fellow of the Townsend Center for the Humanities and was awarded an AMS 50 Alvin Johnson Dissertation Fellowship. She is now working on the book *India in the English Musical Imagination, 1890–1940* for publication.

Malcolm Gillies is President and Vice-Chancellor of City University London. A specialist on Bartók and Percy Grainger, he has authored and edited a large number of publications including *Bartók Companion*; *Bartók Remembered*; and (co-edited with David Pear) *Portrait of Percy Grainger*; *Grainger on Music*; and *Self-Portrait of Percy Grainger*.

Roberto Illiano is General Secretary of the Centro Studi Opera omnia Luigi Boccherini in Lucca, Italy. He is editor of *Italian Music during the Fascist Period*, co-editor of *Muzio Clementi: Studies and Prospects*; and is working on the monograph *Luigi Dallapiccola: un percorso di studio* (with Luca Sala) and on the edited collection *Music and Dictatorship in Europe and Latin America* (with Massimiliano Sala).

Erik Levi is Reader in Music at Royal Holloway, University of London. He has published widely on aspects of German musical life from the 1920s to the end of the Second World War, including *Music in the Third Reich*. He is currently working on a book for Yale University Press provisionally entitled *Mozart and the Nazis*.

Klára Móricz is currently a visiting Valentine professor at Amherst College. Formerly a staff member of the Budapest Bartók Archives, she is editor of a forthcoming volume of the Béla Bartók Complete Critical Edition. She has published articles on Bartók, Liszt, Fauré, Schoenberg and Bloch. Her book *Jewish Identities: Nationalism, Racism and Utopianism in Twentieth-Century Art Music* is forthcoming from University of California Press.

Jann Pasler is Professor of Music at University of California at San Diego. She has published widely on contemporary American music and French music, edited *Confronting Stravinsky: Man, Musician and Modernist*, and has two books forthcoming – *Useful Music, or Why Music Mattered in Third Republic France*, volume 1, and *Writing Through Music* – and one in preparation, *Music, Race and Colonialism in Fin-de-siècle France*.

David Pear is an Associate Professor of The Australian National University. He has co-authored or co-edited with Malcolm Gillies a number of books including *The All-Round Man: Selected Letters of Percy Grainger 1914–1961*; *Portrait of Percy Grainger*; *Grainger on Music*; and *Self-Portrait of Percy Grainger*.

Gemma Pérez-Zalduondo is Professor of Music History at the Universidad de Granada. She has published widely on Hispanic music and concepts of nationalism. Her major publications include *El Compositor José Muñoz Molleda: de la Generación del 27 al franquismo*; and *La música en España durante el franquismo a través de la legislación (1936–1951)*.

Pamela M. Potter is Professor of Musicology and German at University of Wisconsin-Madison and has written extensively on twentieth-century German music and politics. Her major publications include *Most German of the Arts: Musicology and Society from the Weimar Republic to the End of Hitler's Reich*; and *Music and German National Identity*, which she co-edited.

Guthrie P. Ramsey, Jr is Associate Professor of Music History at the University of Pennsylvania. He is a specialist in African-American and American music, jazz, cultural studies, popular music, film studies and historiography and author of *Race Music: Black Cultures from Bebop to Hip-Hop*, which was named outstanding book of the year by IASPM (International Association for the Study of Popular Music). His current book project is *In Walked Bud: Earl 'Bud' Powell and the Modern Jazz Challenge*.

Massimiliano Sala is Vice-President of the Centro Studi Opera omnia Luigi Boccherini in Lucca, Italy. He is on the advisory board for the Opera omnia of Luigi Boccherini and Muzio Clementi, is editor of *Giovanni Battista Viotti: A Composer between the Two Revolutions*; and is working both on the monograph *Muzio Clementi* and the edited volume *Domenico Scarlatti* (with Dean W. Sutcliffe).

Introduction
Music, history, trauma: Western music and race, 1883–1933

Julie Brown

> The aim of judgment in historical or literary-critical discourse, a forensic rather than juridical sort of inquiry, is not that of determining guilt or innocence. It is to change history into memory: to make a case for what should be remembered.[1]

Audiences of today understand a wide range of musics in terms of race. 'African-American Music' is a catch-all label for a variety of musics for which historical, cultural and biological identity are assumed to be irreducible constituent elements. The popular version, 'black music', is even more starkly racial. But concert and operatic music may also have racial meanings for contemporary audiences. The arts media have given wide coverage to recent scholarship about Wagner's anti-Semitism. Decca's 'Entartete Musik' series and related exhibitions have highlighted the fate of Jewish music and musicians under the Nazis, a development that has coincided with the reappearance of music by composers such as Franz Schreker, Erik Wolfgang Korngold, Viktor Ullmann and others in concert programmes. Israeli pianist-conductor Daniel Barenboim's 2001 personal challenge to the exclusion of Wagner from Israeli concert halls has also received wide media coverage, as has his co-founding with Edward Said of the Israeli–Arab peace ensemble, West-Eastern Divan Orchestra, and more recently a centre in Jerusalem for the study of Arab music.[2] Yet if we ask how wide a perspective professional academic work has offered on the matter, the answer is that its perspective has generally been limited. As Ronald Radano and Philip V. Bohlman note in *Music and the Racial Imagination*, the 'specter of race' has until recently largely been erased from historical and musicological writing.[3] Of the historical, ethnographic and theoretical work done, most has concentrated on three broad areas: the anti-Semitic and so-called regeneration theories of

---

[1] Geoffrey H. Hartman, 'Judging Paul de Man', in *Minor Prophecies: The Literary Essay in the Culture Wars* (Cambridge, MA: Harvard University Press, 1991), p. 148.
[2] 'Barenboim's Hopes for Mid East Peace': BBC interview, 27 April 2006. Accessible in the UK only: search for 'Barenboim's hopes for Mid East peace' under BBC Audio and Video at http://search.bbc.co.uk/.
[3] Ronald Radano and Philip V. Bohlman (eds.), *Music and the Racial Imagination* (University of Chicago Press, 2000).

Wagner,[4] music and cultural policy of the Nazi period,[5] and African-American music[6] – that is, on repertoires and discourses about music whose claims to racial meaning are overt.

The present volume explores the waters separating the first two of these areas of professional interest and asks how those topics could have remained islands for so long. In seventeen chapters manifesting a range of archival, historical and critical approaches, the contributors to this book focus on discursive entanglements between Western art music and race in the years (roughly) 1883 to 1933, that is, between Wagner's death and the rise of National Socialism. If the general absence of 'race' from musicology is in itself surprising, perhaps more surprising is its absence from analyses of Western music during a period framed by some of the most explicit discussions of the relationship available to us, and whose framing moments are subject to the most intense scrutiny of the music–race connection to be found in recent scholarship: at one end, Wagner's anti-Semitic and 'regeneration theories'; at the other, the institutionalised cultural racism of Nazi Germany and other European fascist regimes, a racism which, among far worse terrors involving the mass murder not only of Germany's 'inferior races' but also its own 'degenerates', such as homosexuals, the handicapped and the aged, demonised both Jewish and African-American musical influences as degenerate, and sometimes even conflated the two – as in the famous poster for Krenek's *Jonny spielt auf*, which depicts a black

---

[4] See for example Jacob Katz, *The Darker Side of Genius: Richard Wagner's Anti-Semitism* (Hanover, NH: Brandeis University Press, 1986); Dieter Borchmeyer, 'The Question of Anti-Semitism', in Ulrich Müller and Peter Wapnewski (eds.), *Wagner Handbook*, trans. and ed. John Deathridge (Cambridge, MA: Harvard University Press, 1992), pp. 166–85; Barry Millington, 'Nuremberg Trial: Is There Anti-Semitism in *Die Meistersinger*?', *Cambridge Opera Journal* 3/3 (1991), 247–60; and Millington, 'Wagner and the Jews', in Barry Millington (ed.), *The Wagner Compendium: A Guide to Wagner's Life and Music* (London: Thames and Hudson, 1992), pp. 161–4; Paul Lawrence Rose, *Wagner: Race and Revolution* (New Haven: Yale University Press, 1992).

[5] See for example Albrecht Dümling and Peter Girth (eds.), *Entartete Musik: Dokumentation und Kommentar zur Düsseldorfer Ausstellung von 1938*, rev. and exp. edition (Düsseldorf: DKV, 1993); Fred K. Prieberg, *Musik im NS-Staat* (Frankfurt am Main: Fischer Taschenbuch, 1982); Alan E. Steinweis, *Art, Ideology, and Economics in Nazi Germany: The Reich Chambers of Music, Theatre, and the Visual Arts* (Chapel Hill: University of North Carolina, 1996); Erik Levi, *Music in the Third Reich* (Basingstoke: Macmillan, 1994); Michael H. Kater, *Composers of the Nazi Era: Eight Portraits* (New York: Oxford University Press, 2000); Reinhold Brinkmann and Christoph Wolff (eds.), *Driven Into Paradise: The Musical Migration From Nazi Germany to the United States* (Berkeley: University of California Press, 1999).

[6] See for example Guthrie P. Ramsey, Jr, *Race Music: Black Cultures from Bebop to Hip-Hop* (Berkeley: University of California Press, 2003); Ronald Radano, *Lying up a Nation: Race and Black Music* (University of Chicago Press, 2003); Radano, 'Denoting Difference: The Writing of the Black Spirituals', *Critical Inquiry* 22 (1996), 506–44; Radano, 'Hot Fantasies: American Modernism and the Idea of Black Rhythm', in Radano and Bohlman (eds.), *Music and the Racial Imagination*, pp. 459–80; Ingrid Monson, 'The Problem with White Hipness: Race, Gender, and Cultural Conceptions of Jazz Historical Discourses', *Journal of the American Musicological Society* 48 (1995), 396–422; Eric Lott, *Love and Theft: Blackface Minstrelsy and the American Working Class* (New York: Oxford University Press, 1995). Ramsey reviews some important literature in his chapter in the present volume.

American saxophone player wearing a Star of David. It seems astonishing that so little could have been written about the interim period.

This book serves to demonstrate that in key Western centres the issue of race was very much alive during this interim period. Contributors analyse racially inflected musical discourse relating to a variety of geographical centres and language contexts: Austria-Germany (Potter, Deathridge, Brown), France (Pasler, Fry, Fulcher), North America (Frogley, Ramsey), Spain (Pérez-Zalduondo, Christoforidis), Britain (Ghuman, Móricz), Italy (Illiano and Sala). Case studies of individual composers reveal a variety of ways in which the language of race and its associated concepts were co-opted (Christoforidis, Gillies and Pear, Móricz, Fulcher, Ghuman); as do case studies of particular centres of performance activity, such as the *revue nègre* (Fry), and whole spheres of cultural activity (Currid, Bohlman). Several authors trace mutations that Wagner's regeneration theories underwent in the hands of others (Levi, Brown, Móricz). Given this evidence of the variety of ways in which the concept of 'race' circulated in musical discourse during our period, one might legitimately ask why this is the first volume to treat the period in this light.

One explanation for the scholarly silence is the fact that critical and theoretically informed engagement with the way music has, and does, figure in the racial imagination is a relatively recent development in musicology. Radano and Bohlman's book is the first major collection of essays to ask a variety of questions about the discursive category of race in connection with a range of musics. However, another explanation is that for the period tackled the topic amounts to a type of taboo. The largely self-imposed suppression of Wagner's music by Israeli orchestras and concert halls, the anguished and angry responses of some Israelis to Barenboim's breaking of that musical and cultural taboo, and Barenboim's implied and actual challenge that they begin to renegotiate a position for Wagner in their cultural lives are a version of what I am referring to. This sequence of events in the recent cultural life of Israel is a very public expression of the fact that for many Israelis Wagner's music remains indelibly linked with the trauma of the Holocaust. It is not just that Wagner also generated anti-Semitic writings of his own; it is that his legacy came to be directly associated with Nazi ideology by virtue of the ideological and personal embrace that his widow and heirs offered Hitler and National Socialism generally; many Holocaust survivors will also have listened to Wagner as background music to Nazi propaganda, watched footage of Hitler arriving in Bayreuth and being greeted by the Wagner family, and so on. It is not for those of us who have not been through the same experience to seek to deny or underplay the lasting psychological effects of these sorts of memories and associations on Holocaust survivors, even if Barenboim and indeed some other Israelis clearly feel that it may be time to try, tentatively, to move on. Notwithstanding the particularity of the Wagner problem for

Israel, the cultural dynamics to which reappearance of his music in its concert halls has given rise might tell us something about the erasure of other race-linked topics from early twentieth-century music history. In a more muted way the whole musical history of race, and especially the musical history of race in the early decades of the twentieth century – mainly, though not exclusively, in Europe – seem marked by a similar type of trauma.

The idea that a psychoanalytic concept such as trauma might be useful when elucidating the relationship between the present and the past is one that Dominick LaCapra and others explore in their work on the Holocaust.[7] LaCapra feels that a number of the issues arising from such work have broader historiographical import: the significant heightening of the effect of canonisation which occurs when a historian effectively sacralises an historical event is one; another is the tendency, not limited to attempts to represent the Holocaust, to repress deeply unpleasant events when writing history. For him the rhetoric of the unspeakable attaching to the catastrophic events in Germany and Poland serves as a pointer to other levels of historical repression, and ultimately to what he identifies as the return of the repressed in connection with the Holocaust. Recording and processing historical events in memory and writing mimics, in the case of such catastrophic events, the psychological mechanism of repression. We need to recognise the terrible effects of traumatising events such as these on immediate victims and survivors above all; however, we should acknowledge that there can also be a 'transferential relation between the historian or theorist and the object of analysis':

> Victims of severely traumatizing events may never fully escape possession by, or recover from, a shattering past, and a response to trauma may well involve 'acting-out' (or emotionally repeating a still-present past) in those directly affected by it and *at least muted trauma in attentive analysts and commentators*.[8]

The role played by canons in history and historiography has a bearing on this effect – not only canonical texts, but canonical events, and canonical readings of canonical texts and events. It is partly because the Holocaust is not only a canonised, but also a sacralised, event in twentieth-century history that certain issues attaching to it 'tend to be avoided, marginalized, repressed, or denied'.[9] The two processes – canonisation and marginalisation – are mutually reinforcing for LaCapra, because 'In the case of traumatic events, canonization involves the mitigation or covering over of wounds and creating the impression that nothing really disruptive has occurred.'[10]

---

[7] Dominick LaCapra, *Representing the Holocaust: History, Theory, Trauma* (Ithaca: Cornell University Press, 1994). See also LaCapra, *History and Memory after Auschwitz* (Ithaca: Cornell University Press, 1998), *Writing History, Writing Trauma* (Baltimore: The Johns Hopkins University Press, 2000), *History in Transit: Experience, Identity, Critical Theory* (Ithaca: Cornell University Press, 2004).
[8] LaCapra, *Representing the Holocaust*, p. xii. Emphasis added.   [9] Ibid., p. 23.   [10] Ibid.

The notion that a type of 'muted trauma' has characterised post-war discussions of music from this period strikes me as a persuasive explanation for the extent to which race has been absent from post-war discussions of music. Its historical repression therefore adds to Philip Bohlman's detailing of ways in which race is displaced in discourse and otherwise erased from history (this volume). The Holocaust is the point of rupture between a period of discursive openness about race as a determining feature of cultural and specifically musical production on the one hand, and of silence about it on the other. In order to understand the relative absence in the second half of the twentieth century of discussions of music and race emanating from the late nineteenth- and early twentieth-century European musical imagination, it is important, I would argue, to consider the Holocaust's traumatising effects.

Our subject in this book is admittedly not the limit case that historiography of the Holocaust is: no contributor engages directly with the Holocaust – composers who survived the concentration and death camps, for instance, or music-making within the camps.[11] The cultural issues at stake here are of a different order. They are questions of historiography. To what extent can we ever know how discourses of a period considerably distant from our own were understood by its contemporaries? – a question raised long ago by Gary Tomlinson and others, including Michael André Bernstein in the specific context of pre-Holocaust histories.[12] (Bernstein is critical of the misuse of hindsight in historical writing: the tendency to regard as portentously foreseeable events that we know proved significant. In our historical accounts we are in danger of denying the situation of actors at the time: their own sense of an unknown future, their lacking of our wisdom of hindsight.) To what extent should the reputation of a particular composer and his or her legacy be affected by knowledge of his or her subscription to an odious ideology (Fulcher on Honegger)? Is it possible or desirable to 'rescue' the 'purely musical' from non- or extra-musical elements now considered 'tainted' – a long-standing preoccupation of Wagner studies confronted here again by John Deathridge. In her book *The Quest for Voice* Lydia Goehr examines some of the philosophical justifications of this discursive move.[13] Here Philip Bohlman considers the 'purely musical' to be a notion which positively displaces culture and 'race'. Notwithstanding the different order of magnitude between our issues and those of Holocaust scholars, it remains that

---

[11] On this subject, see Shirli Gilbert, *Music in the Holocaust: Confronting Life in the Nazi Ghettos and Camps* (New York: Oxford University Press, 2005).

[12] See especially Tomlinson, *Music in Renaissance Magic: Toward a Historiography of Others* (Chicago University Press, 1993); Bernstein, *Foregone Conclusions: Against Apocalyptic History* (Berkeley: University of California Press, 1994).

[13] See Lydia Goehr, *The Quest For Voice: On Music, Politics, and the Limits of Philosophy* (Oxford: Clarendon Press, 1998).

networks of racialist ideas linked political agenda and cultural practice in complicated ways, such that discussions about music remain linked in the historical imagination, albeit sometimes distantly, with those that led to the extermination of the Jews and Gypsies. The catastrophic events of the Nazi era remain a communal wound, to borrow Lawrence Langer's words; and its repercussions can be traced in many aspects of post-war life and culture and scholarship.

Engaging a range of archival, historical and critical approaches, contributors to the present volume consider a number of mid- to late nineteenth-century developments that played a part in the convergence of racial and musical discourses during the period roughly 1883–1933. Principal among these nineteenth-century developments were global encounters whose imperial desires and racial fears often stood in tense opposition, burgeoning nationalist movements within and beyond continental Europe, and the emerging biologies of race which fascinated nation-builders; there was also the immense shadow cast over Western art music by racially inflected Wagnerism, not only during Wagner's life but perhaps even more so in the decades following his death. Contributors are less concerned with asserting essential links between music and race than with examining ways in which others, including composers themselves, have done so during the period in question. As such, Radano and Bohlman's understanding of 'race' as a discursively unstable signification ('not a fixity, but a signification saturated with profound cultural meaning and whose discursive instability heightens its affective power'[14]) remains relevant to the approaches to the topic here. Guthrie Ramsey's tripartite conceptualisation of race is likewise enabling: he suggests (in this volume) that one might think in terms of 'social race' ('the social experience of being a racialised subject'), 'cultural race' ('the performative dimensions of the social experience') and 'theoretical race' (the 'dense academic (and deliciously speculative) treatments of race in contemporary cultural theory').

Racial categories created primarily by Europeans as a result of their contact with, and subordination of, non-European peoples through colonialism and imperialism vary significantly during this time; sometimes they reflect very closely race science's focus on physical difference, at others they co-opt the term to signify less specific identities; often they move smoothly from one to the other. As the essays in this book clearly demonstrate, 'race' was an extremely malleable category during this period, and for this reason the approach to race taken in this book emphasises the process of racialising. Pamela M. Potter describes much of the language used by writers and composers in German contexts as 'race jargon'; 'race' as 'buzzword'. Gemma Pérez-Zalduondo traces a similar sort of discursive

---

[14] Radano and Bohlman, 'Music and Race, Their Past, Their Presence', in *Music and the Racial Imagination*, p. 5.

looseness in connection with the term 'Raza', whose slippage from one meaning to another served its figural use in explorations of Spain's internal nationalist debates. Alain Frogley describes a similar slippage in the use of racialising terminology in the promotion of Anglo-Saxon music over 'black music' or Jewish influences as an appropriate source for North American art music. Nalini Ghuman attempts to deconstruct a composer's own internalisation and application to himself of a very loosely conceived and quasi-metaphysical notion of race. And as Móricz shows in the case of Ernest Bloch, even if they are understood in such vague terms as a 'feeling', broadly understood concepts of 'racial identity' gave rise to powerful modes of musical creativity.

At the other end of the spectrum Bohlman and Potter discuss the systematic biological applications of racial science in comparative musicology; Potter focuses on the race constructs that German musicology took from the new biologies, noting that applications of craniology to musicology were nevertheless explicitly discredited in the 1920s. The two key conceptions of race, monogenesis (the idea that all races were descended from one) and polygenesis (the idea that there was a separate origin for each human race), as well as the adaptation principle of 'acclimatisation', are all discussed by Jann Pasler, who detects these principles in the methods used to categorise French *chansons populaires* collected in the 1880s and 1890s. A pseudo-philosophical 'cultural race' construct is found in the systematic, but nevertheless non-biological, account of Jewishness found in Otto Weininger's *Sex and Character* (Brown); racial Jewishness is displaced, with gender, into characterology, and ultimately presented within a Kantian philosophical framework as 'type J'. A similar Weininger-like 'typological' or cultural approach to race, whereby 'race' is a set of characteristics that can be 'overcome', is also an idea that Percy Grainger toyed with, though as Gillies and Pear show, he ultimately passed on to explicitly physiological accounts.

It is worth stressing that music was not a passive recipient of processes of racialising. Discursive influence was sometimes in the other direction. As both Potter and Deathridge point out, it was Wagner's interest in the racial theories of Joseph Arthur de Gobineau which seems to have fuelled a Gobineau revival in 1880s Germany. Wagner's influence on the development of Houston Stewart Chamberlain's influential *The Foundations of the Nineteenth Century* is well known; his impact on Otto Weininger's staggeringly widely read anti-Semitic and anti-feminist characterology is less well known (Brown). Futurist artists and musicians likewise influenced the development of racism in 1930s Italy under Mussolini (Illiano and Sala). Mutual influence is traced by Brian Currid, who argues that musicality came to be considered a positive 'natural' trait of both 'gypsy' and 'black' identity via modern discourses of race, while representations of this musicality in opera, operetta and minstrel figures in turn came to be determining for the actual gypsies and black musicians.

For Bohlman, it is also important to think about how racial thinking has resulted in the displacement of peoples and their music. The case of the Romani exemplifies for him several ways in which music and writing about music enact processes of erasure and displacement. Mindful that making use of Romani music and culture to illustrate a scholarly point about music and race is itself an act of discursive displacement, he chooses to open and close his chapter with attempts 'to return some measure of voice to Romani musicians'. Like several other authors here (Pasler, Fry, Brown (introduction)), he also brings his chapter into the present day in an effort to deny us the comfort of speaking only about the music and race in a long-distant past, as if it were somehow separate from us. He closes with the lyrics of a song lamenting the murder of four young Roma in Oberwart, Austria, in 1994.

Nevertheless, questions of personal motivation inevitably come into play when the topic is another person's or another period's stand on what seems, from the present perspective, a morally dubious position. As Guthrie Ramsey notes, those scholars among us prepared to talk about matters of race may have our own secrets to reveal. This observation touches upon the important matter of the subjective content of historical commentary, something which assumes particular significance when moral and ethical issues are at stake – as when an atrocity, or cultural events linked with an atrocity are involved – and is a key concern for LaCapra; acts of reception and interpretation are highly complex, and for a variety of reasons can easily misfire. Yet articulating the ways in which anyone's scholarship and life interact raises its own issues; it would be as unjustifiable to reduce scholarship, as it would be to reduce art and music, to the mere symptom of a life, for instance. However, I would like to suggest that this book, and others like it, mark the beginnings of a scholarly process of working through this collective trauma. For LaCapra, 'Working-through requires the recognition that we are involved in transferential relations to the past in ways that vary according to the subject-positions we find ourselves in, rework, and invent.'[15] As a white country Australian of miscellaneous Anglo-Saxon migrant and convict stock, I have neither Jewish nor Austrian ancestry, and therefore no cultural purchase on the topic of my chapter in any inherited sense, and my links with the Second World War come via a grandparent taken prisoner during the war in the South Pacific, not in Europe. Yet given Australia's painful colonial and penal past and white Australia's lamentable historical relationship with its indigenous peoples I am prepared to accept that I may be working through some other aspects of my identity; I am certainly working through the reasons for my temporary withdrawal from work on Schoenberg's Jewish identity.

---

[15] LaCapra, *Representing the Holocaust*, p. 64.

The book is arranged into three sections, not in order to suggest a reading strategy, but as a workable arrangement for such a diverse collection of individual chapters. Though initially attractive, a grouping arrangement based on geography seemed to me less satisfactory than the present progression from a number of 'issues'-based contributions, via several close-focus individual case studies, through to a series of more broadly based studies. The majority of the essays collected here were presented, in an earlier form, at an international conference entitled 'Western Music and Racial Discourses, 1883–1933' that took place on 11–12 October 2002 at the Institute of Romance Studies, University of London. I would like to express my gratitude to all the contributors for their willingness to participate in this project from beginning to end and for their patience, prompt and willing assistance, and general forbearance during the preparation and publication process. I am also indebted to a number of organisations for their generous support of the 2002 conference: the British Academy, the Jewish Music Institute, the Institute of Romance Studies, University of London, and my own Department of Music, Royal Holloway, University of London for their support both of the conference and of the preparation of this book. Sincere thanks also to Penny Souster, Vicki Cooper and Rebecca Jones at Cambridge University Press for their guidance and support. Above all I thank Štěpán, who has sustained me throughout.

PART I

Overviews and critical frameworks

CHAPTER I

Erasure: displacing and misplacing race in twentieth-century music historiography

Philip V. Bohlman

'The Gypsy Laddie' (Child Ballad no. 200)

1. An English Lord came home one night
   Enquiring for his lady,
   The servants said on every hand,
   She's gone with the Gypsy Laddie.

3. Oh he rode East and he rode West,
   And at last he found her,
   She was lying on the green, green grass
   And the Gypsy's arms around her.

8. It's I can leave my house and land,
   And I can leave my baby,
   I'm a-goin' to roam this world around
   And be a gypsy's lady.

10. Just what befell this lady now,
    I think it worth relating,
    Her gypsy found another lass
    And left her heart a-breaking.

'Djelem, Djelem' – 'I've Traveled, I've Traveled'

1. I've traveled, I've traveled a very long way,
   And I've met many Roma along the way.
   I've met rich and poor,
   As well as their many children.

2. Roma, where do you come from?
   Where do you come from, that you are so many?
   We come from India.
   We Roma are all one large family.

3. Oh, Roma, it was a difficult path
   That we've followed upon this earth.
   With carts and with miserable tents,
   With tears and with pain.
       (performed by Ensemble Milan Jovanović, 1990; recorded and
                                    transcribed by Ursula Hemetek)

PROLOGUE: VOICES OF RACE, DISCOURSES OF RACE

I begin with the voices of race, appropriated, transformed and displaced to lay bare the ways in which they have been woven into the discursive fabric of music. In these two opening songs, the first about Roma people, the second by Roma themselves, the voices of race both are and are not audible. They appear here epigrammatically, as fragments and variants, but as such they appear severed from the racial contexts in which they originally figured. As songs, these two by and about Roma concern themselves intensively with place – the journey of Rom history, the path of the everyday upon which Roma are abundant not invisible – but it is place that separates the Roma from the rest of the world. Unequivocal only is that we encounter the powerful and disturbing discourses of race, discourses ultimately marked by pain, whether or not we choose to listen to those discourses.

The well-known Child Ballad no. 200, 'Gypsy Laddie', reproduced completely in Appendix 1.1 in a version that circulates in oral tradition in the rural region of the American Midwest in which I grew up, gives voice to a discourse about Roma that both is and is not my own.[1] Crucial to the ballad's meanings is not only the wanton employment of stereotype, but also the romantic reimagination of Rom identity over the course of centuries of displacement.[2] That displacement, even if the variant cited above is unfamiliar, has historical, geographical and musical dimensions. It is in the musical dimensions, indeed, that we witness the very realisation of the narrative of displacement.

In the performance of 'Djelem, Djelem' the processes of appropriation are in many ways different from those projected by the American variant of 'Gypsy Laddie' in Appendix 1.1. The variant's text transforms the song into an historical narrative about racism, but extends the historical dimensions of racism to include genocide and holocaust, indeed the Holocaust of the Nazis, in which Roma were among the racial Others Germany incarcerated

---

[1] Many Midwestern variants are the result of historical exchange with the Appalachian Mountains of the American South, especially between the rural settlements of Scottish and Irish immigrant and ethnic communities. Cf. the version in Appendix 1.1 with Jean Ritchie's recording of 'The Gypsie Laddie' on Kenneth S. Goldstein (ed.), *British Traditional Ballads (Child Ballads) in the Southern Mountains Sung by Jean Ritchie* (Folkways Records FA 2301–2); see also Bertrand Harris Bronson, *The Traditional Tunes of the Child Ballads*, 4 vols. (Princeton University Press, 1966), vol. III, p. 216. Most common in folk and popular variants from the folk revival and country music are those circulating widely in the highlands of the mid-Atlantic coast regions of the United States, especially the Carolinas. These songs usually use the names 'Black Eyed Davy' or 'Black Jack Davy' (e.g., in the variant sung by Bob Dylan), which further racialise the stereotypes embedded in the text. For a compilation of variants see Bronson, *The Traditional Tunes of the Child Ballads*, vol. III, pp. 198–250.

[2] Throughout this chapter I employ the following terms to refer to Gypsies: 'Roma' refers to the collective of the Roma as a people; 'Rom' serves as an adjective referring to identity; Romani is a general term referring to the language of the Roma, which nonetheless recognises the many regional and ethnic dialects spoken by Roma. 'Djelem, Djelem', in the variant recorded for the words cited at the beginning of this chapter, was sung in Lovara dialect, widespread in Austria and Hungary.

and murdered in concentration camps. In some variants, the camps, especially Auschwitz, are named explicitly. 'Djelem, Djelem' circulates in oral tradition in East Central Europe, where it has been elevated through written tradition to serve as the 'Anthem of the Roma'. In its many variants, wherever they are sung, 'Djelem, Djelem', nonetheless, bears powerful witness to discourses of displacement.[3]

These songs by and about Roma reproduce the narratives of nationalism and anti-nationalism that have been ascribed to 'Djelem, Djelem', narratives that move a 'people without history' into the modernist narrative of the nation state. As displaced peoples, Roma move across European landscapes, both in the past and in the present, taking their place in Europe by denying place in its political and nationalist geographies. And also by being denied that same place. The denial of place in Europe is a corollary of their racial otherness, which is crucial to the racialisation of the discourses of displacement I examine in this chapter. As songs that are, in fact, relatively well known in their historical and modern versions, 'The Gypsy Laddie' and 'Djelem, Djelem' shift our gaze and our witness from the deeper meanings to the surface features, which in turn reside in the musical dimensions of the song, confirming, or even adding, the link to the chain of racialisation that grows from the discourses of displacement and connects them to music.

THE DISCOURSE OF DISPLACEMENT

The name Arabesque is taken from the country in which this kind of ornamentation reached its most dazzling development. But there the art was one occupying *space*; whereas in the present case it is applied to *time*.[4]

---

[3] Although the song circulates widely among different Roma ethnic groups and in different dialects, it has also been appropriated in popular culture. In his 1993 film, *Latcho Drom*, Tony Gatlif films a performance of the song performed by a Slovak Rom Holocaust survivor, with the following text variant:

> I've traveled, traveled long roads,
> Meeting with happy Roma.
> Roma where have you come from
> With tents on fortune's road?
> Roma, o fellow Roma.
>
> Once I had a great family.
> The Black Legion murdered them.
> Come with me, all the world's Roma,
> For the Romani roads have opened.
> Now's the time, rise up Roma.
> We shall now rise high.
> Roma, o fellow Roma.

[4] Franz Liszt, *The Gipsy in Music*, trans. Edwin Evans (London: William Reeves, 1923), pp. 306–7.

The theoretical focus of this chapter is not specifically the presence of race in music, but rather the ways in which race inflects the ways in which we imagine and talk about music by employing implicitly racial vocabularies. It is this speech about race and music that produces the 'discourse of displacement', whereby I mean to draw in several ways on the themes that the editor and authors have woven into the present volume. Displacement, as I should like to develop the theoretical formulation in this chapter, has many dimensions. There are the more literal dimensions, for example, the reality of peoples who have been displaced, which is to say, forced from the places that allow them fully to embrace their identity and culture. There are the more figurative dimensions, particularly those dimensions that shape processes of representation.

Many, if not most, of the dimensions that accrue to displacement contribute substantially to the ways in which the discourses of displacement are crucial to the construction of race and the unleashing of racism. It is impossible to uncouple the literal and the figurative dimensions of racial displacement, for example, in concepts such as *Blut und Boden*.[5] It is, nonetheless, the very impossibility of uncoupling the racial dimensions that requires alternative discourses, those that deny through erasure a discourse of displacement with particularly pervasive musical dimensions.

'Erasure' is one of the most racialised results of the discourse of displacement, and it therefore requires brief clarification. Erasure does not eliminate the traces of race from the discourses of modernity and modernism, rather it removes them and redeploys them. Erasure, it follows, results from and contributes to specific forms of displacement. Most specifically, erasure results when we shift discourses from the literal to the figurative. In the discursive practices constituting twentieth-century music historiography that shift occurs when the historical and cultural realities of race and racism are replaced with musical dimensions, when, as Béla Bartók famously announced, one applies 'the word racial here to the music itself, and not to the individuals creating, preserving or performing the music'.[6]

---

[5] The slogan, 'blood and soil', provided Germans with one of the historically most persistent justifications for expansion into the lands of Eastern Europe occupied by German *Sprachinseln*, or 'speech islands'. The blood of the German people, according to German racial expansionists, had already laid claim to lands worked by German settlers, occasionally from the Middle Ages, but more often from the seventeenth and eighteenth centuries, when Germans were encouraged to settle in lands vacated by the retreating Ottoman Empire. Genealogy, thus, allowed for the transmission of land ownership through German bloodlines. See, e.g., Uli Linke, *Blood and Nation: The European Aesthetics of Race* (Philadelphia: University of Pennsylvania Press, 1999).

[6] Bartók, 'Race Purity in Music', in Benjamin Suchoff (ed.), *Béla Bartók Essays* (Lincoln: University of Nebraska Press, 1976), p. 29; cf. Julie Brown, 'Bartók, the Gypsies, and Hybridity in Music', in Georgina Born and David Hesmondhalgh (eds.), *Western Music and Its Others: Difference, Representation, and Appropriation in Music* (Berkeley: University of California Press, 2000), pp. 119–42; and Katie Trumpener, 'Béla Bartók and the Rise of Comparative Ethnomusicology: Nationalism, Race Purity, and the Legacy of the Austro-Hungarian Empire', in Ronald Radano and Philip V. Bohlman (eds.), *Music and the Racial Imagination* (University of Chicago Press, 2000), pp. 403–34.

Erasure undergoes a transformation to a racial discourse through the process of replacing the racial dimensions of music with the music itself. Historically erasure has occurred when the West appropriates a music of an 'Other' and transforms it to serve as a music of the 'Self'. We witness precisely this discourse of erasure in the literature of musical and colonial encounter. The Western account concerns itself most extensively with the physical, corporeal dimensions of music-making Others, particularly dance and the collective movement in ritual. In the earliest colonial records, for example, those reproduced by Montaigne from the missionary accounts of Jean de Léry, in which Tupinamba songs from South America were effectively treated as if they were on occasion transmitted through the consumption of flesh by cannibals, the music of the Other was literally regarded as if inseparable from the body itself.[7] The ethnographic space between observing European Self and observed non-Western Other, therefore, turns into a zone of racialisation, where the rationalism can only understand the physicality of non-Western music-making across the chasm of displaced musical discourse. The very notions of difference in music upon which modernist musical thought is predicated arise from the racialised displacement of presumed otherness.[8]

It is, moreover, critical to recognise that many of the major moments of historiographic revolution resulted from the appropriations and transformations of otherness. Such moments recur repeatedly in the Jesuit commentaries on Latin America and by extension the historiography of Latin American music. In the Enlightenment they directly influenced Johann Gottfried Herder and the creation of a discourse with 'Volkslied' as a concept that locates all difference in a distinctively Western discursive domain.[9] At the beginning of the twenty-first century, we witness this discursive appropriation no less in the many different metaphysical practices we call 'world music'.

PLACE AND RACE, DISPLACEMENT AND RACIALISATION

Why do those without place become racialised Others? In what ways does music become the vehicle for racialisation? To answer such questions I should like briefly to discuss the ways in which displacement emerges

---

[7] Cf. Bohlman, 'Representation and Cultural Critique in the History of Ethnomusicology', in Bruno Nettl and Philip V. Bohlman (eds.), *Comparative Musicology and Anthropology of Music: Essays on the History of Ethnomusicology* (University of Chicago Press, 1991), pp. 131–8.

[8] Florian Carl has recently written an extensive study of the musical literature on encounter of Europeans and Africans. I have drawn his notion of a 'Between-space' (*Zwischenraum*) in which music is racialised for my own thoughts. See Carl, *Was bedeutet uns Afrika? Zur Darstellung afrikanischer Musik im deutschsprachigen Diskurs des 19. und frühen 20. Jahrhunderts*, Begegnungen, Geschichte und Gegenwart der afrikanisch-europäischen Begegnung (Münster: LIT Verlag, 2004).

[9] E.g., Herder, '*Stimmen der Völker in Liedern*' and *Volkslieder*, 2 vols. (Leipzig: Weygandsche Buchhandlung, 1778/9).

from theories of African-American history and African diaspora[10] and from more recent attempts to interpret geography and identity as extensions of history and memory.[11] Displacement allows individuals and communities to express their connection to a particular place even when they are not residents of the places from which they draw their identity. In one of the most fundamental ways of understanding the concept, displacement characterises diaspora, in which a people interprets its history as a journey that has the potential of leading them back to a homeland they have not been able to occupy, usually because they were violently expelled from the homeland or because survival in the homeland was for various reasons no longer viable. Diaspora represents a certain type of historical journey, in which, necessarily, the point of departure in the past and return in the present are not usually the same. Displacement, however, can assume many different forms, which in turn bear witness to many different forms of racialisation. Displacement, therefore, is frequently redeployed as a corollary to racism, providing an alternative, an escape, and even a means of survival when racism is most threatening and violent.

Europe is also notable for the ways its historical narratives have been responsible for creating displaced peoples. Racism and ethnic prejudice have prevented Jews, Roma and other minorities from being able to have their own state or from receiving protection from any state. New forms of racism, reimagined from the old, for example in Serbia, Albania and Macedonia, also rely on history as a justification for placing geographical restrictions on peoples without lands of their own. Like its counterparts, racism and nationalism, displacement has the power to generate memory and history, and in this sense, that is, because it forms a counter-history, displacement has powerful historical dimensions that are distinctively European.

There are many denied a place in European history because they do not fit in the nation and its history, perhaps because they speak the wrong language (or fail to speak the right one in a certain way), or because they are explicitly marked as racial Others. Displaced peoples often bear their history with them, in the stories and songs they employ to express selfness and, above all, in the music that allows them both to transmit their narratives of selfness and perform these as expressions of group identity. The music of nationless peoples in Europe is well suited to the processes of displacement. Music that maps history as change and adaptation, an

---

[10] Cf. W. E. B. Du Bois, *The Souls of Black Folk*, repr. ed. by Henry Louis Gates, Jr (New York: Bantam, [1903] 1989); and Paul Gilroy, *The Black Atlantic: Modernity and Double Consciousness* (Cambridge, MA: Harvard University Press, 1993).

[11] Cf. Angelika Bammer (ed.), *Displacements: Cultural Identities in Question*, Theories of Contemporary Culture (Bloomington: Indiana University Press, 1994); Smadar Lavie and Ted Swedenburg (eds.), *Displacement, Diaspora, and Geographies of Identity* (Durham: Duke University Press, 1996); and Winfried Georg Sebald, *Austerlitz* (Munich: Carl Hanser, 2001).

expression of the individual and the collective body, rather than as repertory rooted in the soil, is the music that distinguishes Europe's displaced people. It is perhaps for this reason that the displaced people of Europe have been recognised publicly as peoples whose cultures are marked by music – Roma, Jews and Saami, Travellers in the United Kingdom and Ireland, and minorities of all kinds. Displaced peoples are, indeed, singled out as if their specialities in music were the fragments of the nation they were allowed to occupy, enough to sustain the journey of displacement but insufficient to establish a sense of place in which music and musical style can fully express an authenticity attributed to that place.

What are the conditions that produce displaced peoples? Throughout European history, displacement has resulted when certain groups of people have been denied the ability to occupy and own land. With the emergence of the nation state after the Enlightenment, ownership of property is of particular importance because of the ways it establishes legal relations with the state, thus drawing the citizen into the nation's sphere. Those owning land have legal obligations to the state, and the nation relies on them to expand its own control over the lands within and, in times of military expansion, outside its borders. Just as there are musical repertories that connect people to the land locally, regionally and nationally, there are also those that reflect the mobility of displaced peoples. The folk songs of the Sephardic Jews of the Balkans, for example narrative romances and other ballads among the repertories of *romanceros*, contain references to the lands in which their Jewish singers are living or have lived in south-eastern Europe, but also contain the linguistic and stylistic structure of Andalusia in south-western Europe. Saami and Traveller repertories express the seasonal movement of the groups who cultivate them. For those lacking land of their own, music ascribes identity by not depending on the institutions and processes of collection and inscription that turn music itself into national property.

The music of many displaced peoples in Europe reflects the necessity of negotiating borderlands. Displacement, therefore, becomes a process of juxtaposing diverse styles, repertories, functions and languages. Music responds to placelessness by opening cultural domains between those with the power and means to exclude others and those who occupy no other place. Several border regions of Europe are notable for the ways in which repertories expand because of the capacity to absorb the music of the displaced peoples living in those regions. It is almost futile to divide into national styles the folk-music repertories along the arch of the Carpathian Mountains. The national borders that run along the Carpathians do little to encumber extensive ethnic mixture and the generation of hybrid styles. As a border region and a national crossroads at the centre of Europe, the Carpathians have nurtured musicians whose repertories are enriched from the contributions of fellow travellers. Rom and Jewish repertories in the

Carpathians not only overlap at times, but even form variants that result from folk-song texts with several languages.[12]

Throughout European history, those regarded as non-European have been denied place. The displacement generated by foreignness has deep historical roots, so deep, in fact, that they were firmly implanted long before the Enlightenment and the rise of modern forms of nationalism. Even until the present, the legal restrictions placed on Europe's foreigners have extended primarily to the denial of place. Turkish guest workers in Germany and Algerian labourers in France are pushed to the extremes of the industrial landscape, where they struggle, usually in vain, to acquire the legal status of a citizen, enabling them to cast off the brand of foreignness. Struggles over the building of mosques or the transformation of existing buildings into mosques rage in hundreds of large and small German cities, not unusually focusing on the ways in which the foreigner's music, the call-to-prayer, or *adhan*, would fill and thus take over the urban spaces of Germany.

The most pervasive mark of foreignness is that of Asian origins, however many generations may have preceded extended presence and residence in Europe. Modern attempts to displace Europe's Jews, Roma, Muslims, and even Saami, therefore, construct models of non-Europeanness based on myths of land and culture being taken from Europeans by historical foreigners who had left their own land and culture, those of Asia. The race sciences appropriated by European scholarship during the 1930s and 1940s were quick to seize on the putative traces of Asianness in music of those groups they wished to racialise as foreign, and thus incapable of occupying space in the European nation. Music that confirmed foreignness, therefore, also confirmed placelessness.

The displacement of Europe's nationless peoples almost always had racial dimensions prior to the Holocaust. The ghettoisation and genocide of the Holocaust were themselves forms of displacement, for entire peoples – especially Jews and Roma, who were thought to be anathema to racial nationalism, with its emphasis on *Blut und Boden* – were deprived of the spaces in which they lived, assembled in concentration camps, and there murdered. The vocabulary of race permeated the songs Europeans sang about its displaced peoples, for example, the English-language ballad repertories, in which Roma were always dark-skinned and Jews always lived outside society, thus exaggerating the danger they presumably posed. In the new forms of European nationalism taking shape in the wake of the Holocaust, race has again asserted itself in ways that are sometimes oblique,

---

[12] E.g. Eva Krekovicová, *Zwischen Toleranz und Barrieren: Das Bild der Zigeuner und Juden in der slowakischen Folklore*, Studien zur Tsiganologie und Folkloristik (Frankfurt am Main: Peter Lang, 1998); see also Rüdiger Wischenbart (ed.), *Karpaten: Die dunkle Seite Europas* (Vienna: Kremayr und Scheriau, 1992).

at other times direct. There has been a tendency in some social scientific literature, for example, to claim that difference in Europe, unlike that in the United States, is ethnic and not racial, though more recently the racial dimensions of ethnicity have been undeniable.[13] The recognition, moreover, that 'ethnic cleansing' in south-eastern Europe was at base racially motivated has intensified the concern for the persistence of race as a condition for displacement in Europe today.

MUSIC, SCIENTISM, AND THE DISPLACEMENT OF RACE

[Goethe] spoke about many things with great precision, but throughout his life he possessed a subtle sense of keeping quiet; most likely, he had good reasons to do so.[14]

The science of race and the science of music are sister discourses of modernity. The science of race emerged in the post-Darwinian world of the late nineteenth century, when scientists of various kinds – palaeontologists and anthropologists, sociologists and historians – sought ways to give precise measurement to speculations about the distinctiveness of human populations. By turning to the scientific measurement of human difference, the racial scientists of the late nineteenth and early twentieth century created a new discourse of putative authenticity, one made legible, above all, through the readings yielded by machines and other tools of modernity. The racial discourses of modernist science should have produced languages that were no longer ambivalent in their representational capacities. They should have done so, but, in fact, they did not. Instead, the reactionary modernism of much modernist science, as Jeffrey Herf has labelled it, led to a proliferation of the ways in which the objects of science were perceived.[15]

Modernism and modern science conjoined no less in the shaping of the sciences of music. It would be quite impossible to remove the machinery of scientific modernism from early musicology, for example, from the experiments of Alexander Ellis or Carl Stumpf. Measurement and categorisation were crucial not only to the formulation of new representational vocabularies but also to forging new discourses. It was in the modernist discourses of the nascent sciences of music, moreover, that race made its presence known. We witness these in the schemes of scholars shaping the discourses of the centre of Austro-German musicology, Guido Adler and Erich M. von Hornbostel, for instance, and also those at the peripheries, say, Abraham Zvi Idelsohn, whose recordings of Jewish music in the first

---

[13] E.g. Paul Gilroy, *The Black Atlantic*, and Martin Stokes (ed.), *Ethnicity, Identity and Music: The Musical Construction of Place* (Oxford: Berg, 1994).
[14] Friedrich Nietzsche, *Sämtliche Werke: Kritische Studienausgaben in 15 Einzelbänden*, Giorgio Colli and Mazzino Montinari (eds.) (Munich: Deutscher Taschenbuch Verlag, 1988), vol. V, p. 184.
[15] Jeffrey Herf, *Reactionary Modernism: Technology, Culture, and Politics in Weimar and the Third Reich* (Cambridge University Press, 1984); cf. Andrew Zimmerman, *Anthropology and Anti-Humanism in Imperial Germany* (University of Chicago Press, 2001).

decade of the twentieth century were made specifically to support experiments in linguistic comparison.[16]

The scientism of the new discourses about music recognised race, but the discursive categories placed it at arm's length from music itself. Race informed music at other times and places, displaced and removed from responsibility. It was precisely this criticism that W. E. B. Du Bois raised in his seminal study of race in the United States, *The Souls of Black Folk* (1903), which deliberately wove music and representations of music into its text. The phenomenon of denying the continuity of racial discourses from the past to the present depends on a willingness to displace race, so that it enters music historiography as the problem of another time and place.[17]

Racial discourses permeated the early science of music. They appear in countless guises in the organic notions of music historiography. They are crucial to the musicological construction of otherness through late nineteenth-century colonialism, and in the European models of the Other as displaced – to the East and the South – through a history teleologically drawn to modernity. Race was crucial to musical discourses of nation, nationalism and the rise of the West.

By the early decades of the twentieth century erasure was distinct in musical and in musicological terms. Erasure led to the displacement of race in discourses about music's autonomy. When music expressed race – which is to say, the racialised Other – it was through claims that music was bound to both speech and bodily movement, hence not to music itself as a system of abstract and self-referential symbols. Racialised music, therefore, contains a cluster of symbols that are not self-referential and are ontologically dependent on something other than music *an sich*. In musicological terms, the music of another race could be appropriated through discourse because it was not self-referential, but rather was a function of culture, generated by labour or bound to ritual. The music of the racial Other possessed no metaphysical space of its own, for it had always already been displaced through the discursive representation of music.

RESPONSES TO THE COLLAPSE OF EUROPEAN CULTURAL SPACES

Coupled with European colonialism at the end of the nineteenth century, the new sciences of music provided the laboratory for the establishment of racialised musical discourses. Colonialism in all its forms had encouraged the appropriation, classification and control of the musics of the colonised.

---

[16] Cf. especially Abraham Zvi Idelsohn, *Phonographierte Gesänge und Aussprachsproben des Hebräischen der jemenitischen, persischen und syrischen Juden*, 35. Mitteilung der Phonogramm-Archivs-Kommission der Kaiserlichen Akademie der Wissenschaften in Wien (Vienna: Alfred Hölder, 1917).
[17] Ronald Radano has written brilliantly about the discourse history of locating African American music in a modernist, racial language about music; see especially *Lying up a Nation: Race and Black Music* (University of Chicago Press, 2003).

Erasure: displacing and misplacing race

Figure 1.1: Empress Elisabeth's wedding gift (Multiple texts from the Banat, Romanian, and Serbian border region)

Discourses of displacement were made possible by the dual imperialist projects of collection and control. New categories were created that allowed colonial authorities and various ancillary agents, such as missionaries, to record and transcribe the musics of those living outside the centre of colonial power. The assertion of colonial power through the codification of musical representation was fully globalised by the mid-nineteenth century. The displacement of musical otherness might have seemingly innocuous forms, as in the case of the wedding present from Austria's Emperor Franz Joseph to Empress Elisabeth in 1854 (Fig. 1.1).

The anthology of 'national hymns' from peoples throughout the Austro-Hungarian Empire relied on a fundamental belief in erasure.[18] That belief was hardly limited to wedding presents. The explosion of scientific journals in late nineteenth-century Central Europe was also predicated on a conviction that cultural differences could be gathered in the pages of books or placed in the display cases of museums.[19] Among these imperial projects are those that laid the groundwork for the study of epics in south-eastern Europe, ballads in the German 'speech islands', and even A. Z. Idelsohn's collection of Jewish music in Jerusalem with equipment and funding from the Austro-Hungarian Imperial Academy of Science.

Again, it seems almost remarkable that the colonialist obsession with collecting and controlling cultural otherness should rely on the discourses of the laboratory. A laboratory *mentalité* informed almost all aspects of representations, ranging from the transcriptional decisions employed by Erich M. von Hornbostel for his first commercially conceived set of world-music recordings on wax cylinders to the photographs of racial types that accompanied musical works on nationalism.[20]

The extent to which such erasure could be taken is striking indeed when we listen to early recordings made for imperial academies of science.[21] When the Academy of Sciences gathered soldiers from throughout the Austro-Hungarian Empire to sing 'their musical repertories' as 'our imperial music', musical and cultural differences were reduced to the same scientific space. In 1915, the experimental nature of the imperial recording project even directed soldiers to sing the imperial anthem, the *Kaiserhymne*, in their own languages – German, Czech, Polish, and Hungarian – at the same time. If the texts were lexically meaningless, the music's signification of the power of selfness over otherness was unequivocal.[22] One might argue

---

[18] There were other musical anthologies created on the occasion of the imperial wedding in 1854, and among these there were attempts to extol Habsburg multiculturalism. The chief cantor of Vienna, Salomon Sulzer, for example, gave the imprimatur of the empire's Jewish musical tradition, the 'Viennese Rite', to one such anthology with his composition in Hebrew, 'Psalmodie', thus ensuring that the empire would envoice Jews at an historical moment of perpetuating itself.

[19] Cf. Sara Friedrichsmeyer, Sara Lennox and Susanne Zantop (eds.), *The Imperialist Imagination: German Colonialism and Its Legacy* (Ann Arbor: University of Michigan Press, 1998).

[20] For a comparison of the different scientific roles played by Idelsohn, from psychologist to acoustician to musicologist, see the essays in Sebastian Klotz (ed.), *Vom tönenden Wirbel menschlichen Tuns: Erich M. von Hornbostel als Gestaltpsychologe, Archivar und Musikwissenschaftler* (Milow: Schibri, 1998).

[21] The Phonogrammarchiv of the Austrian Academy of Sciences has been re-releasing the early field recordings commissioned at the end of the nineteenth and the early decades of the twentieth century, thereby employing another discursive process, namely that of historicism. As I write this chapter, I too am involved in one of these CD projects, namely the release of A. Z. Idelsohn's Jerusalem recordings, with commentary. See Bohlman, 'Abraham Z. Idelsohn and the Reorientation of Jewish Music History', commentary for the CD release of Idelsohn's field recordings, Gerda Lechleitner (ed.), *The Collection of Abraham Zvi Idelsohn (1911–1913)*, 3 CDs and CD-ROM (Vienna: Österreichische Akademie der Wissenschaften, 2005), pp. 18–51.

[22] See commentary by Oskár Elschek and Gerda Lechleitner, Austrian Academy of Sciences, *Soldatenlieder der k.u.k. Armee*, series 4: *Tondokumente aus der Phonogrammarchiv der Österreichischen Akademie der Wissenschaften*. OEAW PHA CD 11.

that, musically, it is not possible to make much sense out of the Austrian *Kaiserhymne* being sung in four languages at the same time by soldiers of the Imperial Austro-Hungarian Army. That argument would seem to be confirmed when we realise that this imperial project was given as a commission to Leo Hajek (1886–1975), who was, in fact, a physicist, who accepted the responsibility for the project because it would allow him to work on and improve existing recording technologies. We know from his notes and the quality of his recordings, moreover, that he was particularly skilful at gathering regimental bands and soldiers' choruses together so that as many voices as possible would be captured by the recording horn.[23]

Even more extreme cases of experimentation that led to erasure took place in the prisoner-of-war camps that gathered soldiers from throughout the world as the empires that clashed in the First World War began to implode. Scientists from virtually every field recognised in these gatherings of humanity the possibilities to classify and codify difference, and it should hardly be surprising that musicologists and comparative musicologists were among those who entered the camps. Among those perceiving the promise of such projects were Carl Stumpf and Georg Schünemann for Germany. The very global nature of the First World War, gathering soldiers from throughout Europe, in the first place, but then from the colonies that supplied economic goods from colonies throughout the world, juxtaposed musics and musicians in a truly modern fashion. Béla Bartók, too, found himself attracted to the musical diversity gathered in the garrisons of the Austro-Hungarian army, which had been mustered from throughout Eastern Europe, especially including ethnic minorities.

The prisoner-of-war-camp and army-garrison laboratories became, in fact, very ambitious undertakings. Teams entered the camps, armed with recording equipment and assistants who would translate interviews and photograph the human differences. Linguists, anthropologists and musicologists were engaged to transcribe interviews and recordings designed to enhance comparisons harvested from different ethnic and racial groups. The results of such research in time of war would contribute substantially to the foundations of comparative musicology (*vergleichende Musikwissenschaft*) and the theories of cultural regionalism (*Kulturkreislehre*) that would dominate Central European scholarship for decades.

One project, carried out almost without interruption in the decade following the First World War, produced, which is to say published, its findings under the motto of *eine neue Völkerkunde*, 'a new anthropology'.[24]

---

[23] Ibid.
[24] Wilhelm Doegen (ed.), *Unter fremden Völkern: Eine neue Völkerkunde* (Berlin: Otto Stollberg, Verlag für Politik und Wirtschaft, 1925).

Inhalts-Verzeichnis.

		Seite
1.	Vorwort. Von Wilh. Doegen	5
2.	Einleitung. Von Wilh. Doegen.	9
3.	Rechtsverhältnisse der primitiven Völker. Nach Josef Kohler.	17
4.	Die Farbigen von Nordwestafrika. Von Hubert Grimme.	40
5.	Die Völker der Südhälfte Afrikas und des Sudan. Von M. Heepe.	65
6.	Die Madagassen. Von Paul Hambruch.	80
7.	Die Malaien. Von Otto Dempwolff.	85
8.	Die Tahitier. Von Paul Hambruch.	88
9.	Die Neukaledonier. Von Paul Hambruch.	92
10.	Die Koreaner. Von F. W. K. Müller.	96
11.	Der Hinduismus. Von Helmuth von Glasenapp.	116
12.	Die Gurkhas. Von Heinrich Lüders.	126
13.	Die Radschputen. Von Helmuth von Glasenapp.	140
14.	Die Sikhs. Von Helmuth von Glasenapp.	151
15.	Die indischen Mohammedaner. Von J. Horovitz.	161
16.	Die Iranier. Von F. C. Andreas. (Der Aufsatz wurde aus technischen Gründen an den Schluß des Buches gesetzt.)	376
17.	Die Zigeuner. Von Ernst Lewy.	167
18.	Die Tataren. Von Gotthold Weil.	177
19.	Die Völker des Kaukasus. Von Adolf Dirr.	191
20.	Die Finnisch-Ugrischen Stämme im europäischen Rußland. Von Ernst Lewy.	212
21.	Mordwinische Erzählungen und Lieder, Märchen und Zaubersprüche. Von Robert Pelissier.	233
22.	Die Litauer (nach Bezzenbergers Studie über den Werdegang des litauischen Volkes). Von Theodor Kappstein.	250
23.	Die Juden. Von Gotthold Weil	257
24.	Deutsche Bauernkolonien im alten Rußland. Von Adolf Lane	262
25.	Rußland. Von Clara Körber	275
26.	Die Kleinrussen. Von Hermann Jacobsohn	290
27.	Kurzer Abriß der Musik im östlichen Europa. Von Georg Schünemann	310
28.	Serben. Von Hermann Jacobsohn	318
29.	Romanische Völker. Von Hermann Urtel	338
30.	Die Flamen. Von Markromeo Breyne	351
31.	Der Anglist bei den Engländern. Von Alois Brandl	362

Figure 1.2: Table of contents from Wilhelm Doegen (ed.), *Unter fremden Völkern: Eine neue Völkerkunde* (Berlin: Otto Stollberg, Verlag für Politik und Wirtschaft, 1925)

Figure 1.2 contains a list of those studied by the new anthropologists. The new anthropology thus parsed the world according to political and linguistic otherness, which combined with musical otherness to yield a new racial map (see also Figs. 1.3 and 1.4). Human facial types and melody types were also studied and then represented in the laboratory. Whereas the recording and transcription of music in the camps was very important, it was one of many scientific discourses employed in the laboratory work. We should not, however, underestimate the importance of music, for it was precisely his work in the prisoner-of-war camps that provided Georg Schünemann with the materials for his studies of German music in

Erasure: displacing and misplacing race 17

Figure 1.3: Photographs of Southern African drummers and Africans from Doegen's *Unter fremden Völkern* (facing p. 64)

Figure 1.4: Photograph of Gurka prisoners dancing, 'men dressed as girls' (Doegen, bottom of page facing p. 80)

Eastern Europe and Russia, which were foundational works in Weimar and Nazi comparative musicology.[25]

The erasure made possible by the displacement of racialised music to science justified new and more public racial discourses from the 1920s into the 1930s. In Germany, these discourses were arrogated to the science of the Nazi period. As science, the racial discourses were meant to be taken seriously, which, as we know from Erik Levi's and Pamela Potter's research and from the studies of the history of science from the 1920s and 1930s, had many and different consequences.[26] Indisputably, however, the racial discourses about music proliferated in almost unchecked fashion. Under the name of scientific folk-music study, for example, the German Folklore Union would sponsor a forty-one-volume project that provided a musical map for German expansion in the Second World War. Just as each volume in the *Landschaftliche Volkslieder* project represented the place of a German folk song in a region beyond the borders

---

[25] Cf. Schünemann, *Das Lied der deutschen Kolonisten in Russland* (Munich: Drei Masken Verlag, 1923), and Schünemann 'Zur Tonalitätsfrage des deutschen Volksliedes', in Guido Waldmann (ed.), *Zur Tonalität des deutschen Volksliedes* (Wolfenbüttel: Georg Kallmeyer, 1938), pp. 28–41.
[26] See e.g. Erik Levi, *Music in the Third Reich* (Basingstoke: Macmillan, 1994), and Pamela M. Potter, *Most German of All the Arts: Musicology and Society from the Weimar Republic to the End of Hitler's Reich* (New Haven: Yale University Press, 1998).

of Germany, such as Alsace-Lorraine, Transylvania, or Ukraine, it displaced the non-German speakers (and singers) from those regions. Musical otherness was an explicit ground for erasure.[27]

Musical cartography in the 1930s became more racialised and scientific at the same time. The practices of erasure slid from the figurative to the literal at an accelerated pace as the discourses of music posited that the measurements of skulls and scales were isomorphic (see Fig. 1.5, a map of 'Basic forms of musical thinking within major racial areas').

By the late 1930s, the scientific and racial discourses for music had virtually become one in Central Europe. In his 1939 *Das Rassenproblem in der Musik* ('The Race Problem in Music') Friedrich Blume directed his passionate appeal to science, claiming that 'scientific clarification was especially crucial'.[28] Blume and others appealed to German scholarship to address the 'race question' not from the standpoint of race, but on the basis of the conjuncture of music and science. By 1939, erasure had rendered the discourses of displacement entirely normative.

EPILOGUE: THE CIPHERS OF ERASURE

'Phurde, bajval, phurde'/'Blow, Wind, Blow'

1. Phurde, bajval, phurde
   paj kopča e patra, hej
   te šaj šaradjon de tele
   kodoj laše šave.

   Blow, wind, blow
   The leaves from the trees,
   So that the four Rom boys
   Will be covered.

2. Kurke de teharin
   jaj de kodo hiro šundam, hej
   kaj bombenca mudarde, mamo
   štar romane šaven.

   On Sunday morning
   We received the news
   That four Rom boys
   Were murdered with a bomb.

3. Ašile korkora
   e but cigne šave, hej
   čore taj korkora, mamo
   taj vi lengo nipo.

   Many small children
   Were left behind,
   Poor and alone
   The children and the families.

4. Devlam, Devlam, bara,
   sostar kodo muklan, hej
   te mudaren e gaže, aba
   kodoj terne šaven?

   God, great God,
   How could you allow
   Non-Roma to kill
   Such young men?

---

[27] See Bohlman, 'Landscape – Region – Nation – Reich: German Folk Song in the Nexus of National Identity', in Celia Applegate and Pamela M. Potter (eds.), *Music and German National Identity* (University of Chicago Press, 2002), pp. 105–27.
[28] Blume, *Das Rassenproblem in der Musik: Entwurf zu einer Methodologie musikwissenschaftlicher Rassenforschung* (Wolfenbüttel and Berlin: Georg Kallmeyer, 1939), p. 3.

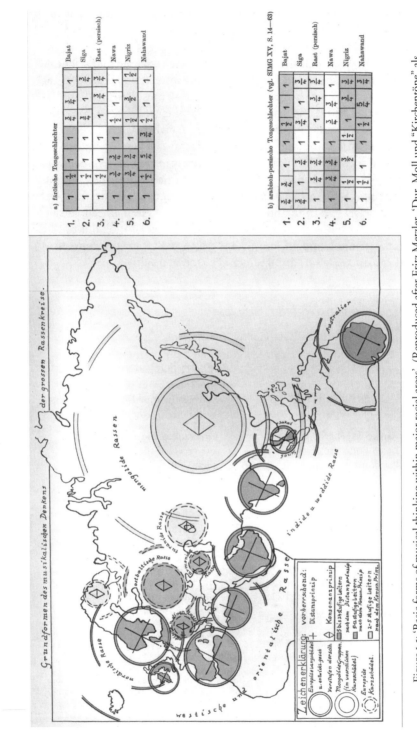

Figure 1.5: 'Basic forms of musical thinking within major racial areas'. (Reproduced after Fritz Metzler, 'Dur, Moll und "Kirchentöne" als musikalischer Rassenausdruck'. In Guido Waldmann (ed.), *Zur Tonalität des deutschen Volksliedes* (Wolfenbüttel: Kallmeyer, 1938), pp. 1–27 (map between pp. 24 and 25)

5. Bara raja Devlam,
šukares mangav tu, hej
žutin e bute Romenge
taj ker amenge pača.

žutin e romenge Devlam
sa pe kadi luma.

Great God,
I beg you from the bottom of my heart,
Help the many Roma
And give us peace.

Help us, God, all the Roma
All over the world.

Text: Ruža Nikolić-Lakatos, 1995
Melody: Traditional Lovara melody
English translation: Philip V. Bohlman

This chapter closes much as it began, struggling to return some measure of voice to Romani musicians. 'Phurde, bajval, phurde' ('Blow, Wind, Blow') was created and sung by Ruža Nikolić-Lakatos to lament the 1994 murder of four young Roma in Oberwart, Austria, one of countless acts of violence against Roma in Europe today that are neither solved nor reported in the international press. Few readers of this chapter are likely to know about these murders, much less about the musical response to them and other acts of violence against Europe's racial Others. Such acts rarely enter modern musical discourse, for they are acts perpetrated on Roma in modern Europe, not on Gypsies in modern music.[29]

Quite deliberately, I have framed the present chapter with Roma and Romani music. On one hand, in our own ethnographic present, at the beginning of the twenty-first century, the massive discrimination and genocide against Roma throughout the world have lessened not in the least. And yet, we ask ourselves, what place do Roma have in the musical discourses of our own time? On the other hand, the Roma, under the signs of musical otherness – as Gypsies, Gitanes, Gitanos, Tziganes, or Zigeuner – have been one of the most distinctive, controllable ciphers of racial otherness, perhaps even more so at the turn of our own century. There is no dearth of writing on gypsy scales or on well-known operatic figures such as Carmen. It is the Roma, themselves, who have won no place in musical discourse, for in that discourse of displacement, the distinction between race and racism has entirely collapsed. Even the most dedicated musical scholars working sensitively among the Roma find themselves writing against the grain.[30]

---

[29] Even when the displacement of Roma briefly makes its way into international news reports, it is quickly silenced, if even by seemingly 'more important' events. The removal of Roma neighbourhoods from districts around the Athens Olympics in summer 2004 received a flash of attention in the spring of that year. As the Olympics drew closer, and completion of the modern athletic facilities seemed certain, the displacement of Roma completely disappeared from international attention, much less concern.

[30] See, especially, Ursula Hemetek, *Mosaik der Klänge: Musik der ethnischen und religiösen Minderheiten in Österreich*, Schriften zur Volksmusik (Vienna: Böhlau, 2001), and Barbara Rose Lange, *Holy Brotherhood: Romani Music in a Hungarian Pentecostal Church* (New York: Oxford University Press, 2003).

The point is that in postmodern discourses of race and music, Rom music lends itself to complete reduction to a sign system that refers to Western music, even to the extent that it acquires non-Romani semiotic meaning. While racism directed against the Roma increases and has even greater consequences, the music of Roma is appropriated for the proliferation of virtually every musical discourse emerging in a postmodern and new-musicological world. Erasure might appear to be complete as racial discourses seemingly yield to musical discourses, as if, for today's musicology and ethnomusicology, that's what music is about. Yet, is it not, in fact, in the music, at least when we hear it and listen to it, that we encounter the very racial discourses we thought we could relegate to the past? Expressed in the music of Roma at the turn of the present century, nonetheless, the racial discourses of music could – and I hope must – resist such displacement and insist that they cannot be erased from the music and the musical scholarship we today call our own.

APPENDIX 1.1 – 'THE GYPSY LADDIE' (CHILD BALLAD NO. 200)

1. An English Lord came home one night
   Enquiring for his lady,
   The servants said on every hand,
   She's gone with the Gypsy Laddie.

2. Go saddle up my milk-white steed,
   Go saddle me up my brownie
   And I will ride both night and day
   Till I overtake my bonnie.

3. Oh he rode East and he rode West,
   And at last he found her,
   She was lying on the green, green grass
   And the Gypsy's arms around her.

4. Oh, how can you leave your house and land,
   How can you leave your money,
   How can you leave your rich young lord
   To be a gypsy's bonnie.

Example 1.1: 'The Gypsy Laddie' (Child Ballad no. 200)

5. How can you leave your house and land,
   How can you leave your baby,
   How can you leave your rich young lord
   To be a gypsy's lady.

6. Oh come go home with me, my dear,
   Come home and be my lover,
   I'll furnish you with a room so neat,
   With a silken bed and covers.

7. I won't go home with you, kind sir,
   Nor will I be your lover,
   I care not for your rooms so neat
   Or your silken bed or your covers.

8. It's I can leave my house and land,
   And I can leave my baby,
   I'm a-goin' to roam this world around
   And be a gypsy's lady.

9. Oh, soon this lady changed her mind,
   Her clothes grew old and faded,
   Her hose and shoes came off her feet
   And left them bare and naked.

10. Just what befell this lady now,
    I think it worth relating,
    Her gypsy found another lass
    And left her heart a-breaking.

CHAPTER 2

Secrets, lies and transcriptions: revisions on race, black music and culture

Guthrie P. Ramsey, Jr

> Here is what race means. Race is a socially constructed process that produces subordinate and superordinate groups. Racial stratification is the key social process behind racial classifications. The meaning of race depends on the social conditions in which it exists.
>
> Tukufu Zuberi, *Thicker Than Blood: How Racial Statistics Lie*[1]

> Searching for the historical essence of black music leads not to a primordial nature but to the second nature of the public sphere, as myths of presence give way to modern representations of blackness as swing, soul, funk, and groove. It is this instability of difference that grants to African-America its special, seemingly miraculous musical power. And it is this same difference that continues to baffle and confuse an American populace still convinced that the blackness and whiteness of sound is fundamentally, essentially, real. The whole, authentic truth of black music becomes but a lie, a social narrative that ascribes difference in order to repress subtexts fundamentally resonant in black and white.
>
> Ronald Radano, *Lying up a Nation: Race and Black Music*[2]

In his study of the black spiritual, *Culture on the Margins: The Black Spiritual and the Rise of American Cultural Interpretation*, Jon Cruz notes that as early as 1845, the year that Frederick Douglass's autobiography was published, the latter had admonished his readers to listen to the spirituals because within these 'songs of sorrow' existed a strong indictment against the institution of chattel slavery. Cruz argues that as abolitionists and other proponents of human rights began to value black music as expressed in the genre of the spirituals, they also began to identify with the slaves as modern subjects. This heightened interest in the slaves and their music was part of a larger, powerful cultural current that he calls 'ethnosympathy', his term to describe 'the new humanitarian pursuit of the inner world of distinctive and collectively classifiable subjects'.[3]

---

[1] Tukufu Zuberi, *Thicker Than Blood: How Racial Statistics Lie* (Minneapolis: University of Minnesota Press, 2001), p. xviii.
[2] Ronald Radano, *Lying up a Nation: Race and Black Music* (University of Chicago Press, 2003), p. 12.
[3] Jon Cruz, *Culture on the Margins: The Black Spiritual and the Rise of American Cultural Interpretation* (Princeton University Press, 1999), p. 3.

This new interest in black subjectivity was linked to other developments in the human sciences. In a ground-breaking study provocatively titled *Thicker Than Blood: How Racial Statistics Lie*, Tukufu Zuberi, a sociologist and demographer, reveals how the quite biased cultural work of 'objective' statistical data became particularly important both in the world of science and the ambitious chore of socio-political domination. Rooted in the fifteenth-century expansion of European nations, race's association with biological differences cemented in the late nineteenth century. Linked to the economics of imperialism and the racialisation of colonialism and slavery, the supposed biological basis of race was a relatively new idea that profoundly shaped America's socio-economic history.[4] It was soon keenly felt in cultural production, especially in the area of music.

If European imperialism was made possible by its superior ships and cannons, then riff, rhythm and repetition became both gifts and curses in the cultural politics of liberation and subjugation of the African-American descendants of enslaved Africans. Along the historical trajectory between early European scientific classifications of human populations and the 'naturalised' notion of white supremacy existed many debates and paradigm shifts.[5] And surely we see the traces of these conversations every time we read a music trade journal such as *Billboard*, *Variety*, *Down Beat*, or *Metronome*, in which broad musical categories, genres and sub-styles often reflect, and in fact, inform racial logic in the social world.[6]

This chapter considers recent strides in research on black musical culture from the mid-to-late nineteenth century up to the 1930s, focusing on how different ideas about 'race' are treated in each. As the twentieth century drew to a close, the 1990s witnessed the questioning and complication of our 'common sense' attitudes about race, especially among academics. Scholars created new ways to discuss the dialogic nature of racial identity and have forever changed how we talk about race in the contemporary moment.[7] These new approaches to race and African-American culture and its interpretation have begun to reorder our view of key historical events, movements, figures and cultural practices.

Collectively, the research under discussion here pushes race discourse in exciting new directions through interventions on several fronts. It explains, among other issues, the strained relationship between late nineteenth-century notions of black uplift and the so-called vernacular musical arts. This work also underscores the importance of the appearance in American culture of the Negro spiritual specifically, reflecting on the processes that it

---

[4] Zuberi, *Thicker Than Blood*.   [5] Ibid., pp. 5–16.
[6] For more on race and genre, see David Brackett, 'The Question of Genre in Black Music', ms., forthcoming, *Black Music Research Journal*.
[7] Shelly Fisher Fishkin, 'Interrogating "Whiteness", Complicating "Blackness": Remapping American Culture', *American Quarterly* 47/3 (1995), 429–67.

underwent to become an index of the cultural and social consciousness of African-American culture and that of the larger communities into which it was disseminated, to be both celebrated and disparaged. Furthermore, it brings into high relief how the 'objective' thrust of scientific investigation has affected the study of African American music historically, from the spirituals to jazz. In fact, attitudes about the nineteenth-century spirituals carried over to that of later musical forms of early twentieth-century black music such as jazz. As we will learn, the philosopher Alain Locke emerges as a key transitional figure in contemporary cultural criticism because of the new light being shed on his views of black culture in the early twentieth century. As a bridge scholar between the spirituals and jazz, one who discussed both genres, Locke's work cleared space for the latter's new pedigree as America's classical music on the one hand, and the notion that black music provided a window into the souls of black folk on the other. Moreover, the acts of notation and recording as mediations of black culture played important roles in the rise of African-American music in the American social consciousness.

Robin D. G. Kelley has written about the 1960s as a time when social scientists converged en masse into urban ghettos in search of a real and authentic black culture that could be explained in measurable terms. What cultural practices these ethnographers 'discovered', however, were more often than not reduced and described as coping mechanisms and survival strategies.[8] Indeed, as I stated above, this search for authentic blackness had begun almost a century before at a time that also marked major shifts in American intellectualism. Cultural practices such as music – particularly the slave song – invited new sites for scientific, objective inquiries into the souls of black folk. 'Their songs', Cruz writes, 'were to be grasped as testimonies to their lives, as indices of their sense of social fate.'[9] Importantly, this view of black song would eclipse the political potency of the literary protest embedded in the slave narratives. The freshly discovered, newly aestheticised and selected-out black spirituals emerged as a powerful vehicle in the Negro liberation struggle. It became a singing testament that would be celebrated as a passage into the secrets of blackness, ones that, at the same time, began to inform America's emerging sense of its own national identity beyond that of a cultural colony of Europe.

One of the most dramatic, transformative gestures during this dynamic process comprised the act of transcribing the spirituals. The spiritual's move from oral expression to literary representation constituted a large symbolic leap and held many consequences beyond the spiritual's accessibility and mass mediation within the larger public sphere. In written form,

---

[8] Robin D. G. Kelley, *Yo' Mama's Disfunktional!: Fighting the Culture Wars in Urban America* (Boston: Beacon Press, 1997), pp. 15–42.
[9] Cruz, *Culture on the Margins*, p. 3.

the spiritual became 'increasingly considered as a modern scientific artifact, a specimen fit for capture by the spreading nets of an emergent ethno-science'.[10] Through this new modality, the spirituals' cultural work in American society musically affirmed black humanity on the margins of society. At the same time, this body of song also served the interests of a modernist scientific impulse to classify and objectify racialised people and their attendant cultural artefacts.

As I have written elsewhere, James Monroe Trotter's 1878 study of nineteenth-century black music, *Music and Some Highly Musical People* – the first of its kind by an African-American writer – demonstrates this desire to write blackness into the consciousness of both the nation and modernity through the discourse of science. He writes in the book's unnumbered opening page: 'The collection is given in order to complete the author's purpose, which is not only to show the proficiency of the subjects of the foregoing sketches as interpreters of the music of others, but, further, to illustrate the ability of quite a number of them (and relatively, that of their race) to originate and scientifically arrange good music.'[11] One certainly gets the message in all of this that (oral) songs did not become 'music' until they were presented in written form. Although Trotter recognised as important 'orally transmitted racial music', he clearly prioritises the written Western art-music tradition, as many of his fellow black intellectuals did.

The space between musical orality and musical literacy is a powerful one and has analogies in other domains of knowledge. Music historian Gary Tomlinson has recently summarised the historical development of the twin quasi-disciplines of ethnography and historiography, and this work can help us understand the spiritual's journey from musical orality to literacy. Tomlinson has argued, for example, that musical practice itself can help us understand the differences and similarities between anthropology and history as disciplines. He opens with a summary of Michel de Certeau's ideas on orality and literacy:

Where ethnography has taken as its object *orality*, historiography scrutinises *written* traces; where the one has wanted to describe an atemporal *space* of culture, the other follows change through *time*; the one starts from a gesture of radical estrangement and *alterity*, the other from an assumption of transparent *identity*; the first analyzes collective phenomena of a cultural *unconscious*, the second the *consciousness* of historical, self-knowledge.[12]

---

[10] Ibid., p. 125.
[11] James Monroe Trotter, *Music and Some Highly Musical People* (New York: Charles T. Dillingham, [1878] 1881). See also Guthrie P. Ramsey, Jr, 'Cosmopolitan or Provincial?: Ideology in Early Black Music Historiography, 1867–1940', *Black Music Research Journal* 16/1 (1996), 11–42.
[12] Gary Tomlinson, 'Musicology, Anthropology, History', in Martin Clayton, Trevor Herbert and Richard Middleton (eds.), *The Cultural Study of Music: A Critical Introduction* (New York: Routledge, 2003), p. 31.

These distinctions and oppositions cut a number of ways and have major implications for music study. Tomlinson insists, for example, that we rethink the commonplace view of musicology's 'birth' dating to the mid-nineteenth century. Rather, he extends it back a century, when the presence of *singing* stood 'at the heart of eighteenth-century accounts of the history of European society, of Europe's relation to other societies, and indeed of the origins of all societies'.[13] Singing or song existed as a category of music-making that linked Europe to its unlettered Others. Gradually, however, between 1750 and 1850, a modern conception of music emerged in Europe, one that was considered aesthetically superior to song. '[M]usic', Tomlinson argues, 'lodged itself at the heart of a discourse that pried Europe and its histories apart from non-European lives and cultures.' He continues: 'Perched at the apex of the new aesthetics, it came to function as a kind of limit-case of European uniqueness in world history and an affirmation of the gap, with the cultural formation of modernity, between history and anthropology. Music, in this sense, silenced many non-European activities that it might instead have attended to.'[14]

The new conception of music included two important and related developments: the rise and privileging of virtuoso instrumentalism and the advancement of the written musical representation thereof. The perceived power of instrumental music peaked over the course of the nineteenth century, and this development was coupled with new views about music's ability to transcend its social setting, instrumental music's non-mimetic expressive capacities, the musical work's perceived fixity and discreteness in notation, and 'even a revising of the human subject that perceived all these things'.[15] For my present purposes, these observations have enormous import for the Negro spiritual and subsequent black music-making in America.

As it did for the new conception of music in European history, the act of notating the Negro spiritual carried out some important cultural work. If notation served to detach or abstract music from its original contexts, then it could be argued that the spirituals' notated form divorced them from black culture. While this may be too severe a view, this move from orality to literacy did impact how observers perceived their access into black culture, albeit an idea of black culture that conformed to the goals of the proto-ethnographers fascinated by them. According to Tomlinson:

The notated work took on almost magical characteristics, projecting spirit outward in legible form, and traversing the distance between musical exegete and composer. The search for the secrets of this written work could in large degree ignore and thus conceal the social interactions of performers and audience at the scene itself of music making.[16]

---

[13] Ibid., p. 33. [14] Ibid., p. 32. [15] Ibid., p. 34. [16] Ibid., p. 39.

This 'black music without the black folk' magic was a complicated matter, indeed. In fact, the search for the secrets of blackness in the spirituals whispered through a notated score seemed to encourage the transcribers to 'overcode' them with meanings that were, in Cruz's view, embedded in the ethnographers' religious frameworks and political agendas if not always in those of the performers themselves. (We have certainly witnessed this development in subsequent genres and historical moments.) Despite the costs of such an abstraction, the act helped to move African Americans from objects of history to bona fide subjects in the American consciousness. Indeed, the desire to 'advance' African Americans through the creation of authoritative texts and artefacts that could be unperformed yet comprehended solely from their notation situated their new modernity in strictly Eurocentric terms, and in some of the same terms that had earlier separated Europeans from their 'simply' singing non-European global neighbours. With one gesture of the pen, untutored orality became lettered culture, space becomes disciplined identity, cultural unconsciousness becomes historical consciousness. Black music would continue this crucial role in African-American cultural politics throughout the next century and beyond.

If Cruz explains how the 'discovery' of the Negro spiritual shaped the course of American intellectual history, and Zuberi has documented the crucial role of racial stratification in the development of social 'objective' science, then Ronald Radano in his exhaustive study *Lying up a Nation: Race and Black Music* adds yet another dimension to this historical moment. Radano argues that the very idea of black music is constitutive of the broader idea of race itself in American history. In fact, his discussion of black music's emergence challenges – with more than a hint of revisionist zeal – the idea that modern black music extends solely from the traditional impulses of a singular black mainstream. Radano's work defies 'those strategies of containment that uphold the racial binaries informing the interpretation of black music. It goes against the grain of a pervasive, yet remarkably underanalyzed assumption that correlates an enduring black music presence with the myth of a consistent and stable socio-racial position of "blackness."'[17]

In Radano's view, African-American music is a modern construction of many racialist discourses that clustered together, gathered steam and culminated in its contemporary form around 1900. Black music has been inextricably linked to our understanding of 'blackness' writ large – as a knowable, learnable and teachable fact of social reality and identity. He believes that this identity has been largely dependent on the aforementioned musical developments. With these arguments, Radano calls for a reinterpretation of contemporary black musical forms, indeed, a radical rehearing acquired from a new set of subversive listening skills. These are tall orders.

---

[17] Radano, *Lying up a Nation*, p. 3.

How does he begin to convince us? He begins with a lie. Drawing on the ethnographic work of Zora Neale Hurston as set out in her *Mules and Men*, Radano relates a story, one that inspired both the title and intellectual licence for his study. Hurston wrote in her 1935 study that as she moved about her native Eatonville, Florida rural community collecting stories and other data, the citizens told what they called 'lies'.

They were not literal lies but, rather, creative expressions of poetic licence – allegories that celebrated the ironic twists of fate giving substance and texture to the art of southern black living. The better the story, the better the lie; the better the lie, the closer one gets to the ironic pleasures and terror of America's racial sublime. In an opening sequence, Hurston, standing back uncharacteristically from the text, requests a story from her friend, George Thomas. Thomas replies matter-of-factly, 'Zora, you come to de right place if lies is what you want. Ah'm gointer lie up a nation.'[18]

Radano's account, an epic act of signifyin(g) and speculation on the very idea of black music in the white, public consciousness, argues for a mulatto understanding of African-American culture in much the same spirit that Albert Murray did in his classic *The Omni-Americans* in 1970. American racial consciousness by its very nature, however, has produced a conflicted affect for black music (or Negro music as it was known earlier). It developed together with American notions of racial difference – as a way to subjugate black humanity and as a way for black Americans themselves to express a musical identity. Thus, nineteenth-century black music represented much more than just sound – or noise, for that matter. It became an audible index of many ideas about race, cultural politics and national identity. Indeed, we have learned that black music has comprised the soundtrack for the dance of an emerging American cultural identity, signifying 'both the integrationist completion of a nation as well as a racial threat to the integrity of whiteness'.[19] In the acts of notating the spirituals, the contemporaneous statistical verification of racial differences, and in the very idea of black music itself, we see several important issues surfacing. They were embedded in nineteenth-century cultural politics, religious ideologies and racialist discourses, all of which carried many implications for the subsequent development and reception history of African-American music throughout the next century and beyond.

The first thirty years of the twentieth century saw a hurricane of creative and scholarly activities that moved African Americans from behind the Du Boisian veil and into modern life. These publishing, musical and entrepreneurial activities were anything but uniform and monotone; they embodied myriad angles, positions and propositions. As a period witnessing the inauguration of the African-American literary-criticism tradition, writers defined the moment with pointed debates about the use of black

---

[18] Ibid., p. 47. [19] Ibid., p. 42.

literature as cultural propaganda and argued publicly not only about the nature of black creativity but also about its relationship to African-American subjectivity. Music also figured prominently during this time, and all manner of music-making and related activities characterised these pivotal years: from western art music to the blues, from the collection and transcription of folk music to the development of non-patronising stances in criticism and cultural interpretation.

All of this work sought to discipline the black muse even as it documented various moments in Afro-Americana's rise from the outhouse of presumed primitive origins to the big house of modernity. The hands, hearts and pens of the 'talented tenth' members of 'the Race' held the belief that intersections with mainstream culture could transform black vernacular music into something worthy of the sceptical white (and black) aristocratic gaze. Or so they hoped.

Of the musical styles that grew from the cultures of Afro-Americana, jazz has inspired the most extensive scholarly attention to date. Beginning with early twentieth-century record-collecting enthusiasts seeking to impose order on an exploding and eclectic discography, the field of jazz studies (as it is now called) is today in the vanguard of academic enquiries into American culture.[20] This new field attracts scholars from many disciplines, including the 'musicologies' (ethnomusicology, musicology, and music theory), American studies, history, cultural studies and sociology, among others. The energy created by this interdisciplinary activity has inspired the feeling among many observers that jazz represents the quintessential American expression, America's classical music, indeed, the country's only true art-form.

The historical grounding of this new pedigree of jazz and its study can be traced back to the 1920s and 1930s when a confluence of discourses converged into heated debates about the future of African Americans and their culture. As the historian and cultural critic Eric Porter has recently argued, writers and musicians such as James Weldon Johnson were faced in this moment with a conundrum. The debates surrounding the supposed biological or cultural racial distinctiveness of black Americans created something of a crisis. Indeed, settling the thorny question of nature versus nurture in African-American culture has become an important concern throughout the history of jazz studies. It is useful to revisit this historical moment in light of recent developments in scholarship because it highlights a shift concerning the cultural work of 'race'.

In his intellectual history of jazz titled *What Is This Thing Called Jazz?*, Porter provides a virtuoso portrait of the 1920s jazz world, a bustling scene

[20] For an example of this interdisciplinary scholarship, see Robert G. O'Meally, Brent Hayes Edwards and Farah Jasmine Griffin, *Uptown Conversations: The New Jazz Studies* (New York: Columbia University, 2004).

in which he depicts African-American musicians as self-consciously participating in the struggles over black representation and social advancement.[21] He charts, for example, an emerging sense of modernity among African Americans themselves, not simply as historical actors unwillingly swept up in a tide of social events but as astute social agents with specific ideas about where they and their creations fit into the larger scheme of things. Musicians such as Duke Ellington, W. C. Handy, James Reese Europe, James Weldon Johnson, Louis Armstrong together with the writers W. E. B. Du Bois, Zora Neale Hurston, Joel A. Rodgers, Dave Peyton and Alain Locke, among others, struggled over some of the pressing issues of the day: most prominent among them, racial uplift on the one hand and the shaking of black (and white) bottoms on the other.[22]

The contested space between 'uplift' and 'get down' existed as a continuum between two poles. At one end rested the idea that African-American achievements within the forms and techniques of Western European music culture would somehow vindicate black citizens within American society and the world. At the other end stood the belief that black music could serve to distinguish black culture from the rest of the nation. While it may be an exaggeration to assert that every musician composed and performed in a heightened state of politicised and racialised identity awareness, Porter convincingly paints a portrait of musicians aware that they were involved in deliberate negotiations of their social world through their creative work. They wanted to make a difference. As Porter argues: 'Making sense of jazz often involved a struggle, for various political and ideological reasons, to elevate the music as a black expression in spite of, or in response to, its precarious place in American life. These debates about music were also a pointed commentary about the liberating and constraining aspects of racial thinking in a segregated, racist society.'[23] Indeed, black music in general, and jazz in particular, represented key figures in racialist discussions throughout the twentieth century with little sign of abating.

Modernism, or better, 'Afro-modernism', as I have called it elsewhere, was a central issue of the Harlem Renaissance, a moment in African-American history self-consciously entrenched in the 'culture as capital' debates of the early twentieth century.[24] Key writers emerged as leaders in this eclectic movement. In *Deep River: Music and Memory in Harlem Renaissance Thought*, Paul Anderson portrays the person who is considered its leading architect, Alain Locke, a writer best known for his editorship of

---

[21] Eric Porter, *What Is This Thing Called Jazz?: African American Musicians as Artists, Critics, and Activists* (Berkeley: University of California Press, 2002).
[22] Ibid., pp. 1–53.   [23] Ibid., p. 18.
[24] On the term 'Afromodernism', see Guthrie P. Ramsey, Jr, *Race Music: Black Cultures From Bebop to Hip-Hop* (Berkeley: University of California Press, 2003), pp. 96–130.

The New Negro (1925).²⁵ As a black intellectual embodying a complex and shifting set of values throughout his career, Locke cuts a fascinating figure. In my earlier work, I, along with many others, believed that Locke's views on culture were simply Eurocentric. Anderson, however, clears the way for other interpretations of Locke's work. This repositioning of Locke and other writers of the period through the lens of black music and social memory allows us to see Locke's vision in all of its nuance and as an important precursor to contemporary black cultural criticism.

Locke emerges as a transitional black intellectual. As a direct heir of the ethno-sympathy strain of the spirituals' transcribers, he took the idea that one could understand the people through their music but coupled it with very strict views about the relative value of oral music and the written, arranged spirituals. Thus he, like his earlier counterparts, privileged the written, more 'modern' renditions of these songs. Furthermore, while he did believe that jazz was a valuable, though raw, musical form, the vernacular music ironically achieved what Locke wanted for black classical music: prestige and currency in America's cultural profile.

Jazz's pedigree grew from several conflicting, though sometimes related discourses. In addition to the view held by Locke, Anderson describes how many white intellectuals of the period invested in jazz with what he calls 'a countercultural aura of erotic liberation'.²⁶ And a younger generation of black intellectuals represented by writers Langston Hughes and Zora Neale Hurston, who eschewed both of these views, argued instead for the self-sufficient relevance of popular music such as blues, jazz and the core-culture Negro spirituals. Thus, three views prevailed. One belief – that black folk music was best expressed in the trappings of modernist concert music – has been most typically linked to Locke. Another view privileged the white gaze of primitivism from the outside in. And the third dispelled both the cultural evolutionary model of the first and the romanticised 'noble savage' ideal of the second, opting instead for a self-satisfied celebration of the everyday blackness of the proletariat. In practice, however, none of these views stood in complete opposition to one another, as Anderson's detailed and compelling intellectual portraits of major figures of this period show us.

Locke's racial and artistic philosophies reveal a complex bundle of ideas, some of which prefigured those of contemporary black cultural criticism. While Locke believed in racial specificity, for example, he also championed the idea of the hybridity of African-American culture – a 'cultural racialism' that would transcend the class boundaries that were an inevitable consequence of the upward mobility of the black middle class. Anderson

---

²⁵ Paul Allen Anderson, *Deep River: Music and Memory in Harlem Renaissance Thought* (Durham: Duke University Press, 2001).
²⁶ Ibid., p. 8.

shows us, however, that Locke's educational experiences, friendships, intellectual attachments and legacies, and the ebb and flow of the contemporaneous debates surrounding his ideas, portrays a thinker free of simplistic binaries and rich with complexity.

One of these complexities is embodied in Locke's views about jazz and other forms of popular music. Locke believed, for example, that black vernacular forms and American art music would be mutually transformative, and 'that the elaboration of African American cultural difference would *not* exclude a mutually transforming integration; integration would be fulfilled only when white racism and its pervasive institutional and ideological effects had been decisively eviscerated'.[27] While Locke's cultural relativism guided some of his writings, one could question whether he truly understood the formal and creative processes of popular forms or even that of the 'universal' formal concert music that he adored. Nevertheless, Locke's notion of cultural racialism has been remarkably influential, and if not directly referenced, certainly prefigures some of the contemporary ideas about jazz and culture that I discuss below.

As I wrote earlier, in Tomlinson's configuration, a complex notational system served to make Western art music more autonomous and prestigious. But black music's journey to this pedigree has been a more contentious and certainly less direct route – if it has reached that pinnacle at all. In fact, it would not be until much later that instrumental jazz would be able even to approach such a distinction when the genre would be separated from the others marketed under the 'race music' rubric. Even in the nineteenth-century quest for scientific representations of the spirituals, the function of African-American music would always be perceived as serving a specific role in America's race industry. It would always perform specific kinds of functional, cultural work for its performers, transcribers and audiences, though not always the same kind. In other words, African-American music would always be tied inextricably to a specific social function.

Ironically, however, recording technology and not notation technology would point black music toward this ideal of autonomy, albeit autonomy with a difference. As Mark Katz argues in *Capturing Sound: How Technology Has Changed Music*, sound recordings carried specific consequences for jazz and its study. Like the transcriptions achieved for the spirituals, recordings disseminated jazz widely, allowing a repeatability that privileged sound over the printed score. 'In jazz', Katz writes, 'the values of the classical world are inverted: the performance is the primary text, while the score is merely an interpretation.'[28]

---

[27] Ibid., p. 134.
[28] Mark Katz, *Capturing Sound: How Technology Has Changed Music* (Berkeley: University of California Press, 2004), p. 78.

Another distinction about recordings can be made here, one that inverts some cultural work that Tomlinson addressed earlier in this essay. Katz makes this point clear when he argues: 'A recorded improvisation ... is music of the moment made timeless, the one-of-a-kind rendered reproducible, the spontaneous turned inevitable.'[29] On the one hand, science in the form of recording technology served similar functions as notation did for instrumental Western European music and for the spirituals: it allowed a musical experience to be engaged outside of the circumstances of its original social and historical contexts. On the other hand, the orality of sound recordings, indeed their decidedly non-literary quality, undermines many modernist ideals that privilege the written as the sole signs of progress, history and consciousness.

Through mass-produced recordings, black music and subjectivity in the public sphere sprouted wings and took flight. Eventually recordings would inspire future kinds of scientific study, first, in the activities of the discophiles that in typical modernist fashion collected and catalogued them, and ultimately in the modern practices of musical analysis and historicist cultural criticism. Mass-mediated, recorded music became an important reservoir of memory, culture-building and pleasure that opened both material possibilities in the marketplace and new dimensions for expression. Katz highlights this cultural work concisely: 'True, mass-reproduced art does lack temporal and physical uniqueness, yet reproductions, no longer bound to the circumstances of their creation, may encourage new experiences and generate new traditions, wherever they happen to be.'[30]

The new repeatable, portable blackness that appeared in the early twentieth century and the score-bound blackness of the nineteenth century beg us to rethink race, particularly when it is used as a unit of analysis in music studies. Music presented both a challenge and rich potential to black intellectuals devising ways to argue for black social equity in the 1910s and 1920s. These musical arguments comprised competing, though not mutually exclusive, 'modernisms' represented in two developing genres: jazz and the spirituals.

In the spirituals, we see the more common modernist idea of cultural evolution: the spirituals could serve best as the raw material for a cosmopolitan art manifested in art song, opera, chamber music and symphonies. Composers such as James Weldon Johnson set the spiritual in modernist dress, canonising these new settings in the concert literature, especially among black musicians. But the unruly muse of recorded jazz presented a challenge to the cultural evolution model. While 'symphonic jazz' experienced a period of popularity during the 1920s and 1930s, jazz has, in many ways, developed along its own trajectory. Jazz has certainly responded stylistically to other genres but it did so without shedding core elements

[29] Ibid., p. 79.   [30] Ibid., p. 15.

of its distinctive character. Thus, jazz represented what might be thought of as a different kind of modernism, one reflecting the sensibilities of the black masses – an Afro-modernism so to speak. Interestingly, neither the spirituals nor jazz monopolised black musical modernism. The appearance of gospel music, for example, could also be considered an important modernist form, one cloaked in the 'folksy' galloping refrains and rejuvenating cries and groans of the storefront, urban black church.

I conclude by offering a way to discuss how this new historical work can help us talk about race in the contemporary moment without falling into patterns of essentialism and in ways that lend to African-American culture the distinctiveness that historical and contemporaneous actors seem to grant it – the quality that allows it to circulate compelling ethnocentric social energies throughout its many worlds. These energies were disseminated through the historical notations and recordings during the late nineteenth and early twentieth centuries, encountering other cultures and taking on new meanings as they moved along. One must take this movement into account as we discuss race as a unit of analysis in musical discourse.

I have begun to think about race as a tripartite concept with porous boundaries separating each stream.[31] Social race embodies the social experience of being a racialised subject. It constitutes the realm of the everyday and is always bound to such variables as geographic location, historical moment, and agency through self-fashioning. Cultural race constitutes the performative dimensions of the social experience. It includes the expressive gestures of speech, music, dance and so on that provide us with a way to communicate to others how we situate ourselves socially in the world. Theoretical race comprises the dense academic (and deliciously speculative) treatments of race in contemporary cultural theory; many of these have sought to deconstruct and de-essentialise racial thinking.

Several points are important within this paradigm. It is useful to keep in mind that as we scholars live race, perform race and theorise race, we participate in the same discursive networks that recordings and transcriptions do. Thus, our scholarship is embedded in the same system of social, historical and cultural contingencies as our objects of study, and our subjectivities are indeed a large part of our 'objective' work. It is not, in other words, autonomous. The new reorientation of blackness in American musical history represented in the research discussed here is a significant step forward in African-American studies. Perhaps, the next step in our re-contextualisation of the past will involve revealing some of our own secrets and lies and how they have shaped the music and work to which we are undeniably devoted. In this way, the lesson of 'blackness', theorised or Other-wise may become not a lie but one of America's undisputed truths.

---

[31] I first wrote about this in 'The Pot Liquor Principle: Developing a Black Music Criticism in American Music Studies', *American Music* 22/2 (2004), 284–95.

CHAPTER 3

'Gypsy violins' and 'hot rhythms': race, popular music and governmentality

Brian Currid

The dissimilarities between the histories of gypsies in Europe and blacks in the United States seem initially overwhelming, the difference between the role of the two groups in the respective economies of Europe and America being only the most obvious. The latter coalesced as a category of identity within the global geopolitical economy of the slave trade, later to be rooted in the subsequent processes of early industrialisation. In contrast, the modern ethnic notion of the gypsy developed within the quite different economy of labour migration within Europe and formed in some sense the remainder and supplement produced and required by the practices of discipline and surveillance that moulded national populations in nineteenth-century Europe.[1] The slippery definitional problem of the gypsy on the margins of European nation-building thus at first seems to bear little resemblance to the overly clear, seemingly continuous identity of imported forced labour in the history of the United States in particular.[2] Not only do these two processes seem to offer little basis for comparison, the two racial concepts circulate differently when seen through a trans-Atlantic lens: on the one hand, the tendency in twentieth-century Europe to conflate a fetishisation of blackness with notions of American identity is not mirrored by any truly similar phenomenon in the case of the gypsy from an American perspective, although we might suggest that the gypsy violinist is indeed an acoustic icon that stands in for a general Europeanness with no specific national identification.

Yet an apparent distinction between these two historical configurations seems less fundamental if we look at the articulation of fetishism and degeneracy that operated within the ideological apparatuses behind and

---

[1] Leo Lucassen, 'Eternal Vagrants? State Formation, Migration, and Travelling Groups in Western Europe, 1350–1914', in Jan Lucassen and Leo Lucassen (eds.), *Migration, Migration History, History: Old Paradigms and New Perspectives* (New York: Peter Lang, 1997), pp. 225–52. See also Leo Lucassen, *Zigeuner: Die Geschichte eines polizeilichen Ordnungsbegriffes in Deutschland, 1700–1945* (Cologne: Böhlau, 1996).
[2] On the historic entanglement of black identity and the economics of the Atlantic see Paul Gilroy, *The Black Atlantic: Modernity and Double Consciousness* (Cambridge, MA: Harvard University Press, 1993).

around both forms of identity.³ But the similarity also goes further than this, not only embracing a structural similarity, but extending to the social forms in which this point of contradiction found resonant form: crucially, in both cases the supremely fetishistic operation of these categories of personhood was from the beginning intimately associated with popular forms of acoustic culture, serving as arguably the two most central racially inscribed acoustic icons of musical practice in the age of mass media.

What kind of conclusions can we draw from these similarities? How can we explain the approximate temporal synchronicity of these two sites of acoustic overdetermination? In the following, I will explore comparatively the relationship of race to popular music in these two cases, along the way proposing ways of thinking about the relationship between acoustic culture, the state and identity formation in the nineteenth and twentieth centuries in both Europe and America. By exploring the contours of these two phenomena, we can go beyond a mere discussion of racial stereotype or appropriation, linking these particularly modern forms of racial fantasy to the emergence of new technologies of personhood in the late nineteenth and early twentieth centuries.

IDENTITY, MUSICALITY AND RACE

In Europe, particularly in Germany and Central Europe, the image of the gypsy has been intimately associated with various forms of music and musicality since the mid-nineteenth century. This conglomeration of musical practices and musical discourse was always accompanied by the simultaneous production of the gypsy as an object of social discipline and control. This link is more intimate than a simple connection in modes of representation. The very emergence of our modern understanding of musical expression and inherent, quasi-genetic musical talent around various forms of musical stardom in the first half of the nineteenth century coincides with the emergence of the gypsy in racialising discourse. First, the gypsy emerged as a fixture of both programme and salon music: composers like Liszt and Brahms made the gypsy a centrepiece of the cultural fantasies of Central European art music.⁴ At the same time, an urban, popular tradition based on gypsy musics and the figure of the gypsy began to develop.⁵ Finally, as a stock character in operettas like *Der Zigeunerprimás* (Emmerich Kalman, 1912) and *Zigeunerliebe* (Franz Lehár, 1908) the 'gypsy

---

³ For more on the gypsy case in Nazi Germany, see Brian Currid, *A National Acoustics: Music and Mass Publicity in Weimar and Nazi Germany* (Minneapolis: University of Minnesota Press, 2005).
⁴ See Franz Liszt, *Gesammelte Schriften*, 6 vols. (Leipzig: Breitkopf und Härtel, 1910), vol. III, *Die Zigeuner und Ihre Musik in Ungarn*. For a detailed discussion of this, see Max Peter Baumann, 'The Reflection of the Roma in European Art Music', *The World of Music* 38/1 (1996), 95–138.
⁵ Ferenc Bóvis, 'Zigeunermusizieren in Ungarn', in Friedrich Blume (ed.), *Musik in Geschichte und Gegenwart* (Kassel: Bärenreiter, 1965), p. 1282.

musician' – and stylised versions of gypsy music – found ready popularity in the cosmopolitan audiences of the growing metropolises of Europe at the turn of the century, filling living rooms, concert halls, opera houses and less reputable establishments of popular entertainment.[6] In literature as well, particularly in the then emergent Germany, the figure of the gypsy was always associated with innate musicality: as but one example, *Friedemann Bach*, Albert E. Brachvogel's historical novel on the 'failed' Bach son, dedicates most of one chapter to his dealings with a gypsy 'horde'. The encounter with the gypsies is inaugurated by the sound of music, and the passage describing Bach's experience of this music is illustrative for the romanticising investment in the gypsy sound:

> At this moment, a deep, wavering tone swelled up, as if a metallic basin had been struck, and a slow, earnest, almost plaintive song rushed down to him with many invisible voices ... The deep pain, the secret, dark belief and a foreign, southern magic that streamed through this melody made an indescribable impression upon him ... a deep, child-like emotion that he had not felt for years came over him, and a longing for love, for a holy something ... hit him with increasing intensity.[7]

This passage is truly remarkable for its over-excited listing of emotional excess engendered in the attempt to describe the acoustic manifestation of otherness. A musical cartography of 'foreign, southern' magic is oddly inverted to become an intensified feeling of self, a 'holy something' that places the listener back in a childlike state, thus revealing the contradictions in both the imagination of the self and the placement of that self within a European cartography of emerging nation states. In the alienated world of modernisation, the acoustics of migrant musics are required to engender a true experience of European selfhood, yet also threaten to seduce the listener away from the proper path of self-improvement and progress. Friedemann Bach's failure is ultimately due to an excessive, undisciplined relationship to self that is 'tragically' disarticulated from modern economies of labour and exchange, a relationship summed up by the sound of gypsy music.

The development of this racial figure shifted at the end of the nineteenth century. While already earliest versions of a modern sense of gypsy identity focused on a vague sense of the exotic and primeval, in the late nineteenth- and twentieth-century version of gypsy discourse, traits which beforehand seemed blissfully and abstractly natural, rooted in a distant, exotic past, were now explained in increasingly 'precise' biological terms. In the more clearly 'racist' mode of this discursive production, like a 1940 article published in the German *Zeitschrift für Ethnologie*, the physical characteristics of the gypsy are produced through a complex apparatus of different

---

[6] On the relationship between Hungarian and gypsy musics, and an introduction to what we know as 'gypsy' style, see Bálint Sárosi, *Gypsy Music* (Budapest: Corvina Press, 1978).
[7] Albert E. Brachvogel, *Friedemann Bach*, 3 vols. (Berlin: Otto Fanke, 1858), vol. III, pp. 9–10.

forms of knowledge production – including photography – and enable claims not about the historical backwardness of the gypsy, but rather their inherent physical inferiority.[8] Although the bulk of the article is dedicated to descriptions of physical or pseudo-physical differences like 'the smell that a gypsy spreads in his surroundings',[9] physiognomic considerations like the 'nose index',[10] and general patterns of gypsy behaviour – 'the gypsy prefers sparkling wine'[11] – this 'anthropology' of the gypsy also includes a brief musical characterisation. In this case, however, musical performance is somehow seen, like in the later description of skull structure, as indicative of a biologically determined 'gypsy soul'. Surprisingly, even here, the musical side of gypsy identity is depicted in a positive light:

> This primitive and animal-like being is however to a large extent balanced out . . . by great musical talent. There is no land on the planet in which gypsies are not known and treasured as musicians [*Musikanten*].[12]

For Gerhard Stein, gypsy musicality was simply one more piece of the puzzle in compiling a complete psychological, anthropological and physiological understanding of the gypsy. Indeed, gypsy music is here a key representation of a racial 'essence': 'It is typical that the already mentioned multifaceted character and variability of the gypsy soul is represented in his music most completely and clearly. Just as he plays, he is in reality.'[13]

The development of the figure of the modern gypsy and his supposed musicality can be seen as a mirror image of a similar historical process in the (Anglo-) American world: over the course of the nineteenth century, as part of the process of the mass-mediatisation of acoustic culture, the figure of the black musician and his supposedly natural musicality emerged in a number of different forms. Dating from around 1830, an early notion of black music and musicality also revolved primarily around romantic tropes of natural rootedness, serving as the authentic counter-pole to white civilisation.[14] Staged in various contexts, from the parlour to the vaudeville stage, this notion of black music and musicality, produced primarily around the minstrel figures of the nineteenth-century American stage and parlour music, bears an uncanny resemblance to Central Europe's gypsies in operetta and salon. More importantly, the relationship between racialising musical tropes and the production of racial identity itself was in both cases highly reflexive: the production of the racial category of gypsy was cemented in these theatrical traditions and modes of domestic consumption, so that later discourses of authenticity mobilised by 'actual'

---

[8] Gerhard Stein, 'Zur Physiologie und Anthropolgie der Zigeuner in Deutschland', *Zeitschrift für Ethnologie* 72/1–3 (1940), 74–113. On the various techniques used to define the gypsy, see Lucassen, *Zigeuner*.
[9] Stein, 'Physiologie und Anthropologie', 77. [10] Ibid., 100. [11] Ibid. [12] Ibid., 89. [13] Ibid.
[14] See Ronald Radano, 'Denoting Difference: The Writing of the Slave Spirituals', *Critical Inquiry* 22 (1996), 506–44.

gypsy musicians were inevitably implicated in the hybrid play that determined the very historical formation of gypsy music itself. In the American context, again in a mirror image of the European practice, the forms of racial drag that both mobilised and produced nineteenth-century notions of race – as particularly seen in minstrelsy – also came to play a definitive role in the production of black music itself.[15]

In European state discourses, the gypsy of the nineteenth century emerged primarily around apparatuses of border control, reflecting the state's interest in controlling mobility in the age of early 'welfare' policies.[16] Similarly, the increasing threat that the migrant black population in the United States was imagined to pose to white civilisation mirrored in many ways the construction of deviant migration in Europe of the same period. This parallel in the development of nation and place was also echoed in the conception of black identity and its relationship to musicality. Again, similar to the figure of the gypsy, the increasing biologisation of racial discourse in the late nineteenth century cast musicality in a new genetic framework: the 'spirituality' from earlier interpretations of the sounds of black voices became increasingly the expression of physical characteristics.[17] This was expressed in both negative and positive depictions of black musicality. In particular, the notion of 'hot rhythms' and an inherent biological configuration of black rhythmic difference served to root the linkage between acoustic culture and twentieth-century configurations of racial personhood.[18]

SOUNDING COSMOPOLITAN: GYPSY BLOOD, HOT RHYTHMS AND THE SOUND OF MODERNITY

Like the Jew in both anti-Semitic and philo-Semitic discourse, the gypsy was a definitionally transnational subject; this transnational character was on the one hand cause for suspicion. The ideological threat provided by embodying the leakage of the modern nation state was translated in European social fantasy into a concrete fear of agential subversion: gypsies were often suspected of espionage. At the same time, the figuration of the gypsy as a sign of the foreign could be retooled in a seemingly 'positive' way: this is particularly interesting in the German case in the 1920s and 1930s. The sound of gypsy music could serve as an icon of travel. This is made clear in an advertisement from 1936: 'A World Full of Music' (see Figure 3.1). The image features a larger-than-life view of a gypsy violinist, emerging from the radio as he plays for the happy German couple at home.

---

[15] Eric Lott, *Love and Theft: Blackface Minstrelsy and the American Working Class* (Oxford University Press, 1993).
[16] Klaus Bade, *Europa in Bewegung: Migration vom späten 18. Jahrhundert bis zur Gegenwart* (Munich: Beck, 2000).
[17] Radano, 'Denoting Difference'.   [18] Ibid.

Figure 3.1: 'A World Full of Music': an advertisement from 1936

The text reads: 'The true to nature play of the radio receiver from the new *Telefunken* year is wonderful. As if the *Zigeunerprimas* played in your room!' The gypsy violinist is depicted in a caricature that comes to inhabit the implicitly domestic space of the German living room through the technology of the radio. Serving as one more sign of the pleasures of commodity capitalism and reinforcing the glamour of this high-end radio receiver, the allure of 'exotic' gypsy music in the home is comparable to that of other commodities that traffic in the exotic. The use of costume additionally produces this music as a would-be visual spectacle: a synaesthetic celebration of the cosmopolitan possibilities of the new mass media, the ad resolutely refuses the dialect of degeneracy, instead integrating the 'true to nature' sound of gypsy music into the very production of domestic intimacy. The technology promises access to a commercial cosmopolitanism, and by placing the gypsy as one figure in an ethnically marked series, engages a fully articulated visual vocabulary of the exotic.

The production of 'gypsy music' as an exotic commodity not only took place in the techniques of advertising, but was rooted in various zones of actual musical practice. If we assume that this advertising was at all intelligible to the audience of the period, we can already conclude that some familiarity with 'gypsy music' is a common denominator of the audience addressed by this advertisement. Again, it indexes a media network around the figure of the gypsy: everyday musical practice in the cities of Germany was dominated in the 1920s by the figure of the gypsy musician in various ways. Hungarian 'ambience' bands were 'a fixture in the band-landscape in Germany' during the Weimar Republic.[19] These bands were most often small trios, quartets or quintets. Led, like many other kinds of bands in urban Central Europe, by the *Stehgeiger* [standing violinist], the band would also include other string players, certainly a cello or bass, possibly a cimbalom and almost always a piano.[20] But this kind of light music was only one of the styles of music linked to the figure of the gypsy: jazz music and jazzy renditions of popular song were intimately associated with the racial figure of the gypsy. Indeed, early performances of jazz on the radio were often described in terms that focused on the 'gypsy blood' of their performers. In a 1927 review of a radio concert of the London Radio Jazz Band, the German commentator described the music of this 'most frequently heard jazz band of Europe', broadcast by 'twenty-five radio stations daily ... through the whole world' with the following racialising inventory:

It is said about the leader of the band, the blonde Hun Sidney Firman that he comes from a gypsy family. Sidney ... won't say anything at all about this ... Similarly with the banjo player, who, as an Argentine, is a true son of the Pampas. The saxophone is also cast according to style: Mr. Leslie is the real Yankee, like in a book. And that the man sitting behind the drum set has Negro blood rolling through his veins almost goes without saying.[21]

The gypsy violinist is here placed as the racial starting point of this cosmopolitan inventory of sound and blood. This trend towards a racial diagnosis of jazz virtuosity was by no means a purely German phenomenon, but rather played a role throughout Europe, linking German popular musics with a broader, cosmopolitan European vernacular.

These multiple forms of popular musical practice insistently return to the locus of gypsy musicality. Even if the linkage to gypsy racial identity is not explicitly mentioned, the context in which they were placed made it clear that the implicit linkage was more than readily understood by its audience. Not only do they traffic in a given set of recognisable musical traits, but these musical traits themselves were seen as icons of cosmopolitan, urban, modern life. The figure of gypsy music and musicality, detached from the specific linkage of place to personhood that determined the operation of the modern, capitalist nation state by the gypsies' mythologised wanderings to and through Europe, remained in this period the locus of cosmopolitan capitalist fantasy, even while the forced removal of

---

[19] Helmut Schröder, *Tanz- und Unterhaltungsmusik in Deutschland 1918–1933* (Bonn: Verlag für systematische Wissenschaft, 1990), p. 91.
[20] Ibid.
[21] 'Hier Charleston auf Welle London! London's Radio Dance Band', *Rundfunk-Rundschau* 2/17 (1927), 331.

gypsies from Germany increasingly became state policy. While the practice of migration was in policy to be limited to cases of the search for work, this music served as the space where the glamour of a work-free life of travel and decadent pleasure could be enjoyed by the non-migrant population.

The link to jazz is of course informative. If in the European case the gypsy link to jazz made gypsy music and musicality an acoustic icon of a hyper-modern cosmopolitan sphere, the American consumption of jazz was repeatedly linked to a staging of the worldly. The hot blood of the gypsy violinist becomes the hot rhythm of the jazz band, and serves in the American national imaginary – and beyond – as a sonic emblem of urban modernity. As Ronald Radano has argued, 'hotness' in music became associated with a particularly American brand of modernity: the racial referent continually harboured both danger and promise, but the linkage of primitivism to a cosmopolitan sphere of modern consumption cannot be overheard. The urban sounds of Gershwin's 'Fascinatin' Rhythm', for example, stand alongside the earlier referents of the bucolic minstrelsy of the same composer's 'Swanee' – always the source of contradiction, black music was aligned on the one hand with the city life of the 1920s and 1930s, while at the same time retaining the folk sounds of a long-distant, and of course never-existent past.

STAGING AUTHENTICITY: THE RURAL SOUTH AND THE *PUSZTA*

If one side of the fetish of black musicality served in both a positive and negative sense as an icon of the modern and 'worldly', black music also exhibited a central, yet uneasy relationship to the production of forms of national authenticity in the United States.[22] As Eric Lott has shown, in the world of nineteenth-century minstrelsy, most importantly, authentic Americanness was produced and inhabited by Irish working-class immigrants who mimed whiteness by imitating a version of 'blackness'.[23] This musical link to national authenticity via a code of black musicality, as it turns out, lasted in this form long into the twentieth century. The slave song, which Ronald Radano has described as 'a site of wholes and origins', went through multiple permutations in American post-war public culture.[24] Indeed, by being continually reproduced in various invented

---

[22] In fact, as Julie Brown has pointed out, authors like Bartók explicitly thematised the links between 'gypsy music', the complex relationship urban/countryside, and registers of cultural capital (aristocrats and fallen aristocrats). See Julie Brown, 'Bartók, the Gypsies, and Hybridity in Music', in Georgina Born and David Hesmondhalgh (eds.), *Western Music and Its Others: Difference, Representation, and Appropriation in Music* (Berkeley: University of California Press, 2000), pp. 119–42.
[23] Eric Lott, *Love and Theft: Blackface Minstrelsy and the American Working Class* (Oxford University Press, 1995).
[24] Radano, 'American Modernism and the Idea of Black Rhythm', in Ronald Radano and Philip V. Bohlman (eds.), *Music and the Racial Imagination* (University of Chicago Press, 2000), p. 466.

sounds, the slave song produced both black music and 'America' as coherent entities across a diachronic axis. Through multiple levels of nostalgic reference, the entertainment traditions of Tin Pan Alley and later Hollywood continually reproduced these earlier versions of black musicality, complementary to and parallel with more modern notions of hot rhythm and cosmopolitan 'sophistication' associated with urban jazz culture – from the early sound films of Al Jolson, which mimicked the earlier processes of Americanisation, through its reference to the by then long-gone minstrel tradition. The 'Swanee' romanticism of Tin Pan Alley and early sound film would later shift to the black-drag of Hollywood singing stars like Judy Garland and Bing Crosby, whose 'bluesy' voices always mimicked a more or less explicitly hued musical past, and continued to exhibit an explicit dependence on black bodies for their claim to American authenticity.[25] Finally, in the 1950s, the nostalgia-times-three exhibited in retrospective films like *Singin' in the Rain* or even *A Star is Born* depends on references to the early sound film of Jolson and others, which itself had depended on the reference to both Reconstruction minstrelsy and a mythical national past of resonant slave songs. As I have argued elsewhere, this tradition of racial reference was key in securing the coherence of Hollywood as a central moment of American national publicity, reclaiming national authenticity ironically through explicit moments of 'naturalised' performance of racial drag.[26]

This dualism in the ideological productivity of the fetish of black musicality also duplicated the situation around gypsy music and musicality in the European sphere. As Julie Brown and others have shown, the figure of the gypsy was always positioned in complex and shifting ways in relation to the musical production of national authenticity in various contexts, and thus provides insight into how contradictory the acoustic national imaginaries of Europe in the early twentieth century in fact were.[27] Popular music in the 'folk' idiom represented a domain of the social where this ideological problem was especially clear. Despite claims to the contrary, 'folk music' in musical mass culture could only serve as a weak support for any kind of attempted ontological linkage with the collective ethnic or racial essence of the audience; instead, 'folk music' functioned as one possible form of exotica among many. In other words, contrary to the ideological terms of its own discursive production, and its obvious attractions for nationalist and conservative politics, the actual use of

---

[25] On the 'bluesy' voice, see Peter Antelyes, 'Red Hot Mamas: Bessie Smith, Sophie Tucker, and the Ethnic Maternal Voice in American Popular Song', in Leslie C. Dunn and Nancy A. Jones (eds.), *Embodied Voices: Representing Female Vocality in Western Culture* (Cambridge University Press, 1994), pp. 212–29.

[26] See Brian Currid, '"Ain't I People?": Voicing National Fantasy', in Radano and Bohlman (eds.), *Music and the Racial Imagination*, pp. 113–44.

[27] Brown, 'Bartók'. See also Katie Trumpener, 'The Time of the Gypsies: A "People without History" in the Narratives of the West', *Critical Inquiry* 18/4 (1992), 843–84.

mass-cultural 'folk music' was always tainted by the folkloristic, and the accompanying problem of inauthenticity. Instead, it was always subject to the threat represented by mass culture more generally. This was especially true in the German case: either suspected of Jewish contamination, or simply linked to the urban distractions which dominated acoustic culture in the 1920s and 1930s, there was no musical practice that could both claim 'down-to-earth' quality and retain and foster the 'purity' of the German *Heimat*.[28]

One more secure way of mobilising the idea of *Heimat* in popular music was displacement. Hungary – as the most clearly nationally grounded political unit associated in the German imagination with 'gypsy' music – provided a powerful locus for this displacement.[29] The 1936 film *Hot Blood* is a particularly useful example of this. A now dispossessed aristocrat, the Baroness Marika, who has lost her home in the Hungarian plains or *Puszta* and the idyll which it represents, has been forced by her officious aunt to come to live and work with her as a schoolteacher in Budapest. As the scene begins, she is seen in her new role, in front of a classroom. When Marika's friend and former servant, Josci (Paul Kemp), arrives, the couple meet on the other side of the classroom's large picture window, the schoolchildren left on their own. Outside, gypsy music begins to sound: in an elaborately orchestrated scene, the music becomes almost a character, positioned between Marika and Josci and the classroom window. As the young *primás* begins to sing, the film opposes his song to a shot of the classroom window, where the children look out longingly to hear the music. This window serves as an unsubtle metaphor for the 'prison' of modernity, outside of which the gypsy's sound of a lost *Heimat* resonates. This becomes even more explicit when the gypsy child drops out of view: hidden by the icons of reminiscence. The film suggests that the music serves as a soundtrack to a flood of nostalgic images in Marika's mind. With a close-up on Marika, a series of shots taken from earlier in the film – superimposed on her face and organised by a series of dissolves – depicts her memory of life on the *Puszta* and the romance with a lieutenant, the male star of the film. The music actually removes us from the space and time of the city, as Marika's face itself dissolves into the image of the lieutenant, upon which scenes of his army regiment are projected. Returning to a shot of Marika, now crying, the gypsy child is shown again, concluding his song.

The gypsy child is explicitly positioned here as the iconic mediation between modernity and the lost *Heimat*; not only does his music accompany Marika's memories, but the syntactic use of the figure separates

---

[28] On the problems of *Heimat* in twentieth-century Germany, see Celia Applegate, *A Nation of Provincials: The German Idea of Heimat* (Berkeley: University of California Press, 1990).

[29] Another film that illustrates this displacement is *Julika* (Harvest) (Bolvary, 1936). A true *Heimatfilm* set in Hungary, *Julika* also uses a gypsy band. Although an Austrian film, it was released by Tobis and played all across Germany.

Marika's reverie from the rest of this scene. On returning to the 'reality' of modern life, Josci encourages the *primás* to play something 'fun', and a *csárdás* begins. Now, the children inside are also swept up by the happy sounds of a would-be *Heimat*, as the window becomes now narratively transparent. This scene suggests that the baroness and the gypsy child are both mourning the loss of their homes, their *Heimat*, in the space of the city. The gypsies in the city serve to musicalise and authenticate urban experience, enabling the baroness to transform modern space into the memories of her 'pre-modern' countryside existence. The musical gypsy child – a frequent icon in the period – thus seeks to both represent and disavow the gap between the modern German city and the *Volk* that the concept of *Heimat* implies.[30] Paralleling the imagination of the American South in the industrialising North of the late nineteenth and early twentieth centuries, the *Puszta* and its 'rooted' inhabitants dancing to gypsy music were a powerful source of collective fantasy, even, if not especially, in Germany of the 1920s and 1930s.

A closer look at the historical emergence of gypsy music and black music in Europe and the United States thus begins to illustrate a deeper structure in the moulding of modern society and its relationship to acoustic culture. Not only were the gypsy and the black key figures in the hardwiring of modern identity, music in both cases provided the backbone for construing difference as ahistorical essence. In turn, this difference was in both cases harnessed in the interest of the nation state to produce ideological surpluses of affect: either as icons of cosmopolitan exoticism, or as tropes of rootedness and authenticity. While 'black' and 'gypsy' musicality were produced as modes of embodiment alternately external and central to notions of national identity, at the same time 'black' and 'gypsy' identity were being radically re-crafted, and arguably reinvented, by the new forms of state organisation emerging in the developing modern structures of what Foucault has termed 'governmentality'.[31] The regimes of governmentality that produced the racial body as a specific site of articulation between various forms of state productivity (the production of population, the production of criminality, the production of biology as a site of regulation and measurement) used the 'gypsy' and the 'black' both as fields to exercise modes of productive regulation that would later extend to other subjects of modern statehood, and to craft the others necessary to secure the 'general population'. In this way, the 'racial discourses' of music can be productively

---

[30] Also in 1938, an especially rabid campaign against gypsies was inaugurated in the Austrian *Burgenland*. This is of course interesting for several reasons: first, the ethnic content of *Puszta* romanticised in the cinema was not unlike that of *Burgenland* itself. Secondly, the campaign focused largely on children. See on this Günter Lewy, *The Nazi Persecution of the Gypsies* (Oxford University Press, 2000), pp. 109–10.

[31] Michel Foucault, 'Governmentality', in Graham Burchell, Colin Gordon and Peter Miller (eds.), *The Foucault Effect* (University of Chicago Press, 1991), pp. 87–104.

linked to quite concrete manifestations of modern nation-state formation. Not only were the operations of governmentality on gypsy and black bodies dependent on the mobilisation of music, this operationalisation also mapped racial embodiedness onto a sense of place: in the American case the 'South', in the European case the '*Puszta*', real-imagined sites of both affective and effective investment in modern economies of the United States and Central Europe.

At issue here is then not merely the undecidability of identity, a more or less abstract notion of the ideological, but rather the production of objects and subjects of state action – or populations – that coalesce around racial notions. These 'concepts' should not be understood on an abstract plane; instead, they were materially produced in the apparatus of the state – be it in the form of legal definitions of blackness in the American case, or the production of the gypsy body as a site of intense discipline and surveillance in the European venue. Looking at the radical historicity of race in its acoustic manifestations, we can begin to see the contours of a clear alliance between emerging forms of governmental practice and hygiene and the production of essentialised, racialised conceptions of population in musical sound. Acoustic culture was not merely a symptom or after-effect of these processes, but instead played a central role in these material practices of everyday life.

CHAPTER 4

The concept of race in German musical discourse
Pamela M. Potter

The mention of 'race' in German musical contexts has had a colourful and infamous history. The first things that come to mind when the words 'German', 'music' and 'race' are mentioned might be Richard Wagner's anti-Semitic diatribes, or the notions of superior and pure Nordic race conveyed in Wagner's *Ring* cycle, or perhaps the graphic depiction on the cover of the 1938 'Degenerate Music' catalogue, which shows a caricature of a black saxophonist with a Jewish star on his lapel. This composite image of a German racist conception of music, one that embraces Wagner, Hitler and everything in between, reflects more a construct of post-Holocaust confrontations with Germany's past than the realities of German intellectual and cultural history. It is certainly true that Wagner raged against an alleged Jewish infection that had taken hold of European culture, and that Wagner's disciples (including his son-in-law Houston Stewart Chamberlain) took this one step further to expound upon the notion of an inferior Jewish 'race'. The linking of the race concept with music continued to float around in the popular consciousness for some time thereafter and emerged off and on well into the 1930s in some of the high-profile debates about the fate of German music and the impact of modernism. Yet it is also true that any systematic study of music and race was dismissed in the early 1920s as scientifically unsound. Despite a brief attempt to resuscitate this line of inquiry after the National Socialist 'revolution', as the new political climate encouraged scholars to revive these questions, the only major work on the subject of music and race one could consult on the eve of the Nazi takeover was that of an SS officer and musical amateur, and any of the handful of specialists who might have recognised the shortcomings of early endeavours had been forced into emigration by the racist policies adopted by universities after 1933.

Rather than following a direct route from Wagner to Hitler, the path of the race concept in musical discourse was a circuitous one, complicated by the blurred lines between science and dilettantism, the growing influence of anti-Semitism as a political movement, and the infiltration of nationalism and utilitarianism into academic disciplines. The application of the race concept to music scholarship was further complicated by the relative newness of the field of musicology, and especially the smaller discipline of comparative musicology (the forerunner to today's ethnomusicology) as well as the indiscriminate use of race jargon in popular musical venues. Rather than proceeding along a teleological *Sonderweg*, the race discourse in music experienced stops and starts prior to 1933, such that music experts in the Nazi years had to grasp at straws in order to cobble together a diffuse body of knowledge which rested on a shaky methodological base. The following study will trace this less-than-direct trajectory by considering the concept of race in European musical discourse before, during and after Wagner; the obstacles facing the development of a scientific study of race in music as an offshoot of anthropology; the popularised use of race terminology in non-scientific musical discourse; and the status of the music/race construct on the eve of the Nazis' takeover.

FROM THE ENLIGHTENMENT TO THE FIRST WORLD WAR

The first loose associations between music and race have been traced to the late eighteenth and early nineteenth centuries in the writings of Rousseau, Herder, Fétis and even Darwin, but aside from these isolated references, there was little impetus to develop such associations until the end of the nineteenth century. In these early references, music was recognised as a central component in social identification and solidarity of groups. For Rousseau, song was the crucial source of group identification because of both its links to language and its emanation directly from the body. And for Herder, it was not just any song, but specifically folk song, that conveyed the purest musical expression of what would come to be known as race. Interest in music as a manifestation of racial difference grew most rapidly as European explorers visited Africa and Asia and recorded their observations with special attention to musical practices, and it was a French musicologist, Fétis, who seems to have drawn the first connections between music and race when he referred directly to the supposed cultural inferiority of the African race.[1] Around the same time Darwin drew attention to the connections between music and race, observing in *Descent of Man* that: 'We see the musical faculties, which are not wholly deficient in any race, are capable of prompt and high development, for the Hottentots and Negroes have become excellent musicians, although in their native countries they rarely practice anything that we should consider music.'[2] Despite the lore that has developed in the last half century, even Wagner failed to develop any systematic ideas about the connections between music and race. In his pseudonymic 1850 essay 'Judaism in Music' Wagner does delve into an

---

[1] Ronald Radano and Philip V. Bohlman, 'Introduction: Music and Race, Their Past, Their Presence', in Ronald Radano and Philip V. Bohlman (eds.), *Music and the Racial Imagination* (University of Chicago Press, 2000), pp. 13–18.

[2] Quoted in Eric Ames, 'The Sound of Evolution', *Modernism/modernity* 10/2 (2003), 304.

ambitious and elaborate exploration of supposed Jewish traits, some of which could be tied to physical characteristics, but never quite crosses over into identifying the Jews as a distinct race and even endorses a process of redemption by which Jews such as Ludwig Börne had supposedly freed themselves from their burdensome legacy.[3] Wagner's own unmasking in 1869 as the author of this rabid attack attracted the attention of newly emerging anti-Semitic race theorists such as Paul Lagarde, Constantin Frantz, and his own future son-in-law Houston Stewart Chamberlain, and soon after its publication in 1878 the *Bayreuther Blätter* would become a forum for anti-Semitic discourse. However, it was only later in life that Wagner came to know the racial theories of Joseph Arthur de Gobineau, too late for him to have had sufficient opportunity to develop the race concept in his own thinking.[4]

It was more the Wagner legacy than the Wagner oeuvre that ultimately lent credence to racial thinking, and then, it seems, still without cultivating any strong connections to music. The fact that Wagner had shown an interest in Gobineau fuelled a Gobineau revival in Germany in the 1880s with the publication of three articles on him in the *Bayreuther Blätter* in 1881. This motivated the young Wagnerian Ludwig Schemann to dedicate his career to proliferating Gobineau's works in Germany and to establish a Gobineau society that accounted for 360 members in 1914.[5] Wagner's impact on later anti-Semitic and racist views was also considerable, especially in the appeal he had to his son-in-law Chamberlain, but the links between music and race in these later writings appeared mainly to reinforce the notion of the special musical proclivities of the Germanic races and otherwise remained at the periphery of the development of racial theories about music. Chamberlain, for example, could wax euphoric on the musicality of the Teuton, tracing a rather circuitous musical lineage from the Teutons to the Goths to the Renaissance composers of the 'Teutonic Netherlands (the home of Beethoven)', continuing on to the 'northern' composer Palestrina and finally to Beethoven, but never makes any claims of racial heredity in any of these contexts.[6] Thus by the turn of the century, the links between music and race were hardly well established, consisting

---

[3] Richard Wagner, 'Judaism in Music', in *Richard Wagner's Prose Works*, trans. William Ashton Ellis, 8 vols. (repr. Lincoln: University of Nebraska Press, 1972), vol. III, pp. 75–122.

[4] Jacob Katz, *The Darker Side of Genius: Richard Wagner's Anti-Semitism* (Hanover, NH: Brandeis University Press, 1986), pp. 116–17; Paul Weindling, *Health, Race and German Politics between National Unification and Nazism, 1870–1945* (Cambridge University Press, 1989), pp. 52, 106–9.

[5] Benoit Massin, 'From Virchow to Fischer: Physical Anthropology and "Modern Race Theories" in Wilhelmine Germany', in George W. Stocking (ed.), *Volksgeist as Method and Ethic: Essays on Boasian Ethnography and the German Anthropological Tradition*, History of Anthropology 8 (Madison: University of Wisconsin Press, 1996), pp. 129–30; Weindling, *Health, Race and German Politics*, pp. 52, 106–9.

[6] See Houston Stewart Chamberlain, *The Foundations of the Nineteenth Century*, 2nd ed. (London: John Lane, The Bodley Head, 1911), pp. 512–14.

mainly of colourful embellishments on the long-established trope of German musical superiority.[7]

Outside the musical realm, any interest in the notion of race had primarily been the domain of linguists in its most serious forms and otherwise the terrain of those advocating Teutonic superiority for political reasons.[8] Already in the eighteenth century, German linguists delved into ethnographical territory in their struggle to understand whether all languages derived from one proto-language and pursued this line of inquiry by categorising languages around the world according to physical, racial and cultural characteristics.[9] By the beginning of the twentieth century, it was all too clear that a strict correlation between language and such physical traits as hair type or skin colour could not hold water. Racial ideologues, however, continued to connect race and language hierarchically, proposing, for example, that blondes were the creators of language, i.e. discoverers of Indo-Germanic language.[10] Colonial expansion changed that dynamic, as it offered new opportunities for scientists from a variety of fields to gain direct exposure to previously unknown populations, inspiring an interest in investigating whether a systematic study of different populations could provide physical data that would test the validity of the race classifications proposed by linguists. Yet throughout its existence, the exploration of race becomes the object of a turf battle between the academy and the politics of Pan-Germanists. The early history of physical anthropology not only illustrates the obstacles that beset any scientific exploration of the race question, but also offers a striking parallel to the later development of the race concept in musical thought.

As carefully outlined and argued by Benoit Massin, the field of physical anthropology in the late nineteenth century strove to assess the validity of the race concept in the face of challenges from the polemical forces of Pan-Germanism, the blurred divisions between science and dilettantism, and the vulnerability of academic disciplines to political and economic pressures. In the 1890s there had been a clear distinction between the practitioners of physical anthropology who had been most critical of Gobineau's theories of racial inequality, on the one hand, and the advocates of Aryan superiority and promoters of eugenics, such as Houston Stewart Chamberlain, on the other. Physical anthropology, a positivistic discipline that relied on measurements and comparisons of the physical characteristics of human populations, continued a course of openly

---

[7] On the history of this trope, see Bernd Sponheuer, 'Reconstructing Ideal Types of the "German" in Music', in Celia Applegate and Pamela Potter (eds.), *Music and German National Identity* (University of Chicago Press, 2002), pp. 36–58.
[8] Massin, 'From Virchow to Fischer', pp. 126–30.
[9] Ruth Römer, *Sprachwissenschaft und Rassenideologie in Deutschland* (Munich: W. Fink, 1985), pp. 39, 124–30.
[10] Ibid., pp. 131–52.

opposing anti-Semitic eugenics arguments, while the other group developed notions of the Jewish and Aryan races and combined forces with nationalist and anti-Semitic political movements. Yet despite this fairly clear ideological demarcation between scientists and dilettantes, any university-based discipline of physical anthropology was still in its infancy, and the vast majority of members of the major anthropological societies consisted of non-professionals.[11]

After the turn of the century anthropology turned far more in the direction of nationalism and a revival of Darwinism, the result of the silencing of voices of opposition and the field's vulnerability as an academic discipline in an increasingly utilitarian environment. Internally, physical anthropology faced a methodological crisis, emerging from the realisation that decades of measuring skulls had yielded little useful interpretive data for understanding the differences among races and calling into question the whole concept of race.[12] Rather than becoming delegitimised, however, the race concept took a new turn as the death of Rudolf Virchow, one of the main protagonists of craniometry and opponents of eugenics, left the field open to the influences of Darwinism, biologism and genetics. These influences breathed new life into the race question in anthropology, as did the concurrent social concerns about racial mixing, nationalism and anti-Semitism, and the proliferation of the term 'race' as a common buzzword in the popular press.[13] Physical anthropologists, engaged in an esoteric discipline, felt additional pressures to justify their existence and demonstrate their usefulness to the state, such that scientists became attracted to eugenics for its political relevance and worked to develop the study of 'race hygiene'.[14] Over the course of the next few decades, the lure of race theories had reoriented the science of anthropology to such an extent that on the eve of the First World War, two decades before the Nazi takeover, German anthropology was already in a prime position to serve the future Third Reich. The war gave further impetus to the race sciences, as feverish nationalism combined with the new opportunities to observe prisoners of war and to speculate on their racial make-up. The POW camps served as unique laboratories for scientists to observe alleged racial distinctions among mainly European populations and to rank them hierarchically. Anthropologists were given full access to study these submissive subjects, and many went on to become leading experts on race science (*Rassenkunde*) in the Third Reich.[15]

---

[11] Massin, 'From Virchow to Fischer', pp. 79–95.   [12] Ibid., pp. 106–14.
[13] Ibid., pp. 126–30.   [14] Ibid., pp. 134–43.
[15] Andrew D. Evans, 'Anthropology at War: Racial Studies of POWs during World War I', in H. Glenn Penny and Matti Bunzl (eds.), *Worldly Provincialism: German Anthropology in the Age of Empire*, Social History, Popular Culture, and Politics in Germany (Ann Arbor: University of Michigan Press, 2003), pp. 198–229.

THE RACE CONCEPT IN MUSICOLOGY AND MUSIC JOURNALISM

Physical anthropology's initially critical assessment of racial criteria fell victim to complications caused by the blurred lines between amateurism and science, the proliferation of a popularised notion of race, and the political forces of nationalism and anti-Semitism that eventually penetrated this vulnerable, nascent academic discipline. Twenty years later, the story of the race concept in musical discourse almost exactly mirrors the experiences of physical anthropology. The study of non-Western musical cultures had been a topic of interest since the early nineteenth century but did not warrant the development of its own methodology until the beginning of the twentieth century. Designated as 'comparative musicology' (*vergleichende Musikwissenschaft*), it took its greatest strides at centres in Berlin (under the guidance of Carl Stumpf, Erich von Hornbostel and Curt Sachs) and Vienna (under Richard Wallaschek and Robert Lach).[16] Comparative musicology's early goals were to use the information gathered from non-Western sources to arrive at clues to the origins of music and to acquire insights into music psychology. By comparing findings from non-Western musical cultures with those of Western music history, it was hoped that one could isolate common denominators among music systems and derive generalisations about music perception. The collection and analysis of musical data for studies of cognition, tonometrical measurements and transcription methods lent the field of comparative musicology all of the outward characteristics of a positivistic, 'objective science'.[17]

With the onset of colonial expansion, the rise of popular interest in exotic peoples, and the opportunities for direct observation offered by the POW camps during the First World War, comparative musicology was able to reap many of the same benefits enjoyed by anthropologists. An excellent example is provided by the *Völkerschauen*, the hugely popular exhibitions touring large urban centres during the late nineteenth century, which imported individuals from African, Asian, North American and some European countries; set them up in fenced-off environments complete with fabricated indigenous structures, flora and fauna; and exhibited them performing their daily routines and ritual customs in front of curious onlookers in public exhibition arenas.[18]

---

[16] Albrecht Schneider, 'Germany and Austria', in Helen Meyers (ed.), *Ethnomusicology: Historical and Regional Studies*, The Norton/Grove Handbooks in Music (New York: W. W. Norton, 1993), pp. 83–5; and Schneider, 'Musikwissenschaft in der Emigration', in Hanns-Werner Heister, Claudia Maurer Zenck, and Peter Petersen (eds.), *Musik im Exil: Folgen des Nazismus für die internationale Musikkultur* (Frankfurt am Main: Fischer, 1993), pp. 189–90. See also Sebastian Klotz (ed.), *Vom tönenden Wirbel menschlichen Tuns. Erich M. Hornbostel als Gestaltpsychologe, Archivar und Musikwissenschaftler* (Berlin and Milow: Schibri, 1998) and Richard Wallaschek, *Primitive Music: An Inquiry into the Origin and Development of Music, Songs, Instruments, Dances, and Pantomimes of Savage Races* (London: Longmans, Green and Co., 1893).

[17] Schneider, 'Germany and Austria', pp. 79–88.   [18] Ames, 'Sound of Evolution', 301.

The impresarios who arranged these exhibits were amateur members of anthropological societies, and well-known scientists not only approved of these displays for their educational value but also made use of them for collecting research data.[19] Comparative musicologists used the *Völkerschauen* as an opportunity to compile a massive collection of sound recordings that could then be analysed in the laboratory.[20] The First World War offered another unique opportunity for these scholars to collect data by recording the speech and songs of prisoners of war, leading to the establishment of the phonographic commission at the University of Berlin under Stumpf and Wilhelm Doegen and furthering the work of comparative musicologists such as Lach, who studied the melodies sung by Russian POWs.[21]

Like anthropology, comparative musicology floated between the worlds of academic rigour and amateur curiosity, except that the 'amateurs' in this case comprised not only non-academic dilettantes but also non-specialists from related academic fields. Comparative musicology never really had a chance to gather a critical mass of experts or to train a generation of specialists. Very few of its pioneers had any musical or musicological training, but rather came from the various fields of chemistry, medicine and psychology.[22] Furthermore, the field's potential sparked the interest of historical musicologists, whose relative dilettantism came through in their naive observations on the usefulness of comparative approaches. Intrigued by the idea that studying 'primitive' cultures could unravel some of the mysteries of prehistoric and early Western music, Georg Schünemann suggested investigating the connections between Gregorian chant and Asian music along with the music of similar 'peoples ... who are not yet acquainted with harmony', tracing the emergence of consonances among 'primitive peoples', looking for the origins of polyphony in the heterophony and parallel organum-like singing in Asia and Africa, and determining similarities between Asian and early medieval notation.[23] When the short-lived *Zeitschrift für vergleichende Musikwissenschaft* was finally launched in 1933, its co-founder Johannes Wolf, another interested bystander from historical musicology, similarly proposed that knowledge of the Orient could contribute to knowledge of the primitive stages of the Occident.[24]

Despite the flagrant references to 'primitives', it is important to remember that the contemporary distinction between the 'peoples of nature' (*Naturvölker*) and 'peoples of culture' (*Kulturvölker*) was not necessarily a

---

[19] Sierra A. Bruckner, 'Spectacles of (Human) Nature: Commercial Ethnography between Leisure, Learning, and *Schaulust*', in Penny and Bunzl, *Worldly Provincialism*, pp. 127–55.
[20] Ames, 'Sound of Evolution', 299–301, 304–8.
[21] Evans, 'Anthropology at War', pp. 208–9; Robert Lach, *Gesänge russischer Kriegsgefangene*, Sitzungsberichte der kaiserlichen Akademie der Wissenschaften Wien (Vienna: Hölder, Pichler, Tempsky, 1926–52).
[22] Schneider, 'Germany and Austria', pp. 83–4, and Schneider, 'Musikwissenschaft', pp. 190–1.
[23] Georg Schünemann, 'Über die Beziehungen der vergleichenden Musikwissenschaft zur Musikgeschichte', *Archiv für Musikwissenschaft* 2 (1919–20), 175, 177, 180, 183–93.
[24] Johannes Wolf, 'Zum Geleit', *Zeitschrift für vergleichende Musikwissenschaft* 1 (1933), 1.

qualitative one, although it seems to have taken on that dimension even in the hands of the most liberal-minded scholars. As originally conceived, this distinction divided the world into populations who recorded their history and those who did not, but without explicitly imposing a hierarchy on them. Rather, it was believed that a comparative analysis of the *Naturvölker* could supply, in the words of Adolf Bastian, a 'set of seminal ideas from which every civilization had grown' that would provide a 'methodological tool for unravelling more complex civilizations'.[25] At the turn of the century, as the ideas of evolutionism gained firmer footing, a hierarchy was imposed to classify *Naturvölker* as 'primitive races' who 'stood closer to the *Urstande* [primal state of humanity] than did the *Kulturvölker*' and who had 'stagnated in their development'.[26] Liberal anthropologists upheld their opposition to racist movements, but even the most open-minded of them had accepted basic principles of racial differences and, although far less callous in their assessments of non-white races than their amateur counterparts, subscribed to a belief in their own racial superiority and to a hierarchy of populations.[27] Similarly, the goals of the early comparative musicologists at the turn of the century were to use the information gathered from non-Western, so-called 'primitive' *Naturvölker* to arrive at clues to the origins of music and to acquire insights into music psychology, but their underlying interest seemed to focus on determining which musical features were uniquely European and therefore representative of the 'higher' stage of development of *Kulturvölker*.[28]

It is important to keep in mind that until the First World War, serious scholars generally drew careful distinctions between the culturally based categories of nation (or *Volk*) and the more biologically based category of race.[29] Andrew Evans has argued that the conflation of these categories and the related supposition that Germans represented the Nordic race solidified only with the POW research, forming the basis of the *Rassenkunde* that was to develop in the 1920s and 1930s.[30] In comparative musicology, there seems to be little if any serious engagement with the race concept until after the Nazis came to power.[31] In the meantime, however, race as a buzzword had

---

[25] Quoted in H. Glenn Penny, 'Bastian's Museum: On the Limits of Empiricism and the Transformation of German Ethnology', in Penny and Bunzl, *Worldly Provincialism*, p. 97.
[26] Willy Foy, *Führer durch das Rautenstrauch-Joest-Museum der Stadt Cöln* (Cologne: M. Dumont Schauberg, 1906), quoted in ibid., p. 113.
[27] Massin, 'From Virchow to Fischer', pp. 98–9. [28] Schneider, 'Germany and Austria', pp. 79–83.
[29] Evans, 'Anthropology at War', pp. 204–8. [30] Ibid., pp. 217–29.
[31] A clear indication of this is found in the somewhat surprising appearance of the bibliographic category 'Race Studies and Folklore' ('Rassen- und Volkstumskunde') following the entry 'Musikwissenschaft' that appeared in *Die Musik in Geschichte und Gegenwart*, published in 1961. Although there is no mention of racial studies in the body of the text, the bibliography includes works on the topic dating back only to 1923, starting with Robert Lach's refutation of the feasibility of race studies in music. All other works listed are published during the Third Reich and appear after the notorious 'Degenerate Music' exhibit of 1938. This would indicate that no scholarly examinations of the race issue existed prior to Lach's response to the proliferation of race rhetoric in the popular press. *Die Musik in Geschichte und Gegenwart* [1st ed.], s.v. 'Musikwissenschaft', col. 1220.

escaped the confines of scholarship and was thrown around haphazardly by other musicologists, music critics and composers. Arnold Schering, an established historical musicologist known for his work on Bach and Beethoven, explored the possibility that an inborn attraction to certain musical styles might be determined by something 'völkisch, racial, cultish, social, i.e. something beyond the individual'. He speculated that 'if the experience of *Klang* is inseparable from the artist as an individual, is inborn, then the entire style of his work will direct itself unconsciously toward the realisation of this "*Klangideal*" and will force his acquired skills into the service thereof'.[32] The Wagner scholar Alfred Lorenz also proposed some racial theories, quoting his father Ottokar in suggesting that 'heredity and propagation of certain ideas are matters of genealogy in the broadest sense of the term'.[33] He gets caught in some contradictions by qualifying that race, rather than serving as a constant, can highlight the conflicts between what is constant, i.e. what is inherited from the father, and the changes brought on by a new generation through the gene pool of the mother. He must further acknowledge the difficulty of applying race concepts to the creative arts.[34]

Composers and journalists also exploited the popularity of the race concept in these years. In his well-known attack on modernism and internationalism of 1917, Hans Pfitzner ridiculed contemporary composers' extensions beyond the traditional diatonic scale as a step backward, forcing Germans 'to understand the music of a wild tribe or the tonal language of past millennia' and adopt practices of 'the Eskimos, Papuans, and Swahili Negroes'.[35] The Icelandic composer Jón Leifs took his own application of the race concept much more seriously, making many attempts to track down the roots of the musical style of the 'Germanic race' in Icelandic folk music while drawing attention to the much neglected culture of his country as a potential source for the rediscovery of the 'Nordic race'. Using the terms 'Nordic' and 'Germanic' interchangeably, Leifs pointed out prominent features of Icelandic folk tunes he regarded as manifestations of Germanic character, such as the frequent intervallic skips that are 'doubtless characteristics of arch-Germanic masculinity which rejects all sweetness',[36] the freely changing metre and accent that are reminiscent of the rhythms of Beethoven and Brahms,[37] and even the ties between Icelandic 'free tonality or atonality' and

---

[32] Arnold Schering, 'Historische und nationale Klangstile', *Jahrbuch der Musikbibliothek Peters* 34 (1927), 31, 32.
[33] Ottokar Lorenz, *Die Geschichtswissenschaft in Hauptrichtungen und Aufgaben* (Berlin: Wilhelm Hertz, 1886), pp. 272–8 (esp. 276); a longer passage is cited in Alfred Lorenz, *Abendländische Musikgeschichte im Rhythmus der Generationen* (Berlin: Hesse, 1928), p. 22.
[34] Lorenz, *Abendländische Musikgeschichte*, p. 23.
[35] Hans Pfitzner, *Futuristengefahr: bei Gelegenheit von Busonis Ästhetik* (Leipzig: Süddeutsche Verlag, 1917); trans. and quoted in Marc Weiner, *Undertones of Insurrection: Music, Politics, and the Social Sphere in the Modern German Narrative*, Texts and Contexts 6 (Lincoln: University of Nebraska Press, 1993), p. 63.
[36] Jón Leifs, 'Isländische Volksmusik und germanische Empfindungsart', *Die Musik* 16/1 (1923), 44–5.
[37] Ibid., 45.

progressive 'Germanic "atonality"'.[38] Race had also become such a common catchword in music journalism that in 1925 Adolf Weissmann responded to its overuse, albeit without rejecting it outright. Weissmann thought to detect explicit 'racial' elements in the 'proclivities' for rhythm (including the attraction to 'Niggerjazz') and the 'inborn predisposition for irony, satire, and the grotesque' of French music, an 'unshakable racial feeling' coming forth in Mussorgsky's use of Russian folk music, and an 'expression of race' in the music of Bartók and Kodály.[39] Still, Weissmann astutely recognised the political force behind the race issue, noting the irony of the Germans' particular enthusiasm for it and observing that 'where racial purity is most controversial, one tries to demonstrate it most'.[40] He singled out the plurality of foreign influences as a unique feature of German *Rassenausdruck*, showing how Wagner had exhibited characteristics that were clearly 'un-German', Mozart 'bonds peoples' and 'negates race and nation', and Germany's music in general revealed shades of 'racial mixing'.[41] In the end, Weissmann believed that race in music would soon become a thing of the past in the industrial world, as was already the case in the American melting pot.

The indiscriminate use of the race concept was widespread enough that one of the pioneers of the Viennese school of comparative musicology, Robert Lach, felt the need to step in and put an end to it in 1923.[42] Lach complained that while the non-specialist assumed that a correspondence must exist between ethnographic divisions of race and tribe and their respective musical styles, the comparative musicologist was simply incapable of determining such a correspondence through scientific means.[43] Lach demonstrated the futility of seeking racial style in scale systems, rhythmic and formal constructions, performance, and the psychology of musical expression. In each instance he illustrated how musical elements thought to be characteristic of one particular nation or race were found to exist among many races at various stages of their musical histories, whether they be *Naturvölker*, intermediate *Halbkulturvölker* or *Kulturvölker*. Lach deflated the claims of others to show at least 'that currently comparative musicology is not yet equipped to demonstrate racial elements and criteria in human musical creation'.[44]

MUSIC AND RACE ON THE EVE OF THE NAZI TAKEOVER

Lach's admonition did not go quite so far as to prompt debates about the validity of the race concept that had dominated similar discourses in

---

[38] Ibid., 46, 51.
[39] Adolf Weissmann, 'Rasse und Nation in der Musik', in Hans Hensheimer and Paul Stefan (eds.), *25 Jahre Neue Musik. Jahrbuch 1926 der Universal-Edition* (Vienna: Universal, [1926]), pp. 94–5, 97, 99.
[40] Ibid., p. 86. [41] Ibid., pp. 101–3.
[42] Robert Lach, 'Das Rassenproblem in der vergleichenden Musikwissenschaft', *Berichte des Forschungsinstituts für Osten und Orient* 3 (1923), 107–22.
[43] Ibid., 107. [44] Ibid., 120.

anthropology twenty years earlier. Wilhelm Heinitz seems to have taken Lach's advice to heart in 1925, when he protested that 'our European adherence to triadic harmony is not the only inspirational system' and envisioned comparative musicology some day eliminating the prejudices inherited from historical musicology.[45] As late as 1931 one still finds a few isolated attempts to look at the simplest musical structures of various peoples in order to classify their practitioners as the most primitive races,[46] but it was mainly a handful of amateurs who came to dominate the discourse, and the only full-scale attempt to explore the race issue in music was the work of one such dilettante, Richard Eichenauer. Modelled on analogous attempts in art history and literature by Paul Schultze-Naumburg and Hans F. K. Günther,[47] Eichenauer's *Musik und Rasse* of 1932 focused on the 'racial soul' (*Rassenseele*) rather than on inherited physical characteristics to gain an understanding of the racial aspects of musical style.[48] Although thoroughly lacking in any scholarly rigour, it nevertheless rose to the status of a reference work in the 1930s and, in the absence of any serious musicological engagements with the race issue, was cited as authoritative after 1933 by all noted musicologists who felt encouraged to grapple with racial questions.

Eichenauer had no formal training as a musicologist; he studied German, modern languages and music in Munich and Leipzig and was certified to teach languages and singing. Having entered the Nazi party in 1932, he then joined the SS and went from *Untersturmführer* (second lieutenant) in 1935 to *Obersturmführer* (first lieutenant) in 1936 and *SS-Führer im Rasse- und Siedlungshauptamt* (Main Bureau for Race and Settlement) in 1938.[49] Eichenauer begins his survey by tracing the roots of the 'Nordic racial soul' to the ancient Greeks; demonstrating the essentially un-German and 'Jewish' nature of Gregorian chant; claiming to find the origins of polyphony, consonance and the triad among the 'Germanic' peoples that include the Notre Dame school; portraying the growth of polyphony as a struggle between the 'alien non-European' (*europafremd*) and the polyphony-friendly Nordic-Germanic forces; and presenting the origins of opera as a form which 'most clearly betrays the influence of the Nordic spirit'.[50] He then focuses the rest of the book on individual composers, lining up their physical and musical traits in racial terms. Bach's physical traits are thus deemed consistent with his Nordic 'passionate soul' (*leidenschaftliche Seele*) and mastery of counterpoint, and

---

[45] Wilhelm Heinitz, 'Vergleichende Musikwissenschaft', *Zeitschrift für Musik* 92 (1925), 435, 437.
[46] Peter Panoff, 'Die Rassen der Erde im Spiegel der vergleichenden Musikforschung', *Die Musik* 23/11 (1931), 797–802.
[47] Michael Meyer, 'Assumptions and Implementation of Nazi Policy toward Music', Ph.D. thesis, University of California at Los Angeles (1970), p. 246.
[48] Richard Eichenauer, *Musik und Rasse* (Munich: J. F. Lehmann, 1932).
[49] Eichenauer file, Berlin Document Center.   [50] Eichenauer, *Musik und Rasse*, p. 144.

despite Handel's preference for Old Testament subjects and any Italian influence detected in his music, he was physically one of the 'purest representatives of the Nordic race'.[51] Gluck reveals his ties to the ancient Greeks by bestowing 'Nordic feeling' on ancient Greek dramas and employing 'Spartan' rhythm,[52] while Haydn displays yet another exclusively Nordic strength, that of melody; and Mozart, racially 'Dinaric-Nordic' like Haydn, displays all of the qualities of the Nordic soul despite the so-called 'Italian "influence"'.[53] Ironically, some of the greatest figures of the nineteenth century pose the most difficulties for Eichenauer's racial analysis: Beethoven's appearance betrays certain eastern influences; Schubert's 'soft' features, the result of racial mixing, come across in his music in the shifts from major to minor, an overall 'harmonic weakness' and a preference for small forms, all manifestations of his eastern genes;[54] and the physical traits of Schumann and even Wagner reveal troubling evidence of potential racial mixing.[55] In his final chapter, Eichenauer digresses with dire admonitions about the insidious threats of the Jews to contemporary German music.

The saga of the race concept in music parallels the developments in anthropology twenty years earlier in yet one other respect: the vulnerability of both academic disciplines. Even by 1933 musicology was still a relatively young and rather esoteric field and, like anthropology at the turn of the century, had gone through a long period of trying to demonstrate its usefulness in an increasingly utilitarian political climate. When the Nazis came to power, the field continued to emphasise its potential to serve the *Volksgemeinschaft* and saw an engagement with the race issue as one way to demonstrate its usefulness to the new leaders. By now, however, it not only lacked any methodological foundation in this area but had also lost to emigration most of the leading personnel who could have perhaps finally put to rest the futile pursuit of racial characteristics in music. As a result of the anti-Semitic policies enforced in universities and research institutes, the scholarly infrastructure of comparative musicology had been all but dismantled within months of the Nazi takeover. The forced emigration of Sachs and Hornbostel left the operation at the University of Berlin in the hands of a few inexperienced students and younger colleagues. Hornbostel's teaching responsibilities went to the twenty-eight-year-old Fritz Bose, while the thirty-year-old Marius Schneider assumed the direction of the Berlin Sound Archive. The Nazi takeover also forced the dissolution of the Society for Comparative Musicology, and its short-lived journal, the *Zeitschrift für vergleichende Musikwissenschaft*, had to terminate publication when its Jewish editor-in-chief, Robert Lachmann, emigrated to Israel in 1935. Psychologists such as Wolfgang Köhler and

---

[51] Ibid., pp. 165–8.   [52] Ibid., pp. 192–3.   [53] Ibid., pp. 205–6.
[54] Ibid., pp. 213–14, 216.   [55] Ibid., pp. 222–4, 227–8.

Max Wertheimer, who had collaborated with the Berlin musicologists, also left Germany upon Hitler's accession, as did a large proportion of the younger generation trained in comparative musicology.[56]

The Propaganda Ministry, the *SS-Ahnenerbe* (Department for Ancestral Heritage), the Rosenberg Bureau, as well as other government and party entities, actively encouraged research and publication in race studies, and a vocal campaign called for the redefinition and expansion of musicology to include ancestry research and biological methods towards an understanding of the musical features of the 'Germanic race'. But the only ones left to take on these tasks after 1933 were the few remaining students of the Berlin school and a host of ill-equipped historical musicologists, most of whom would find refuge in folk-music research rather than grappling with racial and biological issues. Musicologists emerged from all schools of thought to try to reconcile the alleged pioneer work of Eichenauer and other non-musicologist predecessors with the methodologies of their own discipline, but ultimately they generally ignored these difficult questions and acknowledged race only in order to justify their pursuit of more traditional investigations of folk music and the history of German art music.[57]

The temptation to look for a German *Sonderweg* in tracing the development of the race concept has led many to seek out insidious motives lurking behind all German inquiries into the nature and culture of other peoples. Knowing of the fatal outcome of racist and expansionist policies in the hands of the Nazis, one might suspect that the massive involvement of dilettantes and autodidacts in the areas of anthropology, ethnology and comparative musicology led inevitably to the anti-intellectual and politically driven racism of the late nineteenth and early twentieth centuries, and that colonial expansion – limited as it was – only fuelled the already strong desire to demonstrate German racial superiority. Several scholars, however, have shown that the amateur and professional curiosity about other peoples in the various branches of anthropology was part of a much broader movement to compare cultures and share knowledge internationally in order to learn more about humanity.[58] Similarly, the *Sonderweg* theory breaks down when we look at the uneven development of the notion of race in music scholarship. There was no straight line from Wagner to Hitler in the Germans' application of racial thinking to music; rather, Wagner gave it only cursory attention, while his followers such as Chamberlain concentrated on the broader agendas of anti-Semitism and eugenics rather than on the specifics of music. The race concept in music came in and out

---

[56] Schneider, 'Germany and Austria', p. 85; 'Musikwissenschaft', pp. 192–7.
[57] For a fuller exploration of the race concept in musical discourse of the Third Reich, see Pamela M. Potter, *Most German of the Arts: Musicology and Society from the Weimar Republic to the End of Hitler's Reich* (New Haven: Yale University Press, 1998), pp. 32–57, 174–6, 180–99, 209–20, 226–34.
[58] See, for example, H. Glenn Penny, *Objects of Culture: Ethnology and Ethnographic Museums in Imperial Germany* (Chapel Hill: University of North Carolina Press, 2002), pp. 14, 99.

of fashion in the years that followed: it was invoked at points of extreme nationalist protectionism in the wartime polemics of Pfitzner; it caught on as a fashionable turn of phrase in the writings of non-specialists in the aftermath of the war; and it was dismissed summarily as scientifically unsound in 1923 and then similarly questioned for its validity in more popular venues thereafter, lying dormant (save for Eichenauer's peculiar obsession) until artificially resuscitated by political forces after 1933. By that time, any experts who could have re-examined and problematised the issue had fled the country. But even if the pioneers of systematic musicology had been allowed to continue working in Germany, it is doubtful that they would have been taken seriously. A rational, positivistic, scientific approach to studying race and folk culture was not what the times demanded. By the end of the Weimar Republic, emotionally charged terms such as *Volk*, *Gemeinschaft*, *Blut* and *Rasse* defied definition or analysis. Rather, they all stirred feelings of longing for an ideal, unified German nation in an era of political and social fragmentation.[59]

---

[59] Kurt Sontheimer, *Antidemokratisches Denken in der Weimarer Republik: Die politischen Ideen des deutschen Nationalismus zwischen 1918 und 1933* (Munich: Nymphenburger Verlagshandlung, 1962), pp. 244–59.

PART II

Racial ideologues

CHAPTER 5

Strange love; or, How we learned to stop worrying and love Wagner's Parsifal

John Deathridge

Our great artistic aims also have a political meaning.[1]

PRELUDE

Variously described as sublime, vicious or merely decadent, Richard Wagner's *Parsifal* has always fascinated critics who have seen it either as a 'superior magic opera' which 'revels in the wondrous'[2] or as a 'profoundly inhuman spectacle, glorifying a barren masculine world whose ideals are a combination of militarism and monasticism'.[3] More soberly it has been described as a work with an 'underlying insistence on assent to a truth outside itself'.[4] Yet it is precisely the nature of that truth that has been the subject of unending controversy. Is the work's central theme really the 'redemption of an Aryan Jesus from Judaism', as Germany's arch anti-Wagnerite, Hartmut Zelinsky, thinks it is?[5] Can *Parsifal* be interpreted as a Christian work at all, militant or otherwise? Or is it just a benign, and rather feeble millenarianist fantasy – a kind of Armageddon cocktail with large twists of Schopenhauer and Buddha?

One obvious way to interpret *Parsifal* is to look first at the writings and letters of Wagner and his Bayreuth Circle and to conclude that it is really a sermon on the coming of the 'end', the work of a rebel Christian who, resigned and troubled about the progress of modern civilisation, became a heretical admirer of Jesus Christ, the supposed redeemer of a decaying

---

[1] Entry 15 September 1865 in Diary to King Ludwig II of Bavaria, Otto Strobel (ed.), *König Ludwig II. und Richard Wagner. Briefwechsel*, 5 vols. (Karlsruhe: G. Braun, 1936/1939), vol. IV, p. 7 (hereafter *Ludwig–Wagner*).
[2] Eduard Hanslick, 'Briefe aus Bayreuth über Wagner's *Parsifal*', repr. in Susanna Grossmann-Vendrey, *Bayreuth in der deutschen Presse: Beiträge zur Rezeptionsgeschichte Richard Wagners und seiner Festspiele* (Regensburg: Bosse, 1977), vol. II, p. 97.
[3] Peter Wapnewski, 'The Operas as Literary Works', in Ulrich Müller and Peter Wapnewski (eds.), *Wagner Handbook*, trans. ed. John Deathridge (Cambridge, MA: Harvard University Press, 1992), p. 91.
[4] Lucy Beckett, *Richard Wagner: Parsifal* (Cambridge University Press, 1981), p. 126.
[5] Hartmut Zelinsky, 'Die "feuerkur" des Richard Wagner oder die "neue religion" der "Erlösung" durch "Vernichtung"', in Heinz-Klaus Metzger and Rainer Riehn (eds.), *Richard Wagner: Wie antisemitisch darf ein Künstler sein?* (Munich: Text + Kritik, 1978), p. 99 (Musik-Konzepte 5).

Germanic race. To adapt a metaphor once used by the French Bulgarian critic Tzvetan Todorov to describe some authoritarian forms of literary criticism,[6] *Parsifal* turns into a bizarre picnic with Wagner bringing the images and his interpreters their meaning. And yet the Master always reserved his right to make final decisions about what that meaning was supposed to be. 'Although we mercilessly relinquish the Church, Christianity, and even the whole phenomenon of Christianity in history', Wagner wrote to his disciple Hans von Wolzogen, 'our friends must always know that we do it for the sake of that very same Christ . . . whom we want to protect in His pristine purity, so that . . . we can take Him with us into those terrible times that will probably follow the inevitable destruction of all that now exists.'[7] Not much later Cosima Wagner reported in her diaries that Wagner told her: ' "I know what I know and what is in it [*Parsifal*]; and the new school, Wolzogen and the others, can stick to what it says." He then hints at, rather than expresses, the content of this work, "Redemption to the Redeemer" [*Erlösung dem Erlöser*] – and we are silent after he has added, "it's good that we're alone." '[8]

Wagner believed that *Parsifal* had a message that could be correctly decoded, at least by initiates. Yet even in private he was reluctant to be specific. A less dramatic explanation is that he simply mistrusted interpretations that were too sharply defined. He sensed his followers' need for a clear understanding of content; but he also needed himself to shroud that content in a veil of secrecy, to surround it with a noise as it were, that made it less acute. Roland Barthes has said that a photograph whose meaning (though not its effect) is too impressive is quickly deflected, since we consume it aesthetically, not politically.[9] The same could be said of *Parsifal* in the sense that an interpretation of the work that subjects it to a startling array of precise meanings, whether controversial or not, inevitably misfires, because we are affected by its grandeur and the beauty of its music, not because of any doctrinal threads systematically stitched into its allegorical fabric.

I would like to propose, however, that this kind of argument about *Parsifal* is ultimately evasive. The point about the overdetermination of meaning in works of art is of course a commonplace among critics, especially those who still value a dusty connoisseurship that will always promote aesthetics above history. Indeed, those trying to explore the

---

[6] Tzvetan Todorov, *Literature and Its Theorists*, trans. Catherine Porter (London: Routledge, 1988), p. 187.
[7] Letter of 17 January 1880 to Hans von Wolzogen, in *Richard Wagner, Ausgewählte Schriften und Briefe*, ed. Alfred Lorenz (Berlin: B. Hahnefeld, 1938), vol. II, pp. 376–7.
[8] 5 January 1882: Martin Gregor-Dellin and Dietrich Mack (eds.), *Cosima Wagner: Die Tagebücher*, 2 vols. (Munich and Zurich: Piper, 1976/7); *Cosima Wagner's Diaries*, trans. Geoffrey Skelton, 2 vols. (London: Collins, 1978/80) (trans. occasionally modified: hereafter CD).
[9] Roland Barthes, *Camera Lucida: Reflections on Photography*, trans. Richard Howard (London: Vintage, 1993), p. 36.

ideological ramifications of a piece such as *Parsifal* inevitably leave themselves open to the accusation of scholarly taxidermy. Nor is this view confined to the adherents of traditional aesthetics. Slavoj Žižek and Mladen Dolar, hardly part of the right-leaning critical establishment, insist:

> It is easy to show how *Parsifal* grew out of timperial [*sic*], anti-modernist anti-Semitism – to enumerate all the painful and tasteless details of Wagner's ideological engagements in the last years of his life … However, to grasp the true greatness of *Parsifal*, one should absolutely abstract ideas from these particular circumstances; only in this way can one discern how and why *Parsifal* still exerts such a power today … the context *obfuscates* Wagner's true achievement.[10]

Wonderful. But what if the 'painful and tasteless' ideas Wagner lavished on *Parsifal* can help to *explain* the power it still exerts? Has the extremely serious charge of anti-Semitism that has been levelled against it really polarised opinion about it to such an extent that the link between its 'true greatness' and Wagner's far-from-straightforward ideas about race can no longer be convincingly demonstrated? Is the notion of a racist strain in *Parsifal* so absurd and easy to refute that in reality it has come as a godsend to those seeking an excuse to reaffirm the work's status as an incontrovertible musical masterpiece in the Western tradition?

The very idea seems outrageous until one begins to understand the paradoxes of Wagner's racist views and their inseparability from the experience of supposed cultural decay he wanted to share in *Parsifal*, and not just in a series of seemingly madcap polemics in his late writings. This is indeed a disturbing aspect of the work, and it has taken several crude public spats about the gulf that is meant to separate it from its creator's so-called late regeneration essays to deflect attention from what I believe is the contradictory logic of a more subtle discourse about race at its heart, including its music. I want here to make a brief attempt to bring these bits of him together one more time, hopefully by bringing the dramaturgy of *Parsifal* into sharper focus, and by suggesting that, contrary to what both the left and right flanks in the Western cultural establishment are beginning to think, the closer we look at the way its structure has been entwined with the web of ideas inside it, the less our concerns about it are likely to disappear.

SEX AND THE PITY

Critics of a putative inhumanity in Wagner's *Parsifal* will always find it hard to account for the fascinating beauty of its score and the inconvenient fact that militancy and aggression could not be further removed from its

---

[10] Slavoj Žižek and Mladen Dolar, *Opera's Second Death* (New York: Routledge, 2002), p. viii (emphasis SZ and MD).

central idea. Wagner himself called the work his 'most conciliatory',[11] basing it on the notion of compassion (*Mitleid*) borrowed from the philosophy of Schopenhauer and subjected to some characteristically Wagnerian variations. Schopenhauer and Wagner saw compassion as a specific moral response to the violent chaos of the world – a beatific annihilation of the Will, so to speak, achieved through a denial of Eros, and in Wagner's personal version of the doctrine a deep sympathy with the suffering in others caused by the torment of sexual desire.

The idea of compassion also influenced Wagner's radical treatment of his main literary source, Wolfram von Eschenbach's early thirteenth-century romance *Parzival*. Wagner discussed Wolfram and sexual asceticism at length in his letters to Mathilde Wesendonck in the late 1850s (in view of his rapidly cooling feelings towards her after finishing *Tristan* this was perhaps to be expected) and came to the conclusion that he would have to compress the enormous 24,810-line poem into just 'three climactic situations of violent intensity'.[12] In effect he turned the poem into three successive stages of compassion. What begins as a vague feeling in the pure fool (Parsifal) in his response to the Grail ceremony in the first act progresses to a burning insight into Amfortas's suffering at the moment of Kundry's kiss in the second, and ends with two miraculous acts of redemption in the third with the baptism of Kundry and the healing of Amfortas's wound. The epic poem was thus ingeniously transformed into a cathartic theatrical ritual in three cycles, each more drastic than the last.

One of the problems with *Parsifal* is that woven inside its relatively simple outer edifice is not only a skein of memory leading back to a single catastrophic event – Amfortas's serious injury by the spear stolen by his evil rival Klingsor – but also several allegorical threads that are still hard to disentangle. Even the plot is hard to grasp, as Wagner's principal critical enemy Eduard Hanslick discovered. After jettisoning its 'alleged deep, moral significance',[13] he simply related the story, only to find it illogical, at least in the way he tried to tell it. King Ludwig II, too, was puzzled. After receiving the first prose draft of *Parsifal* from Wagner in 1865, he immediately wrote back to ask: 'Why is our hero converted only by Kundry's kiss? Why does this make his divine mission clear to him?'[14] Wagner's reply – a rare attempt to interpret *Parsifal* with more than just riddles – looks evasive at first, though its cautious elucidation of the story's peculiar logic is clear enough:

---

[11] Carl Friedrich Glasenapp, *Das Leben Richard Wagners*, 6 vols. (Leipzig: Breitkopf und Härtel, 1911), vol. VI, p. 555.
[12] Letter of 29/30 May 1859 to Mathilde Wesendonck, in Richard Wagner, *Sämtliche Werke*, vol. XXX: Dokumente zur Entstehung und ersten Aufführung des Bühnenweihfestspiels Parsifal, eds. Martin Geck and Egon Voss (Mainz: Schott, 1970), p. 16 (hereafter SW 30).
[13] *Bayreuth in der deutschen Presse*, vol. II, p. 97 (n. 2).
[14] Letter of 5 September 1865 to Wagner, *Ludwig–Wagner*, vol. I, p. 170.

That is a terrible secret, my beloved! You know, of course, the serpent of Paradise and its tempting promise: 'Ye shall be as gods, knowing good and evil'. Adam and Eve became 'knowing'. They became 'conscious of sin'. The human race had to atone for that consciousness by suffering shame and misery until redeemed by Christ, who took upon himself the sin of mankind. My dearest friend, how can I speak of such profound matters except in comparative terms, by means of a parable? Only someone who is clairvoyant can perceive its inner meaning. Adam – Eve: Christ. – How would it be if we were to add to them: – 'Amfortas – Kundry: Parzifal?' But with considerable caution![15]

Ludwig, whose acute sensibility had immediately recognised, amidst the acres of words in Wagner's prose draft, that this was one of its most crucial moments, seems to have accepted this tentative, and in some ways also rather audacious reading. Only a matter of days after writing it, however, Wagner began sending him one of his most aggressive texts in the form of a diary outlining at some length his plans for the cultural and political renewal of Europe. The text includes disgusting sentences like: 'In nature . . . a dying body is immediately found by worms, which completely tear it to pieces and assimilate themselves. In today's European cultural life, the emergence of the Jews means nothing less.'[16] Ludwig, who all his life had tolerant views about race and religion, does not seem to have noticed.

The young king could have been making a sensible and shrewd distinction between two texts, the one a grandly ambitious artistic project, the other a reckless political corollary of it. But sixteen years later alarm bells began to ring. In the throes of orchestrating *Parsifal* on 19 September 1881, Wagner wrote to his benefactor that he had decided to accept Hermann Levi as the conductor of the first performances of the work, in spite of complaints from several quarters that 'of all pieces, this most Christian of works' was to be conducted by 'a Jew'.[17] Obviously relieved, Ludwig answered: 'It is very good that you do not differentiate between Christians and Jews for your great holy work. Nothing is more repulsive, more unpleasant, than arguments such as these; human beings are basically all brothers, despite their confessional differences.'[18]

Wagner shot back an answer to this almost Masonic largesse, which comes as a shock, even for hardened Wagner scholars:

The only explanation I can think of for my exalted Friend's thoughtful judgement on the Jews is that these people never enter the royal sphere. For you they remain a concept, whereas for us they are all too real. My relations with several of these people are friendly, solicitous and full of compassion; but this is only possible because I regard the Jewish race as the born enemy of pure humanity and everything noble about it. They will be the ruination of us Germans, that is for sure.

---

[15] Letter of 7 September 1865 to King Ludwig II, *Ludwig–Wagner*, vol. I, p. 174.
[16] Entry 21 September 1865 in Diary to King Ludwig II, *Ludwig–Wagner*, vol. IV, p. 19.
[17] Letter of 19 September 1881 to King Ludwig II, *Ludwig–Wagner*, vol. III, p. 223.
[18] Letter of 11 October 1881 to Wagner, *Ludwig–Wagner*, vol. III, p. 226.

Perhaps I am the last German who as an artist knows how to survive the Judaism that's already dominating everything.[19]

Note the phrases 'full of compassion' (*mitleidvoll*) and 'pure humanity' (*reine Menschheit*), both of which have strong resonances with *Parsifal*. And there is plenty more like it from Wagner's pen in the same period: 'Whoever attributes the obtuse clumsiness of our public life', he wrote in 1881, 'solely to the corruption of our blood brought about by a departure from the natural nourishment of mankind, but above all by the degeneration brought about by the mixing of the hero-blood of the noblest races with that of one-time cannibals now trained to be the skilled business leaders of society, is probably quite right.'[20]

WHEN R. MET THE COUNT

Precisely because Wagner's writings are far from being intended as black comedy it has proved more than awkward to separate *Parsifal* entirely from its creator's thoughts on race, which from the 1848 revolution onwards are indeed obsessed with, but by no means limited to, the Jewish question. Hardly a day in the Wagnerian world goes by without some mention of Wagner's justly notorious anti-Semitic essay 'Das Judentum in der Musik' (1850).[21] Far less discussed, apart from some notable exceptions,[22] is the still earlier *Die Wibelungen* (1848–9), with which for the first time, as Ernest Newman rightly says, 'a new Wagner comes into view – a boldly speculative philosopher who takes not only music but all literature, history, and life for his province.'[23] In this essay, running to forty pages of print in his collected writings, Wagner insists that mere 'history' can only ever offer us an incomplete picture of the 'most intimate, so to speak instinctive, motives of the ceaseless striving and urging of whole races and peoples'.[24]

---

[19] Letter of 22 November 1881 to Ludwig II, *Ludwig–Wagner*, vol. III, pp. 229–30.
[20] Richard Wagner, 'Heldentum und Christentum' (1881), *Sämtliche Schriften und Dichtungen*, 16 vols. (Leipzig, n.d. [1911/1914]: Breitkopf und Härtel), vol. X, p. 284; *Richard Wagner's Prose Works*, trans. William Ashton Ellis, 8 vols. (repr. Lincoln: University of Nebraska Press, 1972), vol. VI, p. 284. All extracts are newly translated. (Hereafter SSD and Ellis.)
[21] See e.g., Hartmut Zelinsky, 'Die "feuerkur" des Richard Wagner'; Dieter Borchmeyer, 'The Question of Anti-Semitism' (trans. Stewart Spencer) and John Deathridge, 'A Brief History of Wagner Research', in *Wagner Handbook*, pp. 166–85, 220–3; Marc. A. Weiner, *Richard Wagner and the Anti-Semitic Imagination* (Lincoln: University of Nebraska Press, 1995); Jens Malte Fischer, *Richard Wagners 'Das Judentum in der Musik'* (Frankfurt am Main: Insel, 2000) (insel taschenbuch 2617); Udo Bermbach, *Der Wahn des Gesamtkunstwerks*, 2nd rev. and enl. ed. (Stuttgart and Weimar: Metzler, 2004), pp. 261–82.
[22] E.g. Robert Gutman, *Richard Wagner: The Man, His Mind, and His Music* (New York: Secker and Warburg, 1968), pp. 120–1, 421–2; Joachim Köhler, *Richard Wagner: The Last of the Titans*, trans. Stewart Spencer (New Haven: Yale University Press, 2004), pp. 250–5. Köhler overstates the influence of Hegel on *Die Wibelungen*, however, and ignores its deliberate anti-Hegelian posture against history and philosophies of reason.
[23] Ernest Newman, *The Life of Richard Wagner*, 4 vols. (Cambridge University Press, 1976), vol. II, p. 18.
[24] SSD, vol. II, p. 123; Ellis, vol. VII, p. 266.

The strongest ancient tribes possessed 'the purest of blood from which the entire people descended', but which 'blurred in the course of time'.[25] The 'deepest degeneration' (*tiefste Entartung*) of the Frankish royal race would have retained its identity had it not been for its 'willing acceptance of Latin depravity' (*willige[r] Annahme der romanischen Verderbtheit*) and the predecessor of Karl the Great 'won and ruled the entire German world' by 'getting rid of the deeply degenerate race of the Merovingians'.[26] Indeed, the essay floats the idea more than once that the Germanic races had always to be wary of foreign impurity.

The more one tries to penetrate the unlovely exterior of *Die Wibelungen* the more it becomes clear just how integral to Wagner's intellectual strategy are his racial metaphors of cultural decline and its counterforce, 'the purest of blood'. The four volumes of Count Joseph Arthur de Gobineau's notorious *Essai sur l'inégalité des races humaines* (1853–5) appeared a few years later, soon followed by Bénedict August Morel's now nearly just as infamous *Traité des dégénérescences physiques, intellectuelles et morales de l'espèce humaine et de ses causes qui produisent ces variétés maladives* (1857), which first introduced the concept of degeneration into the pessimistic language and quasi-science of early psychiatric studies devoted to heredity and the alleged decline of the human race.[27] But in many respects Wagner was there before either of them, not only making prominent use of words like 'blood' (*Blut*), 'degeneration' (*Entartung*) and 'depravity' (*Verderbtheit*) to describe racial conflict and decay, but also boldly vandalising the ground rules of political and intellectual history, just as Gobineau was to do, by introducing in their place biological determinism and a free-associative interpretation of myth and ethnology.

Wagner met Gobineau, 'racialism's most illustrious representative', as Todorov calls him,[28] for the first time in 1876 in Rome, but only began to appreciate his work on race – then little known except to a smallish circle – when he invited him to Bayreuth in the early 1880s. He came to regard the Count as a personal friend and cherished confrère in the already thriving industry of doom and gloom in the late nineteenth century, and indeed it is no exaggeration to say that Gobineau's later fame in Europe, including the co-option of some of his ideas by the Nazis, was due in some part to Wagner's advocacy, and in particular to the energy of his disciple Ludwig Schemann, who later translated the *Essai* into German.[29]

---

[25] SSD, vol. II, p. 118; Ellis, vol. VII, p. 261.
[26] SSD, vol. II, p. 118; Ellis, vol. VII, pp. 262–3.
[27] Isolde Vetter, 'Wagner in the History of Psychology' (trans. Stewart Spencer), in *Wagner Handbook*, p. 119.
[28] Tzvetan Todorov, *On Human Diversity: Nationalism, Racism, and Exoticism in French Thought*, trans. Catherine Porter (Cambridge, MA: Harvard University Press, 1993), p. 140.
[29] Joseph Arthur de Gobineau, *Versuch über die Ungleichheit der Menschenrassen*, trans. Ludwig Schemann, 5 vols. (5 = index) (Stuttgart: Fr. Frommann (E. Hauff), 1898–1901).

Schemann notes that Wagner came across the *Essai* after reading a vigorous critique of it by the etymologist August Friedrich Pott.[30] There are at least two interesting things about this. The first is that Pott's scholarly work on linguistics belongs to the pioneering area of research among German academics in the first half of the nineteenth century that laid the foundations of what we know today as Indo-European comparative philology, and upon which Wagner drew extensively for his work on the libretto of the *Ring*. Second, Pott's detailed attack on Gobineau shows that the study of Indo-European languages had inevitably brought with it the issue of race, about which there was already serious disagreement. Wagner once famously claimed: 'Gobineau says the Germans were the last card Nature had to play – *Parsifal* is my last card.'[31] But the metaphor, not to be found in the *Essai*, is actually Pott's, who uses it in a passage laden with irony to sum up Gobineau's absurd notion that around the birth of Christ the Aryan Indo-Germanic races ceased to be '*absolument pure*'[32] because they had opened themselves to racial mixture and hence to eighteen centuries of inevitable decline. After Nature had played its best and final trump card, Pott asks sarcastically, what else was left for it to do?[33]

Pott's book was published in 1856 and obviously Wagner could have come across it at any time after that. There is no evidence to suggest, however, that he was acquainted with it before the early 1880s when he began to look around in earnest for like-minded spirits to support the ideological superstructure he wanted to build around *Parsifal* in readiness for the public unveiling of the work. All we know is that Pott's 'laughable rage against Gobineau', as Wagner's official biographer Carl Glasenapp describes it,[34] made Wagner all the more determined to read the *Essai* for himself. Indeed, when he eventually got hold of a copy with Gobineau's help, he read all four volumes with care, though not without the occasional moan about their length. In particular, the third chapter of the fourth volume entitled 'The ability of the native Germanic races' (*Capacité des races germaniques natives*) seems to have gone straight to his heart, in all probability because it establishes the supposed superiority of the Germanic races with a discussion of, among other things, some of the old literary sources he had used to write the *Ring* (the poetic Edda for instance) and racial conflicts like the one between the Germans and the Merovingians he had already grappled with in *Die Wibelungen*.[35] 'In the evening R. reads to

---

[30] Ludwig Schemann, *Gobineaus Rassenwerk* (Stuttgart: Fr. Frommann (E. Hauff), 1910), p. 237n.
[31] CD, 28 March 1881.
[32] M. A. [Joseph Arthur] de Gobineau, *Essai sur l'inégalité des races humaines*, 4 vols. (Paris: Librairie de Firmin Didot frères, 1853–5), vol. IV, p. 357.
[33] August Friedrich Pott, *Die Ungleichheit menschlicher Rassen hauptsächlich vom sprachwissenschaftlichen Standpunkte, unter besonderer Berücksichtigung von des Grafen von Gobineau gleichnamigem Werke* (Lemgo and Detmold: Meyer, 1856), p. xxxii.
[34] Glasenapp, *Das Leben Richard Wagners*, vol. VI, p. 436.
[35] Gobineau, *Essai*, vol. IV, pp. 34–45 (n. 37).

the Count the pages in his book (Volume 4, Ch. 3) which he so loves', Cosima wrote in her diaries, 'and afterwards he plays the Prelude to *Parsifal*'.[36]

ALTERED STATES

Wagner thought of his relationship with Gobineau's ideas as 'a growing together of two completely independent, but in all essentials deeply related intellectual worlds'.[37] Some friction was bound to occur. A former diplomat who had travelled extensively, Gobineau was far from being a chauvinist or even remotely nationalist. Nor was he an anti-Semite. He regarded the Jews as Caucasians and therefore as a sub-set of the Germanic race which meant, not surprisingly, that on the Jewish question Wagner disagreed with him. Wagner also refused to accept his view that the decline of the Aryan race was unstoppable. The 'absolute purity' of the Aryan race, sullied around the time of the birth of Christ by opening itself to racial mixture, can indeed be aspired to, Wagner thought, by the intervention of a divine hero, who, although himself the product of racial impurity, is capable of compassion and hence able to resist any further adulteration of blood through an intuitive understanding of human suffering.[38] Indeed, the idea of the superior race no longer in possession of its purity, but hoping for salvation, is already to be found in embryo in the last two sections of *Die Wibelungen* where the fallen master race, torn from 'its natural racial origin' (*ihrer geschlechtlich-natürlichen Herkunft*) is left to await its redeemer.[39]

Still, Gobineau was – and these were the two things Wagner particularly liked about him – a pessimist and a racist with an immense knowledge of racial theory that goes back to the heart of the eighteenth century. The overblown scenario of *Die Wibelungen* could not be more different from the smooth elegance of the *Essai*. Yet both writers are at one in their view that race, rather than specific cultural factors, can best explain the trajectory of history; and both give primacy to the undermining of racial origin as the root cause of civilisation's impending disaster. Moreover, they are *d'accord* in bringing the whole issue into close proximity with the sacred. Wagner believed early on, like Gobineau, that the original purity of the Aryan race is to be located in the realm of the gods. And he had no hesitation, too,

---

[36] CD, 12 May 1881.
[37] Schemann, *Gobineaus Rassenwerk*, p. 237 (n. 15). See also Eric Eugène, *Wagner et Gobineau: Existe-t-il un racisme wagnérien?*, with a preface by Serge Klarsfeld (Paris: le cherche midi éditeur, 1998). In contrast to the present essay, Eugène recognises the elective affinities between Gobineau and Wagner, but insists on an 'essential opposition' (p. 177) between them that allows Wagner to escape into a seemingly humane world of racial unity without serious interrogation of his ideology of male heroic supremacy and essential racial difference.
[38] SSD, vol. X, pp. 280–1; Ellis, vol. VI, p. 280.
[39] SSD, vol. II, p. 155; Ellis, vol. VII, p. 295. Also SSD, vol. XII, p. 229 (original ending).

in aligning the pagan and Christian worlds alongside each other: thus the 'abstract highest god of the Germans, Wuotan', is 'completely identified ... with the Christian God'[40] and the Grail is the original relic of humanity containing the hero blood of the slain sun-god Siegfried. In this bizarre scenario, Christ is therefore a reincarnation of Siegfried, and the quest of the Grail replaces 'the struggle for the Nibelungs' Hoard'.[41]

Not even Gobineau was this reckless. But he, too, was scrupulous in keeping racial theory within the confines of Christian belief, even though the central premise behind it – the essential difference between races – fell well outside Christianity's doctrinal boundaries. Robert Young has analysed with considerable skill some of Gobineau's adroit manoeuvres in circumventing the difficulty of justifying the biblical notion of monogenesis (the descent of different human races from a single source) in a treatise predicated on the decidedly un-Christian idea of polygenesis (the descent of inherently distinct races from different sources). The implication in the *Essai* is that the fall itself caused the everlasting separation of species much as 'Babel produced the division of languages' (Young's own analogy).[42]

As Wagner himself believed in a lost purity of racial division long before he read Gobineau – 'everything is according to its kind' (*Alles ist nach seiner Art*), the Wanderer confides to Alberich in *Siegfried* – it is perhaps not entirely a coincidence that in his reply to King Ludwig II's question about Kundry's kiss cited above he makes his heroine a notional participant in the fall. 'But with considerable caution!', Wagner adds, almost as if he were warning that the symbolism of Eve/Kundry's sexual allure is by no means restricted to this biblical imagery, but represents a multitude of non-Christian ideas as well, including – so to speak – the splitting of the racial atom. He describes Kundry to Ludwig not only as a figure who experiences 'constantly changing reincarnations brought about by a primeval curse', which, 'similar to the "Wandering Jew"', condemns her to life for all time,[43] but also as someone marked by radical difference. She is 'as old as time' (*uralt*), yet 'without visible signs of aging'. Her hair is black, 'loose and wild one minute, beautifully plaited the next'. Her eyes are black too, 'darting like burning coals out of their sockets', yet also 'fixed and inert'. And the colour of her skin is subject to startling change: 'now pale, then sunburned and dark'.[44] One only-too-logical conclusion to be drawn from this vivid description of Kundry's visibly different states of being in Wagner's original prose draft of *Parsifal* for Ludwig II is that it is an

---

[40] SSD, vol. II, p. 144; Ellis, vol. VII, p. 287.   [41] SSD, vol. II, p. 151; Ellis, vol. VII, p. 294.
[42] Robert J. C. Young, *Colonial Desire: Hybridity in Theory, Culture and Race* (London: Routledge, 1995), p. 103.
[43] SW 30, 72. (Citations from the original text of the prose draft written for King Ludwig II of Bavaria at the end of August 1865.)
[44] SW 30, 70.

ingenious allegory of essential racial difference that by dint of its creator's own allusion to the fall manages at the same time to remain rooted in the Christian doctrine of monogenesis. But the deep intellectual relationship, which, as Wagner himself thought, exists 'in all essentials' between his work and Gobineau's, goes still further. In the final work, Kundry passes through at least three different lives: the exotic animal-like creature in the first act, the young black-haired seductress dressed in 'roughly Arabic style'[45] in the second, and the pale repentant sinner in the third. Caught between a masculinised Christian community to the north and a feminised world under Moorish influence to the south, she is a potent symbol not just of racial mixture, but also of a supposed sexual attraction between the races, to which her failed seduction of Parsifal in the opera and her successful seduction of Amfortas in the past both attest.

In his *Essai*, Gobineau views the libidinal drive of history almost solely in terms of the attraction of so-called strong masculine races for weaker feminine ones – the idea of gender of course being translated here onto an absurdly generalised level. This leads to a contradiction at the heart of the theory, which Gobineau happily exploits in the name of a universal view of supposed racial inequality.[46] Because of the sexual attraction of races for one another, tribes fuse with other tribes and form nations of higher culture. Therefore miscegenation, the cross-breeding of races, has been inevitable and must account under certain favourable conditions for the existence of successful civilisations. Gobineau even states categorically that the white Germanic races were more inclined to miscegenation and thus stronger and more dominant under certain conditions than the black and yellow races, who have in fact shown greater resistance to racial mixture. The Germanic races have as a consequence become strong and 'civilised' precisely because they have mixed their blood with others.

At the same time, in terms of pure racial division, by which Gobineau and Wagner set great store, the mixing of bloods can only lead to an enfeeblement of racial and cultural vitality. This in turn presents a contradiction that greatly appealed to Wagner: the more a civilisation gains power through racial mixture, the sexual attraction of one race for another, the more it becomes vulnerable to decline and decay.[47] The reason for the civilised strength of the Aryan races, the erotic force that has led to the mixing of blood and the dominance of the strong over the weak, is at the same time its fatal weakness and the source of its inevitable degradation. Indeed, with the contradiction in mind, Kundry's baptism and subsequent death at the end of *Parsifal* can be construed as an allegory of the long-awaited conclusion of this process: the end of racial mixture that caused the whole problem in the first place – the welcome death of hybridity itself.

---

[45] SW 30, 118.   [46] Young, *Colonial Desire*, pp. 107–9.
[47] SSD, vol. X, pp. 276–7; Ellis, vol. VI, pp. 276–7.

BEFORE REDEMPTION

What about the music? At the end of *Parsifal*, saturated chromatic spaces are banished, themes appear to be elevated on high and endlessly consonant harmonic progressions emerge, as if the history of the human races were being embalmed and carried gently to rest by an eternal flame. The music accounts for the perverse sense of inclusiveness in *Parsifal*: the imbroglio of Amfortas and his eroticised wound, Kundry with her fraught existence in radically different types of character, and finally Parsifal, who to gain consciousness of the Divine Code must possess no Enlightenment knowledge and renounce carnal desire as if it were the cause of fractured humanity in the first place, are finally blended together beneath the slogan 'Redemption to the Redeemer' (*Erlösung dem Erlöser*). What does it mean? Probably that the redeemer of mankind is compromised by corrupted blood and is therefore himself in need of redemption by the divine hero, though in the general feelgood wash of sound that ends the work the precise significance of the phrase may not count for much.

Right up to the moment where this high-sounding kitsch begins to take its effect in the mother of all Wagnerian closures, the music is far more interesting. Despite Wagner's differences with Gobineau (and for that matter Schopenhauer) about the supposedly inevitable doom of humanity, the best music in *Parsifal* is more in sympathy with the intransient pessimism of these thinkers than it is with any inscrutable idea of redemption. Humanity is rapidly losing its strength; its best days are gone and a sense of pervading entropy and the inevitable advent of nothingness prevails. The music seems purposefully to avoid forward movement, or rather to propose it at moments, only to take it back again; and the notes seem to repose constantly in motionlessness, reluctant to do anything else.

Wagner achieves this fluid stasis with an array of ingenious technical devices. Egon Voss has pointed out the numerous pauses that interrupt the movement of the music, especially general fermatas lasting an entire bar in places where one least expects them (after Amfortas's first entrance and the words '*Ohn' Urlaub!*' for instance).[48] The modernist interest in new musical processes in *Parsifal* has been shared by others (including Adorno and Pierre Boulez), but rarely has anyone seriously asked how they relate to the dramaturgy of the work where the melancholic sense of stasis and decay among the knights of the Grail – a dynamic nihilism, as it were, that gradually takes hold of a community increasingly in danger of collapsing under the weight of its own history – is clearly reflected by the formal and harmonic processes of the music. Repetitive patterns such as the bells in the Transformation scenes and circular harmonic sequences create movement

---

[48] Egon Voss, 'Die Möglichkeit der Klage in der Wonne: Skizze zur Charakterisierung der *Parsifal*-Musik', in Ulrich Drüner (ed.), *Der Opernführer: Wagner 'Parsifal'* (Munich: PremOp, 1990), p. 187.

while abolishing it at the same time, and indeed the paradox of motionlessness through motion, or motion through motionlessness, pervades the entire score.

Wagner also developed an original relationship between harmony and horizontal line so that both can audibly fold into and out of one another, again creating the possibility of a musical dynamic that paradoxically develops organically by collapsing into itself. Here are a few analytical glimpses at the core of the work. In Amfortas's first mention of 'the pure fool', whom he awaits and envisions as his saviour, a dissonance G, B♭, F, D is introduced at the occurrence of the word 'pure', resolving onto a weaker dissonance G, B♭, E, D (Ex. 5.2). This tiny harmonic moment with a linear trajectory from 'x' to 'y' is then used at certain key junctures throughout the work, normally in closed position with the D either changing during the progression, or already changed, to D♭ (Ex. 5.1). Wagner uses the progression as a kind of musical icon, which, precisely because of its basically unchanging pitch identity, imprints significant moments in the action all the more powerfully on the ear of the listener.

These moments include Gurnemanz's highly charged description in Act I of how Amfortas, drunk with ecstasy in the arms of Kundry, allowed the holy spear to slip away from him (Ex. 5.3) and the peripeteia of the work after Kundry's kiss, which Parsifal rejects in favour of sudden anguished empathy for Amfortas's predicament. In a single chord, the dissonance is fused with its own resolution (Ex. 5.4), only to be unfolded at the beginning of Act III with a striking melancholic melody and quasi-invertible counterpoint. Wagner took great care with this in his sketches, starting with a simple two-dimensional solution in the major key (Ex. 5.5) and eventually arriving at the unforgettable music of the final version in the minor with the D♭ of the harmony placed without the preceding D, and the bottom G approached obliquely with an elongated and highly expressive accented G♭ appoggiatura (Ex. 5.6).

The most controversial moment is in Act III, just after Parsifal's baptism of Kundry, who 'seems to weep passionately' like the *Mater dolorosa*, her former eroticism transformed into religious ecstasy. The solemn moment is underscored with an unexpected harmonic shift towards the recurring iconic harmony (Ex. 5.1), with the linear movement 'x' to 'y' again intact as it was towards the start of the work. Only this time the bottom G of the chord consists of prescient-sounding strokes on the timpani outlining the rhythm of the 'Grail' motif (Ex. 5.7). Wagner was rightly proud of this striking passage: 'the entry of the timpani on G is the finest thing I have ever done', he told Cosima, who described it as 'the timpani's sound of annihilation' (*Vernichtungsklang der Pauke*), or, as Wagner himself explained, 'the annihilation of all existence, of all earthly desire'.[49]

---

[49] CD, 3 February 1879.

78 *Racial ideologues*

All examples in 4/4. Bar numbers from *Sämtliche Werke*, vol. XIV/1–3, Mainz, 1972–3

Example 5.1: Recurring dissonance (pitch identity fixed)

Example 5.2: *Parsifal*, Act I, bars 325–6

Example 5.3: *Parsifal*, Act I, bars 528–9

Example 5.4: *Parsifal*, Act II, bars 994–6

Example 5.5: *Parsifal*, Act III, bars 1–2 sketch (Nationalarchiv der Richard-Wagner-Stiftung Bayreuth, A III m 4^r recto)

Example 5.6: *Parsifal*, Act III, bars 1–2 (final version)

Example 5.7: *Parsifal*, Act III, bars 623–4

TERMS OF ENDEARMENT

The music of *Parsifal* has had a powerful effect on composers such as Mahler and Berg who certainly cannot be accused of sharing in Wagner's barmy racial universe. The distinguished musical lineage is one reason perhaps why many historians have been reluctant to discuss ideas about race in *Parsifal*. A few less cautious scholars, however, have simply distorted history in order to keep the lineage and the undeniable aesthetic power of the work intact. The tactics have been breathtaking, including the one grasped at by Bryan Magee and Frederic Spotts, among others, with the claim that the Nazis found *Parsifal* ideologically unacceptable and always tried to ban it, and indeed succeeded in doing so during the Second World War.[50]

An important source of the Nazis' scepticism, as both Magee and Spotts correctly say, was the party ideologue Alfred Rosenberg. Yet neither of them mention the opinion of seasoned biographers of Hitler and the Third Reich that 'too much has been made' of Rosenberg's role as chief ideologist of the Nazi party,[51] and that he was 'arrogant and cold, one of the least charismatic and least popular of Nazi leaders [who] united other party bigwigs only in their intense dislike of him'.[52] Rosenberg's rejection of *Parsifal* as ideologically unsound, in other words, probably counted for less

---

[50] Bryan Magee, *Wagner and Philosophy* (London: Allen Lane, 2000), p. 366; Frederic Spotts, *Bayreuth. A History of the Wagner Festival* (New Haven: Yale University Press, 1994), pp. 166, 192; see also Robert R. Gibson, 'Problematic Propaganda: "Parsifal" as Forbidden Opera', *Wagner* [Journal of the London Wagner Society], New Series 20 (May 1999), 78–87.

[51] Joachim C. Fest, *Hitler*, trans. Richard and Clara Winston (New York: Penguin, 1974), p. 137.

[52] Ian Kershaw, *Hitler 1889–1936: Hubris* (New York: Allen Lane, 1998), p. 225.

than it seemed to in the Nazi hierarchy, especially if the Führer himself was an admirer of the work.

But even this last point is in dispute. The index to Magee's book has an entry '*Parsifal*: Hitler dislikes',[53] and Spotts states categorically that in a conversation with Goebbels in the winter of 1941 in Berlin Hitler declared that 'after the war ... he would see to it either that religion was banished from *Parsifal* or that *Parsifal* was banished from the stage',[54] which certainly suggests that he harboured significant doubts about it. What Goebbels actually dictated for his diary on 22 November 1941 was this:

> Contrary to what has been reported to me, the Führer does not want *Parsifal* to be performed solely in Bayreuth again; he only means that one should modernize the décor and costumes of *Parsifal* somewhat. Either we have to get away from this Christian mystical style, or *Parsifal* in the long run won't be able to retain its place in the modern repertory. The Führer gives me several suggestions, which I will immediately put into effect.[55]

Far from wanting to banish *Parsifal* or its 'religion', Hitler's qualms were clearly directed at the over-reverential treatment of it by theatre directors who were in danger of alienating modern audiences by mistaking its sacral content for something specifically Christian. Worried that the public would turn its back on *Parsifal*, Hitler wanted a fresh approach to it, and moreover one in keeping with Wagner's own forthright assertion (cited in the second paragraph of this chapter) that, despite its use of imagery and doctrinal niceties borrowed from the Church, it is a denial of 'the whole phenomenon of Christianity in history'.

And how did Goebbels think he was going to implement Hitler's suggestions immediately if *Parsifal* was banned? The simple answer is that a ban did not exist. In fact, there had been a performance of *Parsifal* the previous day in Berlin, and another was due to take place that very evening, both of them with a young Elisabeth Schwarzkopf singing the first Esquire and one of the Flower Maidens. Indeed, we need look no further than Alan Jefferson's biography of Schwarzkopf to see that even during the war groups of three or four performances of *Parsifal* were a yearly, and sometimes twice-yearly feature in the repertoire of the Deutsche Oper, one of Berlin's principal opera houses. Between 1939 up to the end of 1942, when Schwarzkopf began to set her sights on Vienna, there were, according to Jefferson's list of her appearances, no fewer than twenty-three performances of *Parsifal* in this theatre alone.[56]

---

[53] Magee, *Wagner and Philosophy*, p. 391.
[54] Frederic Spotts, *Hitler and the Power of Aesthetics* (London: Hutchinson, 2002), p. 236.
[55] Elke Fröhlich (ed.), *Die Tagebücher von Joseph Goebbels*, II/2 (Oktober–Dezember 1941) (Munich: Saur, 1996), p. 344.
[56] Alan Jefferson, *Elisabeth Schwarzkopf* (London: Gollancz, 1996), pp. 230–6.

Coupled with the fact that the archives of the Deutscher Bühnenverein record no less than 714 performances of *Parsifal* within the borders of the German Reich between 1933 and 1939,[57] which hardly sounds like a ban either, the continued presence of *Parsifal* on German-speaking stages after Hitler's ascent to power does not exactly suggest that either he or Goebbels, whose Propaganda Ministry kept a close watch on theatre repertoire, were lukewarm about its actual content. Wagner's grandsons Wieland and Wolfgang were also witness to Hitler's ideas about the restructuring of the Bayreuth festival theatre after the war that included *Parsifal*.[58] Indeed, the only reservation Hitler seems to have had, apart from his objections to the dated productions already in existence, is that Bayreuth should never again have a monopoly over the work, suggesting that in his view as many people as possible should get a chance to experience it.

Still, setting the historical record straight on Hitler and *Parsifal* is actually less worrying than disentangling the misunderstandings about race that have clustered around the work, particularly after Zelinsky's frontal attack on it in 1982, the centenary of its first performance. Among other things taking his cue from Wagner's description of Kundry's baptism and 'annihilation' in Cosima Wagner's diaries ('annihilation' here referring specifically to a quasi-Schopenhauerian negation of self, and not to genocide), Zelinsky suggested that Kundry is 'the representative of everything that Wagner associated with Judaism',[59] including the wish for its destruction. There is no evidence for this whatsoever, and indeed no one, not even Hitler, had ever made quite such an absurd claim. In the last part of his life, Wagner regarded the Jews as incapable of miscegenation ('if ever Jews are mixed with foreign races,' he claims in another knockabout, unwittingly blackly comic passage in one of his late writings, 'all you get is another Jew'[60]), which would mean according to the historical dynamic of race as he saw it that they are incapable both of civilisation and genuine purity simply because they have never had to reclaim purity from a process of degradation. He did compare Kundry with the 'Wandering Jew', as we have seen, but only in the sense that she, too, is the victim of a 'primeval curse' that condemns her to wander for ever in constantly different guises, never able to die. That does not necessarily turn her into an allegory of Judaism. On the contrary, she seems about as far away from Wagner's idea of the consistent 'purity' of the Jews as she can be – the very opposite of the anti-race she is supposed to represent, which, quite unlike her ability to wander from one type of

---

[57] Drüner (ed.), *Der Opernführer: Wagner 'Parsifal'*, p. 205.
[58] See letter of April 1942 (draft) from Wieland to Wolfgang Wagner in Michael Karbaum, *Studien zur Geschichte der Bayreuther Festspiele (1876–1976)* (Regensburg: Bosse, 1976), p. 109.
[59] Hartmut Zelinsky, 'Rettung ins Ungenaue', in Heinz-Klaus Metzger and Rainer Riehn (eds.), *Richard Wagner: Parsifal*, Musik-Konzepte 25 (Munich: Text + Kritik, 1982), p. 102.
[60] SSD, vol. X, pp. 271–2; Ellis, vol. VI, p. 271.

human being to another, is according to Wagner all the stronger, and hence all the more dangerous, precisely because of its immutable racial character.

If Zelinsky made the mistake of reducing *Parsifal* to an anti-Semitic philippic of enormous banality, the astonishing invective he provoked made matters still worse. 'If Zelinsky is right', Joachim Kaiser thundered:

> James Levine – the conductor of the centenary performance of *Parsifal* – should have himself thoroughly denazified ... If Wagner planned to put anti-Semitism into *Parsifal*, was he too cowardly to *show* it? Cowardice was not Wagner's way. He could be a bit nutty at times; but he was a damned courageous chap![61]

Kaiser's macho blather prevented him from pausing to consider the possibility that the very absence of anti-Semitism inside *Parsifal* could be significant in other ways than simply providing a welcome relief for the work's uncritical admirers. Carl Dahlhaus also weighed in with the opposite tactic of making Wagner's exclusionary ideas about racial identity so generalised that they cease to have any real meaning. Zelinsky omitted to say, Dahlhaus wrote, that Wagner spoke of 'cleansing the redeemer from every Alexandrian-Judaic-Roman despotic deformation'. Thus he meant not just the nefarious optimism of the Jews but also the hidebound church of the Romans and the petrified dogmatism of the Alexandrians. Moreover, in matters of redemption and annihilation Wagner was prepared to include himself as well as ' "the others": the Jews'.[62]

But that does not diminish the role of race in Wagner's way of thinking in the least. As we have seen, it is the Aryan race itself and the inevitable adulteration of its blood with others that is for Wagner the central problem in this dimension of his theory and precisely not the Jews, who are incapable of racial mixture, possess '*Rassenkonsistenz*',[63] and hence neither history nor humanity. In turn, this should not be taken to mean that they had no role to play in his darkly orchestrated jeremiad on the fate of Germany. *Parsifal* may have been intended as an admonition to the German nation, an imploring cry for self-examination of identity and belief, together with an awakening of 'divine compassion streaming throughout the whole of the human race'.[64] But it was premised on the conviction that the failure of the 'noble' races to submit themselves to this arduous process would result in their collapse and a consequent invasion by the Jewish anti-race, who in the wings was supposed to be eagerly awaiting

---

[61] Joachim Kaiser, 'Hat Zelinsky recht gegen Wagners "Parsifal"?', in Attila Csampai and Dietmar Holland (eds.), *Richard Wagner: Parsifal* (Reineck bei Hamburg: Rowohlt, 1984), pp. 257–8.
[62] Carl Dahlhaus, 'Erlösung dem Erlöser: Warum Richard Wagners *Parsifal* nicht Mittel zum Zweck der Ideologie ist', in Csampai and Holland (eds.), *Richard Wagner: Parsifal*, pp. 265–6.
[63] SSD, vol. X, p. 271; Ellis, vol. VI, p. 271.
[64] SSD, vol. X, p. 281; Ellis, vol. VI, p. 281.

the negative outcome of the Germans' painful confrontation with their racial past.

NOT ABOUT REDEMPTION

As Hannah Arendt said long ago, opinions about race in the middle and later nineteenth century were still judged by the yardstick of political reason.[65] As early as 1853 Tocqueville wrote to Gobineau about the latter's doctrines that 'they are very probably wrong and quite certainly pernicious'.[66] We have also heard that not much later a scholar like Pott roundly condemned Gobineau with an entire book, and that no less a person than King Ludwig II of Bavaria eventually plucked up enough courage to congratulate Wagner on his apparent retreat from his rabid anti-Semitism. But Gobineau's ideas about a racial law of decay fired Wagner's enthusiasm to such an extent that they cannot be entirely airbrushed out of the picture we would like to have of *Parsifal* now, particularly as he had already come to his own conclusions about racial conflict since the dawn of humanity well before he had even heard of Gobineau's *Essai*.

I am also suggesting that *Parsifal* is a rather broader fantasy about race than is generally realised, couched as it is, like Gobineau's *Essai*, in terms of a powerful myth about humankind and its supposed demise that is likely to attract like-minded listeners from moderates to zealots for some time to come. It has to be stressed that there is no evidence at all that Wagner considered genocide to be the logical conclusion of his ideas. We can say of him, as Todorov says of Gobineau, 'the victim of his own literary talent', that he 'ought not to have spawned any political activists proposing to rid the world of inferior races'.[67] But that may just be wishful thinking; a more exact insight into the relation between *Parsifal* and race is perhaps unlikely to diminish audiences' love for its sublime music. On one level far from trivial for Wagner, however, its final unity and intensity of utterance is a conciliatory resolution of often-misunderstood ideas about racial identity and decay that are equally unlikely to persuade us to stop worrying entirely.

---

[65] Hannah Arendt, *The Origins of Totalitarianism* (New York: Harcourt, 1985), p. 158.
[66] Ludwig Schemann (ed.), *Correspondance entre Alexis de Tocqueville et Arthur de Gobineau 1843–1859* (Paris: Plon-Nourrit, 1908), p. 192.
[67] Todorov, *On Human Diversity*, p. 140.

CHAPTER 6

Otto Weininger and musical discourse in turn-of-the-century Vienna

Julie Brown

Otto Weininger is principally remembered as turn-of-the-century Vienna's most notorious anti-feminist and anti-Semite. His book *Geschlecht und Charakter* (*Sex and Character*), a racially inflected theory of ethical subjectivity, was a bestseller.[1] Within three years of its 1903 publication it was into its eighth German edition; by 1920 its twenty-first, by 1932 its twenty-eighth (of which the twenty-seventh and twenty-eighth were slightly cut 'popular editions').[2] His posthumous book *Über die letzten Dinge* (*On Last Things*), published in December 1903, also found a very wide readership with about half that number of editions in the same period.[3] Less well known is the fact that Weininger's life as well as his work were heavily inflected with musical import; they also represented a brand of Wagnerism among the most influential in broader European culture of the time.

Based on but controversially extending Weininger's doctoral dissertation, *Geschlecht und Charakter* is a theory of ethical subjectivity fusing a biology of human sexuality and a philosophy of sexual identity.[4] Weininger's thesis was an attempt to rescue the notion of the Kantian intelligible Self in the wake of philosophical thought that had emerged in the late nineteenth century, above all Ernst Mach's explicit rejection of a coherent, unified self or 'ego' in his 1886 *Contributions to the Analysis of Sensations*.[5] Weininger's model consisted of a dogmatic neo-Kantianism positing ideal types 'M' (*Mann*) and 'W' (*Weib*), plus a mediating third type 'Jew'. All ethical, creative and intellectual values are attributed to type 'M', the only intelligible, autonomous subject, while a veritable roll-call of misogynist stereotypes constitute type 'W', the amoral, all-sexual,

---

[1] A new translation has recently appeared from the first edition: *Sex and Character: An Investigation of Fundamental Principles*, trans. Ladislaus Löb, ed. Daniel Steuer with Laura Marcus, intro. by Daniel Steuer (Bloomington and Indianapolis: Indiana University Press, 2005).
[2] For a complete account of successive editions, see Ladislaus Löb, 'Translator's Note', in ibid., p. xlvii.
[3] *Über die letzten Dinge*, with a biographical preface (dated 4 November 1903) by Moritz Rappaport (Vienna and Leipzig: W. Braumüller, 1904); *A Translation of Weininger's 'Über die letzten Dinge' (1904/1907)/On Last Things*, trans. and with an introduction by Steven Burns (Lewiston, Queenston, Lampeter: Edwin Mellen Press, 2001) (hereafter *On Last Things*).
[4] Here I borrow Sander Gilman's words in *Jewish Self-Hatred: Anti-Semitism and the Hidden Language of the Jews* (Baltimore: The Johns Hopkins University Press, 1986), p. 244.
[5] For more on this, see Chandak Sengoopta, *Otto Weininger: Sex, Science, and Self in Imperial Vienna* (University of Chicago Press, 2000), pp. 24–7.

all-irrational feminine principle, the antithesis of the values associated with type 'M'. Though Weininger's type 'Jew' is in many ways identical to type 'W', it stands as the principle of the consciously unethical. Woman and Jew were not autonomous subjects, but mere bundles of sensations;[6] however, unlike 'W', type 'Jew' is capable of moral autonomy: he has simply not chosen it. While one of Weininger's foundational ideas is that human nature is at base bisexual and every real person a mix of all these characteristics, his ideal types betray his fundamental view that ethical human subjectivity belongs to the Aryan male. According to the categorical imperative, man must cease having sex with Woman and overcome his Jewishness if he is to be truly ethical. The extreme asceticism underpinning this recuperation of the autonomous ethical Self would logically mean the end of the human race if it were understood in real terms. In his idealist philosophical terms it signalled the beginnings of man's immortality.[7]

Some of the most famous writers and thinkers of the time were serious Weininger readers, including Ludwig Wittgenstein, Sigmund Freud, Oswald Spengler, James Joyce, Franz Kafka, Elias Canetti, Stefan Zweig, Karl Kraus, Georg Trakl and others. Also among enthusiastic readers were Arnold Schoenberg, Alban Berg, Anton Webern, Alexander Zemlinsky, Franz Schreker and Hans Pfitzner. Lyrical and operatic constructions of women and of the relations between the sexes made by these contemporary composers have been illuminated with reference to Weininger's characterology of Woman. Berg's mystical and superstitious thought has also been linked with Weininger's.[8] However, the connection between Weininger's theory of Jewish character and early twentieth-century music has received little attention. Though it is commonly observed that Weininger's construction of Jewishness in *Geschlecht und Charakter* was not so much racial as characterological, inasmuch as he cast his prejudiced observations in an idealist philosophical framework (Weininger was 'a cultural anti-Semite' and 'most emphatically not a biological racist', Chandak Sengoopta has

---

[6] Ibid., p. 29.
[7] Jeffrey Mehlman describes it as a 'ruthless metaphysical homosexuality', in 'Weininger in a Poem by Apollinaire', in Nancy A. Harrowitz and Barbara Hyams (eds.), *Jews and Gender: Responses to Otto Weininger* (Philadelphia: Temple University Press, 1995), p. 190.
[8] On Weininger's influence on musical constructions of gender, see Susanne Rode, *Alban Berg und Karl Kraus: Zur geistigen Biographie des Komponisten der »Lulu«* (Frankfurt am Main: Peter Lang, 1988), esp. pp. 106–13; Gabriele Busch-Salmen, ' "Menschenliebe im allerhöchsten Sinne": Zu den Frauenrollen in Hans Pfitzners Bühnenwerken', in Carmen Ottner (ed.), *Frauengestalten in der Oper des 19. und 20. Jahrhunderts* (Vienna: Doblinger, 2003), pp. 116–34; Reinhard Ermen, 'Der "Erotiker" und der "Asket": Befragung zweier Klischees am Beispiel der *Gezeichneten* und des *Palestrina*', in *Franz Schreker (1878–1934) zum 50. Todestag* (Aachen: Rimbaud, 1984), pp. 47–57; Lawrence Kramer, 'Fin-de-siècle Fantasies: *Elektra*, Degeneration and Sexual Science', *Cambridge Opera Journal* 5/2 (1993), 141–65. Georg C. Klaren identified Schreker as a likely Weininger reader as early as 1924: see *Otto Weininger: Der Mensch, sein Werk und sein Leben* (Vienna: Wilhelm Braumüller, 1924), p. 229 ('Schreker, der gewaltigste lebende Komponist, hat sogar die Weiningerschen Geschlechtsprobleme vertont, auf seine Bücher wenigstens haben sie stark abgefärbt.'). On Berg's mysticism, see Wolfgang Gratzer, *Zur "wunderlichen Mystik" Alban Bergs: Eine Studie* (Vienna: Böhlau, 1993), esp. pp. 93–101.

recently argued),[9] it remains that he frequently lapsed into discussions of real people: women rather than Woman, Jews rather than (type) Jew. Now that we appreciate how widely read and debated he was it seems likely that his writings contributed to the perpetuation and justification of anti-Semitism in wider intellectual culture, and also to the application of those ideas in works of art. From the very beginning commentators noted a distinctly musical dimension to Weininger's own life, death and work; digging a little deeper reveals that passionate Wagnerism partly accounts for his very construction of Jewishness, even, it seems, his own suicide.

WEININGER'S WAGNERISMS

Geschlecht und Charakter is more than a dry philosophy of ethical subjectivity. The book is curiously multiple in its thematics, and falls into two main sections reflecting views of human sexuality that are fundamentally opposed. The 'First or Preparatory Part', subtitled 'Sexual Diversity', is a biological and psychological account of human nature. Though not experimental, Weininger's approach here is essentially empirical. He draws on diverse contemporary scientific – biological, psychological, physiological – writings to set up his theory of universal bisexuality. The 'Second or Principal Part', subtitled 'The Sexual Types', is a more introspective, speculative account of human nature, foregrounding issues of ethical import. Weininger's approach here is eclectic and involves lengthy and varied speculation about a number of topics: the nature of ego, the nature of sexuality, the nature of genius, logic and ethics, and the supposed Jewish character, characterising human embodiment of, or commitment to, these concepts in gendered terms. An additional section, amounting to about a quarter of the book, is a substantial discursive Appendix of 'Supplements and Proofs'.

Part II may have especially appealed to contemporary creative artists. For if anything anchors the discussion of Part II in a discourse of types, it is the array of creative artists and literary and dramatic characters, including composers and operatic characters, that Weininger brings forward.[10] The hermeneutic sensibility that emerges here is intrinsic to Weininger's theory in many ways; as Slavoj Žižek has noted, Weininger's entire account of subjectivity hinges on matters of creativity and performativity.[11] Though artistic creativity itself is never theorised as such, Weininger co-opts its

---

[9] Sengoopta, *Otto Weininger*, p. 43.
[10] His doctoral supervisor even suggested that in a man of a literary temperament *Geschlecht und Charakter* would have appeared as a piece of theatre or a novel, rather than a psychological theory. Friedrich Jodl, in the *Neues Wiener Journal*, 25 October 1903. Discussed in Jacques Le Rider, *Le cas Otto Weininger: Racines de l'antiféminisme et de l'antisémitisme* (Paris: Presses Universitaires de France, 1982), pp. 41–2.
[11] Slavoj Žižek, 'Otto Weininger, or, "Woman Doesn't Exist"', in *The Metastases of Enjoyment: Six Essays on Woman and Causality* (London: Verso, 1994), pp. 137–64.

terms as the basis for his fundamental distinction between Man and Woman. In the chapter 'Erotik und Ästhetik' (Eroticism and Aesthetics), Weininger argues that Woman's nature is fundamentally 'performative': her beauty is created by Man's love, her ugliness by his hate.[12] As Man's 'creation', whether the screen for his projected aspirations to the spiritual or his own sexual desires and evil tendencies (which can be the same thing to Weininger), Woman is fundamentally an aesthetic object. It is not just that man is creative and woman is uncreative; man is creative and woman is *his creation*.

Weininger's illustrations are never far from musical source material. Though he does not go so far as to theorise musical creation per se, in the context of a discussion of endowment and memory in *Geschlecht und Charakter* he places music at the pinnacle of a hierarchy of the arts, albeit for somewhat idiosyncratic reasons. Because it has no correlative in nature or in the world of experience music requires even more imagination than other artistic and scientific efforts. But despite the familiarity of this idealist appeal to its supposed metaphysical nature, music does not replicate the blind Will and invoke a dreamlike state for Weininger as it did for Schopenhauer. He argues that musical creativity, like philosophy and architecture, depends on 'strong moulding' (*kraftvolle Formung*):

In music in particular what matters is the most articulate sensibility imaginable. There is nothing more definite, more characteristic, more *urgent* than a *melody*, nothing that would suffer more from being blurred. That is why one *remembers* what has been sung so much more easily than what has been spoken, arias always better than recitatives, and that is why the *sprechgesang* takes so much studying by the singer of Wagner.[13]

It is because music requires even more imagination than other artistic and scientific efforts that he considers music to be the art-form furthest removed from the negative feminine principle (in contrast to Wagner's notion of music as Woman to word's Man). Woman's absence from the history of music is offered as support for this view.[14]

Though he does not specifically discuss music any further in *Geschlecht und Charakter*, he takes it up again in *Über die letzten Dinge* where he argues that a composer needs to have a philosopher's intellectual control of ideas:

---

[12] Brünnhilde is one of Weininger's illustrations of this view of Woman as symbolic projection. 'Woman, all the way through, is only an object created by the drive of Man as its own goal, as a hallucination that his delusion is eternally laboring to capture. She is the objectivization of male sexuality, *the embodiment of sexuality, Man's guilt made flesh* . . . What Woman accomplishes through her mere existence, through her whole nature, without being able to do anything else and without ever becoming conscious of it, is only *one inclination in* **Man**, his second, ineradicable, *low* inclination: she is, like the Valkyrie, the "blindly elective tool" of the will of *another*', in *Sex and Character*, pp. 270–1; all emphases – underlinings and bold print – are Weininger's own.

[13] *Sex and Character*, pp. 105–6. [14] Ibid., pp. 104–6.

For questions and ideas [*Gedanken*] are common to both the great artist and the great philosopher. An idea, however, is demonstrable, and so art requires logic no less than science ... In contrast to modern art, which is characterized by a total lack of ideas, and has raised this lack to a principle in that it does not want to hear of ideas in art, it ought to be emphasized that each true art is an art of ideas, and each great artist is a great thinker even if he thinks differently from the philosopher.[15]

Art and music should also be logical – logic, in both *Geschlecht und Charakter* and *Über die letzten Dinge*, being the fundamental manifestation of the ethical principle. In pure logic is the guarantee of the existence of the ego. He extends this observation in an oddly speculative chapter of *Über die letzten Dinge* entitled 'Über die Einsinnigkeit der Zeit' (On the Unidirectionality of Time), arguing – in what appears to be part critique of Nietzsche's idea of the Eternal Return – that morality is also expressed in the unidirectionality of time. The opposite of unidirectional time, such as circular, elliptical and retrograde motions, is immoral – examples being dance music and the Viennese waltz:

To go around in circles is senseless, aimless; anyone who pirouettes has a self-satisfied, ridiculously vain, vulgar nature. The dance is female motion, and indeed is above all the movement of prostitution. One will find that the more a woman likes to dance, and the better she dances, the more of the prostitute she has in her.[16]

By way of further musical illustration, he provides an Appendix to this chapter in which he contrasts the two central approaches to time in purely musical terms. *Tristan und Isolde* provides him with an example of musical 'circularity' (intentionally so, he concedes); by contrast, motivic working in middle-period Beethoven is the paradigm of musical 'becoming', musical confirmation of the unidirectionality of time. Beethoven thus emerges as compositional manifestation of both ethical male subject and a type of hero of ideas, a familiar gambit in Beethoven reception.

As Nike Wagner has observed, *Parsifal* is one of the most quoted works of art in *Geschlecht und Charakter*, being rivalled only by Ibsen's *Peer Gynt*; like *Peer Gynt* it is also the subject of a separate essay in *Über die letzten Dinge*, and emerges as the most important of Wagner's operas to Weininger overall. In that essay he characterises Wagner's motivic working in terms equally positive to Beethoven's, but with a slightly mystical spin:

the characteristic things about the Wagnerian motifs is a maximum of musical *density*, if I may put it this way. They are never diluted, but always say *everything*. Wagner's motifs are characterized by the extreme succinctness, concentration

---

[15] *On Last Things*, p. 131. I have modified this translation slightly, and substituted 'idea' for 'thought' as a translation of the word *Gedanke*.
[16] *On Last Things*, p. 84.

and irresistibility of his melodies, by their great remoteness from any lack of oxygen, and by the opposite of any thinning of the atmosphere and absence of mass. This is especially so where he floats over mountain tops, is intoxicated by glaciers, and breathes that mountain air for which no one had a better sense than he.[17]

Elsewhere Weininger writes about certain types of motifs as expressions of volition that appear to transcend time. This following appears with the aphorisms included in *Über die letzten Dinge*:

The most powerful musical motifs of the world's music are those which attempt to represent this *breaking through* time in time, this breaking forth out of time, where such a rhythmical accent falls on one note that it absorbs the remaining parts of the melody (which represents time as a whole, individual points integrated by the ego), and thereby *transcends* the melody. The end of the Grail motif in *Parsifal*, and the Siegfried motif, are such melodies.[18]

Without specifying it any more explicitly than he does in this reference to the Grail motif, Weininger seems to be trying here to articulate his understanding of Gurnemanz's claim in *Parsifal*: near the temple of the grail '*Zum Raum wird hier die Zeit*' (Here time becomes space).

His liberal use of musical asides and illustrations is certainly never far from Wagnerian source material. Kundry is probably *Geschlecht und Charakter*'s most cited character, exemplifying for Weininger not only Woman's supposed endemic hysteria, but also her lack of a sense of personal value and her indiscriminate motherliness, though he also uses *The Ring* to illustrate this.[19] Kundry's fundamental namelessness exemplifies this supposed lack of a sense of personal value. (According to Weininger, real women are 'nameless' inasmuch as they are willing to

---

[17] *On Last Things*, p. 74. This oddly muscular metaphysical excursus stands in stark contrast to Weininger's account of Wagner's music in the first draft of his dissertation, *Eros und Psyche*, in which his references to Wagner are more akin to existing constructions of Wagner the decadent. He considers Wagner to be a *feminine* musician, and finds both his poetic and his musical imagination wanting, especially as it related to thematic working. Elsewhere in the same draft he wrote: 'music can step in as vicarious sexual relations – *Wagnerei* [Wagner nonsense] especially is often only a better surrogate for coitus.' See Hannelore Rodlauer (ed.), *Otto Weininger: Eros und Psyche; Studien und Briefe 1899–1902* (Vienna: Verlag der Österreichischen Akademie der Wissenschaften, 1990), pp. 148–9.
[18] *On Last Things*, p. 43.
[19] 'The hygienic punishment for Woman's denial of her true nature is *hysteria* . . . **Hysteria**, then, is the **organic crisis of the organic falseness of Woman** . . . But what hysterical women want is hysteria itself: they do not really *try* to be *cured*. *It is the falseness of this demonstration against slavery that makes it so hopeless*. The most noble specimens of the sex may feel that they are enslaved precisely because they wish to be – remember Hebbel's Judith and Wagner's Kundry – but even this does not give them the strength to resist the coercion in actual fact: at the last moment they will still kiss a man who is violating them, or try to make a man their master if he hesitates to rape them. *It is as if Woman were laboring under a curse.* At some moments she may feel weighed down by it, but she can *never* escape from it, because the burden seems too sweet. Basically, all her screaming and raging is a *fake*. It is precisely when she pretends to be recoiling from her curse with the greatest horror that she wishes to succumb to it most passionately.' *Sex and Character*, pp. 239, 240, 251–2.

shed their names when married.[20]) Critically, Kundry exemplifies for Weininger the conceptual link he wants to forge between the Jewish and feminine principles; the Jewish principle represents for him a psychic state, a man's conscious decision to embrace tendencies that are supposedly unconscious in women. He conceived of these supposed tendencies as negative, but they are by no means obviously so, comprising group identification, devotion to family life, lack of individual personality, incapacity for genius, lack of reason, and lack of a sense of humour – though he does admit of Jewish wit, which he distinguishes from humour and appears to value less.[21] '[U]nmistakeably', he claims, 'the shadow of Ahasverus also falls on his Kundry, the most profound female figure in all art.'[22] Forging a conceptual parallel between Woman and Jew was nothing new, of course; but Weininger made a significant contribution to the perpetuation of this myth by formalising it within this all-embracing theory of ethical subjectivity. In his substantial discursive footnotes, he glosses the Kundry-as-Ahasverus comment by boldly proclaiming: 'The problem of Judaism is openly formulated in *Der fliegende Holländer*, in *Lohengrin*, in *Parsifal*.'[23] He also describes Siegfried and Parsifal (the characters), and *Die Meistersinger* as the antithesis of Jewishness, and crowns *Parsifal* 'the most profound work of world literature'.[24] This influential theorist of Jewish character had no doubt that anti-Semitic messages were projected in Wagner's dramas.

Turning from characters in the dramas to the composer himself, Weininger argues that Wagner was more than a genius; he was 'the greatest individual since Christ', and even represented a type of composer parallel to Christ.[25] Such a construction had an ethical meaning for Weininger. In *Geschlecht und Charakter* he presents Wagner somewhat surprisingly as an Aryan creative genius who nonetheless had type 'Jew' characteristics. This is a good thing in Weininger's reading of Wagner's works. For Weininger someone who was 'only a German' could never express the essence of *Deutschtum* in the way Wagner did. His claim follows logically from one made elsewhere, namely that a true creative genius is able to understand and represent characters best when he contains within himself not only the character he is grasping but also its opposite. The implicit parallel he makes between Wagner and Christ is important. He writes: 'An even greater man than Wagner had to overcome Judaism in himself before

---

[20] Weininger quotes Klingsor's words to Kundry at the beginning of Act II of *Parsifal*: 'Arise! Arise! To me! / Your master calls you, nameless woman, / First she-devil! Rose of Hades! / Herodias were you, and what else? / Gundryggia, then, Kundry here! / Come here! Come here now, Kundry! / Your master calls: arise!'. *Sex and Character*, p. 179fn.

[21] For a discussion of the context within which these characteristics were defined, see John M. Hoberman, 'Otto Weininger and the Critique of Jewish Masculinity', in Harrowitz and Hyams (eds.), *Jews and Gender: Responses to Otto Weininger*, pp. 141–53.

[22] *Sex and Character*, p. 289. [23] Ibid., p. 419n. [24] Ibid., p. 310. [25] Ibid.

finding his mission.'²⁶ This is perhaps the key to Weininger's need to attribute to Wagner some Judaism. Weininger considers Christ's defining act, his 'world-historical significance', to have been his redemption of mankind from Judaism, his overcoming of his own racial origin. Weininger implies that Wagner's role in German culture was similarly Christ-like. It was Wagner's special status as creative genius that enabled him to put his '*Beisatz*' (accretion) of Jewishness to ethical use – that is, by creating its opposite, *Deutschtum*, at the highest peak of artistic expression.

It is hard entirely to reject Nike Wagner's claim that *Geschlecht und Charakter* amounts at least at some level to a 'retranslation of *Parsifal* into the language of speculative metaphysics'.²⁷ For her the book is a particularly fervent Wagnerism, a virulent form of German nationalism carried to the heights of moral and metaphysical speculation. Notwithstanding the fact that the book manifests Weininger's assimilation of a large body of philosophical and psychological writings, a prodigious learning, Nike Wagner, Hartmut Zelinsky and Jacques LeRider have all also noted that much of the most controversial material on Woman and Jew in *Geschlecht und Charakter* was written after Weininger's visit to Bayreuth in August 1902 when he saw a performance of *Parsifal*.²⁸ Though it would be easy to dismiss claims of a direct Wagnerian debt from these Wagner-critical commentators, it is worth reviewing the evidence.

Biographies note that Weininger inherited a love of Wagner from his father. He submitted his doctoral dissertation early in 1902 and was examined by 12 July 1902.²⁹ Shortly before submitting he told a friend that he had grown interested in the Jewish Question and in ethical issues, something that Hannelore Rodlauer partly attributes to his reading of the writings of Houston Stewart Chamberlain, who was then resident in Vienna and whom Weininger most likely heard speak on the topic of 'Richard Wagners Philosophie' at the university as early as December 1898. Weininger cites Chamberlain throughout his chapter on Judaism,³⁰ but gives the same chapter an epithet taken (page uncited) directly from Wagner's 'Das Judentum in der Musik': 'Here we must clearly articulate *something* that really exists, rather than trying to give an artificial life to something that does not exist by means of some fantasy.'³¹ The formally examined version of the dissertation has not survived, but the reactions of

---

²⁶ See ibid., pp. 275–6.
²⁷ Nike Wagner, '*Parsifal* et l'Antisémitism Juif à Vienne, Dans les Années 1900', *L'Infini* 3 (1983), 22–32. See also Nike Wagner, *The Wagners: The Dramas of a Musical Dynasty*, trans. Ewald Osers and Michael Downes (London: Weidenfeld and Nicolson, 2000), pp. 118–30.
²⁸ Zelinsky, 'Arnold Schönberg – Gottes Wagner: Anmerkung zum Lebensweg eines deutschen Juden aus Wien', *Neue Zeitschrift für Musik* 147/4 (1986), 7–19.
²⁹ See examination reports in Rodlauer (ed.), *Otto Weininger: Eros und Psyche; Studien und Briefe 1899–1902*, pp. 211–14.
³⁰ Rodlauer, p. 17; for her suggestion.   ³¹ Quoted in *Sex and Character*, p. 272.

his supervisors Friedrich Jodl and Laurenz Müller to the published book testify to significant development of the final chapters on Jews, Women and hysteria between examination and publication – that is, after Weininger's long summer's travelling, which took in both Bayreuth and Ibsen's home of Norway.[32]

Letters and diaries reveal that Bayreuth itself greatly impressed Weininger when he visited in August 1902. The day after seeing *Parsifal* (12 August 1902) he wrote to his friend Arthur Gerber: 'I now have the conviction that I am yet born to be a musician ... Today I discovered a specifically musical imagination in myself, of which I would never have thought myself capable, and which has filled me with a great reverence' – a claim that another friend Moritz Rappaport chose to reproduce in the biographical sketch he wrote for the 1904 posthumous publication of Weininger's *Über die letzten Dinge*, which he compiled and edited. Shortly after this letter (17 August 1902) Weininger wrote again with *Parsifal* still on his mind: 'My journey seems so absurd to me. Only geographically is it right. But as in *Parsifal* one should go on a pilgrimage, a long one, to the end of the earth, and then somehow vanish ... This journey has made me realize that I am also no philosopher. Truly not! But am I anything else? I very much doubt it.'[33] Back in Vienna he set to work between October 1902 and May 1903 writing four new chapters for the published, that is the third, version of *Geschlecht und Charakter*. These crucial final four chapters – 'Erotik und Ästhetik' (Eroticism and Aesthetics), 'Das Wesen des Weibes und sein Sinn im Universum' (The Nature of Woman and her Purpose in the Universe), 'Das Judentum' (Judaism), 'Das Weib und die Menschheit' (Woman and Humanity) – include the anti-Semitic chapter with the Wagnerian epithet, his discussions of *Parsifal* as the greatest poem in world literature, and his conclusions that Woman would cease to exist if Man resisted her.

A review that appeared immediately after *Geschlecht und Charakter*'s publication in 1903 demonstrates that reading it as a type of re-translation of *Parsifal* is not simply the product of hindsight, nor indeed the interpretation of a critical Wagner descendant such as Nike Wagner. Under the heading 'Kundry: Eine Bemerkung zu einem Buche' ('Kundry: A Remark to a Book'), novelist Franz Blei reviewed the book correctly signalling that his review is as much about *Parsifal* as it is about the book.[34] Blei launched immediately to his central point: namely, that the book does an injustice to the opera and its characters by regarding them only as manifestations of

---

[32] See Introduction to *Sex and Character*, pp. xv–xvi.
[33] *Otto Weininger: Taschenbuch und Briefe an einen Freund* (Leipzig: E. P. Tal, 1919), pp. 77, 82. English translation in Martin Dudaniec and Kevin Solway (trans.), *Otto Weininger: Collected Aphorisms, Notebook and Letters to a Friend*, edition 1.12 (Weininger Resources: private publication, ksolway@poboxes.com), pp. 77, 80.
[34] Franz Blei, 'Kundry: Eine Bemerkung zu einem Buche', *Freistatt* 5 (1903), 587–8.

particular Ideas. It is hard to disagree, of course. Ideologically problematic though *Parsifal* is, it is a richly resonant work. Moreover, Weininger's idealist reading of *Parsifal* was not entirely new. It drew not only on Chamberlain, but also in part on an article published in *Wiener Rundschau*, on 15 August 1901, by close family friend Emil Lucka, whom he acknowledges in a footnote near the end of his book. Indeed several of his key ideas closely paraphrase Lucka. Compare Weininger's comments about Kundry ('the most profound female figure in all art') with Lucka's:

> The most masterly form which Wagner created, and one of the most powerful of world literature, is *Kundry*. In this one personality all sides of woman are intertwined. The hallmark of the lack of individuality in the higher sense (meaning the inner – intelligible – identity of all women's characteristics) is simply that one solitary woman stands in opposition to different divergent male characters while she undergoes several metamorphoses under the spell of male hypnosis.[35]

Note also Lucka's concern with ethics:

> The awakening of ethical consciousness is presented with deep artistry in the seduction scene of the second act ... [Parsifal] remembers the mother who died of yearning for him and duty reveals itself to him with tremendous certainty; the veil of the Maya falls from his eyes, physical causality perishes into meaninglessness, and under the musical motives of the first act, which symbolise the transcendent, he grasps the ethical significance of the world and recognises his duty as redeemer.[36]

The value of Blei's 'book review' lies in its testimony that at least one contemporary artist immediately perceived *Geschlecht und Charakter*'s Wagnerian import. While other contemporary critics chose to pick up on Weininger's construction of Woman and sex, it took a novelist to note that behind all the *Zeitgeist* sociobiology, Weininger's method in the second section could be read as fundamentally hermeneutic, with *Parsifal* at its centre.

WEININGER AS MUSICAL *LEBENSKUNSTLER*

With such strong indications that Weininger's ideas about redemption, Jews and Jewish self-redemption were assimilations of Wagner, Nike Wagner's further claim that they actively contributed to his suicide at the age of twenty-three cannot easily be dismissed. Yet it was not only Wagnerian, but also Beethovenian and more general musical import that attached to the Weininger case from the moment his suicide catapulted him into the intellectual spotlight. His decision in October 1903 to rent a room in the house in Schwarzspanier Strasse in which Beethoven had died

---

[35] Lucka, 'Zur Symbolik in Wagners "Parsifal"', *Wiener Rundschau* (15 August 1901), 315.
[36] Ibid., 314–15.

in order to commit an apparently well-planned suicide after a summer's travelling turned his early death into a very public event, something of a performance in fact, and doubtless substantially accounts for *Geschlecht und Charakter*'s subsequent notoriety and publishing success, especially given its fairly quiet release in May of the same year. The choice of venue immediately invited some sort of connection to be made between Weininger, the ethics he propounded and Beethoven, especially when viewed through the lens of his own metaphysics: in *Über die letzten Dinge* Weininger argues that everything is symbol. Almost all accounts of his death note the venue. His father made reference to it on Otto's tombstone:

> This stone marks the resting place of a young man whose spirit found no peace in this world. When he had delivered the message of his soul, he could no longer remain among the living. He betook himself to the place of death of one of the greatest of all men, the Schwarzspanierhaus in Vienna, and there destroyed his mortal body.[37]

In his book on Weininger, family friend Lucka (author of the aforementioned *Parsifal* essay) considered the choice 'no coincidence'. Moritz Rappaport, a personal friend of Weininger, attempted to explain it in a biographical sketch dated 4 November 1903 which he wrote for *Über die letzten Dinge*. Rappaport claimed that what drew Weininger to Beethoven was the danger of evil, the yearning after purity, the terrible suffering, and the enormous struggle, but above all the immense transfiguring joy of which Beethoven alone was capable.[38] Weininger took Beethoven to be, like himself, both a genius and a criminal type. In the chapter 'Begabung und Genius' (Endowment and Genius) in *Geschlecht und Charakter* – which (psycho-)biographer David Abrahamsen suggested in 1948 was essentially an autobiographical tract on Weininger's part[39] – Weininger certainly described Beethoven as a genius, indeed as the ultimate genius. Beethoven exemplified the composer genius able to master any field, who might 'be just as universal, just as adept at traversing the whole inner and outer world, as does the poet or the philosopher', which amounted to a repetition of a philosophical and ethical construction of Beethoven publicly rehearsed between 15 April and 15 June the previous year, when the Viennese Secession Building was turned into a temple of art, with Max Klinger's marble statue representing Beethoven as a type of intellectual,

---

[37] Quoted in David Abrahamsen, *The Mind and Death of a Genius* (New York: Columbia University Press, 1946), p. 96.
[38] 'Vorrede', in Otto Weininger, *Über die letzten Dinge* (1904), p. viii: 'Nächst Richard Wagner verehrte er *Beethoven* am meisten. Er hielt Beethoven für ein Genie, dessen Gefahr das Verbrechen gewesen ist, wie Knut Hamsun, Kant, Augustinus. Die Gefahr des Bösen, die Sehnsucht nach Reinheit, das furchtbare Leiden und der gewaltige Kampf waren es, die ihn bei Beethoven anzogen; vor allem aber jene merkwürdige, verklärte Freude, deren Beethoven allein fähig war.'
[39] Abrahamsen, *The Mind and Death of a Genius*, p. 156.

contemplative Zeus figure at the centre. A musical 'genius' should be held to account in matters other than music, Weininger argues, because genius is the highest manifestation of the creative masculine principle.[40]

Claims about Beethoven's parallel 'criminality' nevertheless remain poorly, if at all, supported by Weininger's own writings: Weininger certainly frequently refers to the criminal in his posthumous papers, just not to Beethoven in this connection.[41] What Rappaport did not spell out in his early biographical sketch, but which seems implicit in his attempt to link Weininger with Beethoven through the figure of the criminal, is that Weininger asserted in a chapter on Ibsen's *Peer Gynt* in *Über die letzten Dinge* that Beethoven was a 'self-hater'. Weininger sometimes invoked Beethoven in underdeveloped, even unjustifiable, ways, as in his characterology of 'Seekers and Priests', also in *Über die letzten Dinge* ('the seeker searches, the priest informs'), where he claims, with little real elaboration, that Beethoven is a 'seeker' in *Fidelio* but a priest in the 'Waldstein' sonata, whose final movement is the highest summit of Apollonian art.[42] In light of the slant of much Weininger reception, his characterisation of Beethoven is extremely important. To Weininger's way of thinking self-hatred is not such a terrible affliction. Self-hatred (*Misautisch*) has many positive sides to it: though self-haters suffer perpetually and are unable to tolerate loneliness, they are also 'the greatest self-observers'.[43] For a champion of Kantian introspection over experimental psychology such as Weininger, self-observation was intrinsically valuable.

Implications of self-hatred have long underpinned accounts of Weininger's suicide, including Rappaport's immediate diagnosis in 1903. Rappaport described Weininger as having taken himself to be a criminal, as having considered his intellectual strivings to be a struggle against the criminal's 'Nothing': he quoted from Weininger's own diaries and writings, 'Before his suicide, he wrote, "I kill myself so that I do not have to kill another person."'[44] Other close friends reported similar things.[45] Abrahamsen noted that Weininger started to show clear, outward critical

---

[40] *Sex and Character*, p. 98.
[41] Weininger wrote many aphorisms about the criminal: see especially his *Taschenbuch und Briefe an einen Freund*. Eva Diettrich buys into this claim by Rappaport in 'Otto Weininger und sein Verhältnis zur Musik', *Studien zur Musikwissenschaft* 33 (1982), 49–53.
[42] *On Last Things*, pp. 68, 70. See also, more eccentrically, his account of sadism and masochism: 'rhythm, which *attends* precisely to every *individual* note, every *individual* syllable, is sadistic; harmony is masochistic, as with truly melodious song (in which the individual notes do not emerge as such).' Wagner, Beethoven and Schumann are also masochists, whereas Verdi is more sadistic. Ibid., pp. 57, 58.
[43] *On Last Things*, p. 28.   [44] 'Vorrede', in *Über die letzten Dinge* (1904), p. xvii.
[45] His closest friend Arthur Gerber relates the events of the night of 18 November 1902, when Weininger seemed almost to have committed suicide, two days after saying extremely grave farewells to his family. According to Gerber amidst an emotionally fraught evening Weininger said: 'I know that I am a born criminal. I am a born murderer.' (In Abrahamsen, *The Mind and Death of a Genius*, p. 62: from *Taschenbuch*).

signs of the effect of his turn to moral philosophy around July 1902, when it became clear to him that he must live in accord with his moral principles.[46] Yet despite Weininger's own positive discussion of *Misautisch, Jewish Self-Hatred*' has become a controversial diagnosis of the particular form it might have taken in his own case. Asserted as a category by Theodor Lessing in 1930, *Jewish Self-Hatred* is also the title of Sander Gilman's more recent history of Jewish anti-Semitism. Though both Lessing and Gilman highlight the Weininger case as almost archetypal,[47] Alan Janik has questioned the label's applicability to Weininger, noting that it assumes the presence of an immutable concept of race in his work and also that Weininger had a Jewish identity in the first place. Janik's observation serves as a useful warning against an overly reductive application of the concept, and yet his objection to its usefulness in Weininger's case ignores the fact that in a footnote in his chapter on Judaism (which he not only openly theorises, but identifies as a cultural disease) Weininger does identify himself as 'of Jewish descent'; the harshly anti-Semitic aphorisms which were initially included in *Über die letzten Dinge* (though eight of the worst were excluded from the second and subsequent editions) are also relevant as signs of his feelings towards his Jewish descent as he approached the point of suicide. Janik also ignores the extent to which Weininger positively valued the profound introspection that he took to be at the heart of self-hatred.

It would be odd, therefore, not to consider his own Jewish descent to have contributed to his suicidal frame of mind, even if it seems unlikely that it alone led him to commit suicide. Not only biographers from his immediate circle but also more historically detached commentators such as Gilman have proposed that a network of psychoses most likely contributed to his decision to commit suicide: a repressed sexual drive, which some have argued was both homosexual and inclusive of sexual sadism; earlier commentators declared him variously an hysteric grappling with feminine traits,[48] a manic depressive,[49] and a schizophrenic, partly withdrawing from reality.[50] The exception to this tendency in psycho-biographical commentary was Karl Kraus, editor of Viennese journal *Die Fackel*, who defended Weininger in *Die Fackel* against both Rappaport's introduction

---

[46] Abrahamsen, *The Mind and Death of a Genius*, p. 66.
[47] Theodor Lessing, *Jüdische Selbsthass* (Berlin: Jüdischer Verlag, 1930), pp. 80–100; Sander L. Gilman, *Jewish Self-Hatred: Anti-Semitism and the Hidden Language of the Jews* (Baltimore and London: The Johns Hopkins University Press, 1986), esp. pp. 244–9.
[48] P. J. Möbius, *Geschlecht und Unbescheidenheit* (1903), pp. 28–9; Wilhelm Stekel, 'Der Fall Otto Weininger', *Die Wage* 45 (November 1904), quoted in Abrahamsen, *The Mind and Death of a Genius*, pp. 101–5.
[49] Ferdinand Probst, *Der Fall Otto Weininger: Eine psychiatrische Studie* (Wiesbaden: Bergman, 1904), p. 39.
[50] Abrahamsen, *The Mind and Death of a Genius*, p. 105.

of *Über die letzten Dinge* and against Ferdinand Probst.[51] He publicly proclaimed Weininger's perfect lucidity and indisputable health. As Jacques Le Rider points out, Karl Kraus found in Weininger an ally for the fight that he had engaged in *Sittlichkeit und Kriminalität* against moral hypocrisy.[52] This idea that suicide might be construed not as symptomatic of emotional instability, but as a step deemed to be logical by a lucid individual who had thought rationally about things moral finds support in Weininger's own writings. Weininger himself wrote about suicide as a preventative measure against performing some sort of 'evil'. His view is clearly linked with the categorical imperative built into his Kantian account of ethical subjectivity, but Weininger gives it a self-redemptive spin. At the end of the chapter 'Logic, Ethics and the Self' in *Geschlecht und Charakter* he discusses the idea that the human being is alone in the world by saying 'he must fulfill the inexorable, non-negotiable, i.e., categorical, demand within him. Redemption! he cries out' – adding in a footnote, 'Cries Schopenhauer, cries Wagner'.[53] In his *Taschenbuch*, first published (posthumously) in 1919, we also find:

> I believe that my powers of mind are surely such that I would have become in a certain sense a resolver of all problems. I do not believe that I could have remained in error anywhere for long. I believe that I would have earned the name of Redeemer, because I had the nature of a Redeemer [*ich war eine Lösernatur*].[54]

There are hints that close personal friends considered there to have been a Wagnerian connection to Weininger's suicide, in the way that Nike Wagner does. In his 1905 book-length study *Otto Weininger: Sein Werk und seine Persönlichkeit* Lucka mentions Wagner several times in connection with Weininger's formulations of the essence of Woman and Jew. He also carefully contrasts Weininger's intellectual anti-Judaism (*geistigen Antijudaismus*) with Houston Stewart Chamberlain's racial anti-Semitism (*Rassenantisemitismus*) – considering Chamberlain's anti-Semitism as the 'preliminary stage' (*Vorstufe*) of Weininger's.[55] Lucka ends his book in such a way as to leave the Wagner connection in our minds: he concludes by saying that if he were to try to identify the lasting value of Weininger's work, he would cite the fact that it is the most ideas-rich theoretical book since the work of Schopenhauer, and that 'the depth with which his books grasped the problem of human life has not been reached since the death of Richard Wagner'.[56] Yet even in his 1903 biographical introduction to *Über die letzten Dinge* Rappaport had immediately noted the profound impact

---

[51] See *Fackel* no. 150 (23 Dec. 1903); no. 152 (16 Jan. 1904); no. 169 (23 Nov. 1904); no. 176 (28 February 1905). Excerpts from Weininger also ran in *Die Fackel* from October 1903 through to 1923.
[52] See Le Rider, *Le cas Otto Weininger*, pp. 144–5. [53] *Sex and Character*, pp. 141–2.
[54] *Taschenbuch*, p. 28; translated by Dudaniec and Solway, p. 42.
[55] Emil Lucka, *Otto Weininger: Sein Werk und seine Persönlichkeit* (Vienna: W. Braumüller, 1905: Berlin: Wilhelm Braumuller, 1921), p. 38.
[56] Ibid., p. 72.

Wagner had on his close friend. It is worth translating his musical comments at length, because they were part of a longer passage in which Rappaport foregrounded Weininger's special interest in music generally.

> He was very musical. In particular, he had a fantastic musical memory; he played no instrument himself. He was most decidedly a music psychologist [*Musikpsychologe*]: i.e. he sensed a psychological phenomenon in every individual melody – a mood in a landscape, which seemed unambiguously and clearly allocated to that melody; so that, for example, he could speak of a heart beat motif, of a melody of the chill of empty space. But these visions were by no means limited to feelings and moods; they very often rose to consider the highest and most general problems. Problems can obviously be rendered musically only through their mood content; one moment this is stronger, the next weaker, exactly to the degree in which problems would be truly experienced. Here this operated in the most extreme manner that can be imagined; and thus with great certainty Weininger would experience in one motif playful [*spielenden*] Monism, in another one resigned separation from the Absolute, in a third original sin, etc. His favourite composer was *Richard Wagner* whom he considered the greatest artist of all mankind. Admittedly in his Avenarius period he had still quite disparagingly commented that: 'Whoever wants to become a psychologist must listen to Wagner'. But in the great conversion he underwent around two years before his death, that position, too, changed enormously. He now considered *Tristan* to be one of the world's greatest works of art; he deemed *Parsifal* to be the absolute pinnacle* in terms of text, and *Siegfried* (especially Act III) the pinnacle in terms of music. The prelude to this act always aroused his admiration; he found his innermost experience expressed in it: '. . . the struggle between All and Nothing, between Cosmos and Chaos, the greatest alternative in the world; and the turmoil of the whole of Nature in this struggle'. – The melody 'Siegfried, Herrlicher, Hort der Welt' meant a great deal to him. – But all this took a second place to the enormous effect that the so-called 'Liebeswonne-Motif' ('Du Wecker des Lebens, siegendes Licht') wielded over him. After a performance of *Siegfried* he once said that he did not undertand how the house could remain standing after this melody. Even in the despairing mood of his last days alive he was terribly shaken by the motif – which he called 'the absorption of the horizon' (because the whole horizon seems to be embraced, devoured [*verschlungen*]). Once more, before the backdrop of the increasing darkening of his mental state, a wide open blue sky revealed itself to him; once more 'siegendes Licht' (victorious light) shone for the clouded eye. – Apart from that, I still want to mention the Regenbogen-motif (*Rheingold*), which to him seemed to contain something of the 'Freedom of the Object'; this too he held in especially high esteem. – Incidentally, in this book he makes several music-psychological remarks about Wagnerian melodies that affected him deeply.[57]

---

* He felt the need to assess as precisely as possible all great men and works of art; his constant striving after clarity demanded this.

Interestingly, Rappaport changed his biography between the first and second editions of *Über die letzten Dinge* in such a way as to downplay

---

[57] 'Vorrede', *Über die letzten Dinge* (1904), pp. vii–viii.

the Wagnerian and general musical influence. In the first edition, quoted above, he was open about the psychological effect that Wagner's music, and music generally, had on Weininger; by the second edition, he no longer describes Weininger as a *Musikpsychologe*; in fact, the word psychology is removed altogether, and philosophy and ideas are emphasised instead ('Weininger associated melodies with philosophical ideas', and perceived in music the 'expression of images of spiritual life'). The detailed account of Weininger's reactions to particular moments in Wagner is likewise deleted; the text now passes directly from the sentence declaring Wagner to have been Weininger's favourite composer to comments about Beethoven, which are virtually identical to those in the first version.

All of this adds a special musical import to the already quite persuasive notion that *Geschlecht und Charakter* was a kind of psycho-biographical tract, the product of someone who, though probably convinced of his own genius, was equally afraid of his 'negative' traits in light of the moral philosophy he espoused.[58] In Barbara Hyams and Nancy A. Harrowitz's words:

> Weininger's transcendental philosophy doomed him to a negation that would never be compatible with earthly reality. In short, Weininger tried to build a science of characterology and totally transcendental religion on the shaky foundation of his own subjective unhappiness.[59]

However, read in conjunction with Weininger's philosophical construction of ethical subjectivity, his comments about his own potential as redeemer, his reactions to *Parsifal* at Bayreuth, his confessional aphorisms and notebooks, plus Rappaport's biographical sketch and Lucka's 1905 book all suggest that at least some people close to Weininger suspected that he styled himself as a kind of self-redemptive Jew of the type called upon by Wagner at the end of 'Das Judentum in der Musik'. As suggested by the epithet his father placed on his tombstone, Weininger's suicide seems to have been a self-redeeming gesture. For Rappaport in 1903 and Hermann Swoboda in his 1911 book *Otto Weiningers Tod* the Beethovenian dimension to his suicide served to indicate that Weininger was the true 'hero' to Beethoven's 'artist/poet'; as Swoboda puts it, whereas the poet expresses perfection and justice in art, the hero goes to death himself 'if justice demands it'. The true hero is an artist of life (*Lebenskünstler*).[60] Whether or not his friends' accounts reflect Weininger's true intention – namely, that he was effectively seeking to out-hero Beethoven – Weininger's choice of Beethoven's death-house for his own suicide served to create a symbol

---

[58] Abrahamsen, *The Mind and Death of a Genius*, pp. 113–15.
[59] Hyams and Harrowitz, 'A Critical Introduction to the History of Weininger Reception', in *Jews and Gender: Responses to Otto Weininger*, p. 8.
[60] Swoboda, *Otto Weiningers Tod* (Vienna: Franz Deuticke, 1911), p. 31. Rappaport had suggested something similar in *Über die letzten Dinge* (1904), p. xvii.

which begged reading both in the light of his own 'philosophy' of ethical subjectivity and of prevailing cultural understandings of Beethoven. Crucially, he posthumously forced his case into broader musical and cultural discourse.

EPILOGUE

It is beyond the scope of the present essay to consider musical responses to Weininger in the context of rising racial anti-Semitism, though the musical gloss that Weininger gave to his racially inflected theory of ethics provided a backdrop for the through-flow of Wagnerian musical anti-Semitism in the popular musical literature that Erik Levi discusses in this volume. It is worth bearing in mind that Hans Pfitzner at least seems to have understood Weininger's suicide in a specifically Wagnerian redemptive sense. In his somewhat self-serving 'Glosse zum II. Weltkrieg' published in June 1945, one month after the war's end, Pfitzner recalls talking to Hitler about Weininger in 1923 when the music-loving but still little-known Hitler paid the composer a visit in hospital where he was having a gall-bladder operation.[61] Pfitzner recalls Hitler bringing Weininger up in conversation, saying that Weininger was the only Jew that he accepted because he had created himself out of the world. Pfitzner seems keen in his essay to create a distance between his own views and those of Hitler; he notes, for instance, that not all Jews 'could be expected to do' as Weininger did. He nevertheless suggests that Weininger's self-hatred (which he accepts and emphasises), and indeed Jewish anti-Semitism more generally, points to the larger picture of anti-Semitism as both a *Weltanschauung* and a racial problem. Most interestingly he implicitly links Weininger's suicide with Wagner's call on 'high-minded Jews' at the end of 'Das Judentum in der Musik'. There Wagner associates redemption from the 'Jew's curse' with Ahasuerus, whom legend says was condemned to eternal wandering for having denied Christ: 'One thing alone can redeem you from the curse that weighs upon you: the redemption of Ahasuerus – *destruction* [*Untergang*]!'[62] Pfitzner writes in 1945, 'In the case of Weininger a willingness to destruction [*Untergang*] is revealed; it shows itself as the Redemption of Ahasuerus.' Pfitzner's self-serving essay remains inherently problematic. Yet even if we can never fully know what he intended by writing this gloss, his record offers two concrete pointers to the music historian: it indicates that in a fairly brief conversation Weininger was either well enough known, or considered of sufficient musical interest, to be the topic of conversation between these two men, one a

---

[61] Bernhard Adamy (ed.). *Hans Pfitzner, Sämtliche Schriften* (Tutzing: Hans Schneider, 1987), vol. IV, part of 'Glosse zum II. Weltkrieg',
[62] Wagner, 'Judaism in Music', as translated in *Wagner* [Journal of the London Wagner Society] 9 (1988), 33.

musician, the other a still little-known politician also interested in music; it also suggests that Pfitzner read Weininger's self-destruction in a Wagnerian spirit.

When we consider Western music and racial discourses in the early years of the twentieth century, it will be important to bear in mind that they sometimes intersected in surprising ways. The musical gloss that Weininger gave to his racially inflected theory of ethical subjectivity, and his very performative 'musical' death, lent his immediate legacy a musical significance that has since been lost. Weininger's writings and his suicide were sensations of their time. Given Pamela M. Potter's observation that links between music and biological accounts of race were far from well established at the turn of the century the musical dimension of Weininger's thoroughgoing philosophical construction of gender and race character is of particular interest to our present understanding of the interface between musical and racial discourses in the first decades of the twentieth century. In considering the impact of Weininger's writings in Vienna and beyond, and also the extent to which musical and racial discourses intersected during this time, the case of Weininger probably ought to be considered part of turn-of-the-century Viennese musical discourse.

CHAPTER 7

Ancestral voices: anti-Semitism and Ernest Bloch's racial conception of art

Klára Móricz

Sidonia, an idealised Rothschild in Benjamin Disraeli's 1844 novel *Coningsby*, explains the indestructible character of Jews as the result of their racial purity. 'You cannot destroy a pure race', he argues. 'It is a physiological fact; a simple law of nature'. As is often the case when racial purity is invoked, Sidonia takes purity as proof of superiority. 'No penal laws, no physical tortures, can effect that a superior race should be absorbed in an inferior, or be destroyed by it', he states. 'The mixed persecuting races disappear; the pure persecuted race remains.'

But there is more at stake than survival. A superior race, Sidonia maintains, even if it is a minority, profoundly affects its environment. Despite centuries of degradation, Sidonia explains, 'the Jewish mind exercises a vast influence on the affairs of Europe'. When Coningsby asks Sidonia about the lack of creative minds among Jews – proof that the stereotype of the uncreative Jew was established well before Richard Wagner's notorious words on the subject – Sidonia proclaims that, on the contrary, the 'passionate and creative genius' is in fact the Jews' most precious possession. The Jews preserved a fervent imagination, which endowed them, Sidonia tells Coningsby,

with almost the exclusive privilege of MUSIC; ... at this moment ... musical Europe is ours. There is not a company of singers, not an orchestra in a single capital, that is not crowded with our children under the feigned names which they adopt to conciliate the dark aversion which your posterity will some day disclaim with shame and disgust. Almost every great composer, skilled musician, almost every voice that ravishes you with its transporting strains, springs from our tribes.[1]

The exaggerated claim that Jews were ubiquitous in the arts was repeated ad nauseam during the course of the nineteenth century. While Disraeli exaggerated out of pride, others distorted reality out of an anti-Jewish bias that, in the form of a new anti-Semitic ideology, was dangerously spreading in countries where political and economical instability helped foster suspicion of the cultural effects of assimilation.[2] Disraeli, preoccupied as he

---

[1] Benjamin Disraeli, *Coningsby; or The New Generation*, The World's Classics (Oxford University Press, 1931), pp. 245–6, 248–9.
[2] Anti-Semitism, a term coined by Wilhelm Marr in 1879, represents a broad, indefinable anti-Jewish ideology that was based on racial (and linguistic) theories that advocated distinction between 'Aryan' and 'Semitic' races. Though claimed to be justifiable biologically, anti-Semitic discourse relied

was with his own position in English high society, seemed to be unaware that what his imaginary Jewish characters like Sidonia proudly asserted could be easily turned into a weapon against real Jews.

Six years after Disraeli's *Coningsby*, Wagner publicly proclaimed his anti-Jewish paranoia in his infamous 'Judaism in Music' (1850). Wagner's chief weapon to fight what Disraeli saw as Jewish pre-eminence in culture was his denial of Jews' ability to participate genuinely in the artistic life of other nations whose language and culture, according to Wagner, 'have remained to the Jews a foreign tongue'. Language is 'not the work of scattered units', he declared, 'but of an historical community', and thus 'only he who has unconsciously grown up within the bond of this community, takes also any share in its creation'. Wagner used this imagined Jewish 'speech impediment' to support his claim that Jews lacked the ability to use spoken words for artistic expression of feelings. Since he believed that music was 'the speech of Passion', Wagner argued that the linguistic barrier that separated Jews and Germans also prevented Jews from creating genuine German music. Whether in speech or music, he asserted, Jews could merely imitate.[3]

Although diametrically opposed, Disraeli's and Wagner's conclusions both exemplified a switch from national to racial discourses, according to which inherent, biological characteristics came to define cultural artefacts.[4] An exception at the time of its publication, Wagner's racial approach to music became pervasive by the early twentieth century. Perhaps the first and certainly the most successful composer to define his art as racially Jewish was the Swiss-born Ernest Bloch (1880–1959). Bloch's willingness to see his artistic personality as racially determined should be understood in the context of a cultural environment saturated with racism.[5] In the aftermath of the Dreyfus affair, which was one of the first political manifestations of the new race-hysteria, it was not difficult for Bloch,

---

mainly on vague cultural categories. Throughout this chapter I use anti-Semitic interchangeably with anti-Jewish, signifying both a general attitude against Jews' presence in society and a specific historical phenomenon strongly related to the racial theories of the late nineteenth and early twentieth centuries. For a bibliography of race theories from that time period see the appendix of Jacques Barzun, *Race: A Study in Modern Superstition* (London: Methuen, 1938), pp. 301–21.

[3] Richard Wagner, 'Judaism in Music', in *Richard Wagner's Prose Works*, trans. William Ashton Ellis, 8 vols. (repr. Lincoln: University of Nebraska Press, 1972), vol. III, pp. 84–6.

[4] About the development of the biological aspects of racial theories see Pat Shipman, *The Evolution of Racism: Human Differences and the Use and Abuse of Science* (New York: Simon and Schuster, 1994); and Ashley Montagu, *Man's Most Dangerous Myth: The Fallacy of Race* (New York: Columbia University Press, 1945). About the cultural implications of race theories see Barzun, *Race: A Study in Modern Superstition*.

[5] Throughout the text I use the term 'racism' according to its primary definition to describe 'the assumption that psychocultural traits and capacities are determined by biological race and that races differ decisively from one another' (*Webster's Third New International Dictionary of the English Language* (Springfield: Merriam-Webster, 1993)). Although the dictionary associates racism also 'with a belief in the inherent superiority of a particular race and its right to domination over others', I use 'racialism' to refer to theories in which racial prejudice, discrimination and racial hatred are predominant.

who was ethnically Jewish, to recognise that he was expected to identify himself artistically as a Jew.[6]

The present study focuses on how specific concepts of race influenced Bloch's artistic vision, self-identity and reception. Disraeli's philo-Semitic and Wagner's anti-Semitic suppositions merged in Bloch's vision of Jewishness. I trace this vision from Wagner to Bloch by way of Bayreuth ideologue Houston Stewart Chamberlain (1855–1927) and Bloch's friend Robert Godet (1866–1950), the French translator of Chamberlain's perniciously anti-Semitic book *The Foundations of the Nineteenth Century*.[7] Though not the only sources of Bloch's widely publicised views on race in music (Bloch enthusiastically propagated the ideas of Gustave le Bon and Hippolyte Adolphe Taine in his lecture in Geneva at the beginning of the 1910s), this Wagnerian lineage affected Bloch most, both personally and artistically. The outcome of Bloch's tale is bitterly ironic. Like many Jewish intellectuals who came to accept their Jewish identity as the basis of their character and creative output, Bloch subscribed to a wide variety of racial prejudices that coincided with prevailing anti-Semitic assumptions. Although the presence of these beliefs in Bloch's conception of Jewishness might put the composer into the category of 'self-hating Jew', the label would unjustly reduce Bloch's complex relationship to Judaism to a cliché.[8] Assimilation to 'a society on the whole hostile to the Jews', Hannah Arendt observed, was possible only 'by assimilating to anti-Semitism also'.[9]

THE PROMISED LAND

In February 1917, shortly after his arrival in the United States, Bloch published his article 'Man and Music' in a new art journal, *The Seven Arts*. In it, Bloch argued that 'music was no longer the emanation of a race and a people, a spontaneous birth out of life. It was a music of musicians'. Bloch's solution was simple. Art 'must have its roots deep within the soil that brings it forth', he declared. 'Needless to say', he added, art 'cannot be the direct output of crowds; but, however indirectly, they must have contributed to its substance'. Bloch's definition of art was a combination of Wagnerian racial theories and Romantic notions of the genius: 'A work

---

[6] I use ethnicity as a cultural category, referring to people's strongly or loosely identifiable cultural backgrounds rather than religious affiliation or biological descent.

[7] Houston Stewart Chamberlain, *Die Grundlagen des Neunzehnten Jahrhunderts* (Munich: Bruckmann, 1899); trans. as *The Foundations of the Nineteenth Century*, 2nd ed. (London: John Lane, The Bodley Head, 1911).

[8] Theodor Lessing, *Jüdische Selbsthass* (Berlin: Jüdische Verlag, 1930). See also Sander L. Gilman, *Jewish Self-Hatred: Anti-Semitism and the Hidden Language of the Jews* (Baltimore: The Johns Hopkins University Press, 1986). For a more detailed argument against designating Bloch as a self-hating Jew see my 'Sealed Documents and Open Lives: Ernest Bloch's Private Correspondence', *Notes* 62/1 (2005), 74–86.

[9] Hannah Arendt, *Rahel Varnhagen: The Life of a Jewish Woman*, rev. ed., trans. Richard and Clara Winston (New York: Harcourt Brace Jovanivich, 1974), p. 224.

of art is the soul of a race speaking through the voice of the prophet in whom it has become incarnate', he claimed. To reach this soul, Bloch wrote, art should be 'created rather by instinct than by intelligence; rather by intuition than by will'.[10] Bloch's emphasis on the intuitive side of artistic creation was a Romantic cliché. His replacement of the social concept of nation with that of the biological category of race as the mandatory basis of musical composition was not entirely new, either, yet it represented a new pervasiveness of racial concepts in art. Bloch's use of race was like that of many others: almost interchangeable with similarly vague, nineteenth-century notions of nation. Yet unlike nation, race – however undefined – carried the dangerous potential of biological determinism.

Bloch's racial conception of music was already familiar to the American public when his essay appeared. Critic Paul Rosenfeld (1890–1946) had elaborated the same ideas in an article that appeared in *The Seven Arts* a month before Bloch's essay. In a racial framework Rosenfeld described Bloch's music as 'a large, a poignant, an authentic expression of what is racial in the Jew'. Publicising the composer's own theories, Rosenfeld distinguished between the 'theatric orientalism of Rimsky-Korsakov and Balakirev' and the 'barbaric and ritual' sound of Bloch's music, the former merely a colouristic effect, the latter the authentic expression of the race. Thus, Rosenfeld based his claim of Bloch's authenticity not on musical specifics, but on assumptions that reeked of Wagnerian racial determinism. He did not invoke biology, but relied on what Etienne Balibar called 'culturalist racism'.[11] The essence of Bloch's Jewish musical expression was based, Rosenfeld wrote, on 'the harsh and haughty accents of the Hebrew tongue' and on the 'abrupt and passionate gestures of the Hebrew soul'.[12] The fact that Bloch himself did not speak Hebrew would hardly have fazed Rosenfeld.[13] Like many others he assumed that race contained an essence deeper and more constant than language. In Bloch's music Rosenfeld discovered 'an element that has remained unchanged throughout all the ages, an element that is in every Jew, an element by which every Jew must know himself and his descent'.[14]

Wagner's presence in Rosenfeld's argument was more concrete than the underlying racial determinism. Sadly, the enthusiastic publicity

---

[10] Ernest Bloch, 'Man and Music', *The Musical Quarterly* 19/4 (1933), 375–6. (The article was first published in Waldo Frank's translation in *The Seven Arts* 1/5 (1917), 493–503.) About the nationalistic inspirations of the group around *The Seven Arts* see chapter 4 of my Ph.D. dissertation, 'Jewish Nationalism in Twentieth-Century Art Music', University of California at Berkeley (1999).

[11] Etienne Balibar, 'Is There a "Neo-Racism"?', in Etienne Balibar and Immanuel Wallerstein, *Race, Nation, Class: Ambiguous Identities*, trans. Chris Turner (London: Verso, 1991), p. 24.

[12] Paul Rosenfeld, 'The Music of Ernest Bloch', *The Seven Arts* 1/4 (1917), 413–15.

[13] In a letter to his mother (14 February 1918) Bloch reported on the numerous reviews of his music in Jewish papers, regretting that he could not understand Hebrew. Quoted in Joseph Lewinski and Emmanuelle Dijon, *Ernest Bloch: Sa vie et sa pensée, 2. La Consécration américaine (1916–1930)* (Genève: Editions Slatkine, 2001), p. 140.

[14] Rosenfeld, 'The Music of Ernest Bloch', 413.

surrounding Bloch's 'authentically Jewish' music seemed to confirm rather than contradict Wagner's anti-Semitic assumptions about Jews' inability to create anything but what Wagner disapprovingly labelled 'Jewish' music. Bloch's success proved, Rosenfeld wrote, that 'Wagner's stricture was just'. Next to the achievement of Bloch, 'who has opened himself to the genius of his race', the works by Meyerbeer, Mendelssohn, Rubinstein and Goldmark – composers 'who have hitherto represented "Judaism in Music"' – seemed 'futile' and 'barren':

They had but to face themselves. They had but to say: 'We are what we have ever been', and the way to freedom, and certitude, and self-possession would have been theirs. A mighty ore lay buried within them. They could have refined it. But they turned shamedly [sic] away, and donned their flimsy masquerades to hide it further. They wanted courage and humility. And so they arrived at nothing. The lordly gold that lay concealed within the race was not for them.

Rosenfeld closed his essay by asserting that in Bloch's music 'the ancient spirit had attained rebirth' because Bloch, unlike other Jewish composers before him, did not 'inhibit any portion of his impulse', and thus revealed his racial heritage in his compositions.[15] In other words, Bloch removed the mask of insincere national idioms and revealed himself as a Jew.

Bloch was far from innocent in the construction of his image as the only authentically Jewish composer. He went even further than Rosenfeld in his willing affirmation of Wagner's anti-Semitic assumptions about Jewish musicians. In an interview with Siegmund Spaeth in April 1917, Bloch publicly endorsed Wagner's assertion about Jews' imitative nature:

The Jewish people have always been remarkable for their faculty of assimilation ... Is it not after all the mechanical side of music that finds its greatest exponent in the Jew? He is by nature a materialist, and in this age of commercialism, when the interpreter is hysterically glorified beyond the composer (a sure sign of artistic decadence, by the way), he naturally takes the quickest and easiest way to fame and fortune.

Some of the best writers of ragtime are Jews. But their creative work is a trick, or a spontaneous expression of self. Your Jew is a wonderful psychologist and a wonderful imitator. He can be more Parisian than a real Parisian and more German than a real German. And because he has always been willing to ape [what] is popular, he has produced no characteristic secular music of his own.

Echoing Rosenfeld, Bloch portrayed himself as the exception. He evoked the cliché of the instinctively creative genius declaring that he composed 'sincerely and from the heart'. The result showed 'strongly Jewish characteristics' despite the fact that, as Bloch claimed, he had 'not written consciously as a Jew, but only as a human being'.[16]

---

[15] Ibid., 416–18.
[16] Siegmund Spaeth, 'Jews Interpreters More Than Composers. Ernest Bloch Says It Is Because In Music, As In Everything, They Assimilate And Imitate – More Sincere Jewish Art To Come', *Evening Mail*, 26 April 1917.

Wagnerian as Bloch's judgement on Jewish composers sounds, his proposed solution shows that, like Rosenfeld, he also misunderstood Wagner's stricture when he assumed that the curse of creative impotence could be lifted from the Jewish composer if he turned to his own race for inspiration. Synagogue music, in Wagner's judgement, was 'the travesty of a divine service of song', a 'sense-and-sound-confounding gurgle, jodel [*sic*] and cackle'. What for other nations was a 'genuine fount of Life amid the Folk', for Jews was only the 'mirror' of 'intellectual efforts'. Only if the Jewish composer would find the 'instinctive' and not the 'reflected', which Wagner indicated was contrary to the Jews' artificial, intellectual disposition, would his art gain genuine racial quality.[17] What Wagner presented was not a solution, then, but a dead end.

For Bloch, emphasis on race instead of nation meant that he could dismiss the question of sources altogether. In an interview with *New York Times* critic Olin Downes (1886–1955) in March 1917 Bloch carefully separated nationalism and what he called 'racial consciousness' in music: 'Nationalism is not essential in music, but I think that racial consciousness is.' Bloch's racial expression, the composer was at great pains to emphasise, did not come from the use of Jewish folk melodies, which, he found, 'on some occasions limits and constrains a composer'. Racial quality 'is not only in folk themes', Bloch explained to Downes:

[I]t is in myself! If not folk-themes, you might ask, then what would be the signs of Jewish music? Well, I admit that scientific analysis of what constitutes the racial element in music is difficult. But it would be unscientific to deny the existence of such elements. Racial feeling is certainly a quality of all great music, which must be an essential expression of the people as well as the individual. Does any man think he is only himself? Far from it. He is thousands of his ancestors. If he writes as he feels, no matter how exceptional his point of view, his expression will be basically that of his forefathers.[18]

Proclaiming 'thousands of his ancestors' as an integral part of his own individuality, Bloch could create racially determined music without relying on the traditional music of his 'race'. The Jewish quality, he announced, 'must be the mind, the emotion, the inner part' of his music.[19] In anticipated self-defence Bloch warned that Jews 'learned in their lore' might not recognise this Jewish quality of his music. Expressing the 'Hebrew spirit' without reliance on a Jewish musical tradition left Bloch free in terms of musical specifics:

---

[17] Wagner, 'Judaism in Music', pp. 90–1.
[18] Olin Downes, 'Ernest Bloch, the Swiss Composer, on the Influence of Race in Composition', *The Musical Observer* 14/3 (1917), 11.
[19] Henry Edward Krehbiel, 'Ernest Bloch's Experiment In the Music of Jewry: A Jewish Composer and the Music Which He Feels To Be Racial – Spirit Versus Traditional Idiom – M. Bloch's Views on Form and the Radicalism of Novices – Themes from His Work', *New York Tribune*, 29 April 1917.

I do not propose or desire to attempt a reconstruction of the music of the Jews, and to base my works on melodies more or less authentic. I am no archeologist. I believe that the most important thing is to write good and sincere music – *my own music*. It is rather the Hebrew spirit that interests me – the complex, ardent, agitated soul that vibrates for me in the Bible; the vigor and ingenuousness of the Patriarchs, the violence that finds expression in the books of the Prophets, the burning love of justice, the desperation of the preachers of Jerusalem, the sorrow and grandeur of the book of Job, the sensuality of the Song of Songs. All this is in us, all this is in me, and is the better part of me. This is what I seek to feel within me and to translate in my music – the sacred race-emotion that lies dormant in our souls.[20]

By emphasising a general Jewish 'essence' rather than identifying any specific type of Jewish music as his source of inspiration Bloch may have sought not only to locate a (racially) 'instinctive' form of expression in Wagner's sense, but also to assure an abstract, yet unquestionably Jewish status for himself. His overall self-construction certainly involved the merging of biological descent and spiritual relatedness into an infinitely elastic expressive category that Bloch identified as both his personal and racial idiom.

ROBERT GODET: THE CONFLUENCE OF ANTI-SEMITISM AND JEWISH IDENTITY

Bloch's ties to Wagner went beyond the composer's adaptation of hackneyed Wagnerian notions of national music. Since the man who most inspired Bloch's ideas about race was a devoted Wagnerian, Bloch's assumptions about art can be traced quite specifically to Wagner. Today Bloch's friend Robert Godet is remembered as Debussy's confidant and one of the earliest Mussorgsky enthusiasts in the West. His friendship with Bloch is little known, and his major work, the French translation of Chamberlain's *The Foundations of the Nineteenth Century*, is long forgotten.

Chamberlain, the son of an English admiral who transformed himself into a prophet of the Teutonic race (he gained admittance into the Teutonic pantheon by marrying Wagner's daughter Eva), intended his 1899 book as the first part of a three-volume study celebrating the century that was coming to its end. Despite its title, Chamberlain's book presented not so much the foundations of the nineteenth century as the foundations of Nazi ideology. Chamberlain's plan was to turn human history into the history of the Teutonic race, culminating, as Cosima Wagner anticipated, with 'the towering genius of the century', Wagner, the artist who, in Chamberlain's view, most truly fulfilled the national, racial mission of

---

[20] Quoted in Guido M. Gatti, 'Ernest Bloch', *The Musical Quarterly* 7/1 (1921), 27. Gatti does not specify his source.

the Teutons.²¹ Chamberlain never completed the projected three-volume study and thus never penned its Wagnerian climax. Still, his enterprise was a fully Wagnerian project that was meant to purify and thus elevate the Teutonic race just as Wagner hoped his music would.

Most Wagnerian was Chamberlain's anti-Semitic passion. Shrewdly disguised behind pseudo-scientific analyses, Chamberlain presented European history as the struggle of racial forces, from which the pure Teutons and the Jews stood out as the most antagonistic. Like most anti-Semites, Chamberlain could never make up his mind whether to consider the Jews a pure race (the anti-race of the Teutons), whose supposed sacred attachment to the 'purity of inherited blood' deserved his admiration, or a mongrel race.²² In opposition to Count Arthur de Gobineau, who in his *Essai sur l'inégalité des races humaines* (1853–5) pessimistically maintained that human races were rapidly declining, Chamberlain argued that the 'sound and normal evolution of man is ... not from race to racelessness, but, on the contrary, to an ever clearer distinction of race'. This confused logic led him to claim that even 'if it were proved that there had never been an Aryan race in the past, we will have one in the future; for men of action this is the decisive point of view'.²³

Chamberlain attempted to build up an entire system of anti-Semitic, racialist views into which he freely channelled anything that served his purpose, even if it required the falsification of his data. The paranoid hatred of the Jews that governed his entire project so strongly distorted his vision that his *Foundations* could be considered one of the most anti-Semitic writings of his time. Indeed, rising anti-Semitism strongly contributed to the book's immense success, which made its author a celebrity overnight. Although criticised for its often incorrect details, the *Foundations* became required reading for European intellectuals.²⁴

Robert Godet prefaced his 1913 French translation with a sixty-three-page essay in which he provided a French context for Chamberlain's theories. Godet downplayed the book's anti-Jewish argument, discussing it in only two-and-half pages of the essay. Yet he seems to have agreed with Chamberlain's major premise about the 'Jewish question'. 'If Chamberlain is right', he concluded, 'it is we who have created the Jewish peril by accepting in our organism an element that it could not assimilate ... We must therefore free ourselves from the Jewish yoke by spiritual means of our own.'²⁵

---

²¹ Geoffrey G. Field, *The Evangelist of Race: The Germanic Vision of Houston Stewart Chamberlain* (New York: Columbia University Press, 1981), p. 171.
²² For more about Chamberlain's inconsistent characterisation of the Jewish 'race' see ibid., especially pp. 180–224.
²³ Quoted ibid., p. 220.
²⁴ For details about the book's reception see ibid., especially chapter 6.
²⁵ Robert Godet, 'Préface de la version française' of H. S. Chamberlain's *La genèse du XIXme siècle* (Paris: Librairie Payot, 1913), p. xlii.

Godet must have been fully aware of the offensive anti-Semitic aspects of Chamberlain's argument, for during the many years he devoted to the translation of the *Foundations* he kept his work hidden from Bloch. Bloch knew only that his friend was involved in an immense collaborative project, which used up all his energies, and, Bloch remarked, turned him into an old, exhausted man.[26] When in 1913 Godet presented the composer with the completed volume, he did it with a certain sense of guilt. Bloch took offence, to which Godet responded with feigned surprise. However disingenuous, Godet's reaction indicates he trusted that Bloch, who shared many of his friend's anti-Semitic ideas, would not be scandalised by the book's anti-Jewish stance.

Godet thought that Bloch's negative reaction to Chamberlain's *Foundations* came from reading only portions of the book and thus missing its essential points.[27] His argument was the same as that of Chamberlain and his advocates, who defended the book against the charges of factual and logical errors by claiming, as one reviewer did, that the book was 'not a mechanical aggregate of assertions and opinions, but rather a living organism', and hence 'it is not to be read as a scholarly argument, but as a deep-moving, dramatic and lively monologue'.[28] Trying to diminish the book's potentially dangerous effect, Godet reassured Bloch: '[W]hat offends you today was written fifteen years ago, and during this period nobody has died of it.'[29]

Reverberations of Bloch's relationship with Godet were still felt in the 1930s. In 1934, detached from the emotional disturbance it had caused when he had received it from his one-time best friend, Bloch belatedly took Godet's advice and reread Chamberlain's *Foundations* in its entirety. Although he recognised how the new German regime could exploit Chamberlain's ideology for its purposes, Bloch maintained that 'in spite of its fanaticism and hypothesis – like Darwin or Marx after all – the book is a great book'. Bloch argued that it was not the ideas but their practical application by 'smaller minds' that could turn Chamberlain's ideology into a 'terrible weapon'.[30] Ultimately, Bloch's opinion did not differ much from that of Godet. He seems to have admitted Chamberlain into the pantheon of great thinkers, noticing, however, the danger Chamberlain's interpretation of history might present, which, in the political climate of the 1930s, was hard not to recognise.

---

[26] Bloch to Edmond Fleg, 2 July 1912, quoted in Joseph Lewinski and Emmanuelle Dijon, *Ernest Bloch: Sa vie et sa pensée*, 1. *Les années de galères (1880–1916)* (Genève: Editions Slatkine, 1998), p. 566.
[27] Godet to Bloch, 25 October 1913, Library of Congress, Washington DC, Ernest Bloch Collection.
[28] Moeller van den Bruck's review appeared in the *Oesterreichische Rundschau* (November 1905–January 1906), quoted by Field, *Evangelist of Race*, p. 230.
[29] Godet to Bloch, 25 October 1913, quoted in Lewinski, *Ernest Bloch* 1, p. 611.
[30] Bloch to Lillian Hodgehead and Ada Clement, 6 July 1934, University of California, Berkeley, Ernest Bloch Collection.

Uncritical acceptance of anti-Semitic clichés prevented Bloch from refuting completely Chamberlain's ideology. Reacting to the performance of his *Sacred Service* by the Jüdische Kulturbund in Berlin in 1934 and to the segregation of Jews and Aryans in Germany, Bloch again referred to Chamberlain as the originator of Nazi ideas:

> I think they [the Jews] can do what they want, between themselves, provided it remains 'Jewish' and no 'Aryans' are allowed! I heard that even they are encouraged to do 'things Jewish', and are not hampered, provided they do not mix with 'Germans' – a queer situation, absolutely *understandable* – though I do not approve it of course! – if one reads the Chamberlain, on which all their ideas – political, religious, racial – are based.

Bloch indicated that he disagreed with Chamberlain, yet he could not repress a malicious remark about his fellow Jews. 'The attitude of certain Jews – in Italy! – and especially here [New York], towards me – and towards everything – seems to justify in a good degree the actual mentality and revolt of the leaders of Germany', he wrote to his friends.[31]

Personal resentment fuelled other similarly disturbing remarks by Bloch. He was particularly sensitive about Jewish audiences who, as the reception of the first performance of his *Three Jewish Poems* showed, could react critically to his self-created Jewish style.[32] Bloch tended to essentialise audiences and critics alike, pointing at their Jewish ethnicity as the reason behind their attitude toward his music. An outsider among both Jews and gentiles, Bloch easily fell prey to anti-Semitic ideology. Due to his ambiguous position, not only the emotional intensity of his relationship but also the anti-Semitic elements in his conception of Jews and Judaism survived the bitter end of his friendship with Godet.

DESCENT TO THE ROOTS

Bloch believed too deeply in racial essences to see Chamberlain's *Foundations* for what it was: dangerous anti-Semitic propaganda. Similarly, Godet's Wagnerian views of art were too embedded in Bloch for him to recognise their dangerous potential. In Godet's judgement following racial instincts was the only way for a composer to achieve genuine expression. Yet racial

---

[31] Bloch to Hodgehead, 6 April 1934, UCB Bloch Col. Bloch's reference to Italy pertains to a review that appeared in Italy in 1934 ('Il "Servizio Sacro" di Ernest Bloch eseguito a Torino e trasmesso per radio', *Israel* XIX/17 [25 January 1934], 3–6). Bloch referred to it again in a letter to Clement and Hodgehead, 23 December 1950 (UCB Bloch Col.): 'the only nasty dissonance in Italy, at the premiere of the Sacred Service (Jan. 1934), the *insulting* article published – again by *Jews*! – in the review "Israel!"'

[32] Bloch wrote to his niece Evelyn Hirsch about the first performance of his *Three Jewish Poems*: 'I've always had the Jews against me: in Geneva, when in 1914 I conducted my *Three Jewish Poems*, the Jews were hostile: "This is not Jewish!" The "Great Rabbi", a title that he granted to himself – Guinsburg, I think, went from one person to the next, criticizing the piece, "there are bells in this work, the Jews don't have bells."' 18 January 1954, quoted in Lewinski, *Ernest Bloch* 1, p. 624.

expression, especially in its initial phase, could also create barriers in communication. Like some of Mussorgsky's works that remained alien to Godet because of Mussorgsky's too specifically Russian language, Bloch's *Three Jewish Poems* (1913), the first performance of which he attended in 1914, also used a musical foreign language, which, Godet believed, was Hebrew. This was a necessary phase, he assured Bloch, preceding the ultimate liberation of the personality:

In order to descend to the roots of pure humanity, where a given race communicates with all other races, one should doubtless follow one by one the inflexions of one's own stem [*tige*], one should keep oneself from believing that one will succeed in getting there in general if one skips any of the particular stages. Ah well, if I rely on my purely musical, immediate and spontaneous impressions, I have the feeling that your *Three Jewish Poems* is one of the stages of the particular that, if everything goes well, will lead you to the depths of a more general reality. This is why, perhaps, the emotion that they stimulate does not completely communicate to someone, who, like myself, comes from a different stem.[33]

Godet convinced Bloch that the particular (in this case the expression of a particular race) would ultimately lead to the universal, to some shared human reality. What Godet presented was the universalistic aspect of Wagner's vision of reaching the eternally human through the descent to humanity's common roots via race.

Wagner found this instinctive, purely human layer in myth, which allowed him, he believed, to reach the foundation of human relations and to identify 'the human shape itself'.[34] For Bloch it was the barbaric that reached this universal human condition. Bloch's attraction to the barbaric coincided with the modernist vogue for primitivism, which, while not completely free of Romantic nostalgia, maintained, as Stravinsky's *Rite of Spring* exemplifies, a fundamentally anti-romantic attitude. Bloch's barbaric mode was different, however. It expressed Bloch's attachment to a romanticised Biblical past, to the presentation of the Biblical Jews as a barbarian tribe of ancient times, with savage rites and a savage God. In the *Three Jewish Poems*, hoarse brass fanfares, shrieking woodwinds and pounding timpani announce the manifestation of Jehovah in his 'terrible grandeur' (three bars after rehearsal number 3). In the *Israel Symphony* the arrival of Jehovah is signalled by similarly barbaric instrumental calls (rehearsal number 4). In 'Yom Kippur', the second section of the *Israel Symphony*, the barbaric music characterises not Jehovah but his people. As the programme note describes, 'irregular, savage rhythms,

---

[33] Godet to Bloch, 6 March 1914, LC Bloch Col.
[34] Richard Wagner, 'A Communication to my Friends', *Richard Wagner's Prose Works*, trans. William Ashton Ellis, 8 vols. (repr. Lincoln: University of Nebraska Press, 1972), vol. I, *The Art-Work of the Future*, p. 358.

fanatic Hebrew motives express the exalted gestures of the crowd that fall down, pitilessly weighted by their sins'[35] (rehearsal number 17).

As his Italian advocate Guido Gatti emphasised, Bloch's music recalled the ancient Jews: 'he seems descended, not from the tribes of Israel dispersed throughout the world ... but from the free sons of Judah'. Gatti's language indicates that his differentiation between the two kinds of Jews was inspired by an anti-Semitic bias. While the tribes of Israel, Gatti wrote, were 'despised and neglected', and were 'still perfecting their terrible weapons, patience, persistency and astuteness', the sons of Judah were 'Asiatic shepherds, wandering from pasture to pasture, today masters and tomorrow slaves, joyous voluptuaries of life and adorers of a warrior-god, the enemy and destroyer of all rival peoples'.[36]

Bloch's attraction to the barbaric, though, was more than a fascination with romanticised Biblical images or a servile adherence to anti-Semitic expectations. One might see the barbaric as Bloch's way of seeking the universally human behind the racially specific. But just as Wagner's desire to plunge into myth in order to reach a pre-national human condition did not weaken the emphatically German characteristics of his racial vision of art, Bloch's emphasis on race calls into question his claim that his music was able to reach the biological roots of humanity, a pre-linguistic past where men communicated with universal gestures rather than with intelligible speech.

A curious episode in Bloch's Rhapsody for cello and orchestra, *Schelomo* (1916), which Bloch left unexplained, might express precisely this descent via race to a pre-linguistic condition. The passage quotes a melody that Bloch remembered his father singing in Hebrew. The words and their meaning got lost in Bloch's memory: only the gesture of singing remained. Deprived of its verbal specificity, the motive assumes an aggressive, barbarous character, and turns into a mechanical rhythmic figure that aggressively intrudes several times to impede the cello's gestures of expressive singing (rehearsal number 30ff). In this way Bloch turned the specific expression of racial identity into a gesture of generic barbarism.

Despite Bloch's universalistic aspirations, the barbaric, pre-linguistic condition that Bloch envisioned as a shared memory of humanity was received by his critics as a specifically Hebrew racial expression. Even after Bloch stopped advertising the racial inspiration of his art, his music remained embedded in racial discourse, which, with its pseudo-scientific pretences, provided a staging post between individualistic Romantic expression and modernist 'objectivity' in art. It shielded artists like Bloch from

---

[35] The programme note, written by Maria Tibaldi Chiesa for the work's Roman performance at the Accademia di Santa Cecilia (22 January 1933) was approved by Bloch. Although with fewer details, Bloch described the piece very similarly in his letter to Hodgehead and Clement (23 April 1925, UCB Bloch Col.).
[36] Gatti, 'Ernest Bloch', 28–9.

the charge of outmoded Romanticism, for, as Bloch kept emphasising, since it sprang from the instinctive, his personal expression was at the same time the artistic utterance of what he and his audience conceived as a racial essence.

Like Disraeli, Bloch, at least for a while, could turn his Jewishness from a social handicap into an attractive, powerful, Romantic posture. Bloch's racial aesthetics of music, like Disraeli's Jewish pose, was the expression of what Hannah Arendt called 'a very real Jewish chauvinism', one that characterised the secularised, assimilated layers of Jewish society.[37] But while Bloch's inflated racial rhetoric assured the initial success of his Romantic Oriental music, the emphasis on his Jewish voice ultimately prevented him from entering the pantheon of universally acknowledged composers. Godet's prediction was false: Bloch's racially specific expression never came to serve as a transitional stage preceding a universal language. Once he declared himself a Jewish composer, Bloch would be permanently confined to the ghetto he had constructed for himself on a foundation of racial theory.

---

[37] Hannah Arendt, *The Origins of Totalitarianism* (San Diego and New York: Harcourt Brace, 1973), p. 74.

CHAPTER 8

Percy Grainger and American Nordicism

Malcolm Gillies
and
David Pear

The Australian-American musician Percy Aldridge Grainger was born in 1882. The development and *floruit* of his career fit almost exactly within the fifty-year focus of this volume. An avid, but amateur, follower of racial theorising, Grainger read a diverse range of the leading authors of these decades: Otto Weininger,[1] Houston Stewart Chamberlain,[2] Roland Dixon,[3] and even the racialists' *bête noire*, Frank H. Hankins.[4] It was, however, through reading the books of the American Nordicists of the 1910s and 1920s that Grainger most clarified his thinking about race, the world, his place in it, and the specifically racial function of his own art.

Race was the binding element of Grainger's personal credo: his personal affiliation as a racial Nordic, while being variously an Australian national, a British subject and an American citizen; his marriage to the Swedish artist, Ella Ström, for whom he wrote *To a Nordic Princess* as a wedding gift in 1928;[5] his approach to language, including the development of his own form of 'Nordic English'; his personal resolution, through the adoption of Nordicism, of the hitherto elusive connection between Scandinavianism and Anglo-Saxonism; his view of Australia, as a 'Scandinavia-of-the-South' and as an Antipodean reservoir of Nordic racial purity;[6] his view of Nordic art as the highest form of individual and communal expression.

Through the mass of documentation held in the University of Melbourne's Grainger Museum, which Grainger built and then stocked during the 1930s to 1950s, it is possible to trace his thinking on race in

---

[1] Otto Weininger (1880–1903), notably *Sex and Character* of 1903. See Julie Brown, 'Otto Weininger and Musical Discourse in Turn-of-the-Century Vienna', this volume.
[2] Houston Stewart Chamberlain (1855–1927), notably *The Foundations of the Nineteenth Century* of 1899.
[3] Roland Dixon (1875–1934), professor of anthropology at Harvard University. Grainger's library contains his *The Racial History of Man* (New York: Charles Scribner's Sons, 1923).
[4] Frank H. Hankins (1877–1970), notably *The Racial Bias of Civilization: A Critique of the Nordic Doctrine* (New York: Alfred A. Knopf, 1926).
[5] This orchestral work was premiered at the Hollywood Bowl concert of 9 August 1928, during which Percy and Ella Grainger were married.
[6] See Malcolm Gillies, 'Percy Grainger and Australian Identity: The 1930s', in Nicholas Brown, Peter Campbell, Robyn Holmes, Peter Read and Larry Sitsky (eds.), *One Hand on the Manuscript: Music in Australian Cultural History 1930–1960* (Canberra: Humanitites Research Centre, 1995), pp. 34–44.

unrivalled detail, and from cradle to grave. Grainger scholarship has, however, often sidestepped questions of race, either through embarrassment that Australia's most famous composer was in such racial thrall, or through a failure to appreciate the significance of race to all corners of his life's work. 'I'm mad about race ... it's to me what religion is to *other* fools,' professed Grainger to a Danish lover in 1907.[7] This was no chance outburst, but a lifelong view which he was to confirm repeatedly in following decades.

THE UNSCHOLARLY OBSERVER

Percy Grainger was a perceptive, but unscholarly, observer of the human race. As a creative artist, he looked for ideas that helped to clarify his own thoughts or provided him with artistic inspiration. He had no training in science, and understood little of the technicalities of heredity, genetics or eugenics. His own racial stirrings came early, however, through boyhood reading of the Icelandic sagas,[8] and through unhappy experiences with his 'dark-eyed' father, who was an alcoholic and had early infected his 'blue-eyed' mother with syphilis.[9] Grainger put his father's weakness for wine and women down to the racial impurity born of increasing urbanism, and, in consequence, harboured lifelong personal insecurities over his own impure Anglo-Saxon inheritance. He feared that these defects might be congenital, as did many in the 1860s to 1920s period.[10] Historic Anglo-Saxonism, on the other hand, offered the young Grainger a heroic, out-of-doors model for life. His move in 1895 from Melbourne to Frankfurt, to study piano and composition at the Hoch Conservatory, added complexity to his early Anglo-Saxonism. Frankfurt was the crucible of his British patriotism, through 'sheer self-shieldment' from German conceit and hostility.[11] There, he made the first of his many Kipling settings; there, too, he first came under the sway of the poetry of Walt Whitman.[12] By 1901, when Grainger left to assay a professional musical career in London,

---

[7] Letter to Karen Holten, 2 February 1907, reproduced in Kay Dreyfus (ed.), *The Farthest North of Humanness: Letters of Percy Grainger, 1901–14* (Melbourne: Macmillan, 1985), p. 95.

[8] Letter, Grainger to Karen Holten, 2 February 1907, reproduced in Kay Dreyfus (ed.), *The Farthest North*, p. 95.

[9] See David Pear, 'Percy Grainger as "Educator-at-Large": The Formation, Expression and Propagation of his Manliness', Ph.D. thesis, University of Queensland (1998), p. 196. Members of his mother's Aldridge family had expressed qualms at her marriage to John Grainger, equating dark eyes with poor character. Hence, Grainger's obsession with eye colour, leading in later life even to a collection of photographs of musicians' eyes, now stored in the Grainger Museum.

[10] See John Edward Morgan, *The Danger of Deterioration of Race from the Too Rapid Increase of Great Cities* (London: Longmans, Green and Co., 1866), p. 25: 'the more prominent causes of enervation, which seem peculiarly associated with a residence in the city ... vitiated air, constitutional syphilis, and the abuse of alcohol'.

[11] Percy Aldridge Grainger, 'Aldridge-Grainger-Ström Saga' (1933–34), W37–153 (Grainger Museum, The University of Melbourne).

[12] See David Pear, 'Walt Whitman and the Synthesis of Grainger's Manliness', *Australasian Music Research* 5 (2000), 61–81.

he was a British patriot, believing in the British *race*, yet aspiring also to the amoralistic democracy of New World nations.

The British were, to Grainger's way of thinking, a mixed race, and thus by definition, a flawed race. In popular interpretation of the turn of the century, the Norman Conquest of 1066 had been a Latin conquest, leading to Grainger's long-held view that the more northerly or Scandinavian Englishness was, then the better; he regretted the progressive contamination of northerly British stock caused both by the Normans and the Celts.[13] Grainger went even further to locate 'the geography of his inspiration' in 'a small area in the North Sea, comprising the English–Scottish border ... and the Faeroes', which he then re-expressed as '"Scandinavians in their Western settlements" with peculiar concentration upon the Faeroe Islands'.[14]

The America to which Grainger hurriedly moved in September 1914 – ostensibly for reasons of his mother's health – was in the midst of a great debate about immigration, in which race was the central issue, and eugenics one of the proposed solutions. William Ripley, professor of political economy at Harvard University, had, for instance, depicted the United States in 1908 as being in the midst of a 'great ethnic struggle for dominance and survival'. This struggle, in Ripley's analysis, was caused by such factors as the radical change in the racial mix of immigrants (from mainly 'Teutons', drawn from the British Isles, Germany, Scandinavia and Canada, in 1870, to a great diversity of Mediterranean, Alpinic, Slavic and Jewish race-types by 1907), with consequential increases in racial intermarriage, urban congestion and ghettoisation.[15] Ripley considered that these ethnic problems were compounded by the 'race suicide' caused by declining Anglo-Saxon birth rates. In 1911, Charles B. Davenport, director of the Eugenics Section of the American Breeders' Association, sharpened these fears in his text *Heredity in Relation to Eugenics*:

The population of the United States will, on account of the recent influx of immigrants from South Eastern Europe, rapidly become darker in pigmentation, smaller in stature, more mercurial, more attached to music and art, [and] more given to crimes of larceny, kidnapping, assault, murder, rape and sex-immorality and less given to burglary, drunkenness, and vagrancy than were the original English settlers.[16]

---

[13] Percy Aldridge Grainger, 'Why "My Wretched Tone-life"?' (1953), in 'Grainger's Anecdotes', 423–89 (Grainger Museum, The University of Melbourne).
[14] Grainger, 'Why "My Wretched Tone-life"?' He identified the Faeroe Islands as the source of his works *The Merry Wedding, The Rival Brothers, Death-Song for Hjalmar Thuren, Father & Daughter,* and *Let's Dance Gay in Green Meadow*. Quotations from Grainger's writings are reproduced by courtesy of the Estate of Percy Grainger (Stewart Manville, White Plains, New York) and The University of Melbourne.
[15] 'Races in the United States', *The Atlantic Monthly* 102/6 (1908), 745–59.
[16] Charles B. Davenport (1866–1944), *Heredity in Relation to Eugenics* (New York: Henry Holt, 1911), p. 219. According to Steven Selden (*Inheriting Shame: The Story of Eugenics and Racism in America* (New York: Teachers College Press, Columbia University, 1999), p. 6), Davenport's book was cited by more than a third of American high-school biology textbooks in the inter-war period.

THE AMERICAN NORDICISTS AND THEIR INFLUENCE

Ripley and Davenport were important influences upon, and sometime colleagues of, two other American Nordicists, Madison Grant and Lothrop Stoddard. Their writings, above all Grant's *The Passing of the Great Race, or The Racial Basis of European History* (1916)[17] and Stoddard's *The Rising Tide of Color against White World-Supremacy* (1920),[18] hugely influenced Grainger, as millions of other Americans, in the way they thought about race, and contributed to long-lasting changes in American attitudes to immigration. Grainger and his mother read the revised edition of Grant's book in 1919–20: it was Rose Grainger's 1919 Christmas gift to her son, who years later noted in the volume, 'The book mother & I enjoyed so greatly in Chicago'.[19] Grainger held, and read, several of Stoddard's books, including *Racial Realities in Europe* (1924)[20] and *The Revolt against Civilization: The Menace of the Under Man* (1922),[21] as well as the earlier *Rising Tide of Color*. Grant, a lawyer by training, and Stoddard, an expert in foreign affairs, were popularisers of racist views, or as they would term them, 'racial theories'. They brought together age-old concepts of blood and race, with the mid-nineteenth-century work on racial diversity of Joseph Arthur de Gobineau, Ripley's turn-of-the-century racial typologies, and the 1890s theories of germ plasm of August Weismann.[22]

Grant's book came to Grainger at a time when he had started to lose faith in Kipling, whom he confessed now to find 'dreary' and lacking in the 'heroic stoicism' of his earlier works.[23] Grant immediately appealed to Grainger through his invocation of the physical markers of goodness that Grainger had known since childhood: eye colour, colour of hair, complexion, stature. Stoddard, in the following year, picked up on Grant's description of the Nordic as the 'high standard' man, requiring healthy living conditions, and 'good food, fresh air, and exercise'.[24] He considered that the industrial revolution had not favoured the healthy Nordic but had favoured the small, dark Mediterranean, who 'adapted himself to the operative's bench or the clerk's stool ... and reproduced his kind'.[25] Both Grant and Stoddard looked to eugenic solutions, brought about by positive techniques – encouraging the superior Nordics to breed – and

---

[17] Madison Grant (1865–1937), *The Passing of the Great Race, or The Racial Basis of European History* (New York: Charles Scribner's Sons, 1916).
[18] (Theodore) Lothrop Stoddard (1883–1950), *The Rising Tide Of color against White World-Supremacy* (New York: Blue Ribbon Books, 1920).
[19] Pencil note stuck in Grainger's library copy (Grainger Museum, The University of Melbourne).
[20] Stoddard, *Racial Realities in Europe* (New York: Charles Scribner's Sons, 1924).
[21] Stoddard, *The Revolt against Civilization: The Menace of the Under Man* (New York: Charles Scribner's Sons, 1922).
[22] See, further, David Pear, 'Grainger on Race and Nation', *Australasian Music Research* 5 (2000), p. 34.
[23] Letter, Grainger to Rose Grainger, 24 April 1919, quoted in Pear, 'Percy Grainger as "Educator-at-Large"', pp. 213–14.
[24] Stoddard, *The Rising Tide*, pp. 163–4. [25] Ibid., p. 164.

negative techniques – requiring inferior types and individuals not to breed, for instance through sterilisation or incarceration. Stoddard dreamed of advances in eugenic science leading to 'clean, virile, genius-bearing blood, streaming down the ages through the unerring action of heredity, which, in anything like a favorable environment, will multiply itself, solve our problems, and sweep us on to higher and nobler destinies'.[26]

The effect of the war upon the racial composition of American manhood was a theme urgently emphasised by another American Nordicist, Henry Fairfield Osborn, in his Preface to the second edition of Grant's book: 'War is in the highest sense dysgenic rather than eugenic. It is destructive of the best strains, spiritually, morally and physically.'[27] And Osborn's 'best strains' were marked by their blue eyes and fair hair. This dysgenic 'Passing of the Great Race' was a theme, too, in poetry of the time, where Edgar Lee Masters penned the lines:

> They were chosen for might in battle;
> For blue eyes and white flesh,
> For clean blood, for strength, for class.
> They went to the wars
> And left the little breeds
> To stay with the women,
> Trading and plowing.
> They perished in battle
> All the way along the stretch of centuries,
> And left the little breeds to possess the earth –
> *The Great Race is passing.*[28]

Even before reading Grant's and Stoddard's writings, Grainger had become an admirer of Masters' poems, particularly the *Spoon River Anthology* of 1916. During 1919–22 he arranged a tune called 'Spoon River' as the first of his *American Folk-Music Settings*.

The heyday of the American Nordicists was the early to middle 1920s. The Second International Congress of Eugenics held during September 1921 at the American Museum of Natural History in New York was a week-long celebration of the advances of the new science.[29] It was chaired by Charles Davenport, of the Carnegie Institution of Washington, and opened by Henry Fairfield Osborn, as director of the American Museum of National History. Madison Grant was the Congress's treasurer and Lothrop Stoddard chaired the publicity committee. The honorary presidency of Alexander Graham Bell lent kudos to the event. These American Nordicists also influenced the course of the immigration quota acts of 1921

---

[26] Ibid., p. 305.
[27] Grant, *The Passing*, Preface to 1919 edition, p. xiii, by Henry Fairfield Osborn (1857–1935).
[28] In *The Open Sea* (New York: Macmillan, 1921), pp. 270–1, by Edgar Lee Masters (1869–1950).
[29] See *Eugenics, Genetics and the Family: Second International Congress of Eugenics, 1921*, Vol. I (Baltimore: Williams and Wilkins, 1923; repr. New York: Garland, 1985).

and 1924, which had the effect of strengthening American immigration from northern Europe for the next forty years, and, through the 1924 Act, stopping immigration by Japanese. Yet, despite their common interests in the eugenic 'science of human husbandry' and questions of migration, each of these Nordicists had a different slant to their racialism. Madison Grant's views were, for instance, part of a wider concern for conservation,[30] not dissimilar to that espoused by President Theodore Roosevelt: a concern for the future of American humanity as well as the country's natural and environmental blessings. Hence, Grant's interests in founding the New York Zoological Society (now the Wildlife Conservation Society), in co-founding the Save the Redwoods League, and in contributing to the founding of the Yellowstone National Park.[31] Stoddard's views on Nordicism, by contrast, need to be seen against the wider backdrop of world racial questions. As a student of world politics, his principal concern was with the ways in which white supremacy was threatened by the yellow, brown, black and red peoples. The White Civil War (Stoddard's name for the First World War) had hugely weakened the white world, he believed, and left it vulnerable to 'colored triumphs of arms'.[32] Principal among these emerging threats were the Japanese, who had shown their might in the Russo-Japanese War of 1904–5,[33] and, more potently, the Islamic world. Stoddard's book of the year following *The Rising Tide of Color* was entitled *The New World of Islam* (1921).[34] In *The Rising Tide* he had already predicted: 'Pan-Islamism, once possessed of the Dark Continent [Africa] and fired by militant zealots, might forge black Africa into a sword of wrath, the executor of sinister adventures.'[35]

GRAINGER'S RESPONSE

From the American Nordicists Grainger gained a simple framework for his racial thinking and new racial terminology; beyond that, he tended to pick and choose what he found personally useful to justify his preferences, prejudices and inspirations. He understood nothing of Mendelian-based science, so steered well clear of any biological discussion. What he gained from Stoddard, via Grant and Ripley, was a basis for determining questions of racial make-up. He even carried around with him a 1924 newspaper

---

[30] Look, with caution, at George McDaniel, 'Madison Grant and the Racialist Movement', *American Renaissance* 8/2 (1997), www.amren.com/9712issue/9712issue.html.
[31] See 'Grant, Madison', *Who Was Who in America, 1897–1942* (Chicago: Marquis, 1966), vol. I, p. 477.
[32] Stoddard's Preface to *The Rising Tide*, p. vi.
[33] Stoddard, *The Rising Tide*, p. 154: 'The Russo-Japanese War is one of those landmarks in human history whose significance increases with the lapse of time.'
[34] Stoddard, *The New World of Islam* (New York: Charles Scribner's Sons, 1921).
[35] Stoddard, *The Rising Tide*, p. 102. Not surprisingly, events since the turn of the millennium have given Stoddard's inter-war works a new lease of life.

cutting by Stoddard, as a kind of racial ready-reckoner.[36] Questions of Jewishness intrigued him, particularly among musicians, although he was confused about blond Jews. In his long essay 'The Things I Dislike' of August 1954 he was still tussling over who among the 'supposed-to-be Jews', such as Delius, Rachmaninov, Tchaikovsky and Wagner, should be included on his 'disliked list',[37] and was especially vexed when he did actually like their music! His thinking about racial purity even started to blur with incest, as he contemplated meeting his blue-eyed mother's extended family again in 1933: 'I feel that no not-Aldridge brood is good enough, clean enough for them to breed with. I long for Aldridges to breed only with Aldridges & to the very core of me I scorn all mere half-Aldridge offspring (the outcome of an Aldridge breeding with a not-Aldridge) as bastards.'[38] His views on eugenics are not clearly documented, but he is on record, in an essay written in the winter of 1920–1 entitled 'The Value of Icelandic to an Anglo-Saxon', as regretting the indifference of most modern populations to adopting serious efforts 'to ameliorate the race (such as prohibition, eugenics, birth control, physical culture, elimination of poverty etc.)'.[39]

From reading Grant's book in 1919 Grainger gained the valuable word 'Nordic', which he had needed to define his own sense of pan-national, high-type people – a grouping not sufficiently encompassed by the terms 'Anglo-Saxon' or 'Scandinavian', and certainly not by 'Teutonic', as proposed by Houston Stewart Chamberlain (whose *Foundations* Grainger first read only in 1926). From Grant he also gained the clearest sense yet of how those Nordic values were coming under threat, in England, for example: through the increasing emphasis on urban communities, which are 'consumers and seldom producers of men'; and through what Grant described as the 'transfer of political power from the vigorous Nordic aristocracy and middle classes to the radical and labor elements, both largely recruited from the Mediterranean type'.[40] Grant considered that the Nordic race was only maintaining its full vigour in Scandinavia and north-western Germany.[41]

Three years later, in *A Study of American Intelligence*, Carl C. Brigham provided a listing of racial mixtures in European countries,[42] with England at eighty per cent Nordic and twenty per cent Mediterranean; Norway, Denmark, Holland and Scotland, eighty-five per cent Nordic and fifteen per cent Mediterranean; Germany, forty per cent Nordic and sixty per cent Alpine; and Ireland, thirty per cent Nordic and seventy per cent

---

[36] Stoddard, 'Racial Realities in Europe', *Sunday Evening Post*, 22 March 1924.
[37] In 'Grainger's Anecdotes', 423–87 (Grainger Museum, The University of Melbourne).
[38] Grainger, 'Aldridge-Grainger-Ström Saga', W37–29.
[39] Reproduced in Malcolm Gillies and Bruce Clunies Ross (eds.), *Grainger on Music* (Oxford University Press, 1999), p. 128.
[40] Grant, *The Passing*, pp. 186–7. [41] Grant, *The Passing*, p. 187.
[42] Carl C. Brigham (1890–1943), *A Study of American Intelligence* (Princeton University Press, 1923), p. 182. Brigham was the father of scholastic aptitude tests.

Mediterranean. Only Sweden emerged as fully Nordic – a statistic that pleased Grainger.

How, then, did Grainger apply this Nordicist knowledge as a musican? His first known response was to intrude the Nordic word into his essays, lectures and letters. In a lecture on 'Nordic Characteristics in Music', given at Yale University on 6 March 1921, Grainger summarised and critiqued Grant's arguments.[43] While he considered Grant's book 'fascinating and provocative', he rejected Grant's 'magic of "blood"', claiming that he preferred to approach issues of racial characteristics in music from an 'utterly cosmopolitan' angle: 'I believe that Jews, Negroes and plenty of other non-Nordic races could and would, if presented with Nordic surroundings and conditions, acquire all the Nordic traits.'[44] Grainger's views are, at this stage of early 1921, still in transformation. He hypothesised that the hard conditions, athletic tastes and pioneering life purpose of Nordics had led to folk music of individualistic melody and lack of harmony, and a repertory characterised by distinctive 'body-warming' dances and music to work to. He recognised and described the different musical characteristics of the two Nordic strands, the Scandinavian and the Anglo-Saxon, as well as different degrees of purity of various Nordic musical characteristics. Grainger, then, had adopted the racial typologies and terminologies of Grant, but still in the service of describing racial art from a reportedly 'cosmopolitan' standpoint. His respect for other musical traditions, notably the 'Negro-American', was still apparent.[45]

Over the following decade Grainger retreated from such overt cosmopolitanism, as is seen in his 1933 article on 'Characteristics of Nordic Music'[46] and the following year's 'The Superiority of Nordic Music'.[47] In the 'Characteristics' essay he expanded Nordic to 'Mongolian-Nordic', here following a highly distinctive line of racial *musical* thinking. His claim for the Mongolian-Nordic tradition was geographically extensive, ranging from Russia to Japan to Thailand. This was Grainger's rather feeble attempt to expand the European racially based musical typology, seen in his 1921 Yale lecture, to musics of all the world. His Mongolian-Nordic hypothesis was also a product of the frisson evoked by the 'exotic' during the era in which Grainger lived. Ironically, the remoteness of the 'Asian' races – sometimes used synonymously with 'Mongolian' – appeared to render them racially 'safer' than so many of the white race-types much

---

[43] Gillies and Clunies Ross (eds.), *Grainger on Music*, pp. 131–40.
[44] Ibid., pp. 131–2. [45] Ibid., p. 140.
[46] Ibid., pp. 258–66. Grainger's 1934 summarised version of the talk is found in Appendix A, 'A Commonsense View of All Music: Lecture 3 – The Mongolian and Mohammedan Influences upon European Music', in John Blacking, *'A Commonsense View of All Music': Reflections on Percy Grainger's Contribution to Ethnomusicology and Music Education* (Cambridge University Press, 1987), pp. 162–4.
[47] Appendix A, 'A Commonsense View of All Music: Lecture 6 – The Superiority of Nordic Music', in Blacking, *'A Commonsense View'*, pp. 172–3.

closer to home. In stark opposition to the Mongolian-Nordic was the Mohammedan (by which he meant Mediterranean) tradition with its 'nervous, passionate, excitable tunes ... that scamper about like the flitting of insects'.[48] These opposing traditions correlated for Grainger with the prevalence of certain physical features, the Mohammedan where 'big or fleshy' noses predominate, while Mongolian-Nordic people had 'smooth, flat faces, high cheek-bones and small turned-up noses'.[49] Grainger again was a product of his racialist age, but here in 1933 he immediately recognised it: 'All these unscientific thoughts about the geographical and racial origins of Asiatic and European music seem to me quite harmless, as long as we entertain them with inquiring and elastic minds and do not claim any scientific authority for our guess-work.'[50] By his 1934 'Superiority' essay, however, Grainger had, with his very title, signalled a further distancing from cosmopolitanism. His first paragraph confessed: '[T]he more I study what I can get hold of of [sic] the world's music, the more convinced I am that the white races have as yet produced no music that can vie with Nordic music, at least in depth, intensity, beauty and complexity.'[51] He went on to claim 'the gradual fading of loftiness into frivolousness' as one moved from the Nordic north to the Mediterranean south.

A 'BREED-ABOVE-BREEDS'

While these were the public claims of Grainger in 1933–4, the private man held stronger opinions. In 1933, during a long sea voyage from Europe to Australia, he penned the vast 100,000-word 'Aldridge-Grainger-Ström Saga', in celebration of his mother's, his wife's and his own lives and heritage. Writing in his Nordic English, Grainger presented a twentieth-century version of the Icelandic Sagas he so loved. His Saga clarified his position in the nature-versus-nurture debate: that people are the product of their circumstance – their race, nationality, class, time-period, religion, education, climate or art – rather than of some intrinsic individuality.[52] Race remained firmly in primary position among the characteristics of 'nature', leading to Grainger's most strident expression of Nordic superiority: 'But why should we mince matters? Must we Nordics go on *forever* shamming that we *do not know* that we are overmen in beauty, soul-depth, spirit-powers?[53] Must we stand by silently forever while the lower races (French, German, Jews), tell us they own powers & gifts that we know they

---

[48] Gillies and Clunies Ross (eds.), *Grainger on Music*, p. 261.   [49] Ibid., p. 262.   [50] Ibid.
[51] Blacking, *'A Commonsense View'*, p. 172.
[52] Grainger, 'Aldridge-Grainger-Ström Saga', W37–91.
[53] Grainger's concept of the 'overman' (*Übermensch*) was Nietzschean, and connected with Grainger's concept of the genius ('oversoul'). See 'Mother a Nietzschean?' (1926), essay appended to 'Sketches for My Book "The Life of My Mother & Her Son"', W35, Grainger Museum, University of Melbourne.

don't?'⁵⁴ For Grainger, the Nordics were the ultimate in bodily and artistic beauty, regardless of the 'half-beauties' other races might, from time to time, be able to produce.

By 1933 a belief in the superiority of the Nordics had come to affect Grainger's view of his personal life, music, use of language, world-view and sense of social responsibility. His first fifty years show a move from being a naive, even playful, racialist to becoming an increasingly intolerant racist. This racial-to-racist transformation was maintained in the remaining three decades of his life. While the American Nordicists found themselves in retreat from the early 1930s because of scientific counter-evidence, as well as growing popular recognition of Hitler's excesses and abuse of eugenic concepts, Grainger's utterances were muted only once the horrors of the Holocaust became known. From his voluminous autobiographical writings of later years it is clear that his views did not significantly change.⁵⁵ To the end, he maintained that racial 'pride' so proudly expressed in his essay of 1927–8, 'The Love-Life of Helen and Paris':

Pride of race above all else. My feelings for my race – for the Nordic race – are deeper & stronger than my feelings for myself. I lose myself in my race as god-loving men lose themselves in the thought of god. My art is only my top-layer ((surface)); but my race is at the very heart of me. No old-time Hebrew felt more fiercely for his race than I do for mine. And Helen [Ella Grainger] is the very vestal virgin of that race; the hallowed priestess of that breed-above-breeds ... O, to be the father of her children – children that could not fail to be whole-Nordics with 2 such begetters ((parents)).⁵⁶

Fate would dictate that the Graingers, as also Madison Grant, remained childless.

---

⁵⁴ Grainger, 'Aldridge-Grainger-Ström Saga', W37–119.
⁵⁵ See chapter 6, 'Self', in Malcolm Gillies, David Pear and Mark Carroll (eds.), *Self-Portrait of Percy Grainger* (Oxford University Press, 2006).
⁵⁶ Percy Aldridge Grainger, 'The Love-Life of Helen and Paris' (1927–8), p. 12 (Grainger Museum, The University of Melbourne). Grainger used these double parentheses to indicate standard English synonyms of his words of Nordic English.

CHAPTER 9

'Persian composer-pianist baffles': Kaikhosru Sorabji

Nalini Ghuman

What earthly connection does the good Mr Frank Denyer (*Letters* 10–16 Dec.) think I have with 'British' Music? I, with no drop of British blood in me ... no contact with a 'musical' group and disliking musicians in general?

That I am a British citizen is nothing to the point – in such matters nationality is nothing ... race and blood on the other hand are all-important, and mercifully unalterable.   Kaikhosru Sorabji, Dorset[1]

'MARGINAL EXOTIC'[2]

The musical and critical works of Kaikhosru Shapurji Sorabji (1892–1988) have long been seen as wilfully unintelligible, idiosyncratic and elitist.[3] Described by one writer as 'a critic with a hundred axes to grind', Sorabji certainly made his likes and, equally, his intense dislikes, very apparent.[4] His writings include two volumes of collected essays, *Around Music* (1932) and *Mi Contra Fa* (1947), contributions to symposia on Ananda Coomaraswamy and Nicolas Medtner, and hundreds of journal articles and reviews.[5] A prolific composer, Sorabji completed over 120 works

---

I am indebted to Roger Parker and Richard Taruskin for their help and advice as I explored Sorabji's identity construction in music; my thanks to them, and also to Bonnie C. Wade, for their critical input on the larger version of this chapter. I am also grateful to Mariane C. Ferme, Paul Singh Ghuman and the late Edward W. Said for their role in shaping my work on identity, race and music. Alistair Hinton has provided generous assistance to me during my visits to The Sorabji Archive in Bath and in correspondence.

[1] 'Letters', *Guardian*, n.d., from Sorabji's clippings in The Sorabji Archive in Bath.
[2] Bernard Holland, 'Pianist of Delicacy as Well as Muscle', *New York Times*, 7 June 1997, 17.
[3] See, for example, Paul Bechert's 'Persian Composer-Pianist Baffles', *Musical Courier*, 2 March 1922, 7 (the source of this chapter's title); and Edmund Rubbra's 'Sorabji's Enigma', *Monthly Musical Record* (September 1932), 148.
[4] Quotation from Scott Goddard, *Music and Letters* 14 (1933), 287.
[5] *Around Music* (London: Unicorn Press, 1932) and *Mi Contra Fa: The Immoralisings of a Machiavellian Musician* (London: Porcupine Press, 1947); 'The Greatness of Medtner', in *Nicolas Medtner*, ed. Richard Holt (London: Dennis Dobson, 1954), pp. 122–32; 'The Validity of the Aristocratic Principle', in *Art and Thought*, ed. K. Bharatha Iyer (London: Luzac, 1947), pp. 214–18. He was a frequent contributor to *The Sackbut* (ed. Peter Warlock) in its first year (1920–1), and wrote music reviews for *The New Age* from 1924 to 1934, and for *The New English Weekly* – henceforth *NEW* – from 1932 to 1945 (both edited at that time by Alfred Richard Orage).

between 1914 and 1984, many for solo piano which make, in the words of one writer, 'demonic technical demands' on the performer.[6] His best-known title, *Opus Clavicembalisticum* (1929–30), is renowned as one of the longest piano compositions in existence: the formidably complex writing is spread across three, four and five staves, covering 253 landscape-format pages and lasting some four hours in performance.[7]

In the past decade, there has been a surge of interest in Sorabji: manuscripts have been prepared for publication, musicians regularly perform and record his works, and his biography has received some degree of attention.[8] As yet, there has been less consideration of Sorabji's music in relation to his cultural milieu. This is perhaps because his music has often been seen as essentially 'Oriental', only superficially belonging to the Western tradition, and therefore only intelligible (or even of interest) to a specialist in Indian or 'Oriental' music. The entry by Cecil Gray in an important musical encyclopaedia of 1930 reveals this attitude all too clearly:

in order to reveal the Oriental mind through a musical medium, a musically gifted Oriental would be needed, one who had mastered the Western musical language well enough to express his conceptions with freedom, yet free from the conventions by which Western minds are unconsciously bound. This is the phenomenon presented by the personality of Sorabji, though naturally his mental equipment does not comprise every conceivable predisposition that might be characteristic even of his own race … Nevertheless, there are certain European influences … in it … But these influences … remain superficial.[9]

'European influences' are, however, central to Sorabji's music, and abundant, as even a glance at the score of *Opus Clavicembalisticum* shows. This is unsurprising, given that the Western European tradition formed the basis of Sorabji's musical experience. *Opus Clavicembalisticum* (a work openly modelled on Busoni's *Fantasia Contrappuntistica*) is typical of his large-scale, multi-movement works for the piano.[10] He professed a

---

[6] Paul Rapoport, 'Sorabji Returns?' *Musical Times* 117/1606 (1976), 995.
[7] Geoffrey Douglas Madge's recording lasts nearly four hours, John Ogden's nearly four and three quarters. Sorabji wrote: 'The work is only intended for pianist-musicians of the highest order – indeed its intellectual and technical difficulties place it beyond the reach of any others. It is a weighty and serious contribution to the literature of the piano, for serious musicians and serious listeners only.' Printed in the booklet to Ogden's recording (Sevenoaks: Altarus AIR-CD-9075, 1989), henceforth CD booklet, 23.
[8] Alistair Hinton, founder of The Sorabji Archive in 1988, has been central to this revival. Rapoport's edited volume, *Sorabji: A Critical Celebration* (Aldershot: Scolar Press, 1992) – henceforth '*Sorabji*' – is an indispensable source book containing, *inter alia*, edited collections of Sorabji's correspondence and criticism and a works-list and discography. Rapoport included a chapter on Sorabji in his earlier volume *Opus Est: Six Composers from Northern Europe* (London: Kahn & Averill, 1978). Marc-André Roberge is currently writing a biography of Sorabji and has prepared a number of critical editions of his music.
[9] Cecil Gray, 'Sorabji', in Walter Willson Cobbett (ed.), *Cobbett's Cyclopedic Survey of Chamber Music* (Oxford University Press, 1930), vol. II, pp. 436–7.
[10] 'This work is admittedly an essay in the form adumbrated by the immortal BUSONI in his great FANTASIA CONTRAPPUNTISTICA', Sorabji, 'Shortform-Analysis of *Opus Clavicembalisticum*', CD Booklet, 22.

'whole-souled' devotion to the instrument and was deeply interested in the music of Alkan, Skryabin and Busoni – key figures in the evolution of virtuoso pianistic modernism.[11] Not only did Sorabji champion these composers in his writings, but his own musical aesthetic was affected by their music and their modernist philosophies.[12]

Even when Sorabji's music has been viewed in the context of both 'Eastern' and 'Western' influence, the former is often misinterpreted as 'essential' or 'integral' and as such remains largely unexamined. Thus, in his chapter on 'Sorabji's Piano Music' from 1992, Michael Habermann writes:

Sorabji's art is equally influenced by Eastern and Western concepts, the former reflecting his heritage, the latter his domicile. But Sorabji's 'exoticism' has nothing to do with the showy and superficial orientalism in works of composers of the 19th century. Eastern elements are an integral part of his music.[13]

The kind of reasoning articulated by Gray, Habermann and others – in part the result of treating Sorabji's own words not as testimony, but as an oracle[14] – rests on false, but familiar, premises. My purpose here is to examine the fascinating process of identity construction discernible in Sorabji's writings and music, and how perceptions of the composer's 'race' have influenced the reception – and the creation – of his music. In doing so, I draw on Stuart Hall's concept of 'hybridity', as well as on Edward Said's critique of Orientalist discourse.[15] I shall suggest that his

---

[11] Sorabji, 'The Greatness of Medtner', 125. His great love and knowledge of the piano and its repertoire is reflected not only in the concentration of his writings about the piano and in the bulk of his output, but also in the amount of time he spent discussing the piano with friends; see Hinton, 'Kaikhosru Sorabji and Erik Chisholm', *Jagger Journal* 10 (1989/90), 27.

[12] Sorabji's writings reveal an intimate knowledge of the music of Alkan, Skryabin and Busoni, especially their piano works: Sorabji attended Skryabin's London recitals in 1914 and reviewed Egon Petri's recitals of Alkan in the 1920s and 30s. His articles and reviews appeared in *The Musical Times*, *The New Age*, and *NEW*; there are many references to Alkan in *Mi Contra Fa* (pp. 109, 195, 196, 203–4), and *Around Music* contains chapters devoted to Alkan's piano works (pp. 213–19) and to Busoni (pp. 21–30).

[13] Michael Habermann, 'Sorabji's Piano Music', *Sorabji*, p. 339. See also Bechert, 'Persian Composer-Pianist Baffles', 7; Christopher à Becket Williams, 'The Music of Kaikhosru Sorabji', *The Sackbut* 4 (June 1924), 315–16; Rapoport, *Opus Est*, p. 166; Ronald Stevenson, 'A Zoroastrian Musician in Dorset', CD Booklet, pp. 4–5; and Charles Hopkins' essay 'Love and Mysticism: Sorabji, Sa'di, and the Sufic Tradition', that accompanies his recording of *Gulistān* (Altarus, AIR-CD-9036, 1995).

[14] Richard Taruskin, 'Revising Revision', *Journal of the American Musicological Society* 46 (1993), 138.

[15] See Stuart Hall, 'Who Needs Identity?' in *Questions of Cultural Identity*, ed. Paul du Gay and Stuart Hall (London: Sage, 1996), pp. 1–17, and Hall's 'Cultural Identity and Diaspora' in *Colonial Discourse and Post-Colonial Theory: A Reader*, ed. Patrick Williams and Laura Chrisman (New York: Columbia University Press, 1994), pp. 392–403. Edward W. Said, *Orientalism: Western Conceptions of the Orient* (London: Penguin 1978, second edition 1995). For further reading on race, identity and music, see Georgina Born and David Hesmondhalgh's 'Introduction: On Difference, Representation, and Appropriation in Music', in their edited volume *Western Music and Its Others: Difference, Representation, and Appropriation in Music* (Berkeley: University of California Press, 2000), pp. 1–58, and Ronald Radano and Philip V. Bohlman's 'Introduction' to their edited volume, *Music and the Racial Imagination* (University of Chicago Press, 2000), pp. 1–53.

music might be better understood as belonging to a Western Orientalist tradition, rather than as the natural product of his 'Oriental mind'.[16]

'HIMALAYAN HERMITAGE'[17]

Leon Dudley Sorabji was born in Chingford, Essex in 1892 to a wealthy Parsi engineer from Bombay (now Mumbai) who was seldom in Britain and was married bigamously in India, and a Spanish-Sicilian operatic soprano, from whom he gained his knowledge of the voice and his early skills at the piano. A precocious child with a thirst for contemporary music, it is said that at the age of thirteen Sorabji travelled alone to Essen to hear Mahler conducting the premiere of his Sixth Symphony.[18] After starting professional life as a music critic, he later realised his true vocation when he inherited enough money from his father to keep him for the rest of his life (although he continued to write on music and other matters for many years).

In the 1920s and 1930s, Sorabji gave occasional performances of his piano music in public, attracting a small but enthusiastic following. Especially valuable were the efforts of his friend Erik Chisholm, founder, in 1929, of the Active Society for the Propagation of Contemporary Music which hosted four successful performances by Sorabji.[19] By the late 1930s, however, owing to his dissatisfaction with the concert-giving scene and with those critical of his music, Sorabji made up his mind never again to give public recitals. More significantly, he withdrew his music from public performance (unless with his consent), declaring that 'no performance at all is better than an obscene travesty'.[20] This 'ban' lasted for some forty years. He subsequently went into almost complete retirement from society, seeing only those of whom he approved and those who had made appointments. This self-imposed withdrawal may seem to have been the result of a whim, the irrational action of an eccentric. However, it may also be seen as an understandable reaction against intolerance and ignorance.

Sorabji's Parsi and Spanish-Sicilian roots meant that he was subjected to a substantial amount of racist abuse which he described in a letter of 1915:

> The English nation ... is persistently nasty to foreigners ... pre-eminently to Indians. Their attitude towards us is one of carefully ... calculated hatefulness ... Insulting and offensive remarks are passed about us in loud tones, we are ridiculed and laughed at to our very faces.[21]

---

[16] Quotation from Orage's 'Foreword' to *Around Music*, pp. ix–xii: 'he is perhaps the first and certainly the greatest composer who has expressed an Oriental mind in modern European technique'; Orage further characterised Sorabji the writer as 'an essentially Oriental mind expressing itself in the European technique of written criticism; and as such it is equally distinguished and unique'.
[17] Sorabji, writing on Busoni, *Around Music*, p. 21.
[18] Hinton, 'Kaikhosru Sorabji and Erik Chisholm', 21. Sorabji refused either to deny or confirm this tale.
[19] Ibid., 20–36. [20] Hinton, 'Kaikhosru Shapurji Sorabji: an Introduction', *Sorabji*, p. 54.
[21] Letter to the Editor, *The New Age* 15 (April 1915), 653.

He recalled one particular incident while on a train in his early teens when a 'dignitary of the C. of E.... After staring long, rudely and offensively first at Ma then at me ... boomed [to the woman at his side] "A BLACK BOY!".'[22] Throughout his life Sorabji kept a file of newspaper clippings and correspondence marked 'Colour Matters'; he also wrote of the misconception that 'nationality' was interchangeable with 'race' and 'citizenship'.[23] His differences and separation from society became a source of strength and he came to see himself as superior to those who despised him, vehemently rejecting attempts to label him English or British: 'I am BY NO MANNER OF MEANS NOR IN ANY WAY ENGLISH ... My racial, ancestral and cultural roots are in civilisations with more millenia [sic] behind them than Anglo-Saxondom has centuries.'[24]

As he became more informed, Sorabji's opinion of his own racial identification changed. In 1916, he viewed himself as '[h]eart mind body and soul ... an Indian and would wish to be nothing else ... "avec un peu d'Espagne autour!"'.[25] By 1932, he wrote of 'our own people, the Parsis who thank God are not "Indians"', and, in the 1950s, referred to the Hindus as the 'scum of the earth'.[26] Much later, in 1977, he identified himself as half-Sicilian 'and much more than that temperamentally and psychologically. Much more my beloved mother's son than my father's'; and by 1980 Sorabji had denounced India as 'that beastly place'.[27]

These changes in attitude were not mere vacillations but important stages in the process of Sorabji's self-definition. Some time during the First World War, he was received into the Zoroastrian, Parsi community and it was then that he changed his forenames to Kaikhosru Shapurji. He became immensely proud of all that being a Parsi stood for, in particular the millennia of their artistic tradition which he saw as having provided everything worthwhile about Indian civilisation.[28] While he was knowledgeable about Zoroastrianism (or Zarathustrianism, as he more correctly called it), he did not practise it. He did, though, tell his friend Philip

---

[22] Letter to F. Holliday (6 September 1958), in *Sorabji*, p. 69.
[23] See, for example, his letter 'Was Delius British?', *Musical Opinion* (February 1952), 297.
[24] Letter to G. Macleod (February 1975), in *Sorabji*, p. 24.
[25] Letter to Philip Heseltine (11 February 1916), in *Sorabji*, p. 221.
[26] The Parsis are a religious community based mainly in the states of Maharashtra and Gujarat, and especially in the city of Mumbai. Their ancestors migrated to India from Persia (Iran) during the seventh and eighth centuries; Parsis use the ancient Pahlavi scriptures and adhere to the Zoroastrianism established by Zarathustra. Quotations are from letters to B. Van Dieren, n.d. (Summer 1932 or 1933, from Bombay), and to N. Gentieu (7 September 1954), in *Sorabji*, p. 222.
[27] Letters to K. Derus (21 August 1977 and 27 November 1980), in *Sorabji*, pp. 215 and 221.
[28] *The New Age* (9 March 1933), 224. Parsis began to visit Britain in 1742, but it was only after the 1850s that they arrived in any significant numbers. In 1861, the Religious Society of Zoroastrians of Europe was founded in Britain; in 1909 the name was changed to the Incorporated Parsee Association of Europe. Sorabji embraced the widely held belief (among Parsis) that Parsis are not 'Indian' and he often pointed to his father's Iranian descent; many Parsis consider Zoroastrians to be unique as a racial, as well as a religious, group. G. M. Towler Mehta, 'Parsees in Britain', *New Community* 10/2 (Winter 1982), 244–5.

Heseltine (the composer Peter Warlock) in a letter of 1915 that 'I am very nearly a Buddhist', explaining that the high standard of Burmese Buddhists' 'morality & personal purity, is with that of my own race – the Parsîs' [sic].[29]

'SCHÉHÉRAZADE-KAIKHOSRU'

Sorabji was an unwitting victim of the Orientalist division of the world into East and West analysed by Edward Said; his personality and music were moulded by it. Rather than submit to his treatment as a second-class citizen, Sorabji turned to his 'roots' for strength, having to learn about the very origins that he was persecuted for having. By birth he had Parsi, Persian (Iranian) and Indian ties, but he knew no Pahlavi nor Farsi, nor any Indian language: he belonged neither in the land in which he was born and educated (and lived for his entire life) nor in the land he acknowledged as his own. He was, in a word, multicultural, exemplifying Said's recognition of the fact that 'human identity is not only not natural and stable, but constructed, and occasionally even invented outright'.[30]

In order to learn about his origins, Sorabji was reliant on texts; hence his knowledge was mediated and, to some extent, formulated, by his Orientalist precursors. Like Gustave Flaubert, for instance, Sorabji spoke of himself as an Oriental;[31] in letters to Erik Chisholm during the composition of *Opus Clavicembalisticum*, he referred to himself first as 'Schéhérazade-Kaikhosru' then as a 'Brahman', suggesting that he considered his Parsi heritage to allow him access to both Persian and Indian traditions.[32] His particular interest in the works of Persian poets (in translation) inspired a number of pieces, including settings of Shamsu'd-Din Ibrahim Mirza, Muslihu'd-Dīn 'Abdu'llah Sa'dī (*Gulistān*, 'The Rose Garden', in particular) and Nuru'd-Din 'Abdu'ı-Rahman Jāmī. It was through Richard Burton's translations that Sorabji gained his knowledge of such works as *One Thousand and One Nights* and *The Perfumed Garden* (the love manual by Sheik al-Nafzawi, translated by Burton at his own expense to avoid prosecution) which inspired the nocturne, *Le Jardin parfumé* (1923). In a letter to Chisholm, he even explained the central 'Adagio' of *Opus Clavicembalisticum* as 'a very beautiful and interesting

---

[29] Letter to Heseltine (6 January 1914), in *Sorabji*, p. 204. He was interested in Roman Catholicism, practised yoga, and dabbled in the occult, astrology, tarot, and numerology.
[30] Said, *Orientalism*, p. 332.
[31] Sorabji, 'Oriental Atmosphere', *Around Music*, p. 147. See also his letter to Heseltine (11 February 1916): he bought a copy of Gustave Flaubert's *Temptation of St Anthony* which contained all three versions; Derus has suggested that *Simorg-Anka* (1924) is a setting of an episode from it, *Sorabji*, p. 222. For Flaubert, see his *Correspondance*, Jean Bruneau, ed. (Paris: Gallimard, 1973–), vol. I, p. 433.
[32] Letters to Chisholm (29 May, and 11/12 June 1930), in *Sorabji*, pp. 306–7 and 308–9.

story about the Sheik and his friend the handsome young prince Nureddior' – an allusion to *One Thousand and One Nights*.[33]

Sorabji was enthralled not only by the civilisation of the East, but also by the exotic, mystical, sensuous Orient of Flaubert and Burton. Intellectually, his view of the Orient, and (paradoxically) of himself, is an essentially Western conception. He wished to be seen as an Oriental in exile, who by nature of his birth possessed certain qualities lacking in Occidentals.[34] It was only later that he understood the crudity of the term 'Oriental' in general, and the assimilation of Parsis and Indians in particular.[35] When Sorabji visited India for the first time in 1932 or 1933, it is not surprising that it did not live up to his expectations: his previous experience of the Parsis had mainly been through the accumulated poetry of over half a millennium. He decided that the modern Parsis (as opposed to their civilised ancestors) seemed to have gone 'pretty rotten'; none of them ever read 'an intelligent book'.[36] Modern Hindus, 'that pestilent foul crew', escaped even less easily.[37] Others before him had experienced a similar shock of disappointment on meeting with the disorientations of a real (rather than textual) society.[38] More recently, V. S. Naipaul's writing reveals an unsentimental, even cynical, view of the country his ancestors left over a century ago, most notably in *An Area of Darkness* (1964) written after the author's first encounter with India, and in the book that followed, *India: A Wounded Civilization* (1977), written after several subsequent journeys to the subcontinent.[39] Sorabji's reaction is revealing: rather than

---

[33] Sorabji expressed great admiration for Burton's *Arabian Nights* translation; see *Sorabji*, p. 325.

[34] See, for example, his letter to Heseltine of June 1917 in which he refers to the 'considerable degree of inner vision and marked supernormal receptiveness' which is inherent in 'Indians ... by right of birth'; *Sorabji*, p. 229.

[35] Sorabji, 'The Validity of the Aristocratic Principle', 214–18.

[36] Letter to Van Dieren, n.d. (Summer 1932 or 1933, from Bombay), in *Sorabji*, p. 222.

[37] Letter to Gentieu (7 September 1954) in *Sorabji*, p. 222. Sorabji's reaction owes much to a predominant attitude among Orientalists, noted by Said: 'the "good" Orient was invariably a classical period somewhere in long-gone India, whereas the "bad" Orient lingered in present day Asia', Said, *Orientalism*, p. 99. In an article on the caste system in India, Sorabji stated that it was not the system which was at fault, but modern Indians, see 'The Validity of the Aristocratic Principle', 214–18.

[38] See, for example, Gérard de Nerval, *Oeuvres*, ed. Albert Béguin and Jean Richet (Paris, 1960), Vol. I, p. 933. The French author and traveller wrote of his disappointment on losing the Orient of the texts: 'I have already lost, Kingdom after Kingdom, province after province, the more beautiful part of the universe, and soon I will know of no place in which I can find a refuge for my dreams; but it is Egypt that I most regret having driven out of my imagination, now that I have sadly placed it in my memory'; quoted in Said, *Orientalism*, p. 100.

[39] V. S. Naipaul, *An Area of Darkness* (London: Deutsch, 1964), *A Wounded Civilization* (London: Deutsch, 1977). For a perceptive commentary on Naipaul's writings on India, see Jeffery Paine, 'Head of Darkness', in his *Father India: Westerners Under the Spell of an Ancient Culture* (New York: Harper Perennial, 1999), pp. 147–76; Paine writes that *An Area of Darkness* 'is the narrative of a young man not finding the India he expected and not liking the India he finds ... [in it] Naipaul blamed India for not living up to his father's vision ... A decade, several trips, and one book [*A Wounded Civilization*] later, Naipaul was still compiling the same indictment [of India]'; pp. 157–8.

discard his pride in the civilisation to which he claimed allegiance, he attempted to keep his dream of the Orient alive with a belief in a past age of greatness.

At the height of his fascination for the 'Orient', Sorabji wrote a chapter on 'Oriental Atmosphere' from a self-appointed position of authorial wisdom as an Oriental.[40] For Sorabji, 'good' Orientalist music possessed rhythmic intricacy, 'melodic lines which, without imitating, suggest by their contours relationship with melodies of Oriental types', and a number of unspecified elements which are 'not perhaps immediately perceptible to the ordinary music lover'.[41] He praised above all Szymanowski's Third Symphony (inspired by the Persian poet Rumi) as 'a work saturated with the voluptuous and passionate languor of a Persian night, richly suggestive and evocative, permeated with that spirit of transcendental, exalted pessimism which is of the East eastern [sic]'.[42] Debussy's best musical qualities were, Sorabji suggested, the result of 'Asiatic affinities'.[43] Likewise he admired Ravel's use of Malayan verse form in his Piano Trio (1914), Bernard van Dieren's 'absorption' of Chinese 'inspiration', Delage and Roussel's 'Indian inspiration',[44] and Delius's use of arabesque.[45] Although Sorabji was unwilling to admit any such influences, examination of his music reveals that the Orientalist aesthetics of the composers he names were refracted through his own imagined identity.

While Sorabji had greater reason to learn about, and embrace, 'Oriental' music than Debussy or Ravel – for him it was not a dalliance, a brief artistic flirtation – he was just as thoroughly schooled as they in the Western tradition, and came to the musics of the 'Orient' equally as a novice. In 'Oriental Atmosphere' he addressed 'Oriental' music as a largely homogeneous body, characterising what he saw as its essential elements; while he appears to have chosen Indian classical music as representative of what he termed 'Oriental music at its best', he does not give a single example.[46] However much Sorabji considered himself to have a 'trained ear' for Indian music, he received no formal instruction.[47] He did, however, attend concerts and lectures in London (and later Bombay), listen daily to the music programme broadcast from the Bombay station, and study the works of Coomaraswamy (including the pamphlet, *Indian Music*) and Arthur Fox-Strangways (*The Music of Hindostan*, which he greatly admired for its scholarly detail and lack of condescension).[48]

---

[40] 'Oriental Atmosphere', *Around Music*, pp. 147–51. [41] Ibid., p. 148.
[42] Ibid., p. 150. See also his chapter on Szymanowski in *Mi Contra Fa*, pp. 178–87.
[43] 'Oriental Atmosphere', pp. 148–9. [44] Ibid., pp. 149–50. [45] *NEW*, 22 April 1937, 35.
[46] 'Oriental Atmosphere', p. 147. [47] *NEW*, 9 February 1933, 398.
[48] Ibid. Sorabji made frequent reference to both authors; see, for example, *Mi Contra Fa*, p. 230, *The New Age*, 2 April 1925, 275, and a letter to the editor entitled 'Rhythmic Music', *Gramophone* 9/107 (1932), 132.

'THE ESSENTIAL PERSIAN SORABJI'?

Indications of Sorabji's interest in Indian music can be discerned in his writings as well as in his own musical works, especially those of explicitly Indian inspiration, which include *Chaleur* (c. 1916–17), a poem for orchestra set in 'Tropical India', two piano variations entitled *Quasi Tambura* (1930) and *Quasi Rag Indiana* (1935–7), *Tāntrik Symphony for Piano Alone* (1938–9) whose seven movement titles are the Sanskrit terms for bodily centres and functions basic to tantric and shaktic yoga, and two *Sutra* [Sanskrit: 'aphorisms'] *sul nome dell' amico Alexis* (1971).[49] It seems clear that this is one musical influence that he wished to be seen.

Yet Sorabji's music is not Indian, and the identification of it as 'Oriental', or of specific elements as 'Eastern', can be misleading.[50] The nocturne *Gulistān*, for instance, has been described (in 1992) as 'representing the essential Persian Sorabji' – a claim that assumes an innate connection between the composer and his father's Zoroastrian ancestors before they left Persia in the eighth century.[51] Likewise, the unusual length of *Opus Clavicembalisticum* has been attributed to Sorabji's (innate) interest in Indian and Persian music (even though he seems to have had no knowledge of the latter).[52] While his penchant for writing lengthy pieces may relate to his interest in *rāga* performance, Sorabji bemoaned the inability of the modern Indian musician to get 'any organic growth out of his material',[53] just as he advocated 'organic technique' as a compositional principle in Western music, and admired the largest works of such composers as Bach, Berlioz and Mahler.[54] In a revealing comment made towards the end of the work's composition, Sorabji wrote of its already unexpected length, explaining that 'The musical necessities and not the convenience or comfort of the audience are what matters in these high regions of Brahman manifesting as Art'.[55] This suggests that the work's length might also owe something to his modernist stance which led him to react against public taste and

---

[49] His writings on Indian music include 'Indian Music and Indian and Western Musical Criticism', in *Mi Contra Fa*, pp. 229–34, 'Music', *NEW*, 24 November 1932, 136–8, and 'Reflections Upon Indian Music', *The New Age*, 9 March 1933, 223–4.

[50] The opening phrase of *Opus Clavicembalisticum* has been likened to 'an Indian *raga*' (Stevenson, 'Opus Clavicembalisticum – a critical analysis', CD Booklet, 32); yet its function and declamatory nature have, perhaps, more in common with the brass calls Sorabji admired at the opening of movements of Mahler's fifth and seventh symphonies, *Around Music*, pp. 188–9.

[51] Hinton, 'Kaikhosru Sorabji: An Introduction', p. 53.

[52] See Rapoport, 'Sorabji Returns?' 995 and *Opus Est*, 166; also Habermann, 'Sorabji's Piano Music', 340.

[53] 'Reflections Upon Indian Music', 224.

[54] Sorabji wrote of 'organic' form and technique in *Mi Contra Fa*, pp. 51–2. See *Around Music*, pp. 178–90 for Sorabji's admiration for Mahler's symphonies.

[55] Sorabji, letter to Chisholm (11/12 June 1930), in *Sorabji*, p. 309.

conventions,⁵⁶ along with his conviction, following Busoni in his *Sketch of a New Esthetic of Music*, that content should mould its own form.⁵⁷

The 'free form' movements of *Opus Clavicembalisticum* (similar in style to his nocturnes, *Le Jardin parfumé*, *Gulistān* and *Jāmī*) have been likened to 'written-out improvisations' suggestive of 'Eastern' music.⁵⁸ Yet, while improvisation is an important element in Indian music, Sorabji saw this as one of the 'inherent defects that prevent it from ever becoming an Art comparable in importance with that of Europe'.⁵⁹ For Sorabji, Indian music's consequent 'lack of architectonic [and] form-sense' was its 'prevailing weakness'.⁶⁰ It is striking that the language and logic of Sorabji's attitude resonate with the conclusion drawn by English journalist, Beverley Nichols in his *Verdict on India*, published after a long visit to India during the Second World War. Nichols denied Indian classical music, whose secret 'lies in the word "improvisation"', the status of an art because 'Art is not . . . a matter of improvisation'.⁶¹

Moreover, *Opus Clavicembalisticum*'s twelve-movement form, structured around four massive fugues each with up to four different subjects and complete with cancrizans and inversions of all kinds, demonstrates Sorabji's commitment to what he called 'the architectonic skill' and contrapuntal techniques of the Germanic tradition, stretching through his avowed models Busoni and Reger back to Bach.⁶² Sorabji's attitude towards structure and composition thus reveals not only its roots in the Western classical tradition, but also his prejudice against the principles of Indian improvisation.

RĀGAS AND JUNGLES

The most explicitly 'Indian' movement of *Opus Clavicembalisticum* is Variation 53 of the *Passacaglia with Eighty-One Variations*, entitled 'Quasi tambura'. The *tāmbūra* is a fundamental element of *rāga* performance, the texture of which Sorabji described as 'melodic, and monodic, harmony . . . only arising as a very subsidiary by-product from the clashes of the curve of an instrumental or vocal melody with the accompanimental background supplied by a continuously thrummed string instrument

---

⁵⁶ Hugh MacDiarmid, *The Company I've Kept* (London: Hutchinson, 1996), pp. 42 and 54. MacDiarmid advised Sorabji not to write a shorter work in order to satisfy public opinion (not that Sorabji was intending to do such a thing); see also Sorabji's letters to Chisholm during the work's composition, *Sorabji*, pp. 300–11.
⁵⁷ Ferruccio Busoni, *Sketch of a New Esthetic of Music*, trans. Theodore Baker; repr. in *Three Classics in the Aesthetic of Music* (New York: Dover, 1962), pp. 78–80. For Sorabji's views on form see *Mi Contra Fa*, pp. 51–2.
⁵⁸ See Rapoport, *Opus Est*, p. 173.   ⁵⁹ 'Reflections on Indian Music', 223.   ⁶⁰ Ibid., 223–4.
⁶¹ Beverley Nichols, *Verdict on India* (London: Jonathan Cape, 1944), pp. 122–36, esp. 111 and 134.
⁶² *Around Music*, pp. 26–7.

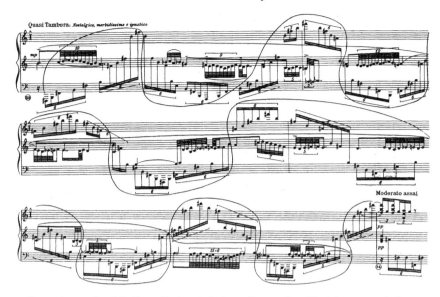

Example 9.1a: Sorabji, *Opus Clavicembalisticum*, Passacaglia with eighty-one variations: 'Quasi tambura' variation

Example 9.1b: Passacaglia theme

tuned in open fifths [*tāmbūra*]'.[63] Given the variation's title, we might assume the B–F#–B ostinato to be suggestive of the *tāmbūra*'s role, while the elaborate turns of the melody function to evoke the unfolding of a *rāga*, each note ornamented from above and below (see Ex. 9.1a[64]). As each phrase comes to rest, the melody interacts ('clashes') rhythmically and harmonically with the ostinato, dwelling on the flat second and flat sixth degrees in a manner reminiscent of certain *rāgas* in performance.

Apart from the creation of an Indian style, 'Quasi tambura' is striking because it is the first (of fifty-four) in which Sorabji converted the passacaglia's ground bass (see Ex. 9.1b), into the melody. Instead of working freely around the melody, however, he added the *tāmbūra*-ostinato that characterises the variation; the only 'free' writing is the ornamentation surrounding each of the theme's pitches. Unlike the pedal figures of

---

[63] 'Indian Music and Indian and Western Musical Criticism', in *Mi Contra Fa*, p. 230.
[64] Variation fifty-three, *Opus Clavicembalisticum* (London: J. Curwen and Sons, 1931). All music examples are reproduced with permission from The Sorabji Archive.

Sorabji's nocturnes (such as *Le Jardin parfumé*) which bear close relation to the left-hand accompaniments found in the music of Chopin, Liszt or Busoni, the '*tāmbūra*-ostinato' includes only open fifths, its pitch and rhythmic outline remains constant and, crucially, rather than being a left-hand accompaniment, the ostinato spans five octaves, thereby transforming the traditional *tāmbūra* figure (often a repeating dominant–tonic pattern of *Pa-Sa-Sa-Sa*) into an idiomatic gesture for piano, shared between the hands.

Significantly, it is in the context of variation form that Sorabji indicated his intention to suggest India musically. In the tradition of character variations, 'Quasi tambura' represents a deliberate evocation of a particular mood or style (here, an Indian style). By way of an effective transformation of the ground bass into melody, Sorabji dressed up his theme in Indian clothes, using irregularly grouped chromatic undulations to decorate the theme's pitches, along with a rhythmic tonic–dominant ostinato; there is no pretence that the theme itself is Indian. We might even hear this variation as an example of Sorabji's penchant for pastiche, evident in his 1922 piano pastiches of Bizet's 'Habanera' and Rimsky-Korsakov's 'Hindu Merchant's Song', or in the later *Malicious and Perverse Variation on Ase's Death by Grieg*. Yet the humour in these pastiches bears little relation to the tone of the 'tambura' variation.

Upon further reflection, the idea of taking a fixed series of pitches (no time signature or solid bar lines) that generally move by step in ascending and descending groups (the passacaglia theme) and unfolding them by way of ornaments and fluid figuration to the accompaniment of an open-fifth ostinato resembles more closely than any other Western musical form the manner of *rāga* performance (the opening unmetered *alap* in which the *rāga* unfolds over the *tāmbūra* drone). Moreover, the principle of variation form, and of the Passacaglia in particular, maintains a historical association with improvisation (the phenomenon of performers improvising variations on a theme). In this way, Sorabji avoids improvisation per se, while effectively signalling it through the passacaglia form.

If the musical texture and form suggest an emulation of Indian music, Sorabji's indications to the pianist, '*nostalgico, morbidissimo e ipnotico*', point to a cliché, pictorial 'India' that has little to do either with *rāga* performance or with the moods traditionally associated with particular *rāgas*. These directions reinterpret the musical material as evocative of certain images of the seductive but dangerous India invented by the colonial imagination. Sorabji's most intense indication, 'morbidissimo', with its associations of the macabre, unwholesome and sickly (given the word's root in the Latin 'morbus'), was evidently considered unsuitable as an interpretive musical pointer by Paul Rapoport; in his 1978 article on *Opus Clavicembalisticum*, he told readers the variation was marked 'nostalgic, very mellow, and hypnotic', thereby replacing Sorabji's desire for the music to be 'very morbid' with the innocuous 'very mellow', and making the 'Indian' music safe to imagine for pianist, listener and reader alike.[65]

The roots of the expressive indications of '*Quasi tambura*', and with them the key to understanding Sorabji's 'Indian' music, can perhaps be found in an earlier work, *Chaleur* (c. 1916–17). This 'Poem for Orchestra', which remains unperformed and unpublished, is the only piece for which Sorabji wrote a programmatic preface:

> It is midday in a grove of Tropical India. The sun does not succeed in piercing the thick roof of leaves overhead, its rays being transformed into a green mysterious twilight. The whole life of the grove seems suspended in the tense quivering heat: not a sound to be heard but the hum of countless insects. Occasionally the subtle evil head of a krait hovers for a moment above the dense undergrowth and vanishes with a venomous hiss. The air is heavy with the narcotic perfume of rare exotics and the languid voluptuous extasy of tropical heat pervades all things.[66]

(Sorabji provided an explanatory note that the krait is 'the deadliest serpent known ... said to be responsible for from 50–75,000 deaths annually in India'.)

Chaleur's programme outlines several Orientalist tropes: first, the idea of a languid, inert land which sedates those who venture in with its 'narcotic perfume' and the cloying 'heat' of the piece's title – providing a context, perhaps, for 'ipnotico'; second, the seductive strangeness, unhealthy atmosphere and macabre dangers of an exotic land – recalled, perhaps, by 'morbidissimo'. Finally, the evocation of India as a tropical landscape, untrammelled by human foot, which resonates with what has been described as 'imperialist nostalgia' for an invented past.[67] Such nostalgia is often associated with domination – mourning the passing of that which colonialism itself has transformed (here an imaginary tropical, pre-industrial India). It is, perhaps, this sense of nostalgia that is invoked by the later 'nostalgico' marking.

The colouristic details of *Chaleur*'s musical material seem to have been created in response to Sorabji's *jangal* scenario; the resulting timbral nuances, orchestral textures and distinctive combinations of instruments recall the scores of Debussy and Ravel. Pianissimo undulating strings divided into twelve rhythmically varied parts play '*dans une Sonorité chaleureuse*', while muted horns and oboes, clarinets and alto flute alternate in setting in relief a '*très languide*' chromatic motif (see Ex. 9.2). If the constantly low dynamic level (often *ppp*) is suggestive of India's inertness and sultry heat ('the whole life of the grove seems suspended in the tense quivering heat') Sorabji recalled this ambience in his 'Quasi tambura' variation with its hushed dynamic.

---

[65] Rapoport, *Opus Est*, p. 174.   [66] *Chaleur*, copyist's manuscript, The Sorabji Archive.
[67] Renato Rosaldo, 'Imperialist Nostalgia', *Culture and Truth* (Boston: Beacon Press, 1989), pp. 68–87.

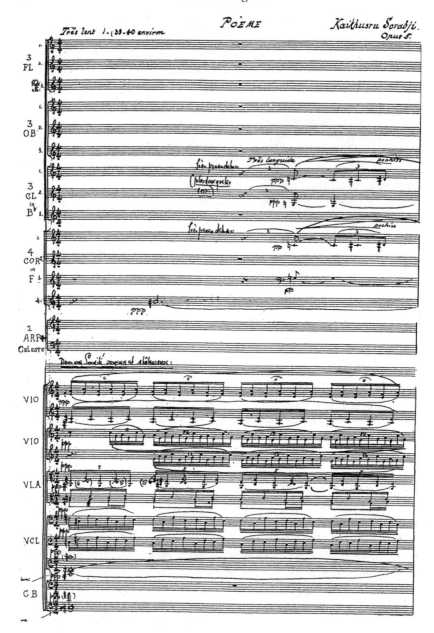

Example 9.2: *Chaleur*, opening

Chaleur's subject – the ominous Indian jungle – had become a resonant European image of India during the late nineteenth and early twentieth centuries. The word itself was derived from the Hindi, *jangal* (Sanskrit: *jangala*). In 1892, Madame Blavatsky published her (translated) travel writings under the title *From the Caves and Jungles of Hindostan, 1883–1886*.[68] Two years later Rudyard Kipling's *Jungle Book* popularised the image of the Indian jungle and, in 1912, Cyril Scott portrayed parts of Kipling's story in *Impressions from the Jungle Book*, a piano suite which includes such movements as 'The Jungle' and 'Morning in the Jungle'. In 1930, when Romain Rolland asked Freud's opinion of the Indian approach to the self to use in his biography of Sri Ramakrishna, Freud replied using the jungle as a metaphor: 'I shall now try . . . to penetrate into the Indian jungle'.[69]

The exotic tropes of *Chaleur*'s programme reappear some twenty years later in the composer's largest work, the three-volume *Symphonic Variations for Piano Solo* (1935–7) which would last some eight hours in performance (it remains unpublished and unperformed). Variation 34, 'Quasi rāg indiana', is marked with the familiar directions, '*nostalgico, languido e morbidissimo sempre*'.[70] The theme of the *Symphonic Variations*, like that of the earlier Passacaglia, is a series of (mainly) stepwise pitches, unhindered by a fixed time signature; it is more extensive though, divided into three parts, and shrouded by static chords (see Ex. 9.3a). As in 'Quasi tambura', Sorabji invoked the structural resemblance to *rāga alap*: he extracted only the theme's outline from its harmonic surroundings and unfolded the subsequent pitch succession in a series of embellished phrases (see Ex. 9.3b). The generic resonance of variation form again suggests a sense of improvisation (emphasised by the score indication '*molto libero in tempo*').

In this lengthy variation, Sorabji used the texture of *rāga* performance to create an extended piece of pianistic virtuosity. An ostinato, outlining B and F#, similar in pitch and shape to that of 'Quasi tambura', is maintained (with only one interruption) at the lowest dynamic level for nine, 'Lento', landscape-format pages. The highly wrought melodic lines span a vast range and are replete with chromatic passages, trills, wide leaps, florid, cadenza-like passages in sixths and sequential figures often suggestive of the tonal and rhythmic inflections of an instrumental *alap*.[71] Indeed, Sorabji did lament what he called 'Occidental equal temperament', advocating instead (after Busoni) the introduction of instruments with 'say, 22 notes to

---

[68] Helena Petrovna Blavatsky, *From the Caves and Jungles of Hindostan 1883–1886*, trans. by the author (London: Theosophical Publishing Society, 1892).

[69] Hermann Hesse and Romain Rolland *Correspondence, Diary Entries 1915–1940* (London: Oswald Wolff, 1978), quoted in Paine, *Father India: Westerners Under the Spell of an Ancient Culture*, p. 102.

[70] Variation thirty-four, *Symphonic Variations for Piano Solo*, manuscript copy, The Sorabji Archive.

[71] Sorabji conjectured optimistically about future temperings of the piano scale (a fifty-five-note octave), and enthused about the experimental keyboards (some containing eighty-one notes to the octave) seen in the Science Museum, South Kensington, which he termed 'marvels of ingenuity'. Marjorie Maulsby Benson, *The Opus Clavicembalisticum* (DMA, The American Conservatory of Music, 1987), p. 5; and *Around Music*, p. 206.

Example 9.3a: Theme of *Symphonic Variations*, opening phrase

Example 9.3b: 'Quasi rāg indiana'

the octave as the hindûs have'.⁷² The figuration might also bear distant relation to Liszt's virtuosic works (in which, as Sorabji noted, decoration takes its part in the melodic structure), or to the *bel canto* style which Sorabji admired in Rimsky-Korsakov's *The Golden Cockerel* and Strauss's *Ariadne auf Naxos*. Although he saw such ornamentation in Western music as exotic, he compares its texture not to Indian music but rather to Chinese embroidery.⁷³ However we conceptualise Sorabji's ornamented lines, they have as little to do with easy-listening Orientalist pastiche as they do with the *rāga* of the variation's title; the melodic lines are difficult both to play and for the ear to grasp, so unhindered are they in range, phrase-length, or by key, melodic mode, tempo, metre or rhythmic cycle.

'ORIENTALIST ORIENTAL'

How, then, might we understand Sorabji's couching of these 'Indian' variations in conventionally exotic performance directions that seem incongruous with the unconventional writing? As Sorabji's racial identification grew more focused, his Indian evocations came less to define the musical material (as in *Chaleur*) than to suggest a texture with which he developed an idiomatic piano style that extended the modernist aesthetics of Alkan, Skryabin and Busoni. Yet, it was the colonial view of an inert 'India' invoked by *Chaleur* (hypnotic, languid, morbid, nostalgic) that he continued to draw on in his piano music. Sorabji's attitude to composition was as eclectic as his approach to religion and culture, though; for him, the modernist Indian-piano idiom was only one of many different styles of writing.

Just as Sorabji's persuasive identification as 'Oriental' has contributed to perceptions of his music as 'Eastern', however, his jungle descriptions and their pianistic resonance have influenced the very language of those perceptions. Chisholm coined the term 'poisonous sweetness' to describe the nocturnes *Le Jardin parfumé*, *Jāmī* and *Gulistān* which, like *Chaleur*, maintain low dynamic levels throughout; Busoni wrote of 'tropical ornamentation [and] luxuriant foliage' after hearing Sorabji play his own first Sonata in 1919;⁷⁴ and, in notes to his 1995 recording of *Gulistān*, Charles Hopkins describes a 'heavily perfumed atmosphere of sub-tropical vegetation – larger sections of other works inhabit the same hypnotic world ... interlaced with sensuous melodic lines ... and rich, exotic ornamentation'.⁷⁵

---

⁷² Letter to Heseltine (11 Jan 1915), in *Sorabji*, p. 216. Busoni discussed similar divisions of the octave in his *Sketch of a New Esthetic*, pp. 89–95.
⁷³ *Around Music*, pp. 47–51.
⁷⁴ Chisholm, quoted in notes to Yonty Solomon's Altarus CD of *Le Jardin parfumé*, AIR-CD-9037. Busoni, letter to Emil Hertzka, quoted in *Sorabji*, p. 254.
⁷⁵ Hopkins, 'Love and Mysticism'. Paul Griffiths invokes a more domesticated jungle in his article, 'Wandering Through a Recluse's Personal Garden', *New York Times*, 18 November 2002, 2.

Yet, our examination of Sorabji's explicitly 'Indian' musical moments, in the context of the composer's relationship to his cultural inheritance and to the racially charged climate of Imperial Britain in the 1920s, 30s and 40s, suggests a way of understanding his distinctive piano writing in terms that extend beyond those such as 'exotic' or 'hypnotic'. These 'Indian' moments in Sorabji's music perhaps reveal a profoundly imperialist nostalgia for an India the composer never really knew, but which he seemed to mourn. That he was appalled by actual knowledge of his 'homeland' – modern urban Bombay – is unsurprising for someone who learned of the paradise of 'Indo-Persia' through its poets and writers, and who mourned its passing in his music. While Sorabji seemed concerned in his music and his writings to break down the racially drawn barriers between India and England, between East and West, his denigration of Indian music's improvisatory style drew its logic from Orientalist arguments, thereby reinforcing those barriers. Sorabji's writings and music in one sense reproduced the colonial view of India, but in another sense they are infused with the awareness of a modernist sensibility. The myriad impingements of empire and its preoccupation with race on Sorabji's sensibility are thus registered in his music and writings in contradictory ways.

As I mentioned earlier, the complex personality discernible in Sorabji's work finds resonance in the contemporary writings on India of Naipaul, which reveal the author's antagonistic relationship to his imagined cultural identity and heritage. As Said noted, Naipaul has (on the basis of his constructed identity) 'allowed himself quite consciously to be turned into a witness for the Western prosecution', yet, 'in the post-colonial world, he's a marked man as a purveyor of stereotypes and disgust for the world that produced him'.[76] The similarity is striking: Sorabji's virtuosic musical evocations of a clichéd India evoked by languor, nostalgia and morbidity, coupled with his increasing disdain for India, its music and its peoples, all expressed from a self-appointed position of wisdom as an 'Oriental', are echoed in Naipaul's work. In the early 1930s, while Sorabji was visiting India, he gave several recitals for the Bombay station; a commentary by H. J. W. Miller, organist of St Thomas's Cathedral, Bombay, was quoted in *The Bombay Man's Diary*:

Sorabji's compositions are most interesting to those who know India, as they illustrate the result of combining Oriental elaboration with Western tradition. Sorabji is an authority on modern music ... Bombay, the home of the Parsis should certainly have some knowledge of his achievements.[77]

[76] Said, 'Intellectuals in the Post-Colonial World', *Salmagundi* 70–1 (1986), 53; and Githa Hariharan, 'The Ignoble Politics of Naipaul's Nobel', *Frontline – India's National Magazine* 18/23 (10–23 November 2001), 71.
[77] Anon, *The Bombay Man's Diary*, n.d., The Sorabji Archive. An article entitled 'Mr. Kaikhasroo Shapurji Sorabji' in *The Indian Radio Times* (1932) indicates that Sorabji gave broadcast recitals on 19 October and 7 December 1932. The Sorabji Archive.

Sorabji drew a line next to this paragraph along with the words, 'keep this carefully', suggesting that he approved of and, perhaps, held pride in the perception (published in a Bombay journal) of a Western-Indian hybrid quality in his music. While many Indians and Parsis did hear his music broadcast on Bombay radio, however, Miller further noted that 'many of the local enthusiasts in the musical world did not share the appreciation [of Edgar Bainton, a musician visiting from England]!'[78]

Sorabji admired many aspects of Indian music: fluidity of rhythm, melodic intricacies and the abundance of ornamentation in particular. Yet he chose a pianistic tradition, and hence a medium, fundamentally unsuited to the vocal/string nuances and use of microtones that are characteristic of Indian music; he succeeded in creating an Oriental atmosphere perplexing to many Westerners and artificial to many Indians.[79] His music is both more and less 'oriental' than suggested in the past: although he draws on technical and expressive aspects of Indian music, some of these were already visible in the music of those Western composers he admired.

One conclusion becomes insistent. It is a mistake to pigeonhole Sorabji as either 'Western' or 'Oriental'; his was an imagined rather than an actual hybrid heritage. He saw the relationship between East and West as neither rigid nor one-sided and in his writings and music he can be seen to be striving towards an end: comparisons between 'Oriental' and 'Western' are a constant theme.[80] Understanding of Sorabji's music has been hindered by the very same arbitrary, yet enormously potent division that was formative of his personality. The mapping of a narrow racial identification onto his music has led to a perception of the composer's human differences (both real and imagined) as musical differences; in this process, described by Ronald Radano and Philip Bohlman as 'locating race "on music"', both Sorabji's 'race' and his music have often been fetishised.[81]

Musically and personally, Sorabji was a kind of 'Orientalist Oriental'. Appreciation of his work thus depends, in part, on how far we wish to understand his music's cultural meanings, and how sympathetic we are towards the personal circumstances that led him to attempt a reconciliation between East and West that is, in many ways, as elusive today as it was when he wrote his Indian musical depictions.

---

[78] Ibid.
[79] Rabindranath Tagore refused to use the piano as he thought it too restricting; B. Chaitanya Deva, *An Introduction to Indian Music* (New Delhi: Publications Division, 1973), p. 115.
[80] See, for example, Sorabji's article on Uday Shankar, *NEW* (2 November 1933), 65–6, in which he draws comparisons between the music of India and that of Mahler and Szymanowski, commenting: 'I do want to hear Mr. Shankar's superb drummer in that unwritten Szymanowski work'; see also 'Music', *NEW* (17 May 1934), 110–12.
[81] Radano and Bohlman, 'Introduction', in *Music and the Racial Imagination*, p. 10.

PART III

Local contexts

CHAPTER 10

Race and nation: musical acclimatisation and the chansons populaires *in Third Republic France*

Jann Pasler

In 1867, soon after Egyptians, Algerians and Tunisians appeared in their first Parisian exhibition, François-Joseph Fétis began his general history of music with the widely espoused opinion that music, like other cultural products, was a key to understanding race and racial differences. In his first sentence, he asserted:

> The history of music is inseparable from appreciation of the special properties belonging to races cultivating it. This essentially ideal art owes its existence to the humans who create it . . . it is the product of human faculties which are distributed unequally among people as well as individuals.[1]

Two beliefs underlie this history, contemporaneous with the emergence of anthropology. First, like many of his contemporaries, Fétis assumed that skull shape and size are links to older times and evidence of intellectual capacity. As he put it, sounds do not affect people the same way because 'a feeling for music . . . is related to the shape of the brain'; for him, that shape determines a person's capacity to understand relationships between sounds.[2] As for anthropologists who looked to human types as a means of measuring and comparing the parameters of a race, Fétis tied an investigation of music to a classification of peoples. He claimed that hearing the music of a people makes it easy to judge their morals, passions and other dispositions – in short, their character.[3] Second, Fétis saw progress, or the ability to develop progressively over time, as characteristic of the Aryan race. This idea harks back to early race theorists of the 1850s, such as Count Gobineau, who saw the white race as the model for all humanity and history (that is, progress) as the result of other races' contact with the white race.[4]

---

[1] François-Joseph Fétis, 'Preface' (26 August 1868), *Histoire générale de la musique depuis les temps les plus anciens jusqu'à nos jours* (Paris: Firmin Didot, 1869), vol. I, p. i. Before this, Fétis had also published 'Sur un nouveau mode de classification des races humaines d'après leurs systèmes musicaux', *Bulletins de la Société d'Anthropologie* 2/2 (1867), 134.
[2] Fétis, 'Avant-propos', *Histoire générale de la musique*, vol. II, pp. i, ii.
[3] François-Joseph Fétis, *Biographie universelle des musiciens*, cited in Jean-Baptiste Weckerlin, *La Chanson populaire* (Paris: Firmin Didot, 1886), p. 188.
[4] Other music scholars of the period concurred. John Rowbotham began his three-volume study, *A History of Music* (London: Trübner, 1885–7), with the assertion: 'The history of savage races is a history of arrested developments' (p. 1).

Throughout the nineteenth century, these two attitudes toward race – the notion of racial types and evolutionary progress associated with Aryans – deeply inflected understanding of indigenous folk song throughout the world, what in France was called *chansons populaires*. Beginning in the 1860s, Jean-Baptiste Weckerlin among other folklorists distinguished art music, which he understood to be universal, from *chansons populaires*. Like the dialects of language, he saw these as specific to race and suggested there are as many varieties as there are races, tribes or peoples.

Chansons populaires, Weckerlin wrote, express a country's 'type, its special physiognomy, particular rhythms, and other characteristics' because they remained relatively 'stationary', while taking on 'new clothes' over time. They also document 'the memory and the history of races that have sometimes been lost or disappeared'.[5] As such, they could function as ethnic specimens, capable of both reflecting and producing notions of race, identity and nation.

In Weckerlin's three influential volumes of music, *Echos du temps passé* (1853–7), *chansons populaires* from Brittany, Normandy, Gascony and Alsace intersperse with those from Mexico, China, Haiti and India alongside songs by Adam de la Halle, Lully and Rameau. All are presented as shards of the past. The 'Chanson mexicaine' is typical in that the original language is maintained and a certain character and memorable distinction are suggested by a recurring rhythmic pattern (Ex. 10.1). Weckerlin begins with a short prose introduction and explains the song's bolero rhythm by noting the presence of Spanish people in Mexico. Then, perhaps remembering the five languages still spoken in France, he acknowledges twenty languages spoken in Mexico, several with distinct grammar and vocabularies. The monophonic song follows above his version for piano and voice. Weckerlin uses two tactics to highlight the original melody – a static accompaniment, alternating octave eighth notes in the left hand and a recurring triplet arpeggio in the right hand, and a piano part that does not double the voice nor offer any competing melodic contours. However, he does make some changes. To support interim harmonic cadences, he alters the end of the internal lines from a third to a falling fifth and ignores upbeat accents that upset the metric equilibrium. The inclusion of a 'Chanson indienne' that Félicien David incorporated in his *Christophe Colombe* and the reappearance of such melodies in Weckerlin's subsequent book on the *Chanson populaire* (1886) – notably those used in *Le Désert* or *Carmen* – suggest that his interest in this music is as emblems of race that composers could adapt and use as signs to exotic cultures.

After 1870 the issues raised by this 'Chanson mexicaine' – the notion of a racial stereotype in music and the argument against race and language alone as the marker of nation – became particularly important. Alsace, Weckerlin's

---

[5] Weckerlin, *Chanson populaire*, pp. 3, 188.

Example 10.1: 'Chanson mexicaine' from J. B. Weckerlin, *Echos du temps passé*

home, was taken as bounty in the Franco-Prussian war and claimed as German because its people spoke mostly the German language. However, Fustel de Coulanges pointed out, 'race is history, the past' and 'language is the remains and the sign of a distant past'; what is 'living' are 'desires, ideas, interests and feelings'. In 1882 Ernest Renan asserted similarly that a nation is 'a common will in the present ... a solidarity made up of the feeling of sacrifices that one has made and that one is willing to make again ... in spite of diversity in race and language'.[6] The challenge after France became a Republic in 1870 was to understand the French as one people, yet speaking many languages, and to construct an identity based on accommodating differences, that is, without opposing the powerful and the powerless.

The *chansons populaires* made an important contribution to this project. They provided a context for discovering similarities within the country as well as rationalising or dismissing differences. Inspired by the Germans and the English, the French had been collecting *chansons populaires* in their own provinces since the 1830s and beginning in 1854, under decree from Napoleon III, as part of building political support and social harmony in the provinces. In the 1860s republicans such as Weckerlin, in the minority during the Second Empire, looked to 'popular' (i.e. folk) poetry and music as 'the treasure-chest' of the common people around the world, a way to understand their legends and their history.[7] For them, *populaire* referred to a utopian sense of the lower classes developed during the Revolution and an association with what was meaningful and authentic in culture, what persevered beyond politics, not as during the Revolution when popular songs often concerned social critique or resistance.[8] Republicans hoped to use this repertoire as 'a rallying cry' to build support for national unity. By contrast, those nostalgic for the *ancien régime* or Empire saw the genre as a way to shift attention from the urban working class to the peasants who, like landed aristocrats, tended to be conservative and had traditionally supported monarchy. After 1879 when republicans took control of the government, this group was concerned with reviving the status of the provinces to diffuse the power of republican-controlled Paris. In the 1880s and 1890s – my focus in this chapter – racial theories were brought in to support both the utopian ideals of the republicans and the desire for distinction and difference among descendants of the *ancien régime*. In this context, the *chansons populaires* collected in France enabled the French not

---

[6] The Coulanges and Renan excerpts are reproduced in Raoul Girardet, *Le Nationalisme français* (Paris: Armand Colin, 1966), pp. 62–9.

[7] Antonin Proust, *Chants populaires de la Grèce moderne* (Paris: Niort, 1866), p. v. This volume of prose poems, some dating to the fifteenth century, contains historical songs, songs from the war of independence, and legends. Beginning in 1867, the republican historian Henri Martin, a disciple of Michelet, published seven volumes of his *Histoire de la France populaire*.

[8] *Populaire* also referred to the need in a democracy to assimilate these classes through education in order to produce informed citizens who would support the political order. In the nineteenth century, it meant not so much what was produced by the lower classes, as what was given them for their consumption to bring their ideals into conformity with those of their leaders. For additional discussion, see my 'Material Culture and Postmodern Positivism: Rethinking the "Popular" in late Nineteenth-Century French Music', in Roberta Marvin, Michael Marissen and Stephen Crist (eds.), *Historical Musicology: Sources, Methods, Interpretations* (Rochester, NY: University of Rochester Press, 2004), pp. 356–87.

only to reflect on their own racial diversity and racial origins, but also to argue for mutually exclusive political agendas.[9]

RENDERING FRANCE AUDIBLE

The first step in understanding French heterogeneity was to collect examples of it, to render France *audible* in all its rich diversity and particularity. Both monogenists, who believed that all races descended from one, and polygenists who believed in a separate origin for each human race, agreed on the importance of collecting and classifying *chansons populaires*.[10] Like anthropological photographs, transcriptions objectified the collector's observations for future study, allowing for not only categorisation, an understanding of the Other as a function of pre-existent categories, but also comparison. Because of the oral tradition, both monogenists and polygenists were convinced that this music communicated unmediated truths about the past. No one seemed particularly bothered by the authority imposed on them by modern, written notation, or by the addition of piano accompaniment. Neither were they troubled by the ahistorical nature of the collections – with no consideration of the religious wars, revolution and imperial expansion affecting France over time that may have influenced this music – nor by the claims to be unveiling the racial unconscious. As with exotic products from the colonies, the point was to capture this music and make it available for new uses.

The collecting proceeded by region. Few who took to the fields were professional musicians – in 1864 Weckerlin published *chansons populaires* from the Alps and in 1883 some from Alsace. Most were literary scholars and amateurs – doctors, clerics, and anyone motivated by an interest in history and local pride. Each song thereafter became associated with the province where it was found, and assumed to convey information about the intellectual and moral life, or '*moeurs*', of the province's inhabitants. In 1885, modelling themselves on the English Folklore Society, the Société des traditions populaires was formed to promote the genre. Among its members were Ernest Renan, the poet Frédéric Mistral, Prince Roland Bonaparte and the medievalist Gaston Paris from the Collège de France. With the advent of two specialised journals, *Mélusine* (1877, 1884–1900) and the society's *La Revue des traditions populaires* (1886–1919), edited by Paris, attention turned to analysing this repertoire. While some looked to it

---

[9] For a study of the genre before 1870, see Jane Fulcher, 'The Popular Chanson of the Second Empire: "Music of the Peasants" in France', *Acta Musicologica* 52 (1980), 27–37. For how the genre served as a malleable symbol for various groups in French society up to the First World War, see my 'The Chanson Populaire as Malleable Symbol in Turn-of-the-Century France', in Yosihiko Tokumaru et al. (eds.), *Tradition and Its Future in Music* (Tokyo: Mita Press, 1991), pp. 203–10.

[10] Among French monogenists were Jean-Baptiste-Pierre-Antoine de Monet de Lamarck, Jean-Louis Armand de Quatrefages and Isidore Geoffroy Saint-Hilaire, and among the French polygenists, Georges Cuvier, Paul Broca, André Sanson, Jean-C.-M.-F.-J. Boudin, and Gustave Le Bon.

for information about the life of the past or the 'soul' of the peasant, others found in its texts legends and myths that were common throughout the world. Most issues of *La Revue* included multiple versions of some story, such as the Medea legend recounted in Laos as well as Greece or an Iroquois fable reminiscent of certain Hindu, Greek and German tales. Such resemblances supported the monogenist project of using culture to suggest similarities among different peoples and assert universals.

The Société des traditions populaires was also interested in the music. For the first ten years their journal included vocal scores. While it had been fashionable to dismiss the aesthetic value of such music, these intellectuals saw it as capable of opening a world of 'unprecedented sensations' and inspiring a 'second youth' in contemporary poetry and music.[11] Along with lectures by musical folklorists, the society sponsored concerts, a 'musical geography'. In 1885, they presented two at the historical society, the Cercle Saint-Simon, introduced by Gaston Paris. In the first, they heard *chansons populaires* from throughout Europe, in the second, those from the French provinces (Figure 10.1). The programme, noting the source of each song and the collector's name, exemplifies both how collective the project of assembling these sources was and how the texts and the music, from Brittany to the Alps, became signs of regional identity. By including songs from the Flemish and Basque regions as well as Alsace, this programme also shows how large they understood the country to be, with Southern Flanders extending into France's 'Nord', the northern Basque country into the south-west, and Alsace and its people, illegitimately appropriated by Germany, still part of the French nation.

When it came to understanding variants in the genre, monogenists, especially monogenist republicans, brought a distinct perspective to interpreting transformation within the genre as well as the music's meaning and value. Like Darwin, they saw variation within the human race as critical to the idea of evolution. They had faith in organisms' capacity for structural and functional adaptation and the environment's capacity to influence people as well as plants and animals. The French had a name for the method, whereby using the principles of science, humans could exploit the forces of nature to assist plants and animals to adapt to new circumstances. They called it acclimatisation. To acclimatise an individual or race of whatever species, as Isidore Geoffroy Saint-Hilaire explained it, meant to remove it from its place of origin and imprint on its organisation modifications that rendered it able to exist and perpetuate its species under these new conditions.[12] The French first began to experiment with trying to

---

[11] Gabriel Vicaire, 'Nos idées sur le traditionnisme', *La Revue des traditions populaires* 7 (25 July 1886), 189–90.

[12] Isidore Geoffroy Saint-Hilaire, *Acclimatation et domestication des animaux utiles* (Paris: Librairie agricole de la Maison rustique, 1861).

Figure 10.1: Programme of the Cercle Saint-Simon, 3 June 1885

acclimatise species foreign to France in 1848. Declaring that only half the globe had been developed for useful exploitation, in 1855 Saint-Hilaire created a zoo (distinct from the Jardin des plantes) that specialised in acclimatisation as well as the creation of racial hybrids: the Jardin zoologique d'acclimatation.

When it applied to people, acclimatisation, or the science of colonisation, made possible assimilation. Both were crucial to those promoting French imperialism. For this reason, many republicans were also monogenists. Republicans advocated foreign expansion not only to assure jobs at home, but also to provide an alternative power base and claims to grandeur strong enough to replace those of aristocratic monarchies. They saw France as the new Rome, the product of assimilating ancient Greek and Roman traditions through the Gauls and German traditions through the Franks. In his *Opuscules sur la chanson populaire* (1874), Weckerlin supported this perspective, pointing to the sun festivals of ancient Greece and the year-end festivals of the Druids as predecessors of popular festivals in the French provinces. Weckerlin also presented variants of songs such as 'Jean de

Nivelle' throughout the country in order to propose a notion of the nation as coherent despite internal differences of language.[13]

Other republican scholars working at the Paris Conservatoire besides Weckerlin, their librarian – his assistant Julian Tiersot and the music historian Louis-Albert Bourgault-Ducoudray – also adopted evolutionist, assimilationist perspectives when attempting to understand diversity within the French population. Bourgault-Ducoudray's understanding of *chansons populaires* came from having collected them in Greece and Asia Minor on two visits in 1874 and 1875, the second funded by the French government, and in his native Brittany for two months in summer 1881. Attempting to 'capture the authenticity', he explicitly sought to 'photograph what he heard'.[14] This meant not forcing the music into the conventions of western tradition, such as changing a melody to adapt to a harmony as Weckerlin had done in his 'Chanson mexicaine'. It also led him to notate not only the music and Greek lyrics of the songs, but also the names of singers and places. Those by Mme Laffon in Smyrna seemed to him particularly authentic because she had an excellent memory and was born in Cyprus, an island visited by fishermen from all the Greek provinces. Still, when Bourgault-Ducoudray performed these songs, he dropped the singers' names and melodies appeared as authorless and placeless, as if to reinforce the collective nature of their composition.

Unlike Weckerlin, Bourgault-Ducoudray's interest was not in regional or national identity. It was the musical modes and the irregular rhythms of the songs. He recognised the modes from plainchant. Yet, referring to the human mummies from the distant past being discovered and dissected in Egypt, he called those in chant musical 'mummies' compared to the 'living melodies of the Orient' with their lively rhythms.[15] In the accompaniment to his transcriptions, he based the harmony – what he called the 'conquest of the modern races' – on the melody's mode and imitated its rhythms and changing metres. He also added performance instructions, extensive accompaniments and sometimes interludes that made them like art songs, easily accessible to Western audiences. His goal was to show that modes were compatible with modern music and could be acclimatised in France, explored and incorporated for the sake of French musical progress. He also performed this music often and in a wide variety of contexts, whether for his colleagues at the Société des traditions populaires or in the chamber music series 'La Trompette', where the songs occasionally functioned as a kind of transitional material between serious music and light

---

[13] Jean-Baptiste Weckerlin, *Opuscules sur la chanson populaire et sur la musique* (Paris: J. Baur, 1874).
[14] Cameras had long provided Europeans with the fruits of explorers' adventures. The phonograph, still in its infancy, was not yet used in fieldwork.
[15] The first intact burial tomb of an Egyptian king was discovered in 1827. In 1881 a French archaeologist discovered over fifty mummies of Egyptian royalty. Louis-Albert Bourgault-Ducoudray, *Trente mélodies populaires de Grèce et d'Orient* (Paris: Lemoine, 1876), p. 7.

repertoire. After his lecture on the Greek repertoire at the 1878 Universal Exhibition, he was made professor of music history at the Conservatoire.

EXCAVATING ARYAN MUSIC

Whereas in his Greek volume, Bourgault-Ducoudray was not troubled by whether the melodies he notated were old or not because he believed they were still 'constructed according to the principles of the ancient scales', in collecting *chansons populaires* in Brittany, he came upon the problem of hearing 'twenty versions of the same air before finding the good one'. This admission is important, for it underlines both Bourgault-Ducoudray's search for origins and a paradox at the heart of his beliefs. If, as he explains in his preface, 'In all men of the same race, there is a common heritage of feelings that are transmitted and perpetuated without being modified', then the 'spontaneous and instinctive' music expressing them should not have changed. However, in Brittany where the melody of *chansons populaires* is tightly linked to the poetry, he encountered two languages: the 'gallot', a dialect influenced by French, and 'Breton'. Not neutral about these differences nor receptive to the kind of assimilation reflected in the gallot, he criticised it for not having 'the character of a pure race' and the melodies using it for being 'half-blood'. In sounding more 'strange' with an 'exotic perfume', he found in Breton the 'character of a race' and its melodies 'pure-blood'. Searching for racial purity put him in sympathy with polygenists who were seeking to understand the origins and distinction of each race.

In the 'Breton' melodies, 'more original and colourful', Bourgault-Ducoudray found echoes of the ancient Greek modes. Refuting the common assumption that most of these were in minor mode, he points out eight diatonic modes. In the north where the 'race is more serious and more reflective', there are songs in hypodorian, associated with the 'serenity, virility and nobility' of Apollo. In the Cornouailles, where the population is 'nervous and passionate', hypophrygian, the mode of Bacchus, dominates. He also found metres used rarely in the West, such as those with five and seven beats. Comparing the fruits of his research with *chansons populaires* in Russia, Ireland, Scotland and elsewhere leads him to a sweeping conclusion. Because of the presence of 'identical characteristics in the primitive music of all Indo-European peoples', he associates them with the Aryan race and dates their origin back to the time when the Aryan race was in its infancy, before 'all the branches of this race' dispersed. Indo-European *chansons populaires* are an 'Aryan music', he asserts, that confirms the hypothesis of shared origins of the Aryan peoples.[16] From this

---

[16] Bourgault-Ducoudray offers an analogously racial hypothesis about the chromatic oriental scale as belonging to Arabs and people whom they've dominated. He found it in *musique populaire*

perspective, Greece was merely 'a smarter and better-situated nation' that knew how to exploit the common heritage, not the inventor of the modes. In an 1884 lecture to an Alpine club, Bourgault-Ducoudray supports this theory in his discussion of *chansons populaires* in the mountainous areas of Europe. There he again found melodies 'not constructed in the system of our modern music, but in that of ancient Greek music and plainchant that comes from it'. Since the mountains have served as 'a refuge for "primitive races"' and were long isolated from the rest of Europe, its 'primitive' music could not have been influenced by the Greeks. In this sense, 'primitive' means that its characteristics 'go back to the oldest antiquity' and is synonymous with racial origins.[17]

This association with the Aryan race, he argues, gives the French a kind of birthright to return to the Greek modes and rhythms as a source of renewal. Believing that the major and minor modes can lead to no further musical progress, Bourgault-Ducoudray wanted to encourage use of the Greek modes as matrices for exploring 'new harmonic formulas'. Like Glinka, he hoped they would tap into this source of Aryan music to generate new music, not unlike the plant and animal hybrids produced at the zoo.[18] With its two modes, hypolydian and chromatic, within the same piece, the tenth of the Greek songs must have been particularly provocative. In 1880, he congratulated his Conservatoire colleague Théodore Dubois for his 'very happy' use of the Greek modes in his song, 'La Chanson lesbienne'.[19]

MUSICAL ACCLIMATISATION

Like Saint-Hilaire, who travelled in the provinces to build the acclimatisation movement and there developed first-hand information about provincial resources, Tiersot collected and classified *chansons populaires* from *all* the French provinces. Romain Rolland called him 'the indefatigable botanist of the *chansons populaires*'.[20] Tiersot's goals were ambitious. In his *Histoire de la chanson populaire en France*, he not only collected and categorised, but also analysed this repertoire. As for other contributors to *La Revue des traditions populaires*, his method was to seek analogies more

---

throughout Turkey, southern Russia, and southern Spain but 'never in countries where the Indo-European element has existed without mixture'. The first of his *Trente Mélodies populaires de Basse-Bretagne* (Paris: Lemoine, 1885) uses this scale. See p. 6, n. 1.

[17] Bourgault-Ducoudray, 'La Musique primitive conservée par les montagnes', *Annuaire du Club alpin français* (1884), 4–5, 9.

[18] The citations of Bourgault-Ducoudray in these paragraphs come from the introduction to his *Trente Mélodies populaires de Basse-Bretagne*, pp. 6, 9, 11–16. His attention was drawn to this repertoire by finding the hypodorian mode in Hersart de la Villemarqué, *Barzaz-Breiz, Chants populaires de la Bretagne*, 2 vols. (Paris: Charpentier, 1839), reissued in 1845 and 1867. In 1882 a local Breton church organist, Charles Collins, had also published his own collection, *Chants de la Bretagne*.

[19] L.-A. Bourgault-Ducoudray 80 (11 June 1880), Bibliothèque nationale, Musique, Paris.

[20] Romain Rolland, *Mémoires et fragments du journal* (Paris: Albin Michel, 1956), p. 63.

than differences among the variants. His conclusions were significant. He understood these songs as reflective of the interests and style of no one class – 'only the chronicles through which the people conserve their memory of past times' – and as moving from one social class to the next, generally starting out in intellectual circles and gradually taken over by the lower strata. He also claimed that this music contains the seed of a musical universal: '[I]n whatever the tonality at hand, antique, modern, French or Chinese, all agree on one fundamental principle: the existence of a tonic and dominant in each scale'. Except in the Basque country, he found 'the sum total of the *chansons populaires* identical from one end of the country to the other'.[21] These results won Tiersot the Prix Bordin, established by the Institut de France in 1885 for the best comprehensive study of the genre in France. The notion of a shared tradition of song also intrigued republicans who were seeking ways to make the French feel unified as a nation and fed the government's desire for a reification and codification of the French past. This led them to increase their sponsorship of travel grants [*missions*] to encourage the collection of *chansons populaires* at home and abroad.

Beginning with his first volume in 1888, Tiersot also published songs from the various French provinces, some of them in local dialects.[22] These indicate the provincial source of the version without commenting on whether Tiersot thought it the original version; singers' names appear only in the preface. Like Bourgault-Ducoudray, Tiersot sought to understand better the origins of French music, what he called 'the charming remaining debris of the primitive art of our race'. He pursued this not in a study of modes, but of melodic types. In some ways, this was a musical version of contemporary work on *la poésie populaire* from the middle ages, for recurring initial melodic patterns in some ways resembled the opening formulas of oral poetry. However, arguing that their 'essences' are more often independent than bound together, Tiersot chose to analyse this music separately from its poetry. In an 1894 essay, Tiersot called on the mechanism of racial transformation in analysing the effects of regional differences on musical production, explaining song variants as the results of 'musical acclimatisation'. By this he meant that melodies were by nature fluid, malleable, susceptible to adapt to various circumstances (e.g. dialects), as monogenists believed about the human race. With 'the people' transforming a tune, modifying its character and accent as Beethoven or Wagner might in the development of a symphony or music drama, the same melodic type could change in allure and accent from one province to

---

[21] Julien Tiersot, *Histoire de la chanson populaire en France* (Paris: Plon, Nourrit et Cie, 1889), pp. v, vi, 1, 287, 356–9. This work gave him a perspective on the exotic music he collected at the 1889 Paris Exhibition and published as *Musiques pittoresques* (Paris: Fischbacher, 1889).
[22] These volumes include the *chansons populaires* performed for the Société des traditions populaires on 3 June 1885.

another even as it conserved some essential elements, such as the opening notes.²³ In this way he explained a song originating in Auvergne that later became known as a Breton song.

As art-song examples of 'musical acclimatisation', Tiersot also performed *chansons populaires* frequently in Parisian concert halls. To facilitate this he 'dressed them with the clothes of harmony' so that in 'transporting them into a context so different from their natural context' they would not be too '*dépaysé* [like fish out of water]' and could be admitted 'into a world that would not accept them in their bare simplicity'.²⁴ Because he added only accompaniments, he did not call his work a 'Suite on *chansons populaires*' or a 'Fantasy on *chansons populaires*'. Still, acknowledging his harmonising work and their resemblance to the texture and style of Tiersot's own art songs, the composer-sponsored Société nationale and the Concerts Colonne presented them as premieres of new music under Tiersot's name. Moreover, on 22 February 1900, instead of including them in the first half with other '*musique ancienne*' – Mozart, Handel, and Borghi – Colonne placed them on the second half, with '*musique moderne*', preceding Schumann, Liszt, Saint-Saëns, Chopin and Enesco. Such contexts raised the status of *chansons populaires* to art.

As the production of hybrids at the zoo increased through the 1880s, advocates increasingly recognised that the project of acclimatisation had problems. De Quatrefages noted that in acclimatising, a race can degenerate, that is, lose or modify the character appreciated most in it. Acclimatisation represents the victory of milieu over an organism that bends to its requirements, but this never takes place without a more or less violent struggle that necessarily leads to loss for both individuals and generations.²⁵ Emile Guimet admitted that it was almost too late to collect *chansons populaires* since there were few regions where the influence of urban popular music from Paris was not yet felt.²⁶ There were also those who were opposed to the republican project of concentrating on similarities throughout the country and wished to protect regional languages and dialects.

RACIAL PURITY

Anti-republican polygenists brought different racial agendas to their understanding of *chansons populaires*. Their theories returned to vogue in the 1890s when colonial efforts at assimilating the Indochinese were failing

---

[23] Julien Tiersot, *Les Types mélodiques dans la chanson populaire française* (Paris: Sagot, 1894); reprinted from *La Revue des traditions populaires*, 9, 29–30.
[24] Julien Tiersot, *Mélodies populaires des provinces de France*, vol. I (Paris: Heugel, 1888), p. 1; and vol. IV (1911), p. 3.
[25] De Quatrefages, 'Acclimatation des animaux et des plantes', *Le magasin pittoresque* (1883), 373–5.
[26] Emile Guimet, *Chants populaires du Lyonnais; Rapport sur le concours pour le prix Christin et de Ruolz* (Lyon: Association typographique, 1882; reprinted from the Mémoires de l'Académie des Sciences, Belles-lettres et Arts de Lyon, vol. XXII), p. 32.

and when anarchist attacks, the Dreyfus affair, and an increasing attraction to Nordic cultures and Wagner threw into question French identity. If, as the polygenists believed, the nature of a people, its soul, is fixed, not alterable by education or environment as Gustave Le Bon argued in his *Les Lois psychologiques de l'évolution* (1894), then what constituted the essence of French identity? In music, this meant seeking the 'purest version' of a song. Acknowledging that environment had influenced the differences between the various people of France – those of Brittany, Normandy, Provence, Auvergne, etc. – Le Bon pointed to the ancient races as those responsible for racial identity, those for whom milieu had negligible influence. Looking to the distant past, polygenists were particularly interested in what resisted invasion and assimilation by the Romans and the Franks, that is, France's Celtic elements. As Edouard Schuré put it in an essay on the legends of Brittany and the Celtic genius, 'The Celtic soul is the deep, interior soul of France.'[27] Bourgault-Ducoudray had argued for certain old and immutable qualities in the *chansons populaires* of Brittany and in his publication was careful to notate the Breton language and vocal timbre. However, his primary purpose was to present these songs as linked to the Greek modes and as Aryan. Schuré and others saw Bretons as Celts and the Celtic tradition as informing the French character.[28] Like the blood of the race, responsible for its vitality, Celtic aspects in music would allow them to locate racial persistence within France.

The composer Vincent d'Indy was among those who looked to the Celts to articulate French identity. His opera *Fervaal*, begun in 1886, is set in an ancient forest of the Cévennes as the country is invaded by barbarians. Steven Huebner finds Celtism central to the meaning of this opera: 'race, nationalism, and Christian faith combine in an allegory about the founding of France out of the Celtic spirit'.[29] When he engaged in collecting *chansons populaires*, however, d'Indy went to his ancestors' birthplace near France's oldest mountains. Because he considered the genre the result of 'impersonal work' and 'time', his sources were not always peasants; the only singer he acknowledged was a baroness. D'Indy too came upon numerous versions of the same songs and, like Tiersot, examining their initial phrases and refrains, catalogued them according to 'type'. He also assumed that while their form might be influenced by various milieux and usages, it was possible to ascertain 'the most primitive' version. As a composer, d'Indy was drawn only to 'the most musically interesting', some of which provided clues to the origins of musical form. The *bourées* intrigued him particularly. He saw the rondo form of the

---

[27] This essay was originally published in *La Revue des deux mondes* (1891) and later appeared as part 4 of *Les Grandes légendes de France*. Cited in Steven Huebner, *French Opera at the Fin de Siècle: Wagnerism, Nationalism, and Style* (Oxford University Press, 1999), p. 324. See also Schuré, *Les Chants de la montagne* (1876).
[28] Ibid. See also Henri Martin, *Etudes d'archéologie celtique* (Paris: Didier, 1872).
[29] Huebner, *French Opera*, p. 326.

fourth one as a predecessor to the cyclicity of the 'eminently French' instrumental suite as well as the sonata and symphony after Beethoven.[30] He used two of these *bourées* in his *Fantaisie sur des thèmes populaires françaises* (1888), and textless melodies he heard sung in the distance in his *Symphonie sur un chant montagnard français* (1886) and Act II of *Fervaal*.

For anti-republican polygenists the subtext of this discourse may also have been political. Many were nostalgic for the *ancien régime*. When Vincent d'Indy and Maurice Denis, for example, elevate the 'humble' and the 'primitive', they wished not just to hail the French qualities of clarity and simplicity or the purported access provided by this music to races from the distant past. The primitive was also that which predated the Republic and its notions of French civilisation as a product of assimilation. It harkened back to pre-modern times. They idiolised not ancient Greece, but the middle ages, the Catholic Church, and the music of Palestrina (considered the last medieval composer and often referred to as primitive). Whereas Bourgault-Ducoudray saw the modal qualities of these songs as remnants of Greek modes, d'Indy interpreted them as having religious origins and offering a way to reconnect with religious faith. After 1900, anti-republican provincials turned to the *chansons populaires* as a way to resist invasion by a more contemporary enemy, the Parisian romance, and helped turn the genre into a symbol of regional identity.

ANALYSING *LA PERNETTE*

An important example of these interpretive differences can be seen in these musicians' analyses of the song, *La Pernette*, one of the country's most enduring 'melodic types'.[31] It concerns a woman who preferred her Pierre to a prince or baron and who went to the grave with her lover for defying her mother's wishes. In his *Chanson populaire* (1886) – probably written for the same 1885 competition as Tiersot's *Histoire de la chanson populaire* – Weckerlin mentions six versions of this song he found from Brittany to the Alps, comparing them to French dialects as he might have in the 1860s. He is not surprised that, 'in its wanderings over the centuries, a *chanson populaire* acclimatises in the different provinces of a country and, with a few transformations, settles in'. However, from a republican and monogenist perspective reminding readers that racial diversity is not an impediment to national identity, he explains, 'Even if certain dialects of our provinces diverge from French, there is at the root of these dialects, except for the Breton language, a spirit of nationality that connects and harmonises them.'[32]

---

[30] Vincent d'Indy, *Chansons populaires du Vivarais* (Paris: Durand, 1900), p. 153.
[31] Tiersot, *Les Types mélodiques*, p. 9.
[32] Weckerlin, *Chanson populaire*, pp. 184–5. The song was also included in his *Chansons populaires des provinces de France* (Paris: Bourdilliat, 1860) and Damase Arbaud, *Chants populaires de la Provence* (Aix: Makaire, 1862–4).

In his *Mélodies populaires des provinces de la France* (1888), Tiersot reproduces a *Pernette* from Franche-Comté, collected by a deputy from the region. He also acknowledges finding it throughout the east and south of the country. This version is interesting because, in spanning an octave, it is implicitly tonal (Ex. 10.2). In the middle of each stanza, which otherwise remains largely within the fifth, E–B, the song moves abruptly to C# and then D on 'tra-la-la'. In his accompaniment Tiersot then adds a D# to prepare a V–I cadence in E minor just before the vocal line reaches up to E¹. Elsewhere too his accompaniment includes the harmonic colours of a contemporary sensibility. Like many published by Tiersot, it is clearly a hybrid conceived for contemporary performance. His accompaniment lightly supports the vocal line, often doubling it, but the work also includes an eleven-bar piano prelude that begins in 2/4 and then shifts to 6/8, introducing the tune as if a musical theme. After the song, he reproduces the nine stanzas for voice alone, yet assumes they will be performed, calling for a different expressive style for each. In his collection of Alpine songs (1903), Tiersot harmonises another *Pernette*, opening with a shorter introduction to the tune's incipit but with almost the same accompaniment.[33] This one, also in 6/8, likewise contains a 'tra-la-la' with a major sixth that functions as a leading tone to the seventh. However, the song never reaches up to the octave and, incorporating this major sixth in the accompaniment, Tiersot creates a modal cadence rather than a tonal one.

Six more *Pernettes* appear in the *Chansons populaires du Vivarais et du Vercors* (1892), collected and transcribed by Vincent d'Indy and annotated by Tiersot. Here Tiersot's assertions go much further than Weckerlin's. He introduces value judgements and suggests origins, calling *La Pernette* the most beautiful of the collection and waxing poetic about its significance. For him it represents 'the force of tradition' that

> imposes itself so imperiously on the people's spirit that, despite any disdain the inhabitants of a region might feel toward this old thing, they could never forget it completely. Like the old melody in Wagner's drama, *die alte Weise*, that resonates in the ears of a wounded *Tristan* . . . it alone survives to teach successive generations what the ancestors sang.

Because the textual verses of so many versions are lost, Tiersot suggests that the melody, more than the poetry, is responsible for being remembered.[34] Explaining the numerous variants of this song as a product of the people's spirit that is 'as capricious and changeable as *l'esprit mondain*', Tiersot isolates something he calls '*le vrai chant*'. This, he asserts, could not

---

[33] Julien Tiersot, *Chansons populaires recueillies dans les Alpes françaises* (Grenoble: Falque et Perrin, 1903).

[34] In his *Chants populaires du Lyonnais*, p. 32, Guimet agrees. This is an important assertion, for the discipline of provincial ethnography was begun and continued to be dominated by literary scholars who collected and studied *la poésie populaire*.

Example 10.2: 'La Pernette, version de la Franche Comté', from Julien Tiersot, *Mélodies populaires des provinces de France* (1888)

Example 10.2: (cont.)

disappear. It is in the blood of the race. Numerous generations 'will keep on repeating it'.

Like the literary scholar George Doncieux in his book on *La Pernette* (1891), Tiersot also finds it to be the oldest in this collection, one version 'belonging almost exclusively' to France's mountainous centre with its 'more primitive and less civilised character'. The song's language is not yet entirely French, and elsewhere it always appears in other forms, especially its ending and use of wide intervals. This leads him to connect racial origins to place, a primitive form of music to primitive peoples. Throughout this volume, Tiersot refers to songs from the mountains as having 'pure inflexions', their notes prolonged by an echo.[35] It is significant, therefore, that the same year d'Indy began contemplating a national French music, he incorporated into his *Symphonie* a *chanson populaire* from these mountains. Its 'primitive simplicity' serves as the basis for both thematic transformation and unity, a kind of noble savage giving birth to civilisation.[36]

In 1900, when d'Indy published his second collection from this region, this time funded by a regional grant, he wrote his own annotations and included texts in their original dialects as well as in French translations. As for Tiersot, his accompaniments reflect his own aesthetic inclinations, leading him to complicate the chordal texture with short contrapuntal lines. His purpose was not only to reiterate the collective nature of this genre and the repository of the past in it, but also to point to its association with regional identity – to 'unveil the Vivaraise soul' – and to look for the origin of 'musical types' in the oldest *chansons populaires*. Like Tiersot, he saw *La Pernette* as 'one of the rare songs that incontestably originate in our mountains' and indeed its verses and modal character resemble more the one Tiersot collected in the Alps than those he found elsewhere.

D'Indy devotes three pages to analysing two versions he collected in the Ardèche. He argues that one was the 'primitive' form: it remained within the interval of a fifth except for a cadential move down a major second below the tonic. Many peasants in the Ardèche knew it and this was the only place where it could still be found. The other he considers an ornamented, more musically developed version. The second line of each verse is a refrain, 'tra-la-la', rising the same major sixth as in Tiersot's versions (Ex. 10.3). D'Indy construes this as added and rendering this version not as 'pure' as the 'primitive' one. He compares the refrain to the melismas in liturgical monody, presumably added over time to pre-existing syllabic chant. In direct confrontation with his anticlerical

---

[35] Vincent d'Indy and Julien Tiersot, *Chansons populaires du Vivarais et du Vercors* (Paris: Heugel, 1892), pp. 2, 29, 32, 39.
[36] Julien Tiersot, 'Une Symphonie sur un thème populaire', *Revue des traditions populaires* (25 April 1887), 181.

	TRADUCTION
1. La Pernèto se lèvo 　Tra la, la la, la la, la la la; 　La Pernèto se lèvo 　Trèis ouras d'avan dzou.　(ter)	1. La Pernette se lève 　Tra la, la la, la la, la la la 　La Pernette se lève 　Trois heur's avant le jour. (ter)
2. Fiälan sa coulougnèto 　　Tra la, etc. 　Fiälan sa coulougnèto 　Amaï soun pèti tou.　(ter)	2. Prenant sa quenouillette 　　Tra la, etc. 　Prenant sa quenouillette 　Avec son petit tour.　(ter)
3. Tçasqué tour que n'en viro, 　　Tra la, etc. 　Tçasqué tour que n'en viro, 　Faï un sospir d'amou.　(ter)	3. A chaque tour qui vire, 　　Tra la, etc. 　A chaque tour qui vire, 　Fait un soupir d'amour. (ter)
4. Sa mèiro li vèn diré: 　　Tra la, etc. 　Sa mèiro li vèn diré: 　—Pernèto, qu'avès vous? (ter)	4. Sa mère lui vient dire: 　　Tra la, etc. 　Sa mère lui vient dire: 　—Pernette, qu'avez-vous? (ter)

Example 10.3: 'La Pernette, version primitive and version ornée', from Vincent d'Indy, *Chansons populaires du Vivarais* (1892)

Example 10.4: 'La Pernette, version ornée' under selections of an Alleluia verse from Ascension Sunday and the Bach chorale, *Jesus Christus unser Heiland*

republican colleagues, d'Indy was seeking to demonstrate that the oldest *chansons populaires*, such as *La Pernette*, have their origins in religious music. To prove his point, he reproduces the ornamented version of *La Pernette* under various sections of a Bach chorale, *Jesus Christus unser Heiland*, then the 'primitive' version under the Bach chorale and an Alleluia verse from Ascension Sunday, reproduced in a Solesmes Gradual (Ex. 10.4). The similar manner in which the three songs open with an ascending fifth and then fill in the interval leads d'Indy to conclude that *La Pernette*, like the Bach chorale, comes from Gregorian chant. Whereas Weckerlin believed that 'it will never be possible to reconstitute an ancient Gaulois song with a hymn' because the oldest songs had adapted and changed significantly with 'the successive invasion of the tonalities of plainchant', d'Indy's search for the origins of French music led to the church, exactly what he wanted.[37]

A single *chanson populaire* thus could support multiple, distinct, pre-existing agendas. As with any other kind of fieldwork, it was not just a remnant of the distant past, but also the product of historically and politically situated observers. Ideally the genre offered a context for articulating some kind of shared political identity, even if in practice this was complicated by conflicting race theories and the political positions supporting them. Whether their perspective was monogenist and they sought to understand what humans shared across regional and even national boundaries, or polygenist and they focused on the immutable racial qualities of the French and their origins, many looked to music for its connection to this past and wished to use it to inspire a sense of French identity. Just as they hoped that racial unity or racial diversity would help regenerate French society as a healthy secular Republic or lead to a decentralised revival of the provinces with ties to the church, both factions hoped that the modal variety and freer rhythms of *chansons populaires*, like

---

[37] D'Indy, *Chansons populaires du Vivarais*, pp. 1, 15–19; Weckerlin, *Chanson populaire*, p. 55.

a blood infusion, would help regenerate French music. They eventually promoted their perspectives not only with publications, but also with educational projects. With his *chansons populaires* for elementary school children (1897–1902), Tiersot aimed to induce shared experiences among the country's children, promote the French language in all regions, and help construct a shared identity for the nation. By contrast, at the Schola Cantorum, a private conservatoire after 1900, d'Indy's colleague Charles Bordes (who collected *chansons populaires* in the Basque country) taught the genre as a way to inspire love of nature, religious music and regional traditions. It is important, therefore, to understand that music in late nineteenth-century France was used to reflect not just on racialised Others, but also on the racialised Self and that this was as complex as the theories underpinning the discourse. At home or within Europe, as this study suggests, the 'primitive' was not disparaged but embraced, and the *chansons populaires* idealised to the extent that they supported racial paradigms.

The question of reconciling the French nation with its population and their many languages has never been resolved. In 1997 the Conseil de l'Europe in Strasbourg put forth a call to take measures to preserve the various languages of France that risk disappearing, such as Breton. However, in 1999 President Chirac refused to sign the document, perhaps fearing the same privilege might be argued for immigrants residing in France. Chirac's response suggests that while monogenist and polygenist theories were both used to support nation-building in the nineteenth century, they grew increasingly problematic by the late twentieth century. The possibility of assimilating people from outside the west raised the fear that their acclimatisation might carry more risks than benefits, that, as de Quatrefages predicted, it might lead to loss of identity rather than progress. France is still a nation of many races and many languages, but without the perspective of imperial expansion, race now seems a destabilising force more than a potentially unifying one, and music too mobile and deracinated to provide the glue a stable national identity would require.

CHAPTER 11

Anti-Semitic discourse in German writing on music, 1900–1933

Erik Levi

Even if one takes some of the major constituents of Nazi ideology at face value, it still seems barely credible that their extremist attitudes could have proved so persuasive to a highly sophisticated and free-voting German population. Yet as many scholars have demonstrated, anti-Semitism was already deeply ingrained into the German psyche well before the advent of the Third Reich. Its influence was so pervasive that in 1918 at a moment of crisis Kurt Weill, a German composer from a proud and strongly Jewish background, was prepared to reiterate stereotypically negative arguments in relation to his own creativity.

The document that exposes this insecurity was a letter written from Berlin to his brother Hans. At the time of writing Weill was a composition student of Engelbert Humperdinck at the Berlin Music Academy. Yet the experience of working under arguably the most distinguished contemporary opera composer after Richard Strauss and Hans Pfitzner proved to be less propitious than he had expected. Humperdinck no longer had the energy to supervise composition lessons, and he soon succumbed to an illness that was to terminate his life one year later. In any case, Weill quickly became disillusioned both by the staunchly conservative outlook of his composition teacher, and by the stifling atmosphere of the Berlin Music Academy. As classes at the Music Academy became less frequent, Weill increasingly turned his attention to politics, then in turmoil with the abdication of the Kaiser. He joined a student commune at the Academy with the intention of joining the fight against the rising tide of anti-Semitism in Germany at that time.

A heady cocktail of disappointment and involvement in the current political turmoil created a serious hiatus in Weill's productivity. He even considered abandoning composition altogether. It was in these depressed circumstances that Weill invoked what appeared to be a deeply ingrained stereotype regarding Jewish creativity. In the letter to Hans he includes the following remarks:

I have already definitely decided to give up this scribbling [*Schreiberei*] altogether and throw myself totally into the conducting business. We Jews are simply not productive and when we are, we have a destructive rather than constructive effect. And if the young movement in music views the Mahler–Schoenberg line as being constructive (as I, alas, do too) then that movement must consist of Jews, or Gentiles with Jewish accents. No Jew could ever write a work like the Moonlight Sonata. The mere idea of pursuing this train of thought is enough to force the pen out of one's hand.[1]

Whilst hardly plunging to a level of Jewish self-deprecation exploited by such figures as Otto Weininger and Karl Kraus, Weill's unguarded remarks are worthy of comment, not least because they invoke a number of familiar tropes about the relationship between Jews and the musical world first aired by Richard Wagner in his 1850 essay 'Das Judentum in der Musik'. One can identify three strands of argument in Weill's letter that broadly replicate those of Wagner: the notion that the Jews' musical gifts seem more suited to the re-creative activities of performance and interpretation than to the creative activity of original composition; the notion that any Jewish influence on composition remains destructive rather than constructive; and the conviction that a Jew was somehow fundamentally incapable of writing music that was essentially Germanic in character.

In view of Weill's pronounced and otherwise consistently anti-Wagnerian outlook, not to mention his much later collaboration with Franz Werfel and Max Reinhardt on the avowedly Zionist *The Eternal Road* (1935), it seems almost implausible that the two composers could ever have occupied any common ground, much less in an area of such great sensitivity as this. At the same time, his comment provides an appropriate impetus with which to explore in greater depth the extent to which Wagner's essay influenced musical opinion in Germany during the first three decades of the twentieth century, particularly in preparing the ground for Nazi formulations regarding the Jewish contribution to music.

Elsewhere in this book Pamela M. Potter challenges the notion posited by such scholars as Jens Malte Fischer that a direct line of thinking can be traced from Wagner's essay to Nazism.[2] Potter argues that there was an uneven development in the application of race to music scholarship from Wagner onwards, and that expressions of anti-Semitism only received widespread currency at moments of extreme nationalist protection. Yet an examination of a selected number of historical studies on music published in book form during this period suggests that an undercurrent of anti-Semitism remained present in populist musical writings throughout this period, even if it was by no means an exclusive thread. Without doubt, the authors of such material – Karl Grunsky, Karl Storck, Rudolf Louis, Walter Niemann, Hans-Joachim Moser, Heinrich Berl and others – were somewhat selective in their interpretation of Wagner's essay, cherry-picking certain ideas whilst overlooking others, in particular the notion of redemption. Yet however ill-digested their

---

[1] Lys Symonette and Kim H. Kowalke (eds.), *Speak Low (When You Speak Love). The Letters of Kurt Weill and Lotte Lenya* (London: Hamish Hamilton, 1996), p. 28.
[2] Jens Malte Fischer, *'Die Nachwirkung', Richard Wagners 'Das Judentum in der Musik'* (Frankfurt am Main: Insel, 2000), pp. 121–33.

reading of Wagner might have been, it is worth pointing out that the majority of books under consideration in this chapter were designed for the general public rather than the academy. Examining such books provides us with a broader cultural picture of the permeation of Wagnerian musico-racial prejudices, not least because a number of the writings enjoyed surprisingly wide dissemination and were reprinted in several editions over a period of many years. As a result of the influential positions held by their respective authors, the trenchant views expressed in these books, though discredited and disputed in academic circles, carried a certain weight of cultural and even intellectual authority, masking their narrow ideological stance. The analysis of an anti-Semitic strain through a sequence of historical surveys of this nature also succeeds in illustrating the manner in which personal opinion and/or ideological agenda managed to merge seamlessly into unchallenged historical truths. The continued presence of such material in the period before the Third Reich helped to facilitate the promulgation of Nazi propaganda with regard to music since the regime was able to tap into ideas that had been already articulated for nearly eighty years.

HISTORIES OF MUSIC PUBLISHED BEFORE THE FIRST WORLD WAR

In many respects, *Musikgeschichte des 19. Jahrhunderts* by Stuttgart-based critic Karl Grunsky set the tone for many of the music-historical surveys to follow it in the first four decades of the twentieth century. First published in 1902, this book was reprinted three times, its final edition appearing in 1924. Although purportedly embracing nineteenth-century music in its entirety, Grunsky's approach is so Germanocentric that only twenty of the 130 pages in its first volume deal with the music of other nations. The book contains no overt traces of anti-Semitism; however some commonplace attempts to marginalise and label Jewish composers as somehow inferior do appear. Grunsky makes sure that his readers are aware that both Mendelssohn and Meyerbeer were sons of rich Jewish bankers, as if to imply that the presumed material advantages they had over their gentile colleagues ought somehow to be brought to bear on appraisals of their creative output. Grunsky relegates Mendelssohn to a position of subsidiary significance in comparison with other contemporaries such as Weber, Schumann and Wagner, all three of whom are accorded extended chapters exclusively devoted to their work as opposed to the few paragraphs allotted to Mendelssohn. Revealing, too, are his brief remarks on Meyerbeer which merely reiterate the antagonistic remarks about the composer that appeared in Wagner's 'Das Judentum':

Meyerbeer was always eager to plunder the riches of Italian, German and French musical styles but without ever achieving a genuine fusion of styles such as one encounters in Mozart... Great musicians and writers such as Schumann, Wagner and Ambros condemned Meyerbeer; their passionate aversion to him was not conditioned by a feeling that he was incompetent, but far more by his unscrupulousness.[3]

In his 1904 *Geschichte der Musik*, critic Karl Storck repeats and even extends Grunsky's arguments regarding Meyerbeer. In a chapter dealing with Parisian opera, he condemns both Meyerbeer and Halévy for pursuing an 'internationalist' style. Such music, Storck claims, lacks sincerity and sounds artificial and contrived, its message remaining far removed from the 'universalism' favoured by masters of pure German origin such as Handel and Mozart.[4] Once again the notion of Meyerbeer's unscrupulousness seems to derive from Wagner's essay, although Storck at least acknowledges the composer's considerable technical skill in handling the vast apparatus of grand opera.

Storck offers a more neutral assessment of Mendelssohn. He reiterates certain leitmotifs that were familiar from critical writing at the turn of the century in challenging the composer's primacy in the overall development of German music. Thus he reproduces the now familiar arguments that Mendelssohn was essentially bedevilled by superficiality and empty virtuosity, that he led an unreal life which never embraced genuine struggle and hardship, and that he manifested an essentially external feeling for folklore.[5] In the latter case, the problem was so serious that even Schumann felt unable to distinguish the national styles contained within his 'Scottish' and 'Italian' symphonies.[6] Whether these negative opinions were determined by a genuine antipathy towards Mendelssohn's music, or by anti-Semitism, is never clear.

In these two books dating from the first years of the twentieth century, Storck's and Grunsky's frequent recourse to the opinions of significant composers of the past – not only Wagner, but also Schumann, as well as the less significant Felix Draeseke – may be read as an attempt to conceal their own racial prejudices. By contrast, the composer, critic and pedagogue Rudolf Louis, author of *Die deutsche Musik der Gegenwart*, first published in Munich in 1909 and reprinted three times before the First World War, is more overt in his attitudes. His book provides a somewhat jaundiced view of contemporary German music; with the exception of Pfitzner and Bruckner, few composers escape his harsh admonishments. But Louis saves some of his sharpest invective for composers of Jewish origin.

In the second chapter, subtitled 'Das musikalische Drama', Louis offers an overview of operatic developments in Germany in the latter part of the nineteenth century, tracing a supposed decline in achievement since the

---

[3] Karl Grunsky, *Musikgeschichte des 19. Jahrhunderts*, 2 vols. (Leipzig: G. J. Göschen, 1902), vol. I, p. 108.
[4] Karl Storck, *Geschichte der Musik*, 4th edition (Stuttgart: Metzler, 1921), pp. 113–14.
[5] Ibid., pp. 151–2.   [6] Ibid., p. 153.

time of Wagner. His opening gambit is to single out two composers, Karl Goldmark and Anton Rubinstein, as exponents of Jewish opportunism. According to Louis, the popular success of Goldmark's opera *Die Königin von Saba* (1875) merely indicated a temperamental and racial affinity with its Old Testament subject-matter on the part of the composer and his Jewish librettist. This explains why Goldmark was unable to capitalise on this success in his subsequent operas, in which he resorted to an artificial appropriation of different styles, none of which he could absorb with any genuine individuality. In *Merlin* (1886), Goldmark tried to imitate the Christian mysticism of Wagner's *Parsifal*, while in *Das Heimchen am Herd* (1896) he attempted to assimilate the post-Wagnerian fairy-tale idiom pioneered by Humperdinck in *Hänsel und Gretel* (1893).[7]

Anton Rubinstein's presence in a book exclusively devoted to German music might seem strange, but Louis justifies the Russian composer's inclusion on the grounds that his opera *Der Dämon* (1875) enjoyed regular performances on the German stage. Yet while Rubinstein may have possessed a refined compositional technique, his musical language remains derivative, and stylistically over-eclectic. Most damningly, both Goldmark's and Rubinstein's penchant for 'Asiatic-Oriental exoticisms' exemplified the fact that these composers were essentially foreigners who occupied positions fundamentally at odds with the German spirit.[8]

Because of their relatively marginal position within German musical life, Louis could afford to consign the assessment of operatic works by Goldmark and Rubinstein to a few paragraphs in his book. It was far less easy, however, to accord similar treatment to Gustav Mahler, whose work only gained wider dissemination in the first years of the twentieth century. In his third chapter, subtitled '*Symphonie und symphonische Dichtung*', Louis confronts the issues surrounding this composer head-on. In charting the most recent developments in German orchestral music, he openly confesses to a problem in conceptualising his antipathy towards the increasing complexities of musical language as manifested in the most recent works of Max Reger and Richard Strauss. No such problem, however, existed with regard to Mahler, a composer whose works he had regularly criticised in his capacity as a critic for *Münchner Neuesten Nachrichten*.[9] Reflecting one of Wagner's dictums again, for Louis, Mahler's music epitomised a fundamental incompatibility between Jewish and Western culture, which manifested itself in a stylistic idiom replete with the language and gesticulations of an Eastern Jew.[10] More

---

[7] Rudolf Louis, *Die deutsche Musik der Gegenwart* (Munich: Georg Müller, 1909), pp. 56–7.
[8] Ibid., p. 58.
[9] For a full English translation of one of Louis's newspaper critiques of Mahler see Karen Painter (ed.), *Mahler and His World* (Princeton University Press, 2002), pp. 338–41.
[10] See K. M. Knittel, '"Ein hypermoderner Dirigent": Mahler and Anti-Semitism in *Fin-de-siècle* Vienna', *Nineteenth-Century Music* 18/3 (1995), especially 267–76, which detail contemporary reactions to Mahler's gesticulating movements as a conductor.

damaging, however, was its claim to warrant serious attention as a product of the German tradition:

> If Mahler's music would *speak* Jewish, it would be perhaps unintelligible to me. But it is repulsive to me because it *acts Jewish* [*jüdelt*]. This is to say that it speaks musical German, if I can put it that way, but with an accent, with an inflection, and above all, with the *gestures* of an eastern, all too eastern Jew. The symphonist Mahler may well utilise the language of Beethoven and Bruckner, Berlioz and Wagner, Schubert and Viennese folk music . . . But those with sharp ears will realise with every phrase that the actual grammar of his musical language simply masks the genuine aspects of the German tradition, as if a comedian from the Budapest Orpheums were to recite a poem by Schiller . . . So, even to those whom it does not offend directly, his musical language cannot possibly communicate anything. One does not have to be repelled by Mahler's artistic personality in order to realise the complete emptiness and vacuity of an art in which the spasm of an impotent mock-Titanism reduces itself to a frank gratification of common seamstress-like sentimentality.[11]

The virulence of Louis's critique illustrates the extent to which he regarded Mahler as a far more dangerous and potentially damaging influence than any earlier composer of Jewish descent. Subsequently, Louis's notion that Mahler's work reflected a materialism and impotence indicative of a perceived decline in German culture proved irresistible to those with a nationalist agenda, especially after Germany's humiliation at the end of the First World War.

Another book that covers similar historical ground to Louis's is Walter Niemann's *Die Musik seit Richard Wagner*. Niemann's survey first appeared in 1913, but was reprinted four times and ultimately reissued in 1918 under the title *Die Musik der Gegenwart und der letzten Vergangenheit*. Yet there are discernible differences in their aesthetic positions. While Louis remained a steadfast opponent of Reger and other composers who were strongly influenced by Brahms, Niemann proved to have a much wider sympathy for this particular line of musical development. Moreover, as a composer, Niemann was actively interested in 'exotic' cultures and developed specialist academic expertise with regard to the music of Scandinavia.

Due perhaps to his broader cultural outlook, Niemann's book is less marked by anti-Semitic subtexts than Louis's, yet certain stereotypical remarks creep in and suggest an underlying prejudice. One obvious example of this can be found in Niemann's discussion of recent developments in the operas of Richard Strauss. In trying to make sense of Strauss's surprising changes of compositional and dramatic approach, from the expressionism of *Elektra* (1909) to the rococo neo-classicism of *Ariadne auf Naxos* (1912), Niemann makes the somewhat provocative observation that the composer's stylistic restlessness is an ingredient more characteristic of

---

[11] Louis, *Die deutsche Musik der Gegenwart*, pp. 182–3.

artists of a Semitic race, a claim that leads him to ask directly whether a Jewish question or problem exists in contemporary opera. Niemann's answer is revealing, if ultimately somewhat ambiguous. The Jewish problem obviously obtains in terms of quantity since nine tenths of up-and-coming theatre composers – he claims – were Jews. Yet at the same time he acknowledges that it is practically impossible to speak in scientific terms of a specifically Jewish style in music. While managing to avoid mentioning any names in his text, Niemann then wonders whether an increasing number of Jewish opera composers represents a danger to the future of the genre. In technical and stylistic terms, the answer to this question must be negative. 'The Jew', he argues, 'is the master of every sparkling burlesque and parody, every desultory and amusing activity and humour, every technical virtuosity that light opera [*heitere Oper*] requires of a composer.' But in terms of spiritual and national feeling, Niemann suggests otherwise; in his opinion Jews are 'incapable of assimilating genuine feelings of identity with Germanic popular and traditional idioms or incorporating a truly Germanic nature [*Wesensart*]' in their musical language.[12]

Notwithstanding his recourse to such commonplace Wagnerian stereotyping, Niemann, in contrast to Louis, mounts a sturdy defence of Mahler's work. He supports the notion that Mahler's symphonic thinking extends developments that originated in Beethoven and to a lesser extent in Brahms. Furthermore Niemann praises the composer for his enthusiastic love of Nature and his sophisticated use of timbre. Although rejecting the contention that Mahler's music has a distinctly Jewish accent, he acknowledges the composer's propensity towards 'tetchy sentimentality, sickliness, artificiality, convulsions, calculating coldness and excessive theatricality', and presents these elements as distinctly alien to the German tradition.[13] Thus, despite offering a very different perspective to Louis, Niemann shared Louis's anxieties with regard to modernism. For Niemann, current developments in music had been suffocated by instant gratification and a superficiality redolent of downmarket cosmopolitan and Americanised culture; Niemann associates this trend with a terminal decline stemming from the increasing preponderance of Jewish opera composers and considers it to be treatable only by musicians once again embracing their national roots.[14]

HISTORICAL SURVEYS PUBLISHED AFTER 1918

The expression of cultural pessimism that concludes Niemann's book might have carried less weight had the First World War turned out differently for Germany. Yet the unstable political situation following German defeat only served to exacerbate polemical arguments both for and against modernism.

---

[12] Walter Niemann, *Die Musik seit Richard Wagner* (Berlin: Schuster und Loeffler, 1913), pp. 89–90.
[13] Ibid., pp. 137–41 (140).   [14] Ibid., pp. 287–8.

Ironically the Weimar Republic's liberal constitution, which outlawed censorship in the arts, encouraged a climate in which conservative writers on music were in a position to give freer rein to their prejudices than might have been the case if political extremism had overtaken Germany. Within this context, therefore, anti-Semitism seemed to prevail more openly than before 1914.

Two books from the early 1920s deal with the issue of Jewish influence on German music, albeit in different ways. Although written from a strongly nationalist standpoint, *Die deutsche Musik und unsere Feinde* by Dr Konrad Huschke, published in 1921, includes only one paragraph which makes any allusions to the Jews; in that reference they are summarily dismissed as 'internationalists' who remained outside the orbit of German national musical development.[15] It seems remarkable, however, that any overview of nineteenth-century German music history could justify leaving out Mendelssohn altogether. Although no existing contemporary reviews of Huschke's book appear to have commented on this strange omission, it is worth noting that after 1933 many writers followed a similar line of argumentation whereby Austro-German Jewish composers were simply written out of music history books, almost as if they had never existed in the first place.[16]

Though published by the highly respected Gustav Bosse Verlag, Huschke's fiercely polemical book makes little pretence at scholarly enquiry. In contrast, the 1920 publication *Das Siegfried-Idyll oder Die Rückkehr zur Natur* by the composer Hermann Wolfgang von Waltershausen follows the prejudicial manner of Rudolf Louis, but claims a degree of academic credibility through the use of extended footnotes. For the series 'Musikalische Stillehre in Einzeldarstellungen', in which a seminal work in the German musical repertoire was analysed and placed in some kind of historical context, Waltershausen's decision to focus his own study on and around one of Wagner's occasional works was no mere flight of fancy.[17] In the context of post-war Germany, *Siegfried Idyll* represented to Waltershausen a beacon of national art that stood in dramatic contrast to the current trend in Germany in which composers had all but lost their roots and, unlike Wagner, could no longer achieve that idyllic return to nature. Waltershausen identifies three 'non-German' composers who supposedly precipitated a dilution of national style: Debussy, Puccini and Mahler – that is, a Frenchman, an Italian and a Jew, Mahler crucially being placed outside the Austro-German tradition. While Waltershausen acknowledges Mahler's strength of personality and the genuine artistic qualities of his Lieder and the middle movements of his symphonies, he argues that there is

---

[15] Konrad Huschke, *Die deutsche Musik und unsere Feinde* (Regensburg: Gustav Bosse, 1921), p. 25.
[16] See in particular Josef Maria Müller-Blattau's *Geschichte der deutschen Musik* (Berlin: Vieweg, 1938) and Otto Schumann's *Geschichte der deutschen Musik* (Leipzig: Bibliographisches Institut, 1940).
[17] The other books in Waltershausen's series were *Die Zauberflöte: eine operndramaturgische Studie* (1920), *Der Freischütz: ein Versuch über die musikalische Romantik* (1920) and *Orpheus und Eurydike: eine operndramaturgische Studie* (1923).

a serious discrepancy between his compositional ambition and his actual achievement.[18]

Identifying certain traits in Mahler's music as manifestations of his Jewishness (specifically a propensity towards asymmetric rhythmic patterns derived from the old Psalms and a melodic style that exploits both false pathos and sentimentality), Waltershausen then deals with the negative aspects of Mahler's influence upon subsequent generations of composers. In claiming Mahler to be the influential leader of a Vienna School Waltershausen goes beyond Rudolf Louis to suggest that Jewish influence was profoundly infecting current developments. Reiterating his belief in the fundamental incompatibility between the Jewish and German temperaments, he focuses particular attention on the music of Franz Schreker as an illustration of the decadent consequences that followed the emancipation of Austro-German Jewry from the ghetto:

> Amongst Mahler's successors in the so-called Vienna School, Franz Schreker stands as the predominant personality. In his works, the rhythm of Jewish Psalms becomes purest cultivation. From this, one senses the environment from which his development comes. Schreker is a major talent. However, to understand this point, we need to consider an additional factor: despite his outwardly strong Jewish identity, in which I see his strengths, he remains ultimately, a rootless Jew, infected with the decline of European culture. Just as germs can totally infect a healthy organism, so the Jew, once liberated from the Ghetto, now finds himself thrust into the arms of European decadence, where its corrupting effects are even more fatal than for the normal European. As such, Schreker's art has become, in effect, a grandiose document chronicling the break-up of Europe as the last decadent residue of the great artistic period which was the nineteenth century. Just as Pfitzner's *Palestrina* expresses in the master's own words the end of one historic Germanic cultural period, so Schreker's art must be seen as the full stop at the end of international artistic development.[19]

It might have been mere coincidence that Waltershausen's brief reference here to the composer of *Palestrina* was published in the same year as Pfitzner's own *Neue Ästhetik der musikalischen Impotenz*. Nonetheless Pfitzner's polemical argument of a post-war conspiracy of internationalist Jewish–Marxist forces bent on destroying German music helped to consolidate a framework of thinking towards the Jewish question which carried considerable weight and authority amongst conservative writers. As Director of the Munich State Academy of Music Waltershausen was in a particularly strong position to promulgate Pfitzner's arguments and continued to do so in a series of articles that appeared in various journals.[20]

---

[18] Hermann Wolfgang von Waltershausen, *Das Siegfried-Idyll oder Die Rückkehr zur Natur* (Munich: Hugo Bruckmann, 1920), p. 100.
[19] Ibid., pp. 102–3.
[20] See in particular Hermann W. von Waltershausen, *Die Politisierung der deutschen Musik*, Deutsches Musikjahrbuch IV, 1926, pp. 39–43 and 'Der Klärungspunkt in der Musikkrise der Gegenwart', *Zeitschrift für Musik* 98 (1931), 369–71.

Another writer who broadly replicated Pfitzner's anxieties was Karl Storck, whose last extended and updated edition of his *Geschichte der Musik* appeared in 1922, along with a new volume entitled *Die Musik der Gegenwart* comprising the final expanded section of the original monograph now published as a book in its own right. Despite the implication that Storck's book embraced the contemporary music scene in its entirety, *Die Musik der Gegenwart* provides as nationalist a bias in its organisation as Grunsky's pre-war study of nineteenth-century music, with eight of its ten chapters dealing exclusively with composers of German origin. Moreover, Storck's prognosis of the current situation in musical development is as prejudiced as those of Waltershausen and Pfitzner. In his new foreword, Storck warns his readers of the threats German music faced from internationalism, claiming that such forces were already damaging national organisations such as the Genossenschaft Deutscher Tonsetzer and the Allgemeiner Deutscher Musikverein.[21] In upholding both Reger and Bruckner as the only genuine standard-bearers of the German tradition, Storck also criticises the increasing support shown for Mahler's music in contemporary programmes – apparently an indirect reference to the high-profile Mahler Festival which took place in Amsterdam in 1920 – emphasising that its ethos was far removed from the German national spirit.[22]

Such an attack on Mahler at this early juncture in the book seems significant. While it is noticeable that Storck, unlike Waltershausen, avoids invoking racial stereotypes when dealing with composers such as Schoenberg, Schreker and Korngold, he seems unable to do so when discussing Mahler. 'Das Problem Mahler', the title of his chapter, appears to refer more to the question of Mahler's racial origins than to any uncertainty that might exist as to the merits or otherwise of the composer's music. Three or so pages into his discussion on Mahler, Storck singles out the composer as an ideal example of *Jüdische Genialität* (Jewish genius). Reiterating Wagner's contention that the Jew can only be a recreative, not a creative artist, he praises Mahler's capacity as a conductor, suggesting that in many ways his achievements in the opera house represent a fulfilment of Wagner's ideals. However, Storck draws a sharp distinction between Mahler's conducting and his compositions. In a construction reflecting cultural commonplaces and the Wagnerian stereotype that although Jews might be capable of volition and have ability, they could never achieve true creative inspiration or reflect the true German spirit, Mahler the composer is charged with the problem of being rootless, and a failure both in his desired attempt to truly absorb German feeling and spirituality, or to

---

[21] In his foreword Storck mentions in particular the internationalist impact on the programme of the 1921 ADMV Festival in Nuremberg. An examination of its programme reveals that a third of the featured composers were Jews – a drastic increase from previous festivals.

[22] Karl Storck, *Die Musik der Gegenwart* (Stuttgart: J. B. Metzler, 1922), pp. 7–9.

identify himself with the German people. As evidence for this supposedly non-Germanic outlook, Storck highlights what he considers to be problems integral to Mahler's melodic writing. Citing passages from Richard Specht's 1913 study of the composer, Storck attacks the use of folk material in Mahler's symphonies. Such material, he argued, sounds contrived and forced – a sequence of wood-cuts conceived with mosaic-like detail but non-integrated and non-symphonic in the truly Germanic sense.[23]

Confirmation that in the 1920s Mahler had become an easy target for anti-Semitic attack is provided by another substantial book, the three-volume *Geschichte der deutschen Musik* (1920–4) by Hans Joachim Moser. In its wealth of detail, this book claims to a depth of scholarship that far surpassed that of earlier general histories discussed here, an authority that was achieved by Moser's specialist expertise in medieval and baroque music. Moreover, having pursued a strongly nationalist agenda in his earlier writings, in particular his seminal article 'Die Entstehung des Dur-gedenkens – ein kulturgeschichtliches Problem' published in the *Sammelbände der Internationalen Musikgesellschaft* (1913–14), Moser was even more resolute in upholding such views during the Weimar Republic.

Two sections of Moser's book continue along the same lines as Karl Storck's. Mendelssohn, for example, is accorded substantial treatment in line with his undoubted significance for the Romantic era. A lengthy footnote at the beginning of his discussion however betrays a recourse to racial stereotyping. While trying to draw some distinctions between Mendelssohn and Meyerbeer in terms of stature, Moser resorts to negative Jewish stereotyping. He mentions, for example, Mendelssohn's tendency to lisp, his highly strung personality and his frequent bouts of illness, claiming that these were character traits typically associated with Jews.[24] Extending his observations to the composer's music, Moser specifically catalogues a series of stylistic features which he regards as being intrinsically Jewish: a lack of German might and profundity in his musical argument, unstylistic imitations of Handelian dotted rhythms, an over-fondness for the compound time-signature of 6/8, an aversion to all music expressive of ambiguous ideas, and an all-too-smooth treatment of pleasant ideas carried out with cosmopolitan suavity.[25] Given that such loaded remarks are confined to a footnote, one might argue that there is far too little evidence of latent anti-Semitism in Moser's assessment of Mendelssohn's music to warrant comment, not least because his initial remarks on Mahler appear more balanced than those of Storck. Noting that Mahler's work

---

[23] Ibid., pp. 168–78.
[24] See Sander Gilman, 'The Jewish Voice – Chicken Soup or the Penalties of Sounding too Jewish' in *The Jew's Body* (New York: Routledge, 1991), pp. 10–37 with special reference to the caricatures reproduced on pages 14 and 15 which ridicule the perceived Jewish tendency to lisp.
[25] Hans-Joachim Moser, *Geschichte der deutschen Musik vom Auftreten bis zur Gegenwart*, 2nd revised edition (Stuttgart: J. C. Cotta, 1928), p. 153.

had aroused strong passions – on the one side regarded as superior to Beethoven, on the other condemned as a fraudster – Moser proposes that a true assessment probably lies somewhere in the middle, a judgement he immediately qualifies, however, by suggesting that his current popularity will fade as quickly as that of the once-famous composer, Joachim Raff. Nevertheless, in trying to offer what he considers to be a fair appraisal of the composer, Moser falls all too readily into the same anti-Semitic clichés as those of Louis, Niemann and Storck:

> I recognise in Mahler only the touchingly tragic appearance of a person striving away, and this with Old Testament prophetic ardour, from the cursed existence of the oriental Ahasuerus to the binding of Catholicism and Germanism. A man who piled gigantic designs full of hysterical dislocation achieving perhaps some delightful detail after commendable struggle, but remaining nevertheless [tied] to that to which he was born.[26]

Further on in his discussion, Moser attempts to exemplify the supposedly non-Germanic elements in the composer's work in more detail. As evidence of his strong influence on the Schoenberg school and ties with international modernism, he cites Mahler's use of a so-called atonal heterophony, manifested in the orchestral introductions to the song cycle *Kindertotenlieder*. Using a musical quotation from the orchestral song 'Revelge', he argues that although the poem refers to the military experiences of a German soldier, the melodic line most readily conjures up visions of a distant Asia or Africa.[27] In summing up Mahler's achievement, Moser concedes that the composer was a 'consuming, passionately driven individual – perhaps the great mythic poet of a foreign nation who with colossal will tries to effect an integration with our own musical language . . . a commendable, not incomprehensible objective, but by no means [that of] a great German musician'.[28]

THE EXTREME POSITIONS OF BERL AND EICHENAUER

Clearly the main leitmotif that runs through so much of the writing I am considering is the contention that a fundamental antagonism and incompatibility existed between Austro-German music and Judaism. Yet ironically this argument was even upheld by those books manifesting a pro-Semitic stance. Consider, for example, Heinrich Berl's *Das Judentum in der Musik* of 1926. A non-Jew who held a teaching post at the Karlsruhe Hochschule für Musik, Berl attempted to define a more subtly nuanced and detailed explanation of Jewish features in Western music than the populist writers considered in this survey. The driving force behind Berl's argument was that of Oswald Spengler's theory of pseudomorphosis which was first expounded in his seminal book *Der Untergang des Abendlandes* (1918). Spengler defined

---

[26] Ibid., p. 399.   [27] Ibid., p. 403.   [28] Ibid., p. 408.

pseudomorphosis as a symptom that resulted from efforts to extend a society's influence beyond its own boundaries. The cultural implications of such action were to create a stunted and sterile expression since the spread of one society's cultural tradition could only smother the creative potential of its unfortunate neighbour.[29]

The first two sections of Berl's book prepare the ground for his application of Spengler's theory by exploring the differences between Western and Eastern musical developments, and then analysing how the latter relate to the music of the Jews. One of Berl's most provocative assertions here is that the triad was alien to the natural musical language of the Jews.[30] Such arguments prepare the ground for the final section of the book in which Berl argues that Jewish 'pseudomorphosis' is the fundamental cause of the Asiatic crisis in European music since the Romantics. With Mahler and Schoenberg begins, he suggests, the era of 'absolute melody' which strongly contrasts with the 'harmonic melody' of the purely European period – a period that ends with Wagner and Pfitzner. Linking this concept of 'absolute melody' to a pre-European, pre-harmonic period, Berl asserts that a more subjective and synthetic approach to musical composition accompanied the increasing emergence of Jews in European musical life. He singles out Mahler's work in particular for its innovative yet intrinsically Jewish features – its lyricism, its triviality and sentimentality, its frequent use of marches and popular melodies, and its penchant for the Asiatic and melodic lines that are prone to lamentation.[31] But far from being a negative influence, Berl suggests that Mahler, and indeed also Schoenberg, rescued European music from its death throes and brought it back to life.

Although he may have drawn a somewhat different conclusion from the positions of some of the other writers discussed in this chapter, it must be stressed that Berl is the only author under consideration here who sanctions the possibility, first aired by Wagner, that certain Jews could be allowed a redemptive role in the development of music. In this context, Berl makes clear aesthetic distinctions between the originality of Mahler and Schoenberg and the largely derivative musical style of the younger Erich Wolfgang Korngold.[32] Inevitably Berl's largely pro-Semitic stance caused a good deal of controversy, judging by the contemporary reviews of the book that appeared during this period.[33] Because Berl was able to encapsulate

---

[29] See Oswald Spengler, 'Historic Pseudomorphosis', in *The Decline of the West*, trans. Charles Francis Atkinson, Perspectives of World History (London: George Allen, 1928), Vol. II, pp. 189–230.
[30] Heinrich Berl, *Das Judentum in der Musik* (Berlin and Leipzig: Deutsche Verlags-Anstalt, 1926), p. 72.
[31] Ibid., pp. 153–67. See also pp. 93–100.   [32] Ibid., pp. 177–82.
[33] For completely divergent opinions regarding Berl's book see Albert Wellek, 'Besprechungen: Heinrich Berl "Das Judentum in der Musik"', *Zeitschrift für Musik* (November 1927), 637–8. Wellek's denunciatory reactions to the author's world-view stands in stark contrast to those of Carl Heinzen, Review of *Das Judentum in der Musik* by Heinrich Berl in *Die Musik* 19/3 (1926), 197. Heinzen describes the book as profound, sincere and optimistic, and showing the way to a revitalisation of the old Europe.

both positive and negative views of the Jewish contributions to music, commentators manipulated his arguments to suit either side of the argument. Indeed as Pamela M. Potter has observed, attempts to produce rational and systematic debates on racial issues in music became increasingly problematic in the polarised political climate of the final years of the Weimar Republic.[34] By this stage, political parties of the Right had exploited the concept of race in German intellectual history far more forcibly, thus allowing anti-Semitism in particular to occupy centre stage. It is significant that although couched in pseudo-scientific terminology, some of the most widely read literature with an anti-Semitic political agenda was written by dilettantes.

Perhaps the most notable and notorious example of this to have appeared in the musicological sphere was Richard Eichenauer's book *Musik und Rasse*, published a year before the Nazis came to power. Unlike most of the authors already mentioned here, Eichenauer neither had any formal training as a musicologist nor occupied a position as a music critic. Depending heavily upon the writings of the racial theorist and university professor Hans F. K. Günther, his book was nevertheless granted enormous prominence during the Third Reich, and was even recommended as a prescribed text for secondary schools. Eichenauer's attempts to equate the racial and physical characteristics of a composer with his musical style were so clearly intellectually suspect that even some Nazi scholars, most notably Friedrich Blume, were prepared to challenge his conclusions. Yet Eichenauer's work appreciably extends the prejudices that had manifested themselves in earlier surveys of general music history to incorporate a pseudo-scientific discourse. In the increasingly xenophobic and paranoid climate of the early 1930s, Eichenauer had effectively managed to turn received opinion into an accepted historical truth, so much so that unlike most of his predecessors he chooses to effect clearly delineated and artificial separation between music composed by Aryans and that of Jews. Significantly, the Jewish issue is reserved for his final chapter where for the most part Eichenauer supports his argument through a mélange of quotations from Storck and Moser. It is hardly surprising too that Eichenauer's last words were drawn directly from Richard Wagner himself – from his essay 'Know Thyself':

A thousand years under the Nordic guidance a racially healthy Europe has withstood the Jewish danger: only after it allowed its race to decay did it lose out to the 'plastic demons for the decline of Mankind' (Richard Wagner).[35]

---

[34] Pamela M. Potter, *Most German of the Arts: Musicology and Society from the Weimar Republic to the End of Hitler's Reich* (New Haven: Yale University Press, 1998), pp. 176–8.
[35] Richard Eichenauer, *Musik und Rasse* (Munich: J. F. Lehmann, 1932), p. 274.

CHAPTER 12

Italian music and racial discourses during the Fascist period

Roberto Illiano
and
Massimiliano Sala

The roots of racism in Italy run deep.[1] Racial policy in Fascist Italy stems from a nationalistic legacy which exalted not only expansionism but also the superiority of the Italian race as a biological 'fact'. Even during the Liberal period, and hence long before the advent of Fascism, racism was already used in the Italian colonies as one of the means by which the supposed 'superior prestige of the Italians' was defined. And even though Italian racists were divided on matters of detail, all prevailing arguments in the late nineteenth and early twentieth centuries were based on questions of biological descent and spiritual heredity. In the same way, the Fascists' anti-Jewish campaign and legislation were not German impositions, but rather initiatives and independent products of the Italian regime itself. A specifically Italian link between political anti-Semitism and (Catholic) anti-Judaic anti-Semitism is found in the first Italian translation of the *Protocols of the Learned Elders of Sion*; this notorious book promulgating the myth of a world Jewish conspiracy was translated in 1921 by Giovanni Preziosi, an anti-Semitic Fascist militant and director of the journal *La vita italiana*,[2] and the priest Umberto Benigni. The Concordat of 1929, which accorded to the Jewish religion the fairly low status of 'permitted cult', was another important milestone in the substantial erosion of Italian Jewish equality in relation to the rest of the citizens.

The road towards state racism followed two principal paths, the colonial-imperialist and the anti-Judaic, and yet it also involved other people who, without being directly affected by persecutory legislation, nevertheless

---

[1] See Gianluca Gabrielli, 'Razzismo', in Victoria de Grazia and Sergio Luzzatto (eds.), *Dizionario del fascismo*, 2 vols. (Turin: Einaudi, 2002–3), vol. II (L–Z), pp. 470–6; and Ruth Ben-Ghiat, *Fascist Modernities: Italy, 1922–1945*, Studies on the History of Society and Culture 42 (Berkeley: University of California Press, 2001); Italian translation by Maria Luisa Bassi, *La cultura fascista*, Biblioteca storica (Bologna: Il Mulino, 2000).

[2] In *La vita italiana* of January 1938 we read: 'It is necessary always to keep in mind race and its danger, in music as in the social and spiritual fields, in science and social life' ('È la razza e il suo pericolo che bisogna tenere sempre presenti, nella musica come nei campi sociali e spirituali, nella scienza e nella vita sociale'). Arthos [pseudonym of Giovanni Preziosi], 'Gli Ebrei e la Musica', *La vita italiana* (January 1938), 108.

suffered from racially inspired repression. Witness, for example, the internment of the Gypsies during the Second World War, the anti-Slav propaganda campaign and the repression of homosexuals. Establishing a connection between colonial racism and anti-Jewish racism is nevertheless important if we wish to be aware of their continuity and also the absence of open manifestations of dissent.

According to a broadly accepted understanding of the term 'race' already rooted in public discourse of the 1920s, the racist ideology of Italian Fascism gave rise to social policies that included such elements as pronatalism and hygienism. Subsidy of the country's mothers and campaigns such as the one against tuberculosis – campaigns also used to justify the segregation of populations in the colonies – could be viewed as Fascist measures taken in defence of the Italian race. In this way racism presented itself as a policy for safeguarding the social body.

In Italian Fascism racism was also exploited for propaganda purposes, for generating consent. It was a political weapon. The repressive measures that accompanied its rhetoric revealed that 'tolerance' was the result of political pragmatism on Mussolini's part, and that it was inevitably followed by initiatives of cultural control and indoctrination of the masses. Specifically, the language of race served to bolster attempts to relaunch the 'Fascist revolution' and restore to the Italian bourgeoisie a secure identity based on a synthesis of history, language and traditions. For a long time the word 'race' was used as a synonym of 'people' and 'nation'. Race thus became a new and particularly attractive discourse within which discussions about national identity and modernity could proceed.

NATIONALISM, FUTURISM, FASCISM

Questions concerning the relationship between culture, music and national identity had been raised by the musicians of the '1880 generation' a decade before the rise of Mussolini's movement. Composers of this period had a strong nationalistic sense that music was a moral and civilising principle, a means of achieving a new ethos to animate the nation. Although this subsequently made them seem a natural part of the (future) regime's programme, one of Fascism's cultural projects, these composers did not necessarily support the regime. There was a significant incompatibility between the new ideals and those of the petty bourgeois class. The petty bourgeois was accused of political mediocrity and was fiercely attacked as a result: though 'to be honest, in artistic terms Puccini could not help but live the lives of mediocrities . . . who were similar to him in intellectual capacity and sensitivity',[3] the new generation could only aim to confirm exceptional

---

[3] Ildebrando Pizzetti, *Musicisti contemporanei: saggi critici* (Milan: Treves, 1914), pp. 76–7.

destinies, in accordance with a 'spiritualistic rebellion against the vulgarity of petty-bourgeois Italy'.[4]

Determined to free themselves from their subjugation to German cultural dominance, musicians of that generation challenged the cultural monopoly of opera and strove to disseminate vocal and instrumental music with its roots in the forms of the past.[5] Ildebrando Pizzetti, who was attracted by the opportunity to rescue Italian music from cultural stagnation, wrote numerous essays from 1908 about the state of contemporary music. He gradually developed a position on musical nationalism by outlining a poetic vision centred on a new concept of drama emancipated from the opera of the preceding century and a desire for renewal associated with the recovery of a glorious musical past.

> Our *Risorgimento* is still not complete. When it is in the consciences of all Italians, through the different, yet concordant, work of all the Italians, then surely we shall have the musician who will sing the greatness of our Country with a song that is new, unprecedented, high and worthy. Italy will then have its Wagner who, by glorifying the strength of the race and the power of the Nation, will also finally glorify the epic actions of the liberators of the nineteenth century.[6]

Two of the key sources to feed into the development of racialised thinking within the Partito Nazionale Fascista (PNF, or National Fascist Party) – in general and specifically in connection with music – were the theories of Cesare Lombroso on the one hand, and of the Futurists on the other. Various members of the party, from its founding in October 1922, apparently took their cue from the work of Lombroso when they took turns in asserting that the racial problem had been a fundamental issue. In his influential book of 1876, *L'uomo delinquente*, anthropologist-scientist Lombroso, considered the founder of criminal anthropology, explained the moral degeneration of the delinquent in terms of specific physical anomalies. By the fifth edition of his four-volume book (1897) he had provided an increasingly detailed analysis of criminal somatic traits (the so-called Lombrosian degenerative characteristics) and proposed a further distinction between crimes on the basis of the specific anomalies of the class to which the criminal belonged. Despite coming under severe criticism in scientific circles, Lombroso's theories exerted a wide cultural influence in the late nineteenth and early twentieth centuries, when they proved fertile terrain for a whole new subculture of doctors and jurists who assembled a series of racist commonplaces and prejudice in the name of 'science'.

---

[4] Giannotto Bastianelli, *La crisi musicale europea* (Pistoia: Pagnini, 1912), p. 12.
[5] See Carlo Piccardi, 'La musica italiana verso il Fascismo', in Norbert Bolin, Christoph von Blumröder and Imke Misch (eds.), *Aspetti musicali, Musikhistorische Dimensionen Italiens 1600 bis 2000*, Festschrift für Dietrich Kämper zum 65. Geburtstag (Cologne: Dohr, 2001), pp. 111–20 and Carlo Piccardi, 'Alla ricerca del grado zero dell'espressione', in Roberto Illiano (ed.), *Italian Music during the Fascist Period*, Speculum Musicae 10 (Turnhout: Brepols, 2004), pp. 191–224.
[6] Ildebrando Pizzetti, 'I cantori del Risorgimento', *Il momento* 7/197 (1909).

Elements within the PNF turned Lombroso's theory about the hereditariness of delinquent tendencies to political ends. Lombroso's biologically justified notion that the delinquent constituted a new 'unfortunate race' not only simplified social issues; it offered an opportunity for those seeking to justify the racial ideology. In *Il delitto politico e le rivoluzioni* Lombroso himself wrote: 'when there is an enormous inequality owing to conditions of race ... a uniform law produces pain and damage, like the same suit of clothes applied to unequal limbs'.[7] For him deviance exists on a spectrum from the born criminal to the honest man. For this reason the PNF felt justified in arguing that if in the social sphere there were different types of man, at a higher level there could be subdivisions into different human races. Those in the PNF making claim to these ideas emphasised the need to limit as much as possible contact between Italians and those who, in a variety of guises, numbered among the 'dangerous' subjects: homosexuals, gypsies, blacks, linguistic minorities, etc.[8] Of the same tenor were the declarations of a part of the PNF, which tended to justify the changed attitude towards the above 'categories' not so much on the basis of biological or chemical diversity, but on the basis of the different spiritual values that different races were alleged to have. They also picked up on Lombroso's idea that a political rebel is always a delinquent, for which reason they could rationalise violence as a necessity: society had to exert violence against the deviant as a means of defence. Because everything that could be considered anomalous had to be controlled, and the 'technician' (i.e. the state apparatus) had to act as guarantor of the politicians' 'norm', laws created according to a simplistic racist argument, such as these, and actions taken against those who broke the law, together served as the mechanism for

---

[7] Cesare Lombroso, *Il delitto politico e le rivoluzioni*, Biblioteca antropologia-giuridica 1/9 (Turin: Bocca, 1890), p. 502.

[8] As regards homosexuality, Nazism in Germany stamped out a homosexual world that was visible, structured and self-aware and that stood as an alternative to what was considered 'normal'. In Italy, paradoxically, if one wanted to fight homosexuality, it was necessary first to make it visible and then to conceal it again. German racism did not take root in Italy because a specifically Italian form of racism already existed. Considering homosexuals as a race meant acknowledging their integration in the Italian social fabric and that completely contradicted the Fascist idea of virility. For this reason – i.e. to negate that there was a homosexual problem in Italy – no special laws were made against homosexuals. And those condemned were either 'political internees' or were dealt with in other ways: they were beaten up, dismissed from public offices or subjected to continuous surveillance by the local police. In Italy it was preferred to leave to the Catholic church the task of controlling and repressing homosexuality: the Catholic church 'covered', and guaranteed the repression of, those areas of behaviour that the Italian Penal Code had intentionally left exposed. As Giovanni Dall'Orto claimed, 'denying even that a persecuted group can constitute a group is the most refined form of racism'. See Dall'Orto, 'Il paradosso del razzismo fascista verso l'omosessualità', in Alberto Burgio (ed.), *Nel nome della razza. Il razzismo nella storia d'Italia: 1870–1945*, Percorsi (Bologna: il Mulino, 2000), pp. 515–25. On this subject, see also Dario Petrosino, 'Traditori della stirpe. Il razzismo contro gli omosessuali nella stampa del fascismo', in Alberto Burgio and Luciano Casali (eds.), *Studi sul razzismo italiano*, Quaderni di discipline storiche (Bologna: Clueb, 1996), pp. 89–107; and Circolo Pink (ed.), *Le ragioni di un silenzio. La persecuzione degli omosessuali durante il nazismo e il fascismo* (Verona: Ombrecorte, 2002).

exerting and retaining political control. It was behind this simple systemic logic that the violence of power was able to act undisturbed.

It was the idea of Nation which became the keystone of a keenly felt spiritual reawakening for many late nineteenth-century and early twentieth-century Italian intellectuals, including the Futurists, who exerted one of the profoundest influences on the shape the Fascist party would take in cultural terms. In his essay 'Music and Politics in Italy', Alfredo Casella argued that Futurism exerted the greatest influence on the cultural roots of Fascism:

> The theory which for 10 years inspired the Futurism of Marinetti was fundamentally the same as that which has since enabled Fascism to rule a nation of 40,000,000 ... The war cry of Marinetti and Boccioni was the first sign of a new and truly artistic consciousness. It was the first affirmation of the 'will to live' of young Italy, awakened at last from the long sleep of the nineteenth century; at the same time it marked the definitive decline of these foreign influences which until then had held most of the intellectuals in bondage.[9]

If one were to give an account of Futurism on the basis of the completed works, one would have to concede that the movement lacked prominent musicians and also seemed to lack a consistent musical aesthetic. As Fiamma Nicolodi correctly puts it, musical Futurism was made up above all of curious, self-taught amateurs; representatives of a musical custom rather than an authentic culture; artists repressed by the academicism of the conservatories; personalities active above all in the theoretical sphere.[10] Much more numerous than actually accomplished works were ideas, projects, manifestos and pamphlets which followed one another in a continuous stream. Despite this, the Italian Futurist movement influenced many currents that thrived at the same time in Europe – principally Dadaism, which associated declamation and all forms of vocal expression with instrumental and noise-making sonorities. The Futurist experience was also shared by exponents of the French group *Les Six* – for instance Satie, whose *Parade* used a battery of noisemakers that included Morse code, pistol shots and toys, and Milhaud, whose *Machines agricoles* called for the noise of tractors and threshing machines. The cult of the machine was also alive in Russia, though there it was associated with factory sounds (as in Prokofiev's *Pas d'acier*), and in the Germany of Hindemith, whose *Suite 1922* calls for very vigorous rhythms, 'like a machine'. For the Futurists themselves, however, the machine was a symbol of liberation, at once an expression of the movement and energy representing the world's future, and a rejection of the conservative past (music like that of Debussy was defined by Pratella as 'rosolio for young ladies').

---

[9] Alfredo Casella, 'Music and Politics in Italy', *Christian Science Monitor* (19 September 1925).
[10] Fiamma Nicolodi, *Musica e musicisti nel ventennio fascista*, Contrappunti 19 (Fiesole: Discanto, 1984), p. 77.

It was by virtue of another of their aesthetic positions that the Futurists found themselves according with Fascism. Given their assumptions and their aspiration to overthrow the conditions in which they lived, the Futurists identified themselves with interventionism, albeit an aesthetically sublimated form of action and conflict. Russian Futurist Vladimir Mayakovsky described war as 'the world's hygiene', since he felt that a new world could be reconstructed through action and by overthrowing the foundations of society. Every warlike action was greeted by the Futurists – who were animated by blind and hysterical nationalism nourished on distorted Nietzschean theories – with a sort of euphoria described by Benedetto Croce as 'an orgy of irrationality'. The force of such distorted patriotic feelings became clear at the outbreak of the Libyan War in 1911, when intellectuals holding utterly different ideas (Gabriele d'Annunzio, Giovanni Pascoli and Filippo Marinetti) adopted the same interventionist stand. The conquest of Tripoli was greeted by Marinetti with a new manifesto in which he claimed that the word '*Italia*' should prevail over the word '*Libertà*', and urged the Italian government to increase its national ambitions and to scorn accusations that Italians had been breaking international law, as per the stupid allegations circulating saying that Italians had been acting as pirates on the high seas. Thus, war was deemed acceptable to the Futurists not only for ideological reasons, as an expression of revolution, but also for political reasons, as the expression of nationalistic integration. Exponents of Futurism saw war as a means of freeing the world from the hypocrisy and conformism of a bourgeoisie which identified itself with the false values of late Romanticism and decadence. However, by glorifying gratuitous violence and nationalism at all costs, the Futurists aligned themselves with the primitive destructive instinct on which Fascism in large part based its authority, and in doing so set out a cultural vision that would easily serve the subsequent imperialist regime.

Yet there was a significant contradiction inherent in the combination of nationalism and revolution that underpinned both the Futurist movement and the Fascist era in general. One who paid the price of this contradiction was Francesco Balilla Pratella, Futurism's finest musician. In him the relationship between folk and art music likewise remained unsolved, for according to his idealistic conception of music, folk elements should be used as a means of expressing the nationalistic dimension of a work (a typical example is his *Romagna* cycle of the years 1903–4). His nationalist ideology aspired to a simple, elemental idiom which returned to the sources of Italian folk song and excluded erudition and refinement; at the same time it nevertheless sought to pursue a revolutionary avant-garde impulse. The composers of the '1880 generation', however, repudiated him and refused to condone such an attempt to mingle avant-garde boldness and folk tradition. A relationship between compositional modernity and popular music is nevertheless found in many authors pertaining to the

European periphery. Through the reactivation of popular traditions, composers such as Grieg, de Falla, Stravinsky, Bartók and Kodály both enfranchised musical tradition in their countries and increased the conventional musical grammar. In Italy, on the other hand, compositional creativity lacked a scholarly awareness of popular music. For instance, Pratella's five symphonic poems of *Romagna* were based on popular songs whose melodies had merely been presented in unison within a simplistic and populist musical structure. Casella, in particular, reproached the Futurist composers for not producing substantial artistic results. An artist of wide and refined culture, Casella could not appreciate declarations of intentional ignorance about the past. In *Ars nova* of February–March 1919 he declared:

> I do not share – in large part, at least – in their [Futurism's] aesthetic and even less their political ideas, and I completely disapprove of their vulgar means of propaganda and struggle; I disapprove of it all the more in that the grave tendency towards coarseness and brutality, which still persists in Italian taste, should be fought strenuously by whoever wants to improve and refine our race.[11]

Use of the term 'Italian race' is unremarkable here, given that during the Fascist period the word 'race' was used in Italian speech as a synonym for 'Italian people', but with especially strong nationalistic overtones.

While Futurist manifestos glorifying the new could reject folklore on purely logical grounds, disavowals of jazz and 'black music' in any given pamphlet seemed substantially to stem from its author's willingness to come into line with post-1930 Fascist ideologies. Initially, however, jazz had been greeted by the Futurists as an expression of the new; an expression of freedom from traditional methods. With its modern, ostinato-like, syncopated rhythms and its melodic improvisation, jazz was considered to be the closest implementation of Futurist principles. In his 1924 manifesto *La musica futurista* and an article published on 14 August 1926 in the newspaper *L'Impero* Franco Casavola strenuously supported the new Afro-American music. However, in doing so he prompted the censorious reaction of *L'Impero*'s editors, former Futurists Mario Carli and Emilio Santarelli. In an editorial note appended to Casavola's text they asserted that such an 'inferior' and 'vulgar' genre was not suited to the Italian people. Marinetti himself disavowed his initial partiality for jazz, worried as he was by accusations that his own art was 'degenerate'. In his manifesto of 1938 *Contro il negrismo musicale*, he launched a racist attack against what he called the 'funereal humour in black pills' and 'funereal asthma' of 'musical negrism', a language that aligned Marinetti's ideas with those of musicians such as Mascagni.[12] A description of 'negro music' as a 'long Puccinian lament asthmatically broken up by punches and the syncopated

---

[11] Alfredo Casella, 'Diffida...', *Ars nova* 3/4–5 (1919), 1.
[12] See 'Mascagni contro la musica jazz', *Corriere della sera* (16 June 1926) and 'Mascagni contro il jazz', *La propaganda musicale* 1/2 (1928).

tam-tam of railway trains' was likewise included in the *Manifesto futurista dell'aeromusica sintetica geometrica e curativa* published on 8 March 1934 and signed by Marinetti and Aldo Giuntini. In this document the usual Futurist formulas were recycled – with the addition of an aeroplane motif, which seems in this instance to have stood for the myth of the war industry created to make people proud to live in a great 'Mussolinian Italy'.

Throughout the Fascist period, however, Marinetti behaved somewhat opportunistically. As an artist and critic of art, Marinetti was without doubt a great innovator, but as a politician he always held very debatable positions: he was wrong not only about the real revolutionary force of Fascism, but also because he agreed to cohabit passively with the reactionary face of the same Fascism. His support of Mussolini's ideas was neither total nor unconditional. His words were certainly exploited and distorted by the regime. When Marinetti spoke of the 'Italian race' his meaning transcended all biological considerations and had exclusively spiritual implications. Marinetti used the term 'Italian race' with the same meaning as other Italian intellectuals who spoke in nationalistic terms, as a kind of source of cohesion in the same native land, a perception of a common cultural identity. Marinetti wanted a political revolution that followed an artistic–literary inspiration, but he knew nothing of economics and the relationships between social classes. The terms that he used in the *Manifesti futuristi* – such as references to asthma – are elements of a provocative, violent and polemical manner of speech, in which his desire to provoke is manifest in disproportionate language. In *Futurismo e fascismo* (Foligno, Campitelli, 1924) the same Marinetti claimed to his movement the formation of the Fascist aesthetic conscience, but also the right to a full autonomy in the creative sphere:

Fascism, born of interventionism and futurism, was fed by futurist principles. Fascism contains and always will contain that amount of optimistic patriotism, proud, violent, superior, warlike, that we futurists, first among the first, foretold to the Italian crowds ... Fascism works politically, that is, within the ambit of our sacred peninsula, which demands, requires, limits, forbids. Futurism works instead in the infinite domains of pure fantasy; it therefore can and must dare dare dare ever more boldly.[13]

Nevertheless, the substantial racism of expressions such as this and Marinetti's unconditional defence of nationalism and exaltation of violence were subsequently adopted by Mussolini when he passed the 1938 Racial Laws.

In this way Mussolini could be considered to have disseminated a model originally proposed by Marinetti. Indeed, Benedetto Croce has argued that

---

[13] Cited from Enrico Crispolti, 'Appunti sui materiali riguardanti i rapporti tra futurismo e fascismo', in Enrico Crispolti – Berthold Hinz – Zeno Birolli, *Arte e fascismo in Italia e in Germania*, I nuovi testi (Milan: Feltrinelli, 1974), p. 52.

for those who have a sense of history, the ideal origin of Fascism is to be found in Futurism. When Mussolini addressed the Italian people, he spoke of the Fatherland and the supremacy of the state; yet when he began to speak of race, the Italians failed to understand what he meant. The Italian people did not care about the ethnicity of the Jews; they wanted the inclusion of all Italians in one common cultural sphere. The war in Abyssinia of 1935 gave shape to the Italian concept of 'race', but it related largely to relationships between Italians and the African populations – mixed unions between Italians and natives were reported – not to the Jews.

The notion that there were Jewish racial issues in Italy – a problem of the Italian nation towards or against the Jews – was stranger to popular feeling. To justify his anti-Semitic politics Mussolini turned to certain concepts expounded by the Futurists (Italian race, nationalism, Italianness, violence) and distorted their meanings. Some Fascist officials, including Italo Balbo,[14] advised Mussolini against passing the Racial Laws, noting that several 'comrades' (*camerati*) were Jewish, and that the race idea was not suited to the spirit of the Italian people. For others racial laws against the Jews had the single purpose of lending a new dynamism to the now ageing Fascism. Mussolini did not have ideological prejudices against Jews. On the contrary, his friends and collaborators included many Jews; Margherita Sarfatti, for instance, was co-director of *Gerarchia*, a monthly journal controlled directly by Mussolini, and author of the first official biography of the Duce. Jews were present in all Italian political parties, including the PNF: Guido Jung was Finance Minister in 1932 and Gino Arias a regular contributor to *Il popolo d'Italia* and *Gerarchia* as well as a main theorist of the corporatist state.[15] Jews appear in the list of charter members of the 'Fasci di combattimento' (*Sansepolcristi*);[16] Jews appear in the lists of martyrs of the Fascist revolution; many took part in the March on Rome; Jews also participated in the 1936 War of Ethiopia. It could be said therefore that until 1936 the greater part of the Jewish population in Italy had maximum confidence in the regime and, above all, in the Duce; he reassured the population many times of Italian Fascism's non-involvement in all manifestations of political anti-Semitism. In the *Informazione Diplomatica* no. 14 of February 1938 Mussolini denied once again that the PFN wanted to inaugurate any anti-Jewish policies.

But Mussolini was a consummate politician. At first he had hoped that the Jews would help him to make the economic sanctions against Italy fail.

---

[14] Italo Balbo (1896–1940) was one of the main protagonists of the Italian Fascism. He was Aeronautics Minister and Governor of Libya.

[15] See Renzo De Felice, *Storia degli ebrei italiani sotto il fascismo* (Turin: Einaudi, 1993), pp. 31–42, and Eleonora Carapella, 'Musicisti ebrei nell'Italia delle persecuzioni: il caso Aldo Finzi', in Illiano (ed.), *Italian Music during the Fascist Period*, pp. 301–26.

[16] The movement *Fasci italiani di combattimento* was constituted by Mussolini in Milan, during the reunion of San Sepolcro (from here the name of *Sansepolcristi*) on 23 May 1919. The movement, which initially comprised trade unionists, revolutionaries, Futurists, merged into PNF in November 1921.

But when such efforts proved useless, Mussolini thought that the international Jewish organisations had turned against him and became convinced that the supposed worldwide Jewish conspiracy against Fascism had to be destroyed.[17] In the *Dichiarazione sulla razza* (Declaration on Race), published in *Foglio d'ordine* of the PNF, on 26 October 1938, we read:

The Great Council of Fascism remembers that International Jewry – especially after the abolition of masonry – has been the encourager of antifascism in all fields, and also that foreign or expatriate Italian Jewry has been – in some periods, culminating in 1924–25 and during the Ethiopian war – unanimously hostile to Fascism.

The immigration of foreign elements – which greatly increased after 1933 – has exacerbated the animosity of Italian Jews towards the Regime, which they do not accept sincerely, since it is antithetical to the psychology, politics, and internationalism of Israel. All the anti-fascist forces are headed by Jewish elements.

POPULAR MUSIC, RADIO AND THE EXALTATION OF THE MASSES

During the developments leading from the foundation of the Fascist movement to its rise to power in October 1922, policy concerning the treatment of the arts was by no means consistent. Unlike other totalitarian regimes that turned radically towards racism and propaganda, Fascism, at first, seemed to be indulgent toward modernist choices in the creative arts and stimulated exchanges with foreign countries, such that Italian intellectuals were led to believe they worked in a pluralistic system. Folk music, in particular, was never the focus of the party's attention, and in the early stages was even ignored. A distinct about-turn came with the PNF's rise to power, however.

The shift to the right that had animated the first phase of the party, and the big propaganda campaign depicting the Italians as warlike and virile, then came to be widely reflected in the music for the masses. The first cultural victim was operetta, guilty of depicting the Italian as a 'mandolin player' and hence clashing with the idea of the virile, proletarian Italian free of the provincialism with which he had been branded throughout the world. The *tabarin* (music hall) met with the same fate; it not only failed to accord with the moralising campaign launched by the government, it was also deemed unsuitable for a people not used to comfort and 'bourgeois laxity'. The combination of these campaigns – which culminated in the midst of the war with the censorship of every non-Italian product, and

---

[17] See George L. Mosse, *Toward the Final Solution. A History of European Racism* (New York: Howard Fertig, 1978), Italian trans. by Livia De Felice, *Il razzismo in Europa. Dalle origini all'olocausto*, Economica Laterza 299 (Rome-Bari: Editori Laterza, 1985), pp. 214–16.

particularly jazz – strengthened the sense of a need for genuinely Fascist musical production.

An important cornerstone of the new cultural production attempting to reflect these views was the myth of Romanism. In it, the history of ancient Rome was de-contextualised and transformed into a 'symbolic universe', in which the cult of the *fascio littorio* (bundles of the lictors) incarnated the aspiration to nationalism and a national identity.[18] In a country with very high levels of illiteracy, music was an especially useful instrument for indoctrinating hatred for the 'other', a hatred that took the form of social discrimination and jeering at foreign powers. All the events of the regime resounded to hymns such as *Giovinezza*, which depicted the young legionaries as heroes: in this particular case the text of the song expressed a desire to settle scores in a nation where the people fought in the name of the *Duce* and died to assert the principles of loyalty to the flag and racial superiority. On the one hand, popular music adopted the form of the traditional-sounding *canzonetta* in an obvious attempt to reach as wide an audience as possible; on the other, it stood in substantial opposition to the status quo, employing new forms and meanings. Propaganda was fully introduced into the actions of the Fascist government and became the main instrument for exercising a politics of consent. And it was precisely in this climate, on the borderline between 'patronage' and 'censorship', that the figure of the regime-composer was born. Of these the best known were E. A. Mario, considered the greatest composer of the regime (he wrote songs like *La leggenda del Piave*, *Passano i Balilla*, *Inno al grano* and *Madonnina d'oltremare*), Libero Bovio, also the author of the famous *Inno del lavoro* set by Pietro Mascagni, and Giuseppe Blanc, composer of *Giovinezza*, the *Inno degli universitari fascisti*, the *Inno dei giovani fascisti* and *Balilla*.

Though related to the activities of repression and censorship typical of every totalitarian state, Italian Fascist propaganda stood apart from that of other totalitarian regimes in its use of methods and dynamics which seemed to belong to the Italian situation alone.[19] Far from having a uniform policy, Italian Fascism constantly wavered between modernity and conservatism, trying to find a balance. At the same time the organs of control and propaganda, such as the MinCulPop (Ministry of Popular Culture), gave their support to a massive ideological conditioning that continually adapted to the requirements of the regime in both form and content.[20]

---

[18] See Luca Scuccimarra, 'Romanità, culto della', in Victoria De Grazia and Luzzatto (eds.), *Dizionario del fascismo*, vol. II (L–Z), pp. 539–41.
[19] See Maurizio Cesari, *La censura nel periodo fascista*, Le istituzioni culturali 3 (Naples: Liguori, 1978).
[20] This explains the numerous indecisions of the party on matters such as the country's cultural policy, its rethinking on operetta or its tolerance towards manifestations that, despite being connected to more internationalist experiences (like jazz), were rehabilitated provided that the title was Italianised and the composer's original name concealed.

Key media for the dissemination of these sanctioned images of the Italian nation were film and radio, both of which lent themselves as tools of propaganda and both of which had an important musical dimension. In 1923 the Istituto LUCE (L'Unione Cinematografica Educativa) was created and entrusted with the production of documentaries and newsreels which the government expected would offer a detailed account of the successes of Fascist Italy. It was only after 21 January 1935, when the Istituto LUCE spawned the Ente Nazionale Industrie Cinematografiche (ENIC), and then again later, with the creation of Cinecittà (a project conceived by Luigi Freddi) and the birth of the Centro Sperimentale di Cinematografia, that the regime started to use cinema to spotlight its achievements. However, because Fascism never attempted to subjugate cinema totally to political propaganda, films continued to be made with a certain degree of autonomy. While encouraging escapist films imitating the American model and stories that did not conflict with Party issues, the censors kept a vigilant eye on didactic documentaries and educational newsreels. Before screening their main features, cinemas disseminated victorious images of Italy in newsreels containing information manipulated in order to show memorable events associated with the regime.

One important film of this context was *Scipione l'Africano* (Carmine Gallone, 1937), with music by Ildebrando Pizzetti. Mainly a political vehicle, it attempted in what was imagined to be 'the august tradition of the race' to legitimate the African enterprise 'as the logical corollary of a glorious past and indisputable reason for life of a fervent present'.[21] The onset of the racial campaign was founded on this hypothetical supremacy. Pizzetti composed the film's music between June 1936 and May 1937 and on 23 May 1937 recorded the soundtrack in Studio 2 of via Veio, with the Orchestra del Teatro Reale dell'Opera di Roma.[22] On 28 April 1937, Pizzetti previewed some of the film music – the *Inno a Roma* (Hymn to Rome) for chorus and orchestra – in Studio 8 of Cinecittà in the presence of Mussolini, on the occasion of the inauguration of the cinematographic studios. The piece *Inno a Roma* immediately became the musical symbol of the film. On 4 August the same year Mussolini heard it again at the Ministero della Cultura Popolare (Ministry of Popular Culture). In a telegram sent to Pizzetti the day after the Duce's viewing, Luigi Freddi seems to guarantee the *Inno* the possibility of becoming the official hymn of the Party.[23]

---

[21] See Massimiliano Sala, 'Dal muto al sonoro: le musiche di Pizzetti per *Cabiria* e *Scipione l'Africano*', in Illiano (ed.), *Italian Music during the Fascist Period*, pp. 157–89. See also Luigi Freddi, *Il cinema*, 2 vols. (Rome: L'Arnia, 1949), vol. I.

[22] The manuscript of the film music (though not the autograph) is conserved to the Biblioteca Palatina of Parma, Sezione Musicale, F. Pizz., Mss B 27.

[23] 'The salient point of its work will become the hymn of our age. Yours Freddi' ('Il punto saliente della sua opera diverrà l'inno della nostra epoca. Suo Freddi'). Bruno Pizzetti (ed.), *Ildebrando Pizzetti. Cronologia e bibliografia*, Materiali 1 (Parma: La Pilotta, 1980), p. 267.

Pizzetti also sent the *Inno a Roma*, reduced for voice and pianoforte, to Mussolini after the success of *Scipione l'Africano* in Venice at the *V Mostra internazionale d'arte cinematografica*, where the film won the Coppa Mussolini. In Pizzetti's 29 August 1937 letter to Mussolini from Cortina d'Ampezzo, the intentions of the composer are clear:

Duce,
To be able to give at least once to the people of one's own nation and one's own time a song which expresses some of their profoundest feelings, some of their purest ideals – I believe that a poet or a musician cannot have a higher aspiration; and to attempt it is not arrogant presumption but an act of love. The Hymn I am sending you, a part of which you already heard in the film *Scipione l'Africano*, is an expression of love by an artist who has always loved his country, his people, his homeland above all else in the world. You who were able to divine the deepest feelings of the Italian people as no one else, illuminate its purest virtues, awaken its most secret energies, you who every day give the Italian people the clearest and most powerful voice to speak the highest words that can be spoken to all mankind, judge whether the Hymn is worthy of being given to the Italian people and sung by them. If you judge it so, I will ask you – though I do not yet dare – to accept that it be dedicated to your name, Duce. Should the Duce wish to hear the Hymn performed by me, I await the command. With the deepest devotion,
  Yours[24]

The aspirations of Pizzetti and Freddi regarding the possible adoption of the piece as official hymn of the party were not ultimately satisfied, since Puccini's *Inno a Roma* (1919) had already entered into the collective imagination, sung on every official occasion with *Marcia reale* and *Giovinezza*.

The Italian colonialism depicted in *Scipione l'Africano* – namely the conquest of Ethiopia (1936) – reflected not only the government's conviction that Italy needed to expand its territories politically and economically, but also its desire to challenge Anglo-French supremacy in Africa. Intent as the party was on celebrating its territorial expansion in the most varied forms (and in particular through music), one comes across references within the party to the spirit of 'Romanism' and Italian 'supremacy' which, although distant from the extremes of Nazi Germany, assumed the semblance of an increasingly overt racism.

Radio however was so thoroughly embedded in the lives of the working classes, that they were immediately open to being manipulated by government propaganda because of the extent to which the regime could exploit the radio medium. Strongly encouraged by Costanzo Ciano (father of Galeazzo, Mussolini's future son-in-law), the first experiments in radio broadcasting took place in Italy between 1922 and 1924. From 1925 to 1929 the only news broadcasts allowed by the URI were the bulletins of the Stefani agency. From 1929 Mussolini was granted full executive

---

[24] An autograph copy of the *Inno* and the letter are in the Archivio Centrale dello Stato, Segreteria Particolare del Duce, Carteggio Ordinario, 5558707.

responsibility, a power which was very soon extended to cinema, radio and cultural events in general. During the early years of Mussolini's regime radio spread in only a limited way; the regime preferred using film and the newsreels from the Istituto LUCE, which became obligatory in cinemas from 1926. Subsequently, however, Fascism reconsidered radio's potential as a medium through which they might influence the masses.[25]

For instance, wide exposure was given to those programmes of government that echoed the new campaign in defence of the 'integrity and health of the race' and pre-announced the regime's new directives on the matter in question.[26] Thanks in part to lower prices and the government's commitment to a policy of ensuring that every family should have a radio set in its home, radio's social and cultural reach increased significantly in the 1930s. The emergence of local stations such as Radio Milano, Radio Roma and Radio Napoli was fully supported by the regime, convinced as it was that increasing the number of radio outlets for the broadcast of Fascist ideology to the masses could only be good for its propaganda campaign.

A marked shift in emphasis on the regime's part from concert music and opera to music better suited to dissemination on the radio came about in 1935. Some of the first provisions involving the Ispettorato del Teatro (Inspectorate of the Theatre) in that year were the censorious measures to be adopted against musics from the countries that adhered to the League of Nations and had therefore adopted economic sanctions against Italy during the Ethiopian War. An official edict declared:

[F]rom the repertories of the opera houses the works of composers belonging to those [sanctioning] nations must be eliminated, while in the case of French works there will only be a reduction in the number of those normally performed.

In the field of concerts and *serious music* in general, the same criterion will be used, while keeping a lower percentage of French and Spanish symphonic and chamber music.

As regards *light music*, on the other hand, all the compositions belonging to composers from sanctioning countries will be eliminated.

As a consequence of the above, at La Scala, instead of *Mignon* by Thomas and *The Legend of the Invisible City* by Rimsky-Korsakov, Giordano's *Siberia* and Cilea's *Arlesiana* will be given. At the Regio of Turin, *L'Elisir d'amore* will take the place of *Werther*. At the Reale dell'Opera, Puccini's *Manon Lescaut* and another Italian opera to be decided on will replace Massenet's *Manon* and

---

[25] See Franco Monteleone, *La radio italiana nel periodo fascista. Studio e documenti: 1922–1945* (Venice: Marsilio, 1976); Alberto Monticone, *Il fascismo al microfono: radio e politica in Italia, 1924–1945* (Rome: Studium, 1978); Gianni Isola, *Abbassa la tua radio, per favore . . . : storia dell'ascolto radiofonico nell'Italia fascista* (Scandicci: La nuova Italia, 1990); Peppino Ortoleva, 'Radio', in Victoria De Grazia and Sergio Luzzatto (eds.), *Dizionario del fascismo*, vol. II (L–Z), pp. 459–63.

[26] See Vincenzo Alaimo, 'La razza in musica nel ventennio fascista', in Illiano (ed.), *Italian Music during the Fascist Period*, pp. 225–49.

Mignon. At the Verdi of Triest, instead of Borodin's *Prince Igor*, Zandonai's *Francesca da Rimini* will be given. The E.I.A.R. has in turn suspended the broadcast of Granados's *Goyescas*.[27]

Although these measures were withdrawn within twelve months, they were early signals for the introduction of autarchy into Italy. And shortly afterwards, the creation of the political and military alliance between Fascist Italy and Nazi Germany was to make repressive measures in the musical field absolutely mandatory.

Wide circulation was also accorded to those popular songs which, by their very nature (e.g. catchy melody and rhythm), best lent themselves to radio broadcasting. One such case was *Faccetta nera*, with words by Renato Micheli and music by Mario Ruccione. Although this song quickly became very popular, it was banned by the party immediately after Racial Laws concerning the populations of the colonies were passed (on 9 January 1937). According to these laws, children born of unions between Italians and Abyssinians were disparagingly defined as '*meticci*' (half-castes), a type of biological attack on the purity of the white race and a treacherous mediation between the two communities. In May and June 1936, all unmarried Italians were prohibited from staying in the colonies for more than six months and the half-caste children of unknown parents were denied the possibility of acquiring Italian citizenship. In January 1937, the Minister of the Colonies, Alessandro Lessona, wrote an editorial in *La Stampa* entitled 'Politica di Razza' where he announced the presentation of a draft law that was to punish mixed unions between nationals and natives. According to this law, one to five years of imprisonment were imposed on the 'white man' who was guilty of 'polluting the race' and who had thereby sacrificed the prestige that stemmed from the fact of belonging to a 'superior race'. *Faccetta nera* was banned because according to the regime it seemed to encourage 'racial commixture' between the Italian and the black girl the song was dedicated to.

In most other popular songs of the period referring to Italy's colonies references to Italic virtues and the prospect of a war of liberation expressed reassuring promises of radiant futures for the coloured populations. However, contrary to the homely folk images found in these songs and the myth of a presumed diversity created by Italian colonialism, the disturbing reality is that mass exterminations of the population on African soil by gas were undertaken by the regime. And though camouflaged beneath the myth of Italians as 'good people', the text of a popular song well known to the soldiers engaged in fighting by the title of *Topolino in Abissinia* includes the lines: 'I have armed myself, I have a sword, a rifle, a

---

[27] Anonimo, 'Notizie', *Musica d'oggi* 17/12 (December 1935), 441–2.

machine gun on my shoulder and a half litre of *asphyxiating gas* in my flask!... As soon as I see the Negus I'll pay him out!'[28]

THE DEBATE ON 'GEZ'

From an exclusively musical point of view, the regime strove to rescue Italian music from foreign invasion. Though it is true that imported music never entirely disappeared from the Italian musical scene, the autarchic policy ensured that firm limitations were imposed on those musics (principally jazz) that, like the *tabarin* itself where it was played, had become absorbed into the connective tissue of the country in patent contradiction with the dictates of the regime.

The actual debate on jazz music[29] – Italianised as 'gez' – focused not so much on musical arguments as on political considerations:

It is deplorable and insulting to tradition, and hence to our stock, to consign to the attic our violins, mandolins and guitars in order to blow into saxophones and beat on timpani with barbarous melodies that survive only thanks to the ephemerides of fashion. It is stupid, ridiculous and anti-Fascist to go into ecstasies over the umbilical dances of a mulatta woman or to welcome like idiots every American vogue that comes to us from across the ocean. It is we who must create for ourselves our forms of life, art and beauty, just as we are creating for ourselves our form of government, our laws and our original institutions.[30]

In a radio broadcast of 1926 jazz music was referred to by the composer Mascagni as a phenomenon made up of 'barbarities', 'opium' and 'cocaine'.[31] Likewise, the performers themselves were subjected to harsh criticism from the Italian musical world. The most violent attacks, however, came from the publications closest to the official organs of the regime:

The first time we heard that tangle of rhythms and that deafening tumult of noises we thought it was a joke of the worst kind. But then we were told it was music and indeed music made to express the spirit, the passions and sufferings of humanity today... And so for some years we have been seeing Negroes playing in our dance halls and whites dancing, parodying the grotesque and sometimes obscene gestures of savages and chimpanzees. A sad sight! In this divine Italy where music and dance have been at every moment of history uplifted and often sublimated by the genius

---

[28] The Negus is the ruler of Ethiopia. See Giacomo de Marzi, *I canti del fascismo* (Genoa: Fratelli Frilli Editori, 2004), pp. 103–8: 106.
[29] On Fascist policy towards jazz, see in general: Luca Cerchiari, *Jazz e fascismo, 1922–1945. Dalla nascita della radio a Gorni Kramer*, I suoni del mondo 4 (Palermo: L'Epos, 2003); Adriano Mazzoletti, *Il jazz in Italia. Dalle origini alle grandi orchestre*, Biblioteca di cultura musicale: Jazz (Turin: EDT, 2004); and, in particular, Franzo Goffrini, 'Sensazioni condite al Jazz', *Cremona* 18–19 (September–October 1940), 125–9; Tullo Bellomi, 'Arte degenerata e *Premio Cremona*', *Cremona* 18–19 (September–October 1940), 356–8.
[30] Carlo Ravasio, 'Fascismo e tradizione', *Il popolo d'Italia*, 30 March 1928.
[31] An expression that Mascagni used in a radio broadcast of 1926: 'Mascagni contro la musica jazz', *Corriere della sera*, 16 June 1926.

of our artists to marvellous expressions of national life, we have received with joyful hospitality hordes of black men who have brought to us and imposed the clumsy delirium of their convulsive, asthmatic music.[32]

According to Adriano Lualdi, jazz was a 'cerebral' fashion and a 'snobbish and decadent travesty of the plain musical primitivism of the African Negroes made by Westerners'.[33] He refers to:

ragtime – irresistible syncopated rhythm – complicated by jazz – a very recent method of orchestration and harmony, in the service of the (by now) rather aged ragtime – these derivatives of barbarous Negro music that have been bastardised and degenerated by contact with the fashions and manners of civilised white music. These laborious, premeditated, contrived returns to brutality and noise, violent and cynical reactions of our age to ages of intellectualism and artistic over-refinement, are the *daguerreotype*, the primitive photograph, of the modern life of the big anti-artistic centres . . . Milan and New York – in their capacities as anti-artistic centres – can now shake hands across the Ocean and admire in the ragtime expressed by jazz a *daguerreotype* of their respective spiritual nostalgias and of the practical reality in which they live. And this is precisely the reason it is difficult to understand why so many people take an interest in jazz in cities like these, which have made jazz their style of life and experience it at all hours of the day.[34]

The autocratic campaign in defence of Italian music involved not only the composers used by the regime (like Gorni Kramer, Pippo Barzizza and Cesare Andrea Bixio), but also all of the media and the press, and not least radio.[35] Even the official newspaper of the Fascist party wrote: 'The autarchic battle must be conducted on all fronts, without exception. One must therefore neglect not even music, a sector in which Italy has nothing to learn from abroad and can glorify in its traditional heritage.'[36]

Italian musical taste firmly resisted the directives of the party, however. Jazz had in fact spread easily and rapidly throughout the country, perhaps partly because Italy's own musical production was scarce at this time. Imported music never disappeared from the radio programmes of the EIAR, which had continued to broadcast jazz. On 7 November 1937, one read in the newspaper *La stampa*:

Italian radio plays too much jazz. We do not know how much is played on the American radio, where jazz music should be an indispensable item: what is certain is that no radio in Europe broadcasts as much jazz as Italian radio. One reason for this preference is easily identified; a great responsibility for this influx of incessant, persistent jazz music on the radio is the Cetra [Orchestra]. The Cetra Orchestra plays jazz music; Cetra-Parlophon records it; and the radio transmits it, either

[32] Guido Carlo Visconti di Modrone, 'Fuori i Barbari!', *Il popolo d'Italia*, 13 September 1929.
[33] Fiamma Nicolodi, *Musica e musicisti nel ventennio fascista*, p. 90, n. 57.
[34] Adriano Lualdi, *Viaggio musicale in Italia* (Milan: Alpes, 1927), pp. 244–5.
[35] Other composers used by the regime include Armando Camera, Enzo Ceragioli, Michele D'Elia and Eldo Di Lazzaro.
[36] *Il popolo d'Italia*, 4 March 1938.

played directly from the studios or recorded on disc. And it transmits it repeatedly, either grouped together at specially designated times or just occasionally, perhaps just to fill a gap.[37]

It is in this light that we must interpret the numerous 'calls to order' made by Mauro Janni, editor of daily newspaper *Il popolo d'Italia* (subtitled *Quotidiano socialista*, 'Socialist Daily', and created on 15 November 1914 by Mussolini himself), to the broadcasting company: '[D]o not forget that radio is made for the people and not for that exiguous band of male and female "fops" that spend much of the day in epileptic vocal – and corporeal – manifestations. Congenital idiocy must not be encouraged.'[38] However, by that time this 'degenerate music' had met with general approval even among the most varied sectors of the population. Moreover, practices such as *camuffamento* (literally, disguise, or the translation of the words of foreign songs) were increasingly common, to the extent that even Janni complained that it had the effect of 'destroying the little – the very little – artistic value that the foreign songs had'.[39]

For fear of potentially distancing the ruling class from the people, Janni rectified the thrust of his declarations, by conceding a certain artistic dignity to the good 'gez' produced in Italy. However, the attempts made by the regime to create legislation that would safeguard the Italian product had scant results. On 7 February 1939 *Il popolo d'Italia* announced that the problem of light music would very soon be resolved by certain legislative measures. One such measure was to be a ban on printing more than twenty per cent of foreign music (in exchange for Italian music published abroad) and an obligation not to exceed the same percentage in performances. However, jazz had by then become a deeply rooted phenomenon in Italian society. In spite of the campaigns of censorship and propaganda in defence of musical autarchy conducted by the regime right from the start, jazz had succeeded in penetrating Italian popular music by various strategies.

Attitudes towards music in Fascist Italy reflect what Gaspare and Roberto De Caro have noted about the Racial Laws of 1937. For these authors, the Racial Laws, which anticipated the Anti-Jewish Laws, 'contradict the widespread, calumnious interpretation of events, according to which racism in Italy was a late Nazi importation, because in the "fatherland of law" there was no need for prompters even on this issue'.[40] Racism

---

[37] *La stampa*, 7 November 1937.
[38] *Il popolo d'Italia*, 7 July 1938. After his rise to power in 1922, Mussolini entrusted this paper to his brother Arnaldo in order to ensure the maximum control; in 1931 it passed into the hands of his nephew Vito. *Il popolo d'Italia* always remained Mussolini's personal instrument and hence the positions it took faithfully mirrored the 'official' thinking of Fascism.
[39] Ibid.
[40] Gaspare De Caro and Roberto De Caro, 'La Shoah di Polanski e l'arte della memoria', *Hortus Musicus* 5/17 (2004), 126, fn. 197; see also Gaspare De Caro and Roberto De Caro, 'Del primato morale e civile degli italiani', *Hortus Musicus* 5/18 (2004), 4–14. For more on the Racial Laws of 1937, see also Luigi Goglia and Fabio Grassi (eds.), *Il colonialismo italiano da Adua all'Impero* (Rome-Bari:

had always been an instrument used to maintain Italian dominion in its colonies; as such, the advent of Fascism did not involve a radical change of approach so much as an escalation of violence. One might add to this that in the heartland of Futurism, there was likewise no need for the importation of Wagnerian cultural regenerationisms. Too often, even in historical studies, comparison with other totalitarian regimes, such as Nazi Germany, has suggested that the Italian situation was some sort of happy refuge. This was by no means the case. In its capacity for repression, Italy's regime was second to none.

Laterza, 1993); Centro Furio Jesi (ed.), *La menzogna della razza. Documenti e immagini del razzismo e dell'antisemitismo fascista* (Bologna: Grafis, 1994); Alberto Burgio (ed.), *Nel nome della razza. Il razzismo nella storia d'Italia: 1870–1945*.

CHAPTER 13

Romanticism, technology and the masses: Honegger and the aesthetic allure of French fascism

Jane F. Fulcher

When considering a composer's politics, one might immediately summon the famous phrase of Stephen Spender that the politics of the artist is the politics of the 'apolitical', decided on for the sake of life and art, and not of politics.[1] Most often construed as essentially an idealist re-assertion of aesthetic autonomy, it evokes the artist as benign opportunist, using politics pragmatically for a transcendent, noble end. More centrally, perhaps, it absolves him of political responsibility for his ideological choices, which appear to be dictated primarily by artistic concerns, and the results of which are negligible politically.

Several figures, however, shatter this paradigm, centrally including Richard Wagner, Louis-Ferdinand Céline, Ezra Pound, Richard Strauss, and in the related field of scholarship Paul de Man. The first three cases indeed make it clear that the artist may employ baleful images in the service of great art, which, because of his political associations or prose, are consequently marshalled toward a malevolent end. The case of de Man raises similar issues about the interpretation of acts and calibration of guilt: can ideologically sordid involvements and politically damaging publications taint subsequent intellectual projects?[2]

Arthur Honegger demands similar interrogations, or further penetration of all of the issues, given the recent awareness of his role in French fascist or 'fascisising' circles in the years between the wars. Not fully aware of the ideological implications, Honegger was enticed by French fascist aesthetics, which held innovation and tradition in taut relation and imbued modern imagery with an emotional, nostalgic tone. This aesthetic, in comparison with those of German and Italian fascism, shall initially provide my focus, but particularly the French fascist enshrinement of the artist, such as Arthur Honegger, as a maker of myths.

---

[1] On Spender's views concerning politics and the artist, see his article, 'Poetry and Revolution', originally published in *New Country* in 1933 and reprinted in Stephen Spender, *The Thirties and After: Poetry, Politics, People (1933–75)* (London: Macmillan, 1978), pp. 43–53. On his own political involvements, see pp. 13–33.
[2] On the case of Paul de Man, see Alan Spitzer, *Historical Truth and Lies About the Past: Reflections on Dewey, Dreyfus, de Man, and Reagan* (Chapel Hill: University of North Carolina Press, 1996), pp. 61–85.

From here I shall turn to the nettlesome issue of what is 'in' Honegger's music, or the relation of its style and images to the movements that promoted it, and how his political associations affected construal in his day. My focus here will be on *Jeanne d'Arc au bûcher*, its nature and impact in 1939 and during Vichy, as well as Honegger's role in encouraging politicised perceptions, or misappropriations, of its meaning. This will lead me in the end to the issue that musicology has so often dismissed of the role and the impact of images and symbols in politics, in shaping understandings or in beguiling the public. The question of race is central here, for music and the discourse around it played a significant part in the moulding of racial images, and specifically those deployed by anti-Semitic rhetoric, in twentieth-century France. Honegger participated in a tradition of thought and behaviour that included other figures discussed in this section, such as Vincent d'Indy, who are similarly absolved in current scholarship as simply naive artists, using common parlance to advance their noble cause. Clearly, this transposes the question of political opportunism for artistic ends into a different key: are those who participated in their art's appropriation as a noxious symbol free of guilt?

HONEGGER AND 'NON-CONFORMISM' IN THE 1930S

Like Francis Poulenc, Arthur Honegger was not an enthusiastic supporter of the Left coalition of the mid-1930s, the Popular Front, although he did participate in its programmes and *fêtes*. Honegger, just as Poulenc, was sincerely attracted to 'the popular' as a concept, but not in the narrowly partisan sense as conceived by the government between 1936 and 1938. For this government, the goal of art was to project a contemporary, democratic and enlightened mass culture, as opposed to the archaic, hierarchic, and often Romantic models of the German fascists. Indeed, Honegger's own tastes were distant from the Popular Front aesthetic of a modern but accessible music that avoided complicated architecture as well as traditional or sophisticated techniques.

Yet, as so many artists in the 1930s, Honegger took a true interest in ideological movements and social questions, confronted by mass politics and parties as well as by the social and political trauma of the decade. His search was for the right kind of relation between his aesthetic proclivities, which were both traditionalist and modern, and the projected broad audience that he sincerely wished to attract through his art. This would lead him to other movements that sought a different social and aesthetic future, which, as Honegger discovered, were not, like most colleagues in *Les Six*, within the Republican tradition.

Already, at the beginning of the 1930s, Honegger had turned to a literary and philosophical circle associated with a new generation of French youth seeking a 'spiritualist' solution to the political impasse. Referred to as the 'non-conformist' movement, some of its groupings would attract certain younger French composers, however with a slight delay, as the Popular Front crested and then declined. But Honegger was immediately drawn to specific aspects and themes of this movement, and particularly to one of its journals, the cultural concerns of which mirrored his own. For he was unquestionably an intellectual – an avid reader, aware of the implications of contemporary movements of thought, most of which, during this period, were responding to political, social and ideological crisis.[3]

Non-conformism crossed a broad spectrum and ranged from groupings that were closer to the Left or the Right, and which could ultimately lead either to a complicity with fascism or to unequivocal refusal. However, they were united by 'a general rejection of liberal values and institutions of the Third Republic' and 'an acute anxiety about the future of France'. This tendency, of course, embraced such movements as Communism and Christian Democracy, and it also included French fascism, which would become a powerful intellectual current.[4] But the non-conformists specifically rejected an approach to man as an 'atom', as in liberal democracy, or as merely a unit within a totalitarian series. Emphatically anti-materialist, they envisioned man as a responsible, spiritual being, tied to others in a communitarian vocation, free of political, national or social boundaries.[5]

One of the many non-conformist journals of the early 1930s was *Plans*, directed by Philippe Lamour, a supporter of Mussolini, who would later found a *Parti Fasciste Révolutionnaire*, and then grow close to the Vichy regime. Its spirit was one of both modernity and reform, which undoubtedly appealed to Honegger, as did its myth of the ideal 'plan' for the technological state of the future. *Plans* was a journal that also emphasised geographic and cultural regionalism, or the relation of man to the soil, to his race, his community, and to his cultural tradition.[6] Honegger, as we will recall, was

---

[3] Honegger may well have been introduced to non-conformist ideas by one of his literary collaborators of the period, a fellow Swiss, Denis de Rougemont, who moved to Paris in 1930 and became involved with the non-conformist journals *L'Ordre nouveau* and *Esprit*, while also collaborating on the *Nouvelle revue française*. It was he who later wrote the libretto for Honegger's *Nicolas de Flue*, based on the story of one of Switzerland's national heroes. See 'Rougemont, Denis de', by Pascal Balmand, in Jacques Julliard and Michel Winock (eds.), *Dictionnaire des intellectuels français: les personnes, les lieux, les moments* (Paris: Seuil, 1996), pp. 1006–7.

[4] See Robert Wohl, 'French Fascism, Both Right and Left: Reflections on the Sternhell Controversy', *Journal of Modern History* 63/1 (1991), 91–8.

[5] The larger rejection of liberal values may explain Honegger's involvement in a Communist project. He wrote the music for a short film, *Visage de la France*, a gift from the French Communist Party to the Soviet Union in 1937, in honour of the twentieth anniversary of the October Revolution. See Harry Halbreich, *Arthur Honegger*, trans. Roger Nichols (Portland, OR: Amadeus, 1999), p. 146. Honegger also wrote several short *chants de masses* for the Communist *Editions du chant du Monde*.

[6] See Jean-Louis Loubet del Bayle, *Les Non-conformistes des années 30* (Paris: Seuil, 1969), pp. 92–6. *Plans* was considered '*moderniste*' and '*réformateur*', as was *L'Ordre nouveau*, which was edited by Robert Aron and Armand Dandrieu. See Olivier Corpet, '*La Revue*', in Jean-François Sirinelli (ed.), *Histoire des Droites en France* (Paris: Gallimard, 1992), p. 178. On the '*planisme*' of *Plans* and Philippe Lamour's myth of the ideal plan of '*l'Etat technicien*' (which included Le Corbusier's urban models)

in fact a Swiss national living in France, born and raised by German-Swiss parents in Le Havre, and restlessly in search of a firm collective identity.

He was thus attracted not only by the journal's emphasis on the role of culture and race, as opposed to nationality, but also by its attempt to provide a synthesis of scientific, economic, political and aesthetic advances of the period. Like other non-conformist journals, one of its fundamental themes was the necessity of youth projecting and creating a new world, one that would be both progressive and spiritual. Hence the editorial committee included those who were drawn not only from a variety of sympathetic social perspectives, but from different fields or cultural disciplines. On it, for example, were not only Honegger but Le Corbusier (a Swiss who became naturalised French), the writer René Clair and the artist Fernand Léger. The first issue of the journal, in fact, contained an article by Le Corbusier in which he presents his theory of a new kind of architecture and social order, 'La Ville radieuse'. But it also included an article by Honegger which, like Le Corbusier's, advocates a marshalling of the latest techniques of his art in the interest of a new social vision.[7] Its subject is music for film, which had interested Honegger since his earlier collaborations with Abel Gance on the silent films *La Roue* (1923) and *Napoléon* (1927). Now, with the economic depression, Honegger was increasingly drawn into film, and was concerned with both the process of 'sonorisation' and with balancing musical continuity (as opposed to pastiche) with the continual demands of the action.[8]

Entitled 'Du cinéma sonore à la musique réelle' (From sound cinema to real music), it begins by addressing the technical problem of reconciling cinematic exigencies with musical form. But it ends with a telling metaphor that reveals a great deal about Honegger's vision of the aesthetic and social goal of his art and its ties to a certain trajectory within non-conformist thought: 'Music can ... become herself, enter into reality, be like the cinema, and with it, a genuine, unanimous, collective force, no longer subjected to the anarchic revisions of individualities, but applying itself with all its force to a transported crowd.'[9]

---

see Romy Golan, *Modernity and Nostalgia: Art and Politics in France Between the Wars* (New Haven: Yale University Press, 1995), pp. 76 ff. Also see Georges Lefranc, 'Le Courant planiste de 1933 à 1936', *Le Mouvement social* 54 (January–March 1966), 69–89.

[7] See Loubet del Bayle, *Les Non-conformistes*, pp. 94–6, and Le Corbusier, 'Invite à l'action', *Plans* (January 1931), 5. Also see Golan, p. 76. She notes that all the editors of the journal criticised '*l'homme économique*' of the Marxists and '*l'homme abstrait*' of the democrats, promoting rather '*l'homme réel*' or '*concret*'. As the opening editorial of *Plans* put it, their goal was 'the blossoming of a more human civilization, where man, dominating the tyranny of the machine ... would retrieve his place in the universe'. Ibid.

Politically, Le Corbusier tended to support those governments that were willing to use their authority in the interest of the 'masses', and particularly in creating an architecture for them. On Le Corbusier see Mark Antliff, '*La Cité française*: Georges Valois, Le Corbusier, and Fascist Theories of Urbanism', in Matthew Affron and Mark Antliff (eds.), *Fascist Visions: Art and Ideology in France and Italy* (Princeton University Press, 1997), pp. 134–70.

[8] See Halbreich, *Arthur Honegger*, p. 377 on *La Roue*, and on Honegger's article in *Plans*, see 525–7.

[9] Arthur Honegger, 'Du cinéma sonore à la musique réelle', *Plans* (January 1931), 74–8.

SEEDS OF THE FRENCH FASCIST AESTHETIC
IN '*PLANISME*'

Honegger's stress on the collective, on the force and reality of the emotions that unite it, and on the use of technology toward an anti-materialist end was by no means an isolated discourse. Rather, it tied in with the journal's adaptation of Sorelian rhetoric (or that characteristic of the syndicalist leader, Georges Sorel, during the period (*c.* 1907) when he allied himself with the nationalist Right), and to its elaboration in the 1920s by Sorel's follower, Georges Valois, who then became (for several years) a fascist. Both thinkers emphasised the importance of the spiritual, of re-sacralising an atomised, materialistic society so that the classes would ultimately work together, fused through the force of a galvanising collective myth. Tapping intuition, as opposed to reason, was thus paramount for them in realising these values, as was altruism and sacrifice, which similarly demanded a myth that would both impress and unite.

Here the artist was central; indeed, for Sorel the aesthetic dimension of myth was essential in both inspiring and effecting all subsequent political action. For aesthetic forces could 'manifest' the new order as well as the new sensibility sustaining it, and thereby not only transform consciousness, but unite and inspire consequent acts. As a result, artistic myths had criteria in order to arrive at the desired social end: they had first to be attuned to the sensibility of the masses, which required dynamism, precision and speed. One might immediately note the connection to the Futurist strain within fascism in Italy, which is indeed no coincidence since Mussolini (as Valois noted) similarly traced his roots to the Sorelian circle. For Valois such imagery was also tied to violence, which was a necessary ethical and regenerative force: spiritually, physically and politically, it was a revolt against decadence and a source of creativity.[10]

This, in turn, fostered the image of rebirth, based upon the return to a past that was 'pure' or more glorious – to healthy eras in national history as sources for true regeneration. Again, we encounter a parallel with fascism in Italy, with its cult of 'Romanness', or reactionary nostalgia, which could be combined with certain vital Futurist elements. For Italian and French fascists in the 1920s, cultural traditions were to form the basis of a new civilisation that combined the revolutionary and conservative, addressing both the past and the future at once. As a result, in both Italy and France, as opposed to Germany, fascist aesthetics covered the gamut from abstract or 'advanced' artistic trends through various historicist and traditionalist styles. Sorel himself had idealised the medieval guild as well as monastic communities,

---

[10] Antliff, '*La Cité française*', p. 152 and the 'Introduction' to *Fascist Visions*, by Matthew Affron and Mark Antliff, p. 15. The French were well aware of Italian fascism since Italian fascists were 'implanted' in over twenty French towns, and included 2,400 of Mussolini's secret police, unofficial agents, and 'provocateurs'. See Eugen Weber, *The Hollow Years: France in the 1930s* (New York: Norton, 1994), p. 89.

associating both with the art of the people, as had Ruskin and the pre-Raphaelites. In this spirit, he similarly enshrined Jeanne d'Arc as the incarnation of '*la cité française*', or the nation's common spiritual values and the political system that expressed them within French geographical borders.[11]

But the machine was also a resonant symbol, particularly for Georges Valois, who believed that rational technological planning could be imbued with a creative or intuitive spirit. Technological modernism and vitalism (or the cult of an unreflective 'life-force') were thus one, and considered a part of the fascist mystique not only in Italy but in France, as well as in German 'reactionary modernism', as Jeffrey Herf has shown. Indeed, in Italian Futurism the machine became a model of social integration, of social and political organisation and the functional harmonisation of man and nature.[12]

It is, then, little surprise that Valois's *Faisceau*, the first fascist party in France, founded in 1924, was quick to appropriate the urbanist ideals of Le Corbusier. In search of an organic order that was superior to modern democracy, they adapted his concepts to their own Sorelian, anti-materialist and corporatist social programmes. The architect was received with enthusiasm within the French fascist party, having been attracted to its circle in 1927 and giving a slide presentation to a fascist rally.[13]

THE AMBIGUITY OF *JEANNE D'ARC AU BÛCHER*

Honegger's trajectory was different: his attraction to groups openly supporting fascism would not occur until the later 1930s, although he was previously well aware of their ideas. Not only was he friends with Le Corbusier, working with him on *Plans* and on subsequent projects, but in the 1920s he had made contact with Gabriele d'Annunzio, who had himself become a fascist. But this was the decade when Honegger collaborated with a number of highly engaged artists across the entire political spectrum, which undoubtedly raised his own ideological awareness. These included not only Abel Gance, but also Romain Rolland, with whom he worked on the trenchant and controversial anti-war play entitled *Liluli*.

Honegger's collaboration with d'Annunzio was on *Phaedre*, after he had met the politician and poet through the intermediary of Ida Rubenstein, the originally Russian dancer and entrepreneur. The first performance of *Phaedre* in Rome led to violent protests and a near riot when young fascists

---

[11] Affron and Antliff, 'Introduction', pp. 10 and 17, and Antliff, '*La Cité française*', pp. 146, 149. Also see Matthew Affron, 'Waldemar George: A Parisian Art Critic on Modernism and Fascism', in *Fascist Visions*, p. 195.

[12] See Antliff, '*La Cité française*', p. 161. Also see Jeffrey Herf, *Reactionary Modernism: Technology, Culture, and Politics in Weimar and the Third Reich* (Cambridge University Press, 1984) and Andrew Hewitt, *Fascist Modernism: Aesthetics, Politics, and the Avant-Garde* (Stanford University Press, 1993), pp. 133 and 147.

[13] Affron and Antliff, *Fascist Visions*, pp. 15 and 18, and Antliff, '*La Cité française*', pp. 131, 134–5, 137, and 149–51.

in the audience became enraged at the absence of their hero, d'Annunzio, who had been sent to prison.[14] Honegger, well aware of d'Annunzio's takeover of Fiume and his fascist associations, did not now sever his relations with the writer, and in fact subsequently paid him a visit on his Italian estate. Moreover, he was undoubtedly apprised not only of the early French fascist aesthetic but also its affinity with the Italian, especially their dual emphasis on the past and the future.

The natural proximity of Honegger to this aesthetic is clear in several of his early works, but perhaps most patently in his first *mouvement symphonique*, entitled *Pacific 231*. Here he suggests the impression of speed, or acceleration through mathematical rhythmic means, gradually increasing the rhythmic subdivisions while also decreasing the tempo. But the modern machine-like imagery serves to mask the traditional form subtending the work: cast as a kind of chorale prelude, the theme is stated grandiosely as a cantus firmus in the end.

Honegger was no fascist in this period, but these aesthetic proclivities would ineluctably lead to his appropriation, like Le Corbusier, by fascist circles in the course of the 1930s, and with his consent. The work that eventually won the most extensive praise among fascist sympathisers in the 1930s and during Vichy was Honegger's *Jeanne d'Arc au bûcher*, the ideological uses of which would be encouraged by his later political involvements. It was shortly after his activities with *Plans* that Honegger composed the work, which does, in fact, parallel some of the Sorelian circle's aesthetic values.

A conversation between Ida Rubenstein, Honegger and the musicologist Jacques Chailley (who had participated in attempts at the Sorbonne to recreate medieval theatre) led to the proposal of Jeanne d'Arc as the subject for a modern version of a mystery play. Claudel was selected to provide the text, but apparently hesitated to do so because of the number of recent and politicised works on Jeanne d'Arc in France. Claudel particularly wished to distance himself from contemporary, left-wing versions of the story, and so avoided any reference to the present, preferring an elevated, universalised version.[15] This lofty approach, as well as the musical style and Honegger's further intellectual activities, would all become factors in subsequent political and ideological appropriations of the work. The score was completed by 1935, shortly before the advent of the Popular Front, and was later reworked as an oratorio, but not performed in France until 1939. As we shall shortly see, in the tense, reactionary climate of the later 1930s, and given Honegger's popularity with the widely read pro-fascist press, the work won immediate and enthusiastic acclaim.

---

[14] See Arthur Honegger, *I am a Composer*, trans. Wilson O. Clough (New York: St. Martin's Press, 1996), p. 107, and James Harding, *The Ox on the Roof: Scenes from Musical Life in Paris in the Twenties* (New York: St. Martin's Press, 1972), p. 124.
[15] Halbreich, *Arthur Honegger*, p. 701.

Honegger's goal was to write a simple but powerful kind of music that, in keeping with his professed aesthetic position, would not require sophistication on the part of the audience. In order to bring the text alive, he attempted to synthesise a diversity of styles and genres, and employed an imaginative orchestration which included both saxophones and *ondes Martenot*.[16] Honegger also incorporated authentic folkloric elements into the work, and, inevitably, their rural and reactionary associations would cause a political problem in 1936.

Created before the style employed was considered politically inimical to the Popular Front, *Jeanne d'Arc* was ready for production in 1936, when both religion and peasant folklore were closely associated with the Right. Honegger's stylistic choices were based upon what he considered to be appropriate to the nature of Claudel's text, and perhaps to some of the 'vitalist' aesthetic values that he had developed in the circle of *Plans*. For Honegger the element of folklore was central to the full realisation of the text, and so he attempted to incorporate folkloric elements, especially authentic *chansons populaires*. He not only employed but emphasised such chansons, as well as other relevant musical materials that were associated with those geographical areas related to the text – Laon, Beaune and Troy. In addition, he made frequent reference to older liturgical music, including Gregorian chant as well as early sacred polyphony.[17]

The premiere was planned for the Paris Opéra in 1936, and then pushed back to May 1937, and there are several explanations as to why neither performance occurred. Among them are lack of adequate preparation as well as the financial constrictions being widely felt in France at the time, which made such a large-scale production difficult. But here it is significant to note that in 1936 the Chamber of Deputies actually voted the Opéra additional funding of 450,000 francs. This was intended to aid presentation of new works by French composers, and undoubtedly contributed to the lavish staging of a composition by Charles Koechlin (a strong supporter of the government), his opera *Oedipe*. It is therefore unlikely that the premiere of *Jeanne d'Arc* was cancelled due to lack of funds: a more plausible explanation is its stylistic and political inappropriateness in 1936 and 1937.[18]

---

[16] Marcel Delannoy, *Honegger* (Geneva: Slatkine, 1986), pp. 181–3.
[17] On the style of other works about Jeanne d'Arc in the period see Delannoy, *Honegger*, p. 175. Also see, for example, Manuel Rosenthal's *Jeanne d'Arc. Suite symphonique en 5 parties. Après la 'Jeanne d'Arc' de Joseph Delteil* [the Surrealist] (1937). This work, significantly, is dedicated to Rosenthal's mentor and friend, Maurice Ravel, who had originally planned to set Delteil's avant-garde treatment of the story as a musical drama.
[18] See Honegger, *Ecrits*, ed. Huguette Calmel (Paris: H. Champion, 1992), p. 331. Also see Halbreich, *Arthur Honegger*, p. 172; José Bruyr, *L'Ecran des musiciens*, 2nd series (Paris: Corti, 1933), p. 186; Geoffrey Spratt, *The Music of Arthur Honegger* (Cork University Press, 1987), p. 253; Myriam Chimènes, 'Le Budget de la musique', in Hugues Dufourt and Joël-Marie Fauquet (eds.), *Musique du théorique au politique* (Paris: Klincksieck, 1991), p. 268; and Jean Zay, *Souvenirs et solitude* (Paris: Talus d'Approche, 1987), p. 191.

Not surprisingly, when the work finally premiered on 12 May 1938 in Basel, Switzerland (under Paul Sacher) it was those politically conservative or pro-fascist French journals that immediately expressed enthusiasm. The French premiere did not occur until 8 May 1939 in Orléans, in conjunction with the annual festival of the saint, made a national holiday in 1922.[19]

FRENCH FASCISM AND ITS USES OF MUSIC

The work's reception in France was heavily influenced by Honegger's image in the press, especially the traditionalist, conservative press of the Right and that with more 'fascisising' tendencies. Here it is important to recall the nature of French fascism as it evolved in the 1920s and 1930s, more as an 'ideal type' or intellectual model than as a political force. Of course, much disagreement remains over whether we can properly label a larger sympathy or mood, as opposed to a coherent political organisation or regime, as authentically 'fascist'. Equally at issue is the question of whether fascism as a movement was inherently French (as Zeev Sternhell argues) or merely a foreign importation that lay outside the main French political traditions.[20]

However, there is general consensus among scholars concerning the distinctive character of the fascist 'climate' as it developed in France and finally crested in the late 1930s. Most historians agree that fascist influence in France was spread by a small coterie of intellectuals, journalists and men of letters, but one that wielded considerable influence. Hence fascism in France, despite the existence of small fascist parties, such as Valois's and Doriot's, was more an intellectual and cultural than a significant political movement.[21]

The ideology that French fascists espoused in the 1930s shared certain traits with other European fascisms – a revolt against liberal democracy and bourgeois society and a systematic refusal of all materialism. They too believed that the state alone properly represented all the classes of society, and thus it was incumbent on the nation to realise a harmonious and organic collectivity. But the fascism of French intellectuals was far less 'volkish' in emphasis than the German variety, less inclined to glorify a mystical 'Volk soul' or the masses as its embodiment. And it similarly emphasised an ethic – that of a 'virile, pessimistic, and puritanical new world', or one that was founded upon an abiding sense of duty and selfless sacrifice.[22]

---

[19] Spratt, pp. 253–4.
[20] Affron and Antliff, p. 8, and Wohl, pp. 95–8. Also see Robert Soucy, 'Barrès and French Fascism', *French Historical Studies* 5/1 (1967), 67, and his 'French Press Reactions to Hitler's First Two Years in Power', *Contemporary European History* 7/1 (1998), 21–2. Also see his book, *French Fascism: the Second Wave, 1933–1939* (New Haven: Yale University Press, 1995).
[21] Serge Berstein, *La France des années 30* (Paris: Armand Colin, 1993), pp. 98ff. Also see Soucy, 'Barrès and French Fascism', p. 72, and Zeev Sternhell, *Neither Right nor Left: Fascist Ideology in France*, trans. David Maisel (Princeton University Press, 1995), p. 23.
[22] Sternhell, *Neither Right nor Left*, pp. 21–7 and Soucy, 'Barrès and French Fascism', pp. 67 ff.

Because of this emphasis on duty and 'vision', French fascists continued to promote both the sacred and subjective, articulating their goals in ethical and aesthetic terms, here recalling the Romantic movement. For fascist intellectuals like Pierre Drieu La Rochelle and Robert Brasillach, French fascism was synonymous with a new 'mystique', or a new kind of social imagination. As we have noted, although modernist in projecting an industrial utopia, they were nevertheless regressive in spirit, emphasising the theme of a necessary return to an imagined purity of origins. Finally, French fascists were less concerned with political doctrine or a utilitarian aesthetic (as opposed to German fascists) than with lyricism and affective themes, exalting emotional and moral values. French fascism thus addressed itself primarily to the imagination and feelings, its proponents seeking above all directly to affect the sensibilities of their readers. In quest of a new 'style' of collective life and a poeticisation of the political world, they strove to confront a de-sacralised society with subjective moral and aesthetic conceptions.[23]

If the rhetoric of French fascism made consistent use of music it was because here, especially, it could apply its nebulous spiritual and social values with both cogency and coherence. Far from being neglected, the imagery of music provided French fascist rhetoric with a powerful conceit, a language and legitimation through association with a lofty 'high art'. In music, as in literature, the cardinal values of 'elite' French fascist thinkers were emotion and lyricism, with a stress on the group (as opposed to the individual) and on the 'pure' realm of the spirit. Earlier, d'Indy and the Schola Cantorum had associated these ideals directly with symphonic music, the German classics, Germanic forms, and with techniques and genres carrying religious associations. These were indeed the models promoted in the fascist journals *Gringoire*, *Candide* and *Je suis partout* by prominent critics, some of whom had attacked them decades before.

HONEGGER'S ROLE IN BERGERY'S *FRONTISME*

This climate and aesthetic would indeed influence the reception of *Jeanne d'Arc au bûcher* which, like Honegger's other works, was hailed with panegyric in the French pro-fascist press. But another important influence

---

[23] Although the fascist utopia was an industrial society, dominated by the state, it was spiritually reactionary, questing for a return to an imagined purity of origins. See Jane F. Fulcher, 'Musical Style, Meaning, and Politics in France on the Eve of the First World War', *Journal of Musicology* 13/4 (1995), 425–53. On those aspects of Hitler and German fascism that French fascists did not like, see Soucy, 'French Press Reactions to Hitler's First Two Years in Power', p. 22. Also see Paul Sérant, *Le Romantisme Fasciste: Étude sur l'oeuvre politique de quelques écrivains français* (Paris: Fasquelle, 1960), pp. 94–5 and 112. As Soucy points out, in 'Barrès and French Fascism', p. 272, French fascism was 'less taken with the "*Führer prinzip*", and less attached to the principles of totalitarianism'. Berstein, *La France des années 30*, pp. 97–9, stresses French fascism's activating 'mystique' and exaltation of vitalist values. On the literary manifestation of French fascism, see David Carroll, *French Literary Fascism: Nationalism, Anti-Semitism, and the Ideology of Culture* (Princeton University Press, 1995).

here was Honegger's own evolving political associations, by now not distant from the press that consistently gave his works such vociferous praise. By 1938 Honegger had grown close to the circle of Gaston Bergery, originally a centrist, Radical-Socialist deputy, who had turned against the Popular Front. As Bergery and his followers gradually perceived the failure of the Left coalition, they began to criticise the Prime Minister, Léon Blum, and to denounce all established political parties.

Bergery then broke with the principal league of the Left, the *Ligue des Droits de l'Homme*, assuming an anti-war stance despite fascist threats in Italy, Germany and Spain. Publicly, however, he remained discreet, avoiding all overt statement of his feelings with regard to the current fascist movements and regimes in Europe. Still, it was clear that Bergery valued certain aspects of fascist regimes – their anti-liberalism, their economic *dirigisme*, and the state's organisation of social life. In addition, he was anti-Semitic, although as Philippe Burrin has put it, 'artfully so', blaming the Jews themselves for anti-Semitism by stressing their comportment, as opposed to race.[24] Bergery was here defining himself, as an assimilated, upper-class French Jew, against recent poor Jewish immigrants who refused cultural conformity and thus entry into the national entity, often referred to earlier in the century in terms of 'race'.

The movement that Bergery began, '*Frontisme*', was politically ambiguous in 1938 and 1939 since he called for the reform, not abolition, of the Republican state. During this period he was actively courting both intellectual and artistic circles, and in 1938 he formed a club to support his journal, called *Les amis de La Flèche*.[25] Among the *Comité d'Honneur* it counted not only André Gide, but also Arthur Honegger, as well as Honegger's choreographic collaborator, Serge Lifar. By 1938 Bergery's movement was clearly veering to the Right, just ahead of the general defeat of Republican values that would become manifest in the Munich accords. As Robert Paxton has pointed out, the '*Frontiste*' movement in the later 1930s was an 'antiparliamentary, anticapitalist appeal for national unity against communism and against "the trusts"'.[26] And so Bergery, he observes, indeed 'sounds objectively fascist', although publicly he denounced fascism for its racial, as opposed to cultural, anti-Semitism. Pétain's government (during Vichy) would share this stress on cultural assimilation as opposed to race, making Bergery, who

---

[24] Bergery, although Jewish by birth, saw himself as culturally different from Jews in certain other countries, and apparently did not feel threatened by the racial laws of the fascist regimes. See Philippe Burrin, *La Dérive fasciste. Doriot, Déat, Bergery 1933–1945* (Paris: Seuil, 1986), p. 238. On Bergery's break with the *Ligue des Droits de l'Homme*, see pp. 219–21.

[25] Bergery's journal, *La Flèche*, had grown regularly in its subscriptions, from 4,500 in 1936 to 10,000 in 1938. On Bergery and '*Frontisme*' see Robert O. Paxton, *Vichy France: Old Guard and New Order, 1940–1944* (New York: Columbia University Press, 1972), pp. 273–4.

[26] Ibid., p. 214.

in fact was Jewish, its ambassador to the Soviet Union and then to Turkey.

'*Frontisme*', in retrospect, has historically been identified with the process of 'fascisisation', for by 1938 it shared significant values with all the major fascist movements. These included a desire for a homogeneous national body, achieved through exclusion, a sense of the necessity of taking charge of the nation forcibly, and a belief in the integral role of the leader in doing so. Hence having initially been a movement to combat fascism (when Germaine Tailleferre supported Bergery), '*Frontisme*' ended by approving of certain fascist ideals. This was the moment when Arthur Honegger lent his name openly in support of Bergery's journal and, by extension, in the mind of the public, to his ideological programme.[27]

Certainly, Honegger did profit from his public association with the journal *La Flèche*: reaching an elite and influential readership, it consistently supported his music in highly favourable reviews. And it promoted Honegger not only in print but in performance, for *La Flèche*, like *Action française* before it, sponsored concerts not only to obtain contributions but for 'symbolic capital', and they proudly featured his work.[28] *La Flèche*, like other pro-fascist journals, emphasised Honegger's stylistic traditionalism in order further to dissociate him from the now maligned aesthetic of *Les Six*. So did André Coeuroy (a future collaborator), who asserted in the openly fascist *Gringoire* that Honegger would go down in history as the leading musician of his period in France.[29] In addition, the rabidly anti-Semitic and fascist critic of the arts, Lucien Rebatet, was a vocal supporter of Honegger's music in several journals, including the pro-fascist *Je suis partout*. Honegger was indeed to benefit from such constructions of himself as an artist, particularly as the aesthetic and political opposition to the Popular Front triumphed upon its fall. And this would have an unquestionable impact on public construal of *Jeanne d'Arc au bûcher* when the work finally premiered in France on 8 May 1939.

HONEGGER'S TRIUMPH ON THE EVE OF AND DURING VICHY

Honegger's star had been rising steadily in the course of the later 1930s: now frequently performed, and with wide approbation, he was elected to the Institut de France. But his greatest triumph of the period was unquestionably *Jeanne d'Arc au bûcher* which, although it premiered in Orléans,

---

[27] Bergery made a trip to Italy in the summer of 1937 and, according to a contemporary, Georges Izard, was highly impressed with the fascist regime there. Burrin, *La Dérive fasciste*, pp. 223–5.
[28] On *La Flèche* see Michel Winock, *Le Siècle des intellectuels* (Paris: Seuil, 1997), pp. 235–7. I am using 'symbolic capital' here in the sense made current by the sociologist Pierre Bourdieu.
[29] André Coeuroy, *Gringoire*, 18 February 1938.

was widely reported in the Parisian and national press.[30] Now the moment was right for *Jeanne* – indeed it was perfect for a work that ritualistically celebrated a national saint, employing both religious and folk traditions. Reception was closely linked not only to Honegger's image in the pro-fascist and conservative press, but to shifts in French political and cultural values by 1939.

Critics, in large part, were ecstatic: in the climate of mounting anxiety over the future of France, the work appeared to reflect the current plight of the nation, linking it to the past and sustaining new hopes. Given the conservative stylistic priorities of the period, most critics predictably praised Honegger's use of traditional popular chansons, of Gregorian chant, and of Renaissance-like polyphony. Most fulsome of all was the article by André Coeuroy in the conservative *Mercure de France*, which focused on the way in which the composition responded to contemporary French emotional needs. For Coeuroy, it was a great work – meaningful, noble, profound and human – replete with '*poésie populaire*' and powerfully invoking those 'shared memories and traditions that nourish us'. The theme of 'the soil' is also prominent in his article; Coeuroy invokes it in connection with the chansons employed in the work, which he nostalgically associates with the healthy, the authentic and the naive.[31]

Not all reviews were so positive, especially those of critics espousing Republican and democratic values, if now intrepidly so, against the growing French reactionary tide. The work premiered in Paris shortly after the lavish premiere at Orléans, at the Théâtre de Chaillot – unstaged, and thus without the choreography of Ida Rubenstein and the sumptuous sets of Alexandre Benoit. Writing in *La Nouvelle revue française*, Boris de Schloezer pronounced Honegger's music troubling, for behind the 'magnificent orchestral clothing' and impressive vocal writing he perceived a 'poverty of thought' as well as a reliance upon 'effect'.[32]

But Honegger, although a Swiss national, if residing in France (a fact ignored in the press), was widely lauded as the very incarnation of those traditional, if still contemporary, values characteristic of true French art. This would sustain his career throughout Vichy, when Honegger and his music were omnipresent in both the occupied and unoccupied zones, with many

---

[30] Honegger was elected to the Institut de France in 1938. His melodrama, *Le Cantique des cantiques* (of 1926) was presented at the Paris Opéra, choreographed by Serge Lifar, on 12 February 1938. See Halbreich, *Arthur Honegger*, p. 178. *Jeanne d'Arc au bûcher* was performed in Orléans as a result of the initiatives of both the mayor and the archbishop. See Antoine Prost, '*Jeanne d'Arc à la fête. Identité collective et mémoire à Orléans depuis la Révolution française*', in Christophe Charle, Jacqueline Laloutte, Michel Pigenet and Anne-Marie Sohn (eds.), *La France démocratique: Mélanges offerts à Maurice Agulhon* (Paris: Publications de la Sorbonne, 1998), p. 398. On *Jeanne d'Arc au bûcher* and its performances in the early 1940s, see François Porcile, *Les Conflits de la musique française (1940–1965)* (Paris: Fayard, 2001), p. 39.
[31] Review of *Jeanne d'Arc au bûcher* by André Coeuroy in *Mercure de France* 293 (l July 1939), 194–9.
[32] Review of *Jeanne d'Arc au bûcher* by Boris de Schloezer in *La Nouvelle revue française* 53 (July–December 1939), 153–5.

recordings and two festivals devoted to his music in 1942 (in Paris), one of which included a performance of *Jeanne d'Arc au bûcher*. This now timely work was also performed in the unoccupied zone, on 4 July 1942, in Lyon, and then in several other cities in the south-west in July and August. When performed in the unoccupied zone it resonated with Vichy's conservative French nationalist rhetoric; despite German fears of such expression in the occupied zone, the authorities nevertheless approved its performance.[33]

Honegger indeed seemed to transcend the boundaries between conservative and progressive factions at Vichy, and between what Stanley Hoffmann has referred to as 'defensive' or involuntary '*collaboration d'état*' and deliberate collaborationism'.[34] But at Vichy Honegger did not fit in closely with the followers of Charles Maurras (of the Action Française) and their stress on class, hierarchy, discipline and stability, although they did appreciate his traditionalism in form. Rather, he was closer to the small group of former political leftists at Vichy, who had since moved into marginal groupings that were anti-Communist and anti-trust, now stressing the need for authority and state planning. This included Gaston Bergery, who had continued to support his old friend Honegger, and who was active behind the scenes at Vichy before becoming one of Pétain's ambassadors. It also included Hubert Lagardelle, made Minister of Labour in April 1942 (under the pro-German Laval), the other prominent '*planiste*' of the 1930s, who had grown hostile to parliamentary socialism and, in fact, had introduced Mussolini to the works of Sorel.[35]

Honegger, perhaps because of his mixed identity, assimilated well into collaborationist circles in Paris as principal music critic for the prestigious, now collaborationist, journal *Comoedia*. This indeed led to his censure by the Resistance circle of musicians in Paris, which finally repudiated Honegger as one of its own because of the articles that he wrote in the journal, now under the control of the German Institute.[36] Relevant, perhaps, to explain his participation is Stanley Hoffmann's observation

---

[33] Honegger also composed music for documentary films in this period. On the performances of his music and his activities during Vichy, see Yannick Simon, 'Les Jeunesses Musicales de France', in Myriam Chimènes (ed.), *La Vie musicale sous Vichy* (Brussels: Editions Complexe, 2001), p. 210, and in the same volume, Alexandre Laederich, 'Les Associations symphoniques Parisiennes', p. 228, Guy Krivopissko and Daniel Virieux, 'Musiciens: une profession en Résistance?', p. 551, Philippe Morin, 'Une nouvelle politique discographique pour la France', p. 261, and Josette Alviset, 'La Programmation musicale à Vichy: Les Apparences de la continuité', p. 404. Also see Véronique Chabrol, 'L'Ambition de "Jeune France"', in Jean-Pierre Rioux (ed.), *La Vie culturelle sous Vichy* (Brussels: Editions Complexe, 1990), pp. 175–6, and Nadia Margolis, *Joan of Arc in History, Literature, and Film* (New York: Garland, 1992). See Porcile, *Les Conflits de la musique française*, p. 39, on the performances of the work and Honegger's collaboration on *Comoedia*. On the performance of *Jeanne d'Arc au bûcher* by the '*Chantiers*', or groups organised to give work to the unemployed, including musicians (here some 250 performers for the piece), see Serge Added, *Le Théâtre dans les années Vichy 1940–1944* (Paris: Ramsay, 1992), p. 57.

[34] Stanley Hoffmann, 'Collaboration in France during World War II', *The Journal of Modern History* 40/3 (1968), 376 and 381.

[35] Paxton, *Vichy France*, pp. 273–5.   [36] Krivopissko and Virieux, 'Musiciens', p. 338.

that the collaborationists in France were drawn by their search for order and authority in a new Europe, which they believed that German victory would bring about. Honegger was attracted to the European ideal, which provided him with a collective identity, although not to the idea of a totalitarian party that would help to realise a heroic, virile, and ultimately redeeming action.[37]

Honegger, then, fitted several categories, including collaborationists and former leftists at Vichy, while remaining an idealist but also a pragmatist, who sought above all to put his art first. His politics of the apolitical thus led to the efflorescence of his career during Vichy, but also to its ignominious decline in its wake, as he indicates so bitterly in the *Incantations aux fossiles* (1948). And so, what conclusions can we draw? Was Honegger the misunderstood, stoic hero, as depicted by Geoffrey Spratt, or Michel Faure's ignoble bourgeois, who helped to prepare for the collaborationist mentality?[38]

Nuance, perhaps, is the key to identifying shades of grey between simple black and white, or guilt and innocence, and an awareness that a composer may be impelled by 'pure' creative intentions, but that his compromised acts may affect construal of his art. Opportunism or political naivety in the service of great art is not insignificant: the 'politics of the apolitical' can lend force to those symbols that may have politically noxious, even deadly effects. For symbols can convince and legitimise: they are part of the myriad vectors of ideological diffusion, or networks of impregnation of ideology that historians have stressed in the recent history of modern France.[39] Not as guilty as some, but not innocent, Honegger did indeed pay the price for his actions, not only as an artist but as a man, seeking whatever means necessary to advance the noble cause of 'great art'.

---

[37] Hoffmann, 'Collaboration in France', 394 and 381–2.
[38] See Spratt, *The Music of Arthur Honegger*. The theme of Honegger as heroic and victimised by circumstances runs throughout the book. Also see Michel Faure, *Du Néoclassicisme musical dans la France du premier XXe siècle* (Paris: Klincksieck, 1997), especially pp. 258–62 and 338.
[39] These concepts appear implicitly as well as explicitly in Jean-Pierre Rioux's collection, *La Vie culturelle sous Vichy*, as well as in the second volume, '*Cultures*', of Jean-François Sirinelli (ed.), *Histoire des Droites en France*.

CHAPTER 14

Racial discourses in Spanish musical literature, 1915–1939

Gemma Pérez-Zalduondo

During the period from the nineteenth century until well into the 1940s the term *raza* or 'race' can be found in most texts published in Spain and reflecting on Spanish music. However, these appeals to race reflected a range of ideas and assumed a number of different contextual meanings. In this first study of its kind, I consider the use of the term *raza* in literature spanning the period from the return of Spanish musicians from Europe to Spain at the beginning of the First World War up to the end of the Spanish Civil War in 1939, a period during which the political and social life of Spain was profoundly affected by the spirit of nationalism.

In broad terms, reflections on Spanish music up until 1915 tended to focus on its supposed decadence; composers and critics wrote profusely on this perceived problem, reflecting a frustration that had pervaded Spanish thought in general and composers' thoughts in particular since the loss of Cuba in 1898.[1] Consider, for example, the exclamation in 1914 of young composer, Conrado del Campo, a teacher of future generations of Spanish musicians and a staunch defender of Wagnerism:

What question can more urgently torment the spirit of all those who in some way or another are concerned with music than this: the miserable, precarious and as-never-before distressing situation of an Art which ought to shine delightedly, even

---

[1] For more reading on nationalism in Spain, see: Celsa Alonso, 'Nacionalismo', in Emilio Casares (ed.), *Diccionario de la música española e hispanoamericana* (Madrid: Sociedad General de Autores de España, 2000), vol. VII, pp. 924–44; Emilio Casares, 'La música española hasta 1939, o la restauración musical', in *Actas del Congreso Internacional España en la Música de Occidente* (Madrid: Instituto Nacional de las Artes Escénicas y de la Música, 1987), vol. II, pp. 61–322; Carol A. Hess, *Manuel de Falla and Modernism in Spain, 1898–1936* (University of Chicago Press, 2001); Joaquina Labajo, 'Política y usos del folklore en el Siglo XX español', *Revista Española de Musicología. Actas del XV Congreso Internacional de la Sociedad Internacional de Musicología* 16/4 (1993), 1988–98; Beatriz Martínez del Fresno, 'El pensamiento nacionalista en el ámbito madrileño (1900–1936). Fundamentos y paradojas', in *De musica hispana et aliis*. Miscelánea en honor al Prof. Dr. José López-Calo, S. J. (Universidad de Santiago de Compostela, 1990), vol. II, pp. 351–97; 'Nacionalismo e internacionalismo en la música española de la primera mitad del siglo XX', *Actas del XV Congreso de la Sociedad Internacional de Musicología. Revista de Musicología* 16/1 (1993), 640–57; Gemma Pérez Zalduondo, 'El nacionalismo como eje de la política musical del primer gobierno regular de Franco (30 de enero de 1938–8 de agosto de 1939)', *Revista de Musicología* 18 (1995), 247–73; Jorge Persia, *En torno a lo español en la música del siglo XX* (Granada: Diputación de Granada, 2003).

if for no other reason than the fact that it might bring solace to the soul of a race as depressed and without hope as the Spanish?[2]

With an awareness of crisis that is typical of Spanish regenerationism, del Campo uses the word 'race' here to identify the Spanish as a people. At this time, composers, critics and musicologists were in broad agreement that the only way out of Spain's state of cultural 'decadence' was the creation of a kind of music that would reflect a particular 'Spanishness'. While cultural nationalism was taking shape among regional and local elites in the last years of the nineteenth century, archaeologists and anthropologists were attempting to discover the ethnic identity of a far-off antiquity, one which they hoped might justify the nationalist aims of the moment: Manuel Murgía wrote on Galicia, Telesforo de Aranzadi on the Basque Country and Boch Gimpera on Catalonia; anthropologist Manuel Antón Ferrándiz, educated in Paris, Federico Olóriz Aguilera and others also published studies explicitly inquiring into the 'Spanish race'.[3] From then on, a combination of the dialectic between the Spanish, the European and the universal, the portrayal of a diverse national and regional consciousness in music, and the fact that different interpretations of history became available, meant that the term 'race' was used with different meanings and according to different applications. The invocation of 'race' during this time always related in some way to the history of Spanish thought.

Though never clearly defined in musical literature, the term 'race' rarely had biological connotations in Spain and only very rarely acquired the type of radically ethnic meaning that it does in the following statement of 1923 by José Forns:

Just as the history of the fatherland is an eternal battle of reconquest, in which the Spanish people have fought tenaciously and bravely to pluck back the land inch by inch from the invaders, with the unflinching will to maintain the superiority and supremacy of their race, so the musical history of our country is an incessant struggle of the Spanish spirit against interference, which though less bloody, is just as harmful.

This ethnic and ideological war of independence is of special interest in the aesthetic domain; our people were always a fertile terrain for all things foreign and they gathered in everything from strange lands with maternal affection, which they so often denied those who saw the light of day here for the first time.[4]

In contrast to sentiments of this sort, discourses of race have almost always been linked with the cultural expression of the soul of each regional group of people. Marcelino Menéndez Pelayo, who performed an

---

[2] Conrado del Campo, 'Sobre la situación actual de la Música Española', *Revista Musical Hispano-Americana* 1 (1914), in Conrado del Campo, *Escritos* (Madrid: Alpuerto, 1984), p. 317.
[3] José Álvarez Junco, *Mater Dolorosa. La idea de España en el siglo XIX* (Madrid: Taurus, 2001), pp. 268–70.
[4] José Forns, 'La música española. Manuel de Falla', *Harmonía. Revista Musical Ilustrada* 1/5 (1923), 1.

intellectual analysis of Catholic nationalism in his *Historia de los heterodoxos españoles, 1880–1882*, included birth and blood in the race concept, but also 'a way to be and to think, characteristics of which include, crucially, religion, in this case catholicism'.[5] I will focus here on two approaches to this concern, approaches that are particularly relevant to the period 1915–39, namely, via roots and religion. Race was usually identified with roots and folk music in the context of musical, literary and even political texts, where the word race was applied to the particular mentality of each regional group. Race came to be identified with religion, however, in the context of traditional and Falangist ideologies.

THE DIALECTIC BETWEEN SPANISH, EUROPEAN AND UNIVERSAL MUSIC

Language invoking the concept of 'race' emerges with particular importance in texts that consider the musical sensibilities of different groups of people, texts that were important not only for shedding light on the causes of the supposed decadence of Spanish music, but also for formulating strategies for overcoming it. In 1920 the music critic and avid follower of Wagnerian thought, Rogelio Villar, pointed out in his book *El sentimiento nacional en la música española* that the 'sensibilities' of different races are what determine the differences in intensity of popular art in different countries. These sensibilities depend, in turn, on climate and religion. This approach led him to conjecture that differences among races depend on their artistic temperament.[6]

The differentiation between northern and southern races, a feature of European thinking at the turn of the twentieth century, also left its mark on Spanish music and thought.[7] José Ortega y Gasset, a philosopher who would influence both Spanish thinking and Spanish musical thought after 1914, felt that one of the causes of Spanish decadence was the difficulty Mediterranean people had with subjective thought; the Spanish people could never have been modern, he postulated, because it lacked the subjective thought which had been a characteristic of European culture during the modern age. Only when this idea of subjectivity changed would another era begin in which Spain would be able to wake up to life and history.[8] For Ortega y Gasset, in order to discover life as a radical reality

---

[5] Junco, *Mater Dolorosa*, p. 457.
[6] Rogelio Villar, *El sentimiento nacional en la música española* (Madrid: Artes Gráficas Mateu, 1920), pp. 36–7.
[7] See Lily Litvak, *España 1900. Modernismo, anarquismo y fin de siglo* (Barcelona: Anthropos, 1990), pp. 155–258.
[8] In José Abellán, *Historia del pensamiento español de Séneca a nuestros días* (Madrid: Espasa, 1996), p. 562.

man needs to overcome the idealism typical of Nordic societies. The main and primary fact, and the basis of philosophy, is living itself.

The various writers who shaped discussions about the formation of Spanish musical identity likewise reflected upon the different ways in which northern people – developed and industrialised – and southern people – undeveloped – have felt, expressed and written music in the context of their cultural and religious traditions. Three such authors were the critic Rogelio Villar, the composer Felipe Pedrell, and the latter's pupil, Manuel de Falla, who led the vanguard of Spanish music in the twentieth century. Villar defines the difference between the music of the Northern and the Latin peoples very clearly. While he recognises the musical superiority of the former, he considers the Northern and Latin sentiments to be opposed to each other:

Because of the musical tradition of these peoples (Germany and Austria), the technical procedures of these schools (of the North) are the most perfect. As such, they seem to us Latins somewhat nebulous, dark, sometimes heavy and cold; they lack the feeling of proportion, of unity of style, of spiritual balance. They are altogether the opposite of what for me expresses the true concept of the word beauty, that is, expression, grace, lightness, elegance, ease, simplicity (simplicity is perfection), intensity, depth that is not apparent . . .

Let us recognise that nationalist tendencies in universal music, and 'colourism', its natural consequence, have revived with freshness and health the musical atmosphere that was slightly stuffy from the pessimistic philosophism of the schools of the North, impregnated as this is with an exaggeratedly idealistic, romantic, and sometimes tiring sentimentalism; for when diaphanous inspiration wells up in them in melodies of ineffable beauty, the Latin spirit [is] what brings them to life with the flame of its inextinguishable fire.[9]

Villar goes on to explain that Bach, Mozart, Schubert and Wagner were all inspired by Latin, Italian and French sources.

Drawing on these opposed traditions, some authors maintained that Spanish composers should use musical forms and procedures created and developed by their northern counterparts, adapting them to their own character, their own race and their own feelings. As early as 1891 Catalan composer Felipe Pedrell pointed out in his influential essay *Por nuestra música* – notwithstanding his admiration for Wagner – that the new theory of poetry of the German composer was 'different from the character of our Latin spirit':

Wagner has created a new theory of poetry, German, forthright, incalculably advanced, yes, but different from the character of our Latin spirit; admire as much as you like the fertile philosophical-aesthetic basis on which all his creation is founded: the more we admire it, the more convinced everyone will become that in art, whether it be music, literature, or whatever artistic genre, feelings that persist

---

[9] Villar, *El sentimiento nacional en la música española*, pp. 36–7.

will always be the hallmark of the nations of the North, just as feelings that explode will always be the hallmark of the nations of the South ... Artists of the South, I shall repeat here and always: let us breathe in the essences of that purely human ideal form, which does not belong exclusively to any nationality, but let us breathe them in sitting next to our southern gardens.[10]

Several years later, Manuel de Falla, on his return to Spain at the outbreak of the First World War, incorporated the idea of racial difference into his defence of the anti-Romantic movement. He argued that the reason for Spanish decadence lay in the influence of Classical and Romantic forms and procedures which were far removed from the Spanish character.

[T]he purely musical methods [of masters such as Beethoven and Wagner] cannot be applied in a general way to works written by composers of other races without impairing their individual and national character.[11]

Starting from this premise, Falla submits that the way forward for modern music lies in the recovery of pre-seventeenth-century musical stylistics. His final point is another transcendental one, namely, the creation of an identification between race and tradition: '[T]he weight of tradition is so overwhelming to composers belonging to that race, that neither Strauss, nor even Schoenberg, has been able to free himself from it.'[12]

Falla's rejection of northern music led to his search for models in Spanish music history, his avant-garde use of folk music and his rejection of Romanticism as un-Spanish. Almost twenty years later, Falla would tone his argument down, but only a little; he still believed that 'Wagner's influence on composers of a different race to his own' might serve as a 'great stimulus for everyone to make an effort ... to reflect in their works the characteristic spirit of their nation and race'.[13] On the fiftieth anniversary of Wagner's death in 1933 Falla adopted a less extreme tone, but his opinions remained essentially the same. In his prologue to Adolfo Salazar's translation of *La música francesa contemporánea* by Jean-Aubry, Falla expressed his hope that the First World War would serve to settle 'what we might call racial boundaries'. He continued: 'These have been increasingly and constantly blurring, and together with them those values that characterize art created by a particular race.'[14] For Falla, there was a risk that the values held by the people in Spain's

---

[10] Felipe Pedrell, *Por nuestra música. Algunas observaciones sobre la magna cuestión de una escuela Lírica nacional* (Barcelona: Henrich, 1891), ed. facs. Barcelona, Institut de Documentació i d'Investigació Musicològiques 'Ricart i Matas' (Universitat Autónoma de Barcelona, 1991), 27–8.

[11] Manuel de Falla, 'Introducción a la música nueva', *Revista Musical Hispanoamericana* (December 1916), in Manuel de Falla, *Escritos sobre música y músicos* (Madrid: Espasa Calpe, 1988), p. 38; Manuel de Falla, *On Music and Musicians*, trans. David Urman and J. M. Thomson (London: Marion Boyars, 1979), p. 18 (hereafter *Escritos* and *On Music and Musicians*).

[12] *Escritos*, p. 39; *On Music and Musicians*, p. 19.

[13] Manuel de Falla, 'Notas sobre Wagner en su cincuentenario', *Cruz y Raya* 6 (September 1933), 77–8.

[14] Manuel de Falla, 'Prologue to the Spanish translation of G. Jean-Aubry *La música francesa contemporánea*', *Revista Musical Hispanoamericana* (Julio 1916), in *Escritos*, p. 43; *On Music and Musicians*, p. 22.

various regions would eventually come to resemble one another and ultimately blend into a universal formula. Written in 1916, his prologue reflects something of the radicalisation that took place in this debate around the First World War years.

Though the figure of Wagner is ubiquitous in the literature and criticism of that time, it is difficult to find references to other contemporary Austrian, German or British composers.[15] The prolific critic Adolfo Salazar, a champion of the musical avant-garde, admired and respected Schoenberg but, like Falla himself, considered Schoenberg's thinking alien to the way in which the Spanish feel their music. In 1931 he stated that Webern was not a model to follow either.[16] But if references to music from central and northern Europe were scarce (with the exception of Russian music), it was rarer still to find news of contemporary Italian music. In spite of their supposed racial proximity (because of their common Latinism and Mediterraneanism) and above all in spite of the similarities in Spanish and Italian musical thinking at that time, there was no reflection in the Spanish musical literature of any shared musical interests with Italy. The harmonious co-existence of Spanish and Italian composers in Paris until 1915, personal relationships, common interests in researching their respective historical and traditional musics, and the similarity of the national projects initiated by Falla and Alfredo Casella, for example, were not reflected at all in Spanish musical literature.[17] This somewhat surprising fact is hard to explain. It might partly reflect the fact that the Spanish public's enjoyment of Italian opera, and the influence of the latter on the Spanish *zarzuela*, meant that Italian influence was considered as undesirable as the influence of German opera. It might stem from the fact that it was French music that interested avant-garde Spanish composers; France was where such composers found an internationalisation of their own language.[18] It might equally reflect the fact that the concept of racial difference between regional musics found a properly national expression centring on the search for characteristics peculiar to the (national) Spanish race. The presence of contemporary Italian music in Spain was thus an exception. It was found mainly in Catalonia, where Mediterraneanism developed as antagonist to northern culture within the setting of *neucentism*: inspired by intellectual and occasional music critic Eugenio d'Ors, *neucentism* contrasted

---

[15] An exception is the article 'Crónica de viajes. La joven música vienesa', *El Sol*, 16 August 1922, p. 2.
[16] Adolfo Salazar, 'La IX reunión de la S.I.M.C. en Oxford', *Ritmo* 42 (1 November 1931), 6–8. Adolfo Salazar, 'La Vida Musical. Historias y Propagandas. Las Orquestas. Obras nuevas', Ibid., 6 February 1922. Catalogue number AMF 6411/4. Salazar expresses indignation over the trivial and, according to him, nefarious interpretation of Spanish music given in *Die Musik der Gegenwart* by Karl Storck.
[17] See Montserrat Bergadà, 'La relación de Falla con Italia. Crónica de un diálogo', in Yvan Nommick (ed.), *Manuel de Falla e Italia*, Colección Estudios, Serie Música 3 (Granada: Publicaciones del Archivo Manuel de Falla, 2000), pp. 17–62.
[18] The fertile influence of French music on Spanish national music is explained in detail in the work of Jean-Aubry, *La música en las naciones*, published after the First World War, translated by Adolfo Salazar. This book was widely publicised.

the tragic life sentiment of the 'northern peoples' with the order, measure, fullness, calm, serenity, constraint and balance – that is, the classicism of antiquity – of the peoples of the Mediterranean.[19]

From the 1920s onwards, considerable optimism spread about the development of the music of the south in relation to that of the north. In 1922 Jean-Aubry spoke of the renaissance of Spanish music; in 1930 an exultant Salazar wondered if Madrid could not take over the musical leadership that Paris had lost; in the same year Alfredo Casella published his article 'Il *Renacimiento* musicale iberico', in which he observed that the Spanish renaissance was very similar to its Italian counterpart.[20] In 1934 the music critic Vicente Salas Viu wrote:

> Music today is at one of those moments in which one stage finishes and the sunrise of a new cycle begins. Is this perhaps a return to Latin supremacy, after three centuries have passed in which the greatest musical values have been Central-European? Is this the beginning of another era of dominance by the countries of Southern Europe? Is the supremacy of musical creation returning to them, just as in the seventeenth century it left them and went to Germany? Nowadays, when the great Germanic instrumental forms are fading, this would mean no more nor less than giving life to a Latin *symphonism*. For what we cannot expect at all is that if it were to predominate, the supposed asymphonism of Mediterranean music could lead to an abandonment of instrumental music.[21]

After this lively rejection of the idea that symphonic instrumental music need be strictly northern, Salas wonders about the possibility of a renewed concept of the symphonic, which would presumably be Mediterranean. To go towards it, to 'add one's contribution, is the new goal which is offered to the *renaissance of Spanish music*'. The way to achieve it is by following Pedrell's proposal, namely, pursuing folklore and history.[22]

Latinism started as a nationalist idea which sought the affirmation of what was Spain's own as against the influence of what it considered to be alien. And yet its internationalisation conflicted with this underlying nationalism. Salas Viu, a defender of nationalism, is only one of those who argued that the Spanish ought not to use forms, procedures or languages that were typically German or Italian on the grounds that to do so would amount to writing alien music. The nationalist way – that is, the way involving the use of folk-music traditions – was the only way. Yet even here, cultural anxieties led to considerable speculation about origins. For instance, the philosopher Miguel de Unamuno argued that Iberian roots were to be found in the folk traditions of the rural population, when

---

[19] See, for example, 'Glosas. Glosas nuevas sobre lo de Salzburgo', *ABC*, 21 August 1923, 4–5.
[20] Alfredo Casella, 'Il *Renacimiento* musicale iberico', *Pègaso* 7 (1930), 57–66.
[21] Vicente Salas Viu, 'Más o menos música española. Traba del folklore y holgura de lo sinfónico en nuestro arte', *Cruz y Raya* 31 (October 1935), 76. '*Sinfonismo*' appears in italics in the original, as does '*renacimiento de la música española*' in the following excerpt.
[22] Ibid., 80.

in reality these traditions had existed prior to Latinism and Romanisation. And this is only one of the alternatives to the theory of the Latin renaissance. Notwithstanding certain differences in nuance, we find a similar sentiment in Rogelio Villar:

[B]efore the Roman, Visigothic and Saracen invasions, we Spanish had a popular art (the Ibero-Oriental) as testified by certain Latin writers who describe the songs and dances of Spain. From the writings of Martial and Juvenal we may deduce that popular Spanish music had distinctive characteristics, not excluding, nevertheless, Arab and Moorish influences.[23]

THE DEBATE ABOUT SPANISH MUSICAL IDENTITY

While these debates about Spain's position in European and even broader cultural contexts proceeded, different and opposing conceptions of Spain and its regions emerged in the second half of the nineteenth century, which were influenced by the many specifically Spanish interpretations of nationalism. Peripheral nationalisms (Basque, Catalan and Galician) and Spanish nationalism were viewed from two distinct perspectives: some viewed the first as part of the second; others considered them to be quite different. For Rogelio Villar Spanish popular music manifests the 'ideal unity of the race'; in spite of the particular characteristics of the different regions, he suggested, they almost all 'sing with the same sentiment'. By contrast, Francisco Gascue, a defender of folk tradition and critic of Villar's work, defended the qualitative differences among the various traditional forms of Spanish musical expression. For him Spain is made up of different races, even what he calls 'antithetical' ones:

While Spain is an aggregate of races that are different, and on occasion, antithetical, we are not able to talk about a synthetic Spanish art which would express the sentiment of the entire Spanish State. It is impossible to reconcile the character of Catalan melodies with that of Basque, Asturian and Andalusian ones.

Precisely in this marked difference between races and musics lies the possibility that there exists in the Peninsula a powerful musical art, in which all the peoples who form part of the general State would contribute their feeling, their way of expressing themselves, their own songs, etc. . . . At the present time one may talk about a Castilian, Andalusian, Basque or Catalan art, but a chemical combination of those simple bodies is not possible.[24]

Though not in agreement about the syncretisms involved, all these writers attribute cultural idiosyncrasies and their expression in folk music to racial difference.

---

[23] Villar, *El sentimiento nacional en la música española*, p. 14.
[24] Francisco Gascue, 'Publicaciones musicales y de libros. *El sentimiento nacional en la música española*, por don Rogelio Villar', *Revista Musical Hispano-americana* (September 1917), 11.

This romantic idea of folklore had been taken on board by intellectuals and composers in previous years, as we can observe in the love of flamenco shown by Falla in the *Cante Jondo* or 'Deep Song' Competition held in Granada in 1922 and *El amor brujo* (1914), or Federico García Lorca in *Romancero gitano* (1928) and *Bodas de sangre* (1933). In Andalusian musical criticism of the 1920s, a time in which there was an extraordinary musical resurgence, folk music was the vehicle used for exalting the sentiments of regional differentiation. A similar phenomenon occurred in the rest of the Spanish regions (Castilian, Asturias, Aragón, La Rioja, etc.), and even in the peripheral nationalisms (Basque, Catalan and Galician), and did not run contrary to the process of reflection about Spanish national identity. The folk music of each region was used by composers to consolidate the region's own particular identity and was understood by critics to represent the crystallisation of a collective consciousness. The idea of regionalism infused not only musical reflection and creation, but also musical institutions. For example, a number of public and private institutions in the Basque country felt compelled to contribute to the rescue of folk music, choral music and Basque musical theatre.[25] Indeed, much Spanish musical thought of this time is tinged with shades of regionalism or nationalism, even that of the most ardent defenders of Europeanism and internationalism.

This contradiction was often resolved via an invocation of race. Consider, for instance, Adolfo Salazar's racial construction of 'universality'. Referring to Basque composers who used their own folklore to distinguish themselves from the rest of Spanish music, Salazar explains that 'being universal' consists of:

a deeper capacity, more in contact with the vital nucleus of the person, in that place where characteristics of individual variety fade in the face of the strong, profound definition of the collective soul. Universality is not a similarity of languages, which in music is reflected in a homogeneity of styles, but an intimate penetration into the roots through which the personality drinks the sap of race. In the past we would have said 'of humanity', but this is perhaps too complex and we prefer the clearest concept of race, clarity for the conscience, in spite of all the ethnological difficulties.[26]

For Adolfo Salazar infusing 'racial' music with 'racial' values would be a basic prerequisite of attaining universality. In fact, he contrasts the 'superficiality of western styles' to the 'profound statement of the will (of Basque musicians) to create their own expression, absolutely at one with the musical sentiments of their race'.[27]

---

[25] María Nagore Ferrer, 'La realidad musical vasca en el periodo de entreguerras', in Javier Suárez-Pajares (ed.), *Música española entre dos guerras, 1914–1945* (Madrid: Publicaciones del Archivo Manuel de Falla, 2002), pp. 151–5.
[26] Adolfo Salazar, 'La música natural y los músicos vascos', Supplement of *El Sol*, 30 August 1919, 3.
[27] Ibid.

Salazar also had recourse to racialist thought in 1915 when he defended Falla's *El amor brujo* against detractors who criticised the Frenchness of its style. In doing so, however, he resorted to expressions imbued with the romantic and exotic concept of an Alhambra-like Andalusia ('rhythms that sound of Moorish lands, of Arabia, with their heavy aromas of the oasis'), the very type of superficial language he had on many occasions reproached the French for using. Only 'natural music', music with 'a strong racial character' could be saved from the dangers of the superficial and the picturesque.[28] The triviality of 'the picturesque' was one of the hazards that Salazar found in a musical nationalism based only on what he describes as 'the purely apparent, without any true deep-rootedness in the character and in the psychology of our race'. For him: 'This means that one can be truly "nationalist" without resorting to popular themes (as Ravel in France or Pfitzner in Germany do).'[29] It was by identifying race as a characteristic and a psychological peculiarity in this way that Salazar was able to dissociate musical nationalism from folklore.

In short, racialist language about Latin and Anglo-Saxon peoples and their respective musical traditions imbued discussions of Spanish music conducted by defenders of both conservative and avant-garde musical positions. In the debate about the musical identity of Spain, of its regions and its nationalities, different ideological points of view about the definition and composition of Spain were presented. Both positions were based on the concept that differences among peoples were not only cultural, 'sentimental' or psychological in nature; they formed part of folklore and were racially constitutive. Twenty years later the deepening of these differences would ultimately allow for a move away from the superficiality of nationalism.

'MEDITERRANEANISM' AND 'SPANISHNESS'

The 1920s also witnessed the publication of texts in which elements were already taking shape that were to forge the political ideology of Spanish Falangism, a doctrine that resembled Italian Fascism but was also profoundly anti-French. The art of guitarist Regino Sáinz de la Maza inspired Falangist ideologist Ernesto Giménez Caballero to pen the following gloss to one of his performances for the magazine *La Gaceta Literaria*:

Mediterranean: South. Regino Sáinz de la Maza presses the guitar to his chest like a shield against the western violin, blond, plaited, with plaited strings. The vigorous Germanic blood of the violin turns into Mediterranean wine. Greece, Rome, Rome, Spain. And Russia. A – new – fascist or Soviet symbol. (Sitar, balalaika, vihuela). Mexico, Volga, Seville, Naples, Coimbra, Buenos Aires. The new dawn.[30]

---

[28] Ibid. [29] Adolfo Salazar, 'La vida musical', *El Sol*, 6 February 1923, 2.
[30] Ernesto Giménez Caballero, 'Itinerarios jóvenes de España. Regino Sáinz de la Maza', *La Gaceta Literaria*, 1 February 1929, 7.

In addition to the surprising fascination Spanish Falangism showed for Soviet art, it now lent to Mediterraneanism a new meaning; Falangism embraced not only Greek and Roman antiquity, but also Portugal and Latin America, hinting at the idea of *Hispanidad* or 'Spanishness', conceived as the antithesis of pan-Latinism. At the beginning of the twentieth century Spanishness had been an element of historical imaginings; Falangism would see it, by contrast, as common to all Hispanic peoples, a permanent distinguishing characteristic comprising its missionary character and religion, despite its variety of races and languages.[31] In 1934 Ramiro de Maeztu, one of the most influential twentieth-century Spanish intellectuals, published *Defensa de la Hispanidad* from material developed as individual texts in the magazine *Acción Española*. The concept of nation expounded in it by Maeztu does not depend on growth, race or economy: 'What forms the single one and only mother country is a nexus, a spiritual community that is, at the same time, a value of universal history.' This spiritual community, composed of American people, was described as *Hispanidad* and evangelised by Spaniards and the Iberian people, including Portuguese, as a specific development of Spanish humanism.[32] This identification of race with religion had no aggressive implications, even between 1936 and 1943, the first years of Francoism. Rather it was used inside Spain as a source of cohesion, and for the purposes of propaganda. This is shown by the fact that in 1941 Manuel de Falla, who was living in Argentina by then, was not only appointed to the *Consejo de la Hispanidad*, or 'Spanishness Council', in an attempt to take advantage of his prestige; until the 1970s he was also classed as a Christian missionary and mystic by Spanish music historiographers.[33] In this way, Spanishness was also a pretext for rejecting European modernity and rationality.

RACE, RELIGION AND TRADITION DURING THE FIRST YEARS OF FRANCOISM

During the Spanish Civil War, myths supported by propaganda about such things as Spanishness and the imperial past, and about concepts such as Race, Homeland, Nation, State, Empire and Religion reflected the ideology and culture of Franco's regime. Patriotism was linked to the notion of race, which in turn was a synonym for Catholicism. Under Franco official culture insisted less on folk music and more on a tradition of mysticism and religion. 'Racially' Spanish music was now thought to be

---

[31] See Ernesto González Calleja and Fredes Limón Nevado, *La Hispanidad como instrumento de combate. Raza e Imperio en la prensa franquista durante la Guerra Civil española* (Madrid: CSIC, 1988).
[32] See Pedro Carlos González Cuevas, *Maeztu. Biografía de un nacionalista español* (Madrid: Marcial Pons, Editores de Historia, 2003), pp. 310–12.
[33] *Orden de 7 de Enero de 1941* (Ministerio de Asuntos Exteriores) (Boletín Oficial del Estado 8 January 1941).

that of the polyphonists of the Renaissance, and religious spirit to be the distinguishing characteristic of all truly Spanish music. Consider the following fragment of text dating from 1939, in which Regino Sáinz de la Maza provides a description of Manuel de Falla:

> Explorer of the musical roads of Spain, the temperament of the race expresses itself in him with its own attributes, with the character that distinguishes the creations of a Vittoria, of a Saint John of the Cross, of a Cervantes. With the same grandeur, the same austerity, and an identical expressive force. The ideal unity of form and substance on which he succeeds in focusing his thoughts demands a truly supernatural force of concentration and capacity of abstraction. Traces of this effort were to be seen on his face, and were captured by the great Zuloaga when he painted it on canvas, rendering a translucent, unsubstantial image. The soul triumphed over the material.[34]

Such a passage reflects the view that the Spanish race was an amalgam of different peoples united not by biological or anthropological traits, but rather by religious, historical and moral orientations, as well as a common psychological structure. This imagined Spanish race rejected the materialism of modern empires.

It is precisely in Catholicism that we find a breach between the Spanish Falangists' thoughts about music and those of their European counterparts – this despite Falangism's enormous fascination for German Nazism, with whom they shared views as to the potential role of music and art as elements of State propaganda.[35] Activity carried out by the Third Reich in this connection was of great interest to the Spanish Falangists. The scholarly infrastructure for the pursuit of ethnomusicology was dismantled after the Civil War – likewise during the months of the Nazi takeover.[36] This and a subsequent delay in Ethnomusicology's development were the most important characteristics of the discipline in Spain, features it shared with musicology and anthropology. Marius Schneider, head of the folklore section at the Spanish Institute of Musicology (founded in 1943), had previously been director of the Berlin Sound Archive. Many of the authors who wrote about music were amateurs, young performers or critics without scientific education in the field of the investigation. The work of dilettante Richard Eichenauer – discussed elsewhere in this volume by Pamela M. Potter – was also studied by the Falangists.[37] In a special 1939 issue of *Vértice* dedicated to discussion of Germany Sáinz de la Maza wrote:

---

[34] Regino Sáinz de la Maza, 'Manuel de Falla', *Vértice* 21 (1939), s.p.
[35] Regino Sáinz de la Maza, 'Pasado y presente de la música alemana', *Vértice* (1939), s.p. (This is a special edition about Germany.) Musical policies and directives of the Third Reich were explained in the Spanish press, as were the essentials of Richard Eichenauer's work, *Musik und Rasse*.
[36] See José Antonio Gómez Rodríguez, 'La Etnomusicología en España: 1936–1956', in Henares Cuéllar, Cabrera García, Pérez-Zalduondo and Castillo Ruiz (eds.), *Actas del Congreso Dos Décadas de cultura artística en el franquismo 1936–1956* (Universidad de Granada, 2001), p. 211.
[37] Pamela M. Potter, 'The concept of race in German musical discourse', this volume.

Hitler's Germany has put music on the right road and directed its course towards its glorious traditions. The nation that has given the world the most eminent figures of music, embodying the profoundly musical spirit of its soul, could not lose itself in theories that carry within them the seeds of decomposition. This need for salvation had already been felt and expressed by Ricardo Eichenauer [*sic*] in 1932. In his book *Música y Raza* he defends the future of European Music from the snares that are threatening to destroy it. His thesis is that European Music, based on harmonic and polyphonic scores, is a Northern invention, whose tradition only the Northern races have created and conserved.

In Germany today we see a nation that is ready to direct the destinies of art, realising its cultural and spiritual value, and the moral influence that it exerts.[38]

For the Falangists Catholicism affirmed the universality of humanity, and it is here that we find the point where Falangist thought on music diverged from that of its European counterparts. And yet traditionalism, another of the ideologies that gave rise to the revolt of July 1936, was also extremely influential. Indeed, the traditionalist Catholic Right held great sway in Spanish music from then on, and was the only group to remain influential after 1943, when the power of the Falange began to diminish. The ideology of this group was founded on a never satisfactorily explained concept of tradition which, as far as music was concerned, became a new synonym for the Spanish 'race'. Joaquín Turina, composer and director of the Commission of Music in 1941, described the role of the international avant-garde in Spanish music before the outbreak of the Civil War by acknowledging:

when all this gimmickry intruded on Spain, its aim was to do away with the racial elements which gave it all its colour, all its atmosphere. And those who composed in the Spanish style were in grave danger from the assaults of the international group.[39]

In writings about the crisis and development of Spanish music between 1915 and 1936 we therefore see a thoroughgoing infiltration of the sorts of racial nuances that were also present in Latin and northern European artistic and intellectual circles. In spite of the awareness of Spanish composers and critics of belonging to a Latin or Mediterranean race, and the variety of proposals regarding musical forms and procedures to be used, we see hardly any references to Italy in the Spanish musical press; for its part, the avant-garde looked towards French music. The notion of a Spanish 'race' was linked to the cultural expression of each regional group's particular sentiment, though without biological connotations. It was always identified by means of its folk music. As such, the concept of 'race' appears in debates about musical regionalism and nationalism on the one hand, and Spain's possible clash with Europeanism and universalism on the

---

[38] Regino Sáinz de la Maza, 'Pasado y presente de la música alemana', *Vértice* (1939), s.p.
[39] Joaquín Turina, 'Desenvolvimiento de la música española en estos últimos tiempos' (lecture given at the University of Oviedo in 1941), in Joaquín Turina, *Escritos* (Madrid: Ed. Alpuerto, 1982), p. 221.

other. Finally, in Falangist and Francoist discourse, the concept of a 'Spanish race' incorporates in effect a cluster of 'races' and cultures united by a common psychological structure, with Catholicism as an essential component. To some extent tradition, conceived as spiritual and religious values, took the place of folklore in discourse on Spanish music. Philip Bohlman's and Ronald Radano's observation about 'race' holds true for Spain – namely, that ' "race" defines not a fixity, but a signification saturated with profound cultural meaning and whose discursive instability heightens its affective power'.[40] Several concepts of 'race' are traceable in the discursive constructions of Spanish musical nationalism, concepts that are reinterpreted into different Spanish ideologies until the end of the Civil War in 1939. It is impossible to study Spanish musical thought without taking these deeply ideological constructions into account.

---

[40] Ronald Radano and Philip V. Bohlman, 'Introduction: Music and Race, Their Past, Their Presence', in Ronald Radano and Philip V. Bohlman (eds.), *Music and the Racial Imagination* (University of Chicago Press, 2000), p. 5.

CHAPTER 15

Manuel de Falla, flamenco and Spanish identity
Michael Christoforidis

Throughout his career, Manuel de Falla sought to create a Spanish identity in music, and until 1920 foregrounded his Andalusian origins in order to achieve this.[1] Flamenco and gypsy culture formed the cornerstones of his construction, even though by the late nineteenth and early twentieth centuries these elements had become problematic in Spain. The perceived exoticism and otherness of flamenco and gypsy culture, both within and outside the country, led to a questioning of their relevance in emerging debates on Andalusian and Spanish nationalism and race. Falla became a key figure in overturning these views, transforming contemporary Spanish appreciation of flamenco both by his general advocacy of the genre and via his own flamenco-influenced creative output. He helped to shape Spanish perceptions of flamenco, and did so partly by relating racial categories to accounts of its origins and performance style.

ANDALUSIA, EXOTICISM AND THE MUSIC OF MANUEL DE FALLA

Falla's assertion of a distinctly Andalusian identity can be traced to his earliest works from the turn of the twentieth century and reflects ideas of Andalusia as a region with a distinct culture, which had become prevalent in the second half of the nineteenth century.[2] Unlike other constructions of Spanish nationalism, especially in the Basque and Catalan regions, Andalusian identity was not predicated on notions of racial purity. Andalusia's unique identity was often defined by the very multiplicity of cultural and racial layers from which it had evolved.[3] By the nineteenth century only the gypsy population maintained a separate racial status, while still forming an integral part of Andalusian culture.[4]

---

[1] Manuel de Falla was born in the port city of Cádiz in the Southern Spanish region of Andalusia. This region has the highest concentration of gypsy inhabitants on the peninsula and is closely associated with the origins and development of flamenco.
[2] There was a clear aspiration to self-government, coinciding with the rise of federalist models and the rise of regionalisms/nationalisms in Spain. These ideas led to the *First Charter of the Andalusian Country* (1883) which proposed a federation of the Andalusian provinces.
[3] Including Greek, Roman, Visigoth, Byzantine, Moor, Gypsy, over a 'Spanish' substratum.
[4] Timothy Mitchell has outlined some of the theories of Spanish authors since the 1930s who have contested perceptions of the gypsies of Spain in purely racial terms. These include ideas that Jews and

As Gerhard Steingress has pointed out, the region's resistance to French invasion and its 'exoticism' in the eyes of European Romantics were traits that fascinated many Spanish intellectuals, both conservative and liberal. Given the lack of socio-economic development in Andalusia, often a cornerstone of other European nationalisms, folklore acquired added significance in the emergent Andalusian ethno-nationalism, and flamenco was one of its most striking and unique features.[5] Studies of Andalusian folklore and flamenco by Antonio Machado y Álvarez, Manuel Balmaseda and Hugo Schuchardt appeared from the early 1880s and were complemented by folk-song collections of the region, the most comprehensive being that of Eduardo Ocón.[6] Despite these developments, the musical expression of Andalusian identity in Falla's early works was initially modelled upon exotic elements in Romantic salon music and the *zarzuela* (Spanish operetta), which often had recourse to folk melodies taken from anthologies. Yet even at this early stage Falla was searching for new ways of representing flamenco and gypsies. In his first opera, *La vida breve* (1905), Falla drew on notes he had taken of flamenco rhythms and guitar figurations and employed a flamenco singer (*cantaor*) on stage. The opera's protagonist, Salud, is a gypsy who is portrayed sympathetically rather than as a stereotype in the mould of Carmen. By going beyond the token gypsy presence as merely an element of local colour Falla broke away from common practice in contemporary *zarzuelas*.[7]

During his Paris years (1907–14) Falla's output became more clearly indebted to Romantic and Impressionistic imagery of Spain, with its perceptions of Andalusia as the nearest manifestation of the Orient. He began to read the seminal French texts by François René Chateaubriand, Victor Hugo and Théophile Gautier which disseminated the nostalgic vision of the Andalusian town of Granada, and by extension Spain, as the last European refuge of Arab culture and presented its gypsy dwellers as their progeny or exotic substitutes.[8] Though predating Falla's arrival in Paris, such nineteenth-century representations of Spain had culminated in

---

Moors escaped deportation by claiming gypsy status, and that there has been a conflation with gypsiness of other (at times nomadic) groups dedicated to marginal trades, such as the *quinquis*. *Flamenco Deep Song* (New Haven: Yale University Press, 1994), pp. 51–71.

[5] Gerhard Steingress, 'Ideología y mentalidad en la construcción de la identidad cultural', in Gerhard Steingress and Enrique Baltanás (eds.), *Flamenco y Nacionalismo: Aportaciones para una sociología política del flamenco* (Seville: Fundación Machado, 1998), p. 166.

[6] Eduardo Ocón, *Cantos españoles. Colección de aires nacionales y populares* (Málaga: Unión musical española, 1876). Four editions of this work were published to 1906.

[7] See for instance the song delivered by a gypsy woman in the opening scene of Federico Chueca's *La alegría de la huerta* (1900).

[8] Falla's reading lists include references to Chateaubriand's *Le dernier Abencérage*, Hugo's *Les orientales*, and Gautier's *Voyage en Espagne* from this period. Falla's extant personal library at the Archivo Manuel de Falla (hereafter *AMF*) includes his annotated copies of Alhambrist texts like François René Chateaubriand, *Le dernier Abencérage* (in French and Spanish translation), Inventory Number *AMF* (IN) 2598 and 3401, Washington Irving, *Cuentos de la Alhambra*, IN 2014, and Théophile Gautier *Loin de Paris*, IN 3866.

1900, at the Exposition Universelle in Paris, in a 'theme park' entitled 'Andalousie au temps du Maures', which was established on the fringe of the official colonial pavilions at the Trocadero. The Moorish monuments of Spain were displayed through reproductions of the Giralda tower of Seville, and a more capricious conflation of a patio from the Alcazar of Seville with the Patio of the Lions from Granada's Alhambra. A racial ambivalence was also present in the exhibit, in which a variety of North Africans, Spanish gypsies and even the odd Frenchman provided the human local colour. Spanish dance troupes dominated the entertainment, with many flamenco numbers performed by the gypsy contingent. The irony of presenting Spanish folk and flamenco styles that had evolved over the previous century within a medieval Moorish and often primitivist setting was not lost on some contemporary commentators.

Some of Falla's Parisian output alludes to the literary themes of nineteenth-century exoticism and is even indebted to the means employed by Romantic composers to denote Spanishness in numerous espagnolades, while *Noches en los jardines de España* (1909–16) draws on various impressionistic evocations of Spain in its poetic conception and style.[9] However, a few months after returning to Madrid in August 1914, Falla commenced work on a radically different composition: the *gitanería* (gypsy scene) *El amor brujo* (Love the Magician), which was written for the popular gypsy entertainer Pastora Imperio and her troupe. In this work, Falla reinterpreted visions of the gypsy in light of the primitivist aesthetic that he and many in Paris had so admired in the productions of the Ballets Russes, particularly *The Rite of Spring*.[10] While most of the numbers in *El amor brujo* can be identified as stylisations of flamenco forms, some of the more popular numbers, such as the 'Romance del Pescador' (The Fisherman's Romance, originally entitled 'Magic Circle') and especially the 'Danza ritual del fuego' (Ritual Fire Dance), defy such classifications, though they display some gestural and intervallic affinities with Andalusian music.[11] To recreate the primeval rites of the gypsies Falla consulted examples of ritual music from the Far East. He believed that this more

---

[9] These include the 'Seguedille' from *Trois mélodies* (1910) and the *Siete canciones populares españolas* (1914). See Michael Christoforidis, 'Manuel de Falla's *Siete canciones populares españolas*: The Composer's Library and the Creative Process', *Anuario Musical* 55 (2000), 213–35.

[10] For a discussion of the impact of primitivism on Falla's construction of flamenco see Michael Christoforidis, 'Un acercamiento a la postura de Manuel de Falla en El 'Cante Jondo' (canto primitivo andaluz)', in Manuel de Falla, *El 'Cante Jondo'* (canto primitivo andaluz), facsimile edition (Granada: Ayuntamiento, Archivo Manuel de Falla, Imprenta Urania, 1997).

[11] In his extensive monograph on this work, Antonio Gallego repeats the often vague flamenco descriptions given by Adolfo Salazar, and authorised by Falla, in the initial programme note, which include references to distant now-forgotten dances of the gypsies and the dance of the tarantula for the 'Danza del terror': Antonio Gallego, *Manuel de Falla y el amor brujo* (Madrid: Alianza, 1991), pp. 173–6. Despite consulting secondary sources and raising the matter with leading Spanish folklorists and flamencologists such as Josep Crivillé y Bargalló and José Blas Vega in private conversations, no satisfactory flamenco precedent has been cited for these numbers.

closely resembled the type of music that characterised the gypsies in prehistoric times, given his belief that they had originated in India. This assumption was based upon the speculations of Sales Mayo, which Falla had underlined in Francisco Manzano Pabanó's 1915 book on the history and customs of the gypsies.[12] In his search for primitive musical elements which could be explored in the ritualistic passages of his drama Falla turned to Judith Gautier's *Les musiques bizarres*, which included transcriptions by Benedictus of Oriental music heard at the Paris Exposition Universelle of 1900.[13] In doing so Falla paralleled some of the exoticist strategies of French composers and the type of cultural conflation evident in 'Andalousie au temps du Maures'.

Falla copied Gautier's commentaries on the influence of Arab music, and was especially interested in the transcriptions of the *Danse javanaise* and the Ceylonese *Danse du diable*. From the two dances Falla noted various effects that he would employ in *El amor brujo*, most notably in the 'Danza ritual de fuego'. These include the insistent repetition of a single note, the ritualistic repetition of a short phrase, loudly and softly, the employment of arpeggiated but harmonically static bass lines, and the use of the extended trill. In *El amor brujo* Falla also drew from musical traditions which had closer ties to the Iberian peninsula and flamenco forms. He stated that this work's peculiar orchestral colouring was not only due to his attempts to imitate the guitar; it sprang from his desire to evoke 'primitive Arab instruments', which he associated with the Hispano-Arabic tradition.[14]

While *El amor brujo* is now viewed as a quintessential representation of Spanish gypsiness, and even Spanish musical nationalism, contemporary commentators were estranged by Falla's primitivist and orientalist conception of flamenco, and by his modernist musical language. These were at odds with the employment of flamenco as an element of local colour in the *zarzuela* and its harmonic and rhythmic domestication in the *cuplé* popular song style of the early twentieth century.

Over the following years Falla continued to draw parallels between the music of the Orient and that of Andalusia, which in turn informed his composition of *El sombrero de tres picos* (1917–19) and the *Fantasia Baetica* (1919). This process had intensified with his greater exposure to performances of *cante jondo* – a term which denominates certain flamenco song forms[15] – particularly during the composition of *El amor brujo* and in the

---

[12] F. M. Pabanó, *Historia y costumbres de los gitanos* (Barcelona: Montaner y Simón, 1915).

[13] Judith Gautier, *Les musiques bizarres a l'Exposition de 1900* (Paris: Ollendorff, 1901), IN 1455, *AMF*.

[14] Falla's draft for a programme note of the work, unclassified papers, *AMF*. Most of the texts he read and annotated on Arab music highlighted the use of double-reed instruments and percussion, and he evoked their sonorities in many sections of the score.

[15] For Falla this term included the forms of the *Caña, Martinete, Serrana, Soleá* and *Siguiriya gitana*. It did not include such forms as the *bulería, alegrías* and *tango*. See Manuel de Falla, *Escritos sobre música y músicos* (Madrid: Espasa Calpe, 1988), p. 183; Manuel de Falla, *On Music and Musicians*, trans. David Urman and J. M. Thomson (London: Marion Boyars, 1979), pp. 102, 112 (hereafter *Escritos* and *On Music and Musicians*).

course of his journeys to Andalusia in the company of Serge Diaghilev and Léonide Massine in 1916 and 1917. Falla's perspectives on flamenco were undoubtedly conditioned by the value accorded to the primitive artefact and the Orient in his European cultural milieu. His association with the Ballets Russes prompted Falla to argue that oriental influences were responsible for the similarities between Russian and Spanish music, and this claim was echoed by his admired friend Igor Stravinsky, who stated in 1921:

> It is not solely a matter of curiosity. Between the popular music of Spain, and that of Russia, I perceive a profound affinity which is, without a doubt, related to their common Eastern origins. Certain Andalusian songs remind me of the melodies from Russian provinces, awakening atavistic memories in me.[16]

Was this merely cultural rapprochement based on aesthetic sympathy?[17] Falla's orientalist conception of flamenco resonated with emerging constructions of Andalusian identity, which had cultural, racial and political dimensions, most notably in relation to Spanish expansionism into Morocco.[18] Similarly, Stravinsky's fascination with flamenco's supposed Eastern origins may have drawn on his contemporary interest in radical proto-fascist Eurasian theories that highlighted the Oriental substratum of Russian identity.[19]

GRANADA AND THE *CANTE JONDO* COMPETITION

In 1920 Falla realised his long-held dream of moving to Granada, one of the emblematic Andalusian towns known for its Moorish legacy, large gypsy population and flamenco traditions. Within a year Falla became concerned with the progressive contamination and possible extinction of 'pure' *cante jondo* styles. In doing so he was echoing contemporary notions of the 'vanishing rarity' of the primitive artefact.[20] Falla's response was to organise, in collaboration with the poet Federico García Lorca and a circle of artists and intellectuals, the first *Cante Jondo* Competition in Granada in 1922, a pivotal event in the revival, dissemination and broader acceptance of flamenco in Spain and abroad.

To coincide with this event Falla wrote an extended essay entitled '*Cante Jondo*', in which he identified three historic factors that had an impact on

---

[16] Quoted in Scott Messing, *Neoclassicism in Music: From the Genesis of the Concept through the Schoenberg/Stravinsky Polemic* (Ann Arbor: UMI Research Press, 1988), p. 120.
[17] Falla wrote notes on his discussions with Stravinsky regarding the similarities between Spain and Russia, which included the Castilian plains and the Russian steppes, the expression of religiosity, the folk types and colours used for ornamental designs. For details see Christoforidis, 'Un acercamiento', p. 13.
[18] See discussion of Blas Infante's ideas in the final section of this chapter.
[19] See Richard Taruskin, 'Stravinsky the Subhuman', in *Defining Russia Musically: Historical and Hermeneutical Essays* (Princeton University Press, 1997).
[20] Glenn Watkins, *Pyramids at the Louvre: Music, Culture, and Collage from Stravinsky to the Postmodernists* (Cambridge, MA: Harvard University Press, 1994), p. 72.

Spanish music history: 'the adoption by the Church of Byzantine chant, the Arab invasion, and the settlement in Spain of numerous groups of gypsies'. Falla echoed here late nineteenth-century anthropological constructions of Andalusian identity in which, in Steingress's words, 'flamenco was viewed by many liberal intellectuals as an aesthetic manifestation and [atavistic] memory of the various "races" that had set foot in Andalusia.'[21] Of the gypsies Falla claimed: 'Those tribes, who arrived from the East, according to the historical hypothesis, give Andalusian singing a new character which consists of the *cante jondo*.' By underlining the historic role of the gypsies in the definitive formation of its styles, Falla consciously sought to give pre-eminence to the primitive Indian roots of flamenco. He then proceeded to trace the origins of most flamenco songs to the (gypsy) *siguiriya gitana* and pointed out that 'it is perhaps the only European song which preserves in all its purity ... the highest qualities of the primitive song of oriental people'. In comparing 'the essential elements of *cante jondo*' with 'the songs of India and of other oriental countries', Falla observed various similarities including: the use of enharmonic intervals melodically and as a means of transposition, restricted melodic range of a sixth, and the repeated, even obsessive, use of one note, frequently accompanied by an upper or by a lower appogiatura.[22]

Despite stressing its Oriental origins, Falla highlighted the importance of local Spanish conditions and the influence of the 'Spanish race' in shaping flamenco forms:

It must not be thought, however, that the *siguiriya* and its derivatives are simply songs that have been imported from the East. At the most, it is a grafting or rather, a case of the coincidence of origins that certainly did not reveal itself at one particular moment, but that is the result, as we have already pointed out, of an accumulation of historical facts taking place through many centuries in our peninsula. That is why the kind of song peculiar to Andalusia [*cante jondo*], although it coincides in its essential elements with those developed in countries so far away from ours, shows so typical, so national, a character, that it becomes unmistakeable.[23]

Falla conceived of *cante jondo* as a folk manifestation of Andalusia and one of its principal markers of identity, although he believed in its relevance for all Spaniards. In doing so he positioned gypsy culture in the peninsula as an integral component of Spanishness.

One of the principal aims of the organisers of the *Cante Jondo* Competition was to encounter 'unadulterated' renditions of this repertory

---

[21] Steingress, 'Ideología y mentalidad en la construcción de la identidad cultural', p. 168.
[22] Falla also noted performance practices such as the use of ornamental features at certain moments to express states of relaxation or of rapture, and the shouts with which the public encourage and incite singers and performers. Manuel de Falla, *El 'Cante Jondo' (Canto Primitivo Andaluz)* (Granada: Urania, 1922), reproduced in *Escritos*, pp. 168–71; *On Music and Musicians*, pp. 101, 102, 103.
[23] Falla, *Escritos*, p. 171; *On Music and Musicians*, p. 105.

from amateurs and they therefore excluded professional *cantaores* (flamenco singers) from competing, although they were employed among the jury.²⁴ In setting these criteria Falla was not primarily invoking notions of purity versus contamination, which had racialist overtones at this time. Rather, he was echoing writers from the late nineteenth century, such as Antonio Machado y Álvarez, who had bemoaned the commercialisation of flamenco and its loss of purity in the *tablaos* (flamenco taverns) and *café cantantes*, due to the professionalisation of artists and the formation of new styles in combination with Andalusian popular idioms. Machado had argued that flamenco songs were losing, bit by bit, their primitive character and originality. On the eve of the *Cante Jondo* Competition Falla echoed these concerns:

> We would not have gone to the trouble of organising this competition for the sake of flamenco songs now in vogue ... What we propose is to bring about a renaissance of an admirable Andalusian folk art that was about to disappear for ever, victim of the *couplet* and modern flamenco songs, which are about as Andalusian as I am Chinese.²⁵

While it may not have been Falla's intention, this position has been taken as a critique of the gypsies' pivotal role in the professionalisation of the genre. Some flamenco purists had argued, partly on racial grounds, that the contamination of the pure *cante jondo* style was predominantly due to gypsy innovations in the *tablaos* of the second half of the nineteenth century. However Antonio Mairena's later influential revindication of pure *cante jondo* styles was predicated on bringing the gypsy elements to the fore.²⁶

ANTIFLAMENQUISMO AND GYPSIES

Although several prominent Spanish intellectuals signed a proclamation of support for the *Cante Jondo* Competition, many expressed their misgivings.²⁷ Flamenco music and its subculture were seemingly incompatible with the calls for greater Europeanisation or the search for a new Spanish

---

[24] Some flamencologists have criticised Falla for failing to understand that the *tablaos* and professional *cantaores* were integral to the evolution of flamenco forms in the nineteenth century. On occasion, they have failed to recognise the esteem that Falla had for many professional *cantaores*. He admired the renditions of *cante jondo* by professional *cantaores* such as Chacón or La Niña de los Peines and wanted such professionals to form part of the judging committee at the *Cante Jondo* Competition. See Christoforidis, 'Un acercamiento', pp. 6–7.

[25] Notes held at the *AMF*.

[26] Félix Grande, *Memoria del flamenco* (Madrid: Alianza, 1999), p. 412. The equation of *cante jondo* elements of flamenco with gypsiness is still prevalent, although it has been viewed as problematic by recent scholarship on flamenco. See Timothy Mitchell, *Flamenco Deep Song*, pp. 198–215.

[27] Its supporters included Fernando de los Rios, Juan Ramón Jiménez, Ramón Menendez Pidal, Azorín, Tomás Borrás and Miguel Salvador. Among its most vocal critics were Francisco de Paula Valladar. See Jorge de Persia, *I Concurso de Cante Jondo* (Granada: Archivo Manuel de Falla, 1992), pp. 28–35, 41–6.

identity steeped in the values of Castile, which were espoused by the intelligentsia of the cultural Generation of 1898. In the aftermath of the Spanish–American War and loss of Empire, and the ensuing search for identity, many of the intellectuals associated with the Generation of 1898 aimed their criticism at flamenco and its associated contexts.

Debates on *antiflamenquismo* first came to a head in the late nineteenth century in the context of a flamenco spectacle organised for the foreign delegates to Madrid's Congreso Artístico y Literario Internacional of 1887. Gaspar de Núñez de Arce, president of the Asociación de Escritores y Artistas argued vehemently for the cancellation of the spectacle, attacking the custom of presenting foreigners with flamenco acts that graced Madrid's popular stages. By the turn of the century the popularity of flamenco, especially in Madrid, was such that intellectuals became obsessed with it, identifying it with Spain's supposed decadence, an attitude evident in the *antiflamenquismo* of writers such as Miguel de Unamuno, Pio Baroja and José Ortega y Gasset. Writing in the 1930s, Carlos and Pedro Caba pointed to the roots of this *antiflamenquismo*, in their classic work *Andalucía, su comunismo y su cante jondo*:

Another prejudice of the [Generation of 1898] ... was the *espagnolade*, the florid writings with which a Byron, a Gautier or a Mérimée presented Spain ... they gave such great importance to the judgements of these literary tourists, [and] were so alarmed at the thought that Europe could believe that Spain could be like that ... that they ended up venting their spleen on bullfights and flamenco.[28]

For the *antiflamenquistas* flamenco and its associated contexts (including taverns, jails and bordellos) were seen as grotesque caricatures of Spanishness which encapsulated the backwardness of the peninsula in relation to Europe. The perceived lower-class, low-life and immoral associations of its public and settings – which did not preclude aristocrats and intellectuals slumming it at the *tablaos* – was also linked by the *antiflamenquistas* to contemporary stereotypes of the genre's gypsy protagonists. There had been numerous Spanish royal decrees dating from the seventeenth and eighteenth centuries that had attempted to outlaw and later assimilate the gypsies within Spanish society, and many had settled in southern Spain (as so-called 'New Castilians'). Unlike the case in much of Europe, many gypsies became established in sectors of Andalusian towns by the nineteenth century – such as the Albayzín in Granada – and did not form part of an itinerant transnational population. However, this did not preclude an exoticising attitude and they were often still considered outsiders. Writing at the time of the *Cante Jondo* Competition, Vicente Manzanares highlighted both an identification and an overriding sense of

---

[28] Carlos and Pedro Caba, *Andalucía, su comunismo y su cante jondo* (Madrid: Biblioteca Atlántico, 1933). Cited in Yvan Nommick and Antonio Alvarez Cañibano (eds.), *Los Ballets Russes de Diaghilev y España* (Madrid: Centro de Documentación de Música y Danza, 2000), p. 171.

otherness, noting that the people of Granada had no social contact with the gypsies until a few years before; however, 'the passion and artistry of gypsiness had infiltrated into the heart of the city. Who in Granada had not felt the temptation to seduce a gypsy? ... Who in Granada has not heard of a man who has died, or rather has been killed, in search of a crazy love in the Albayzín.'[29]

The racialised characterisation of the gypsy as foreigner or exotic Other is encapsulated in the writings of authors of the generation of 1898 like Pio Baroja, as can be seen in this passage from *La Busca* describing a *bailaor* (flamenco dancer):

a gypsy of chocolate skin stood up and began an [Andalusian] tango, a dance with negro origins; he twisted himself, throwing his abdomen forward and his arms back. He finished the [twisted] movements of his feminised hips creating a complicated plait of arms and legs.[30]

Baroja's description is similar to that of numerous commentators who conflated the gypsy and flamenco with the African and resorted to a gendered, highly corporeal, and often deprecating description of flamenco dance. Baroja's comments reflect numerous damning critiques of flamenco dancing, especially aimed at its male protagonist, the *bailaor*, and his subversion of masculinity. The following description of a *bailaor* appeared in the popular newspaper *El Cronista* in 1887:

Far sadder and more incomprehensible is the fact that men, forgetting their dignity and stature, agitate and move themselves with ridiculous feminised gestures. The dance in this case becomes vice in all its ugliness, something repugnant and disgusting, the relaxation of all sense of morality.[31]

Most of the *antiflamenquistas* were not of Andalusian origin, as was the case with Eugenio Noel, the author from Madrid who led a series of campaigns against both flamenco and bullfighting. He dedicated much of his writing from 1911 to this end, as can be seen in his numerous critiques of flamenco singing and dancing that highlighted the otherness of the form and its detrimental effect on Spanish culture. His comments on flamenco dancing reflect those cited above and are not restricted to men, but present female dancers as similarly cheap illustrations of lowly sexual decadence:

One of the evils of *flamenquismo* has been the detrimental effect it has had on our dances. We have no sense of voluptuousness, refinement or subtle grace. Our *bailaor* is an indecent, androgynous and tortured being, and his partner is a disgraceful woman who handles her body as she does her soul, without art or science and in order to gain a few pesetas.[32]

[29] Quoted in De Persia, *I Concurso de Cante Jondo*, p. 52.
[30] Pio Baroja, *La Busca* (Madrid: Caro Raggio, 1904).
[31] *El Cronista*, 23 June 1887; quoted in Manuel Ríos Ruiz, *Ayer y hoy del cante flamenco* (Madrid: Istmo, 1997), p. 58.
[32] Eugenio Noel, *Campaña antiflamenca* (Valencia: Editorial Sempere y Cia., 1919).

Noel's description of the *cantaor*'s singing brings to mind racialist contemporary accounts of deformity and mental retardation among gypsies.³³

To sing [flamenco] one needs a very special vocal quality, an exceptional mucous membrane in the throat and artistic taste that is so grotesquely exaggerated and absurd that it reflects . . . voluntary stupidity and tones produced or accompanied by mysterious convulsions.³⁴

And yet Noel was also highly knowledgeable of flamenco forms and this sensibility is evident in many of his essays. His critique of the dancer Pastora Imperio acknowledges her artistry while lamenting the consequences of her gypsy art for the progress of Spanish culture:

If only this spirit contained something of an artistic ideal! . . . What great surprises it could have offered. But it is indomitable, steely, brutal, rough, crude and gypsy. Her gypsiness is savage and pure; there is nothing more genuine or lamentable.

I have long been a student of gypsiness. I know that it is the cause of our civil and moral decline. But this disconcerting woman has convinced me that gypsiness is the supreme formula of our art at present. Damn this art . . . as it is an implacable movement backwards!³⁵

Noel's ambivalence is palpable and in his comments on Pastora Imperio's dance one senses his difficulty in disparaging something that is so deeply rooted in his culture and sensibility.

Racial stereotypes of gypsies also precluded them in the eyes of some commentators from having contributed to the formation of flamenco genres. This was due to their perceived appropriation of the cultural artefacts they came into contact with. Well into the twentieth century Spanish writers on music, and even flamenco, have remarked on the gypsies' supposed limited musical talent, creativity and their lack of poetic ability.³⁶ Some authors, like the eminent philosopher Miguel de Unamuno, have gone so far as to deny on racial grounds the overall importance given to the gypsy element in Spanish culture, claiming that the image of gypsy Spain was historically false:

We are, in effect, convinced that the base of the Spanish people is, racially, one of the most homogenous, consisting of a Romanised Celtic-Iberian substratum, and that the various invaders and immigrants, numerically very small, were soon mixed with it . . . And we come to believe that a people [like the gypsies], who pushed into Spain uninvited, without a homeland, history, literature or great historical figures . . . has been given more importance than it deserves. Can people believe that in Spain there is more gypsy blood than that of the Visigoths?³⁷

---

³³ Such notions are alluded to in Pabanó's 1915 *Historia y Costumbres*.
³⁴ Eugenio Noel, *Señoritos chulos, fenómenos, gitanos y flamencos* (Madrid: Renacimiento, 1916).
³⁵ Eugenio Noel, *Escenas y andanzas de la campaña antiflamenca* (Madrid: Libertarias/Prodhufi, 1995), p. 241. Original edition: Valencia: Editorial Sempere y Cia., *c.* 1913.
³⁶ Bernard Leblon, *Gypsies and Flamenco. The Emergence of the Art of Flamenco in Andalusia* (Hatfield: University of Hertfordshire Press, 1995), pp. 81–2.
³⁷ Miguel de Unamuno, 'Gitanadas y judiadas', *El Sol*, 27 January 1932, 3.

Antiflamenquismo persisted in the debates surrounding the *Cante Jondo* Competition of 1922, with many intellectuals wary of reviving interest in music that had been so closely associated with exoticising and derogatory images of Spain.[38] However, the leading modernist critic, Adolfo Salazar, pointed out that one should not reject such incredible sources of 'popular' music 'because of the ways in which they have been abused by bad musicians, and if this abusive *casticismo* [Hispanic traditionalism] has degenerated into a topic, it is no less a topic to reject [flamenco] in the name of a second-hand Europeanism'.[39]

By the late nineteenth century the onus of creativity within flamenco performance had begun to rest with the individual and this gradually translated into the rising status of the gypsy *cantaor/a*, *bailaor/a* and *tocaor/a* (guitarist). Even *antiflamenquistas* such as Noel suggested that flamenco owed more to the caprices of its latest performer than to its lengthy historical genealogy.[40]

Falla and Lorca's espousal of flamenco and the gypsies' contributions to Andalusian and Spanish culture helped transform the attitudes of intellectuals and the subsequent cultural Generation of 1927.[41] Lorca's characterisation of the gypsy as encapsulating the ideals of the Andalusian race is presented in the introduction to his *Romancero gitano* (1924–7):

> The book as a whole, though entitled 'Gypsy', is the poem of Andalusia. I have called it gypsy because the gypsy epitomises the loftiest, the most profound, the most aristocratic characteristics of my country; he is the most representative of its way of living, the keeper of the flame, the blood, and the alphabet of a truth both Andalusian and Universal.

FALLA AND DEBATES ON THE RACIAL ORIGINS OF FLAMENCO

The primacy accorded the gypsies in Lorca's constructions of flamenco and Falla's notion of the origins of *cante jondo* were not always in accord with contemporary Spanish cultural and musicological perspectives. The importance Falla gave to the Indian roots of flamenco contrasted with the thoughts of his Andalusian compatriot Joaquín Turina, who speculated on the defining role of Arab music in the transformation of Southern Spanish music, in line with his own Hispano-Arabic Orientalist musical style. Falla's essay provoked a bemused response from Turina, who wrote to him on 7 October 1922, 'I am now completely disorientated. Do you

---

[38] Valladar noted that 'there are no means of ridding ourself of the *espagnolade* in foreign lands and it is true that Spaniards are to blame'. Quoted in De Persia, *I Concurso de Cante Jondo*, p. 29.
[39] *El Sol*, 16 February 1922; as quoted in De Persia, *I Concurso de Cante Jondo*, p. 37.
[40] Eugenio Noel, *Martín el de la Paula en Alcalá de los Panaderos* (Madrid: La Novela Mundial, 1926).
[41] Taking their cue from Falla and Lorca, other authors of the Generation of 1927, such as Rafael Alberti and Luis Cernuda, were powerfully influenced by flamenco and its literary, visual and musical manifestations.

really believe that *cante jondo* comes from India? Are we making Indians of ourselves?'[42] (a colloquial expression in Spanish for making a fool of oneself).

Falla also disagreed with his teacher Felipe Pedrell's assertion that the persistence of musical orientalism in various Spanish popular songs was solely the result of 'the influence exerted by the most ancient Byzantine civilisation', and that even Andalusian song 'does not owe anything essential to the Arabs'.[43] While Pedrell did give some credit to the role of gypsies, whose origins he traced to upper Egypt, it was only to stress their role in transferring Syrian influences and thus reinforcing the Byzantine legacy. Pedrell's promotion of Byzantine music as the possible conduit for Oriental influence can also be seen as an attempt to marginalise the Arab and Jewish legacies in Spain. Theories advancing Arab and Jewish influence on the evolution of flamenco only became more prominent from the 1930s.[44] *Antiflamenquistas* at times referred to the mixed origins of flamenco but generally regarded its hybrid nature as a negative.

While Falla had also alluded to Byzantine influence, he respectfully challenged Pedrell's ideas by admitting the Hispano-Arabic cross-influences on the rhythmic contours and instrumental timbres associated with some of the dance forms. He specifically related aspects of the *sevillanas*, *zapateados* and *seguidillas* to the Moorish Andalusian music of North Africa, and had even made attempts to bring a group from Morocco to perform for the 1922 *Cante Jondo* Competition.[45] At this time and later in 1930 Falla also considered visiting Morocco to study Arab-Andalusian music.[46] In a 1932 letter to the eminent music critic Adolfo Salazar, he expanded on the possible Arab influences on flamenco styles and even cited the sources he had studied:

As far as Arab-Andalusian influences are concerned, I have only found these in the music for dance. (Independently, of course, of the evident relationship of the purely Andalusian *cantos* with those of Oriental origin). You have the Yafil

---

[42] Mariano Pérez Gutiérrez, *Falla y Turina a través de su epistolario* (Madrid: Editorial Alpuerto, 1982), p. 111.

[43] Falla, *El 'Cante Jondo'*, p. 166. For an extensive discussion of Falla's essay and the sources of his ideas see Christoforidis, 'Un acercamiento'.

[44] In terms of Arab influence see for instance Aziz Balouch, *Cante jondo: Su origen y evolución* (Madrid: Ediciones Ensayos, 1955), and in terms of Jewish influence see, for instance, Medina Azara, 'Cante jondo y cantares sinagogales', *Revista de Occidente* (1930). Falla's reticence to admit Jewish influence may have also been due to a degree of anti-Semitism inspired by his Catholicism. For some progressives the 'cultural pluralism of the high Middle Ages were a source of patriotic pride' (see Carolyn P. Boyd, *Historia Patria. Politics, History, and National Identity in Spain, 1875–1975* (Princeton University Press, 1997), p. 84), and these ideas became even more prevalent during the Second Republic.

[45] See copy of a letter from Isidro de Cagigas to José Martínez Ribóo, *AMF*.

[46] Falla's proposed trip to Morocco to listen to Arab-Andalusian music is referred to in a letter from Prosper Ricard (February 1922, *AMF*). J. B. Trend's descriptions (and transcriptions) of Moroccan music are found in letters to Falla from March 1930 (see especially letter dated 2 March 1930), *AMF*. In a postcard dated 15 March 1930 Trend attempted to organise a trip to Marrakesh for Falla, *AMF*.

collection. Look at numbers 17 and 22 (Tuchiats Ghrib and Sika): Sevillanas and Zapateado... But how can one know if the origin of both is Moorish or Spanish? In any case, both examples are interesting.[47]

Falla's personal library includes copies of the Collection Yafil which display the composer's annotations.[48] It is also evident from Falla's remarks to Salazar that he did not discount the possibility of the influences travelling in the other direction, from Spain to North Africa.

Despite admitting the possible, if somewhat limited, influence of the Arabs on certain flamenco forms, Falla denied their more generalised impact upon Spanish music. While displaying interest in Julián Ribera's initial studies on correspondences between Spanish and Arab music, Falla became openly critical of Ribera's more controversial affirmations,[49] which signalled the impact of the Arabs upon a wide spectrum of Iberian music, from the Aragonese *Jota* to the medieval *Cantigas de Santa María*. Some of the tenets of Falla's position can be viewed within a tradition of Spanish scholarship which sought to minimise the Arab influence on the Spanish peninsula, its culture and race. The *Reconquista* (the Christian reclamation of the Peninsula from the Moors and the Jews) was interpreted as a defining force in Spanish Nationhood and identity and the disastrous contemporary military campaigns against the Moroccans (1919–22) were viewed by some commentators as a continuation of that struggle.[50] Falla's identification of pan-Andalusian elements in flamenco that cross the Ibero-African divide also parallels contemporary cultural-political theories of identity, such as those of the modern father of Andalusian nationalism Blas Infante, who sought to incorporate Northern Morocco as an integral part of the Andalusian state within Spain.[51]

In the early 1920s Falla's musical nationalism progressively assimilated some of the ideals of the Generation of 1898, most notably their Castilian bias and modern European aspirations. His music shifted from evoking Spanish folklore, and especially the flamenco genres of Andalusia, to exploring Spain's musical past in the light of emerging neo-classical trends, a style followed by most musicians of the cultural Generation of 1927. However, Falla retained elements of flamenco and the musics that had supposedly played a part in its evolution.[52] Examples of this shift include

---

[47] Manuel de Falla, letter to Adolfo Salazar, 7 March 1932, *AMF*.
[48] The Touchiat Sika referred to in the above letter is marked 'Sevillana' and Falla's annotations provide a rudimentary harmonisation while transforming the metre indicated in the score. See IN 937.
[49] Adolfo Salazar, letter to Manuel de Falla, March 1932, *AMF*.
[50] Both Catholic conservatives and progressives embraced the concept of the *Reconquista*, although progressive commentators were more ambivalent about its significance. While celebrating the triumph of the Spaniards (with concepts of nation and political rights) over the Arabs, they recognised the extraordinary achievements of Hispano-Arabic culture. Boyd, *Historia Patria*, p. 84.
[51] Steingress, 'Ideología y mentalidad en la construcción de la identidad cultural', p. 188.
[52] For instance, in *El retablo de Maese Pedro* elements of the prosody and harmony are indebted to flamenco practices, and there are references to Indian ragas in the sketches.

works like *El retablo de Maese Pedro* (Master Peter's Puppet Show, 1918–23), the puppet opera based on passages from Miguel de Cervantes' *Don Quixote*. He also projected a scenic cantata based on El Cid, the legendary figure of the *Reconquista*.[53] It could be argued that the climax of *El retablo de Maese Pedro* reflects something of the ideals of the *Reconquista*, and possibly even the contemporary Spanish campaigns in Morocco, with its destruction of an army of puppet Moors by a deluded yet chivalrous Don Quixote.

Issues of race and identity were central to the cultural politics of Falla's time, and they are evoked whenever his writings and music addressed flamenco. While his ideas and compositional output also reflect many of the primitivist ideals prevalent in Paris, Falla achieved a new modernist construction of flamenco, which highlights its multiracial origins and the defining influence of gypsies in its evolution. Falla's musical construct of flamenco eventually prevailed with Spanish audiences and, perhaps more importantly, his thoughts on the genre and gypsiness helped shape Spanish cultural consciousness and identity. The ongoing significance of this vision of flamenco is demonstrated by more recent manifestations of cultural exchange, in which Spanish gypsies have engaged with and reinterpreted Falla's music and Lorca's poetry.[54]

---

[53] See Federico Sopeña (ed.), *Correspondencia entre Falla y Zuloaga (1915–1942)* (Granada: Ayuntamiento de Granada, 1982); Michael Christoforidis, 'Hacia un nuevo concepto de ópera en los proyectos de Manuel de Falla (1911–1921)', in Emilio Casares Rodicio and Alvaro Torrente (eds.), *La Opera en España e Hispanoamérica. Una creación propia* (Madrid: Fundación Autor, 2002), vol II, pp. 363–71.

[54] Versions of Falla's music have been recorded by musicians such as Paco de Lucía and Ginesa Ortega.

CHAPTER 16

'The old sweet Anglo-Saxon spell': racial discourses and the American reception of British music, 1895–1933

Alain Frogley

The subject of race and art music in the English-speaking world has until recently been almost entirely neglected.[1] One problem is that in discussing virtually any aspect of art music during the decades either side of 1900, music history has always tended to reduce Britain and America to a sideshow; another is that the dramatically explicit musical racism which emerged before, during and after this period in Germany and Austria has inevitably thrown issues of music and race in other countries into the shade. Yet if we consider the geopolitical power relationships of this period, or imagine a discussion of race in the turn-of-the-century novel, or in poetry of the 1920s, then the idea of viewing Britain and America as peripheral begins to seem decidedly strange. The lack of attention musicology has given to imperialism and postcolonialism until quite recently might be attributed, at least in part, to the low status of Britain, the leading imperial power, in the established narratives of music history for this period. Yet a hundred years ago London was in many ways the capital of the world, the centre of a vast empire which dominated the globe, not only by virtue of its military and economic power, but also for important cultural reasons; some four hundred million people, close to a quarter of the world's population, were subject to British rule, and Britain played a crucial role in articulating and defining the West's encounters with other peoples and cultures. During the same period Britain was developing more and more common ground, especially in thinking about what was then understood as 'race', with the United States, its former colony, where Anglo-Saxon predominance was giving way to an unprecedentedly diverse, and increasingly explosive, mix of ethnic groups.

---

[1] For a long time the one major exception was MacDonald Smith Moore, *Yankee Blues: Musical Culture and American Identity* (Bloomington: Indiana University Press, 1985). Since the present chapter was completed several new contributions on the subject have appeared, the most substantial of which is Beth E. Levy, *Frontier Figures: American Music and the Mythology of the American West, 1895–1945*, unpublished Ph.D. thesis, University of California, Berkeley (2002). Levy and others largely confirm Moore's arguments, however, and like him do not make the connections with British music that I pursue here. In contrast to art music, popular music in Anglophone countries has of course received much attention from a racial perspective; of recent contributions see in particular Nicholas M. Evans, *Writing Jazz: Race, Nationalism, and Modern Culture in the 1920s* (New York: Garland, 2000).

At this time Britain and America were only just beginning to make an impact in the field of modern art music to compare with that of Germany, France, Italy, or even Russia. Yet this situation was rapidly changing; perhaps more importantly, even when they appeared compositionally peripheral in performance, education, criticism and other areas Britain and America had emerged as central forums for the negotiation and renegotiation of the cultural values of Western art music as a whole. This position was reinforced by their leading roles in applying the new technologies of recording, broadcasting and film, and by deteriorating political and economic conditions in continental Europe during the inter-war years, which led eventually to a massive musical exodus west to both countries. Indeed, though beyond the scope of this discussion, there are many respects in which British and American musicians even came to see themselves as safeguarding the values of European musical traditions which were now threatened or already eclipsed in their countries of origin.

From our perspective in the early twenty-first century it should come as no surprise that ideas about race contributed significantly, overtly and covertly, to the debates in the English-speaking musical world surrounding these upheavals, not least in the emergence and promotion of distinctive national schools of composition in Britain and America. This was especially true of America. In this chapter I focus on what can perhaps best be described as a pan-Anglo-Saxonism in debates surrounding new American music during this period, a discourse that reached explicitly across the Atlantic, and implicitly spanned the globe. This is a preliminary study, and the emphasis will be more on historical exposition than on discourse analysis. Nevertheless, it clearly exemplifies not only the unusually pivotal role often played by music in encounters with Others increasingly defined by theories of race, but also the inherently contradictory and hence unstable character of so much racial discourse – especially in the forms dominant around 1900, in which biology and culture were for the most part hazily conflated. Since the mid-eighteenth century, cultural values had increasingly been viewed as heritable, and thus portable through migration, yet also by implication resistant to social assimilation in new contexts. In the United States, a nation built on immigration, this became an especially critical debate.[2]

THE SPECIAL RELATIONSHIP

A particularly vivid quotation will serve to set the scene in the domain of music. In 1931 Daniel Gregory Mason (1873–1953), American composer,

---

[2] For a concise survey of the evolution of the modern concept of race and its relationship to music see the editors' 'Introduction: Music and Race, Their Past, Their Presence', in Ronald Radano and Philip V. Bohlman (eds.), *Music and the Racial Imagination* (University of Chicago Press, 2000), pp. 1–53, especially 10–16.

widely read and influential writer on music and Professor at Columbia University, lamented over the state of American music:

[O]ur whole contemporary aesthetic attitude toward instrumental music, especially in New York, is dominated by Jewish tastes and standards, with their Oriental extravagance, their sensuous brilliancy and intellectual facility and superficiality, their general tendency to exaggeration and disproportion.[3]

He goes on to quote an article written eleven years earlier in which he had broached these same themes: 'For how shall a public accustomed by prevailing fashion to the exaggeration, the constant running to extremes, of eastern expression, divine the poignant beauty of Anglo-Saxon sobriety and restraint?'[4] He then crystallises the whole matter in one striking phrase: 'The Jew and the Yankee stand, in human temperament, at polar points; where one thrives, the other is bound to languish.'[5]

This bitter polemic serves as a useful window onto the main themes which I will pursue here. Mason's anti-Semitic stance is probably familiar to anyone who has read the standard literature on American music. His remarks have been quoted in several prominent sources, for instance the path-breaking survey by Gilbert Chase, and most recently by Richard Crawford, but they have been presented in a way that has tended to obscure or neglect a good deal of their significance.[6] First, the views they represent have for the most part been treated as largely isolated and marginal (Chase says he quotes Mason's remarks 'merely as a curiosity in our musical literature'[7]); second, the emphasis has been placed almost exclusively on their anti-Semitism, rather than their position within a broader discourse

---

[3] *Tune In, America: A Study of Our Coming Musical Independence* (New York: A. A. Knopf, 1931), p. 160.
[4] Ibid., p. 161. Mason quotes from his article 'Is American Music Growing Up? Our Emancipation From Alien Influences', *Arts and Decoration* 13 (November 1920), 7–10.
[5] *Tune in, America*, p. 160. Mason attempted – not very convincingly – to distance himself from these remarks later in the decade, in response largely to the outrage of his Jewish friends, most notably conductor Ossip Gabrilovich: see *Music In My Time and Other Reminiscences* (New York: Macmillan, 1938), pp. 324–5.
[6] See Chase, *America's Music, From the Pilgrims to the Present* (New York: McGraw-Hill, 1955), p. 402; this passage appears unchanged in the revised second edition of the book, published in 1966. By the time of the third edition (Urbana: University of Illinois Press, 1987) Chase had slightly expanded his discussion of Mason's remarks (pp. 471–2), and contextualised them a little more widely, but he still marginalises Mason, dubbing him a 'fossil'. Richard Crawford, in *America's Musical Life: A History* (New York: Norton, 2001), p. 782, quotes Chase's earlier discussion rather than referring directly to Mason. Between Moore's *Yankee Blues* and the recent Levy and Evans sources cited in n. 1, the only extensive published discussion of these issues appears in David Schiff, *Gershwin: Rhapsody in Blue* (Cambridge University Press, 1997), pp. 86–100, especially 87–92; Schiff was also the first author to make significant reference to Moore. For a fuller treatment of aspects of the construction of Jewish musical identity during this period see Klára Móricz, *Jewish Nationalism in Twentieth-Century Art Music*, unpublished Ph.D. thesis, University of California, Berkeley (1999), and the same author's contribution to this volume. Ernst Bloch is a particular target of Mason's in *Tune in, America*. British musical anti-Semitism deserves extended consideration in another forum.
[7] Chase, *America's Music*, 1st ed., p. 402, n. 9. Although it remained in place in the second edition, this sentence disappeared in the third, where the passage has been substantially rewritten; the later version does not mention any other instances of musical anti-Semitism, however.

of race and music; and, third, the emphasis on their *pro*scriptive anti-Semitism has obscured the *pre*scriptive part of Mason's message, the cure for the ailment, as it were. An important element in this last was an urge to turn to the cradle of the Anglo-Saxon race: for Mason, contemporary British composers and British musical life set a salutary example for American musicians, and provided inspiration for those wishing to reconnect with America's historic Anglo-Saxon 'racial' roots.[8]

Mason's views, though certainly not unchallenged, were far from eccentric, either in the musical world or beyond: they reflected broader debates in American society, and his high opinion of contemporary British music, which he preferred in some cases to that of other European nations, was shared by a good number of influential peers. Indeed, the impact of British music and musicians is an important and largely untold story of twentieth-century American art music.[9] In the transatlantic traffic of performers, composers and critics, of compositional influences, and of shared ideas and ideologies, there are many connections that have yet to be fully traced. Important here is the traffic of ideology, specifically a brand of racialist thinking which helped shape musical relationships between the United States and Britain. From the mid-1890s, when discussions of American musical identity entered an especially intense phase, until the onset of the Great Depression in the early 1930s, debates concerning new American art music and surrounding the early phases of the Anglo-American folk-music revival were caught up in this discourse. (The Depression years and the Second World War brought important new elements into play and as such deserve a separate treatment.[10])

That this story has remained untold is perhaps surprising. British influences on earlier American music, and in the popular realm, are widely acknowledged. And there is a wider suggestive context: that network of cultural ties and geopolitical common interests conveniently gathered under the so-called 'special relationship', which continues to shape the world in ventures such as the First and Second Gulf Wars and to influence culture in such products as the Austin Powers films.[11] Whatever its contradictions and ambivalences, this relationship has remained remarkably

---

[8] I shall return to Mason's arguments briefly below; I discuss them at greater length in a forthcoming article on the American reception of Vaughan Williams.
[9] The only coordinated exploration of the subject occurred under the wider umbrella of the Third American Music Conference, held at Keele University in July 1983 and entitled 'British-American Musical Interactions'; the conference generated special issues of *Musical Times* (124/1685, 1983) and *American Music* (4/1, Spring 1986), which published articles derived from the conference proceedings or closely related to its subject-matter. There appears to have been no consideration of the racial issues under discussion here, however.
[10] I deal with aspects of this in my article on Vaughan Williams reception cited in n. 8.
[11] The literature on Anglo-American relations is, not surprisingly, vast. For a stimulating introduction concentrating on the twentieth century see David Dimbleby and David Reynolds, *An Ocean Apart: The Relationship Between Britain and America in the Twentieth Century* (New York: Random House, 1988); and, with a more detailed treatment of the cultural domain, Christopher Hitchens, *Blood, Class, and Nostalgia: Anglo-American Ironies* (New York: Farrar, Straus and Giroux, 1990).

resilient, and its origins and evolution are directly pertinent to my concerns here. The modern rhetoric of the special relationship is founded primarily on that of the Anglo-American alliance of the Second World War and the Cold War, which was dominated by the themes of combating tyranny and totalitarianism, and of championing democratic government and individual freedoms. On the surface it emphasised shared history, especially democratic traditions, rather than shared racial origins, which from the polyglot American side were politically problematic. Yet the wartime alliance grew out of a more extended rapprochement between the former adversaries, which had begun towards the end of the nineteenth century and which involved a strong and explicitly racial component; this was a blurred concept of race, typical of the era, which allowed even a predilection for democratic government to be seen as the product of racial biology as much as that of political history.[12] Since the mid-1870s at least, and spurred on in that decade by the colonial nostalgia surrounding the American centennial of 1876, influential voices on both sides of the Atlantic had been stressing with growing force the significance of the two nations' shared heritage and values in a rapidly changing world, and advocating closer practical co-operation. This movement sprang from a variety of closely interwoven factors; among others, these included the emergence of America as an economic powerhouse, America's establishment as an imperial power through the Spanish–American War of 1898, and increasing challenges to Britain's own imperial dominance on the global stage, especially from European rivals. But there was more to the new Anglo-American axis than a marriage of convenience. In the English-speaking world as much as anywhere else in Western society during this period, theories of race were ever more called upon to explain the history and future of the world; the increasingly unstable international scene was viewed by many as a Darwinian struggle between races as much as between nations.[13] At the high noon of British imperialism, and the dawn of America's role as a world power, it became a common belief in Britain and America that the Anglo-Saxon 'race', however hazily defined, had been charged with a divine mission to civilise the peoples of the world. This discourse could cut across national boundaries in complex ways. It was also malleable in its boundaries in that according to discursive requirements an already broad racial category, the Nordic, could extend racial kinship

---

[12] For an introduction to the early phases of this Anglo-Saxonist movement see Stuart Anderson, *Race and Rapprochement: Anglo-Saxonism and Anglo-American Relations, 1895–1904* (Rutherford, NJ: Fairleigh Dickinson University Press, 1981); for broader and comparative treatments see Cushing Strout, *The American Image of the Old World* (New York: Harper and Row, 1963), especially chapter 8, and Hitchens, *Blood, Class and Nostalgia*, chapter 4. Strout discusses contradictory forces in Anglo-American relations, including Irish-American and German-American opposition to closer ties, but also shows that such dissent was largely swimming against the tide, at least after the advent of the Second World War.

[13] See Anderson, *Race and Rapprochement*, *passim*, esp. chapter 3.

beyond the Anglo-Saxon world and include all of northern Europe; indeed, such notions inevitably mutated with the times, especially as Germany gradually emerged as an enemy of modern Anglo-Saxon democracy.[14]

Yet despite its literally global implications, for turn-of-the-century Americans Anglo-Saxonism was resonant more because of developments on the domestic front than on the international scene. Not only did Anglo-Saxonist rhetoric echo America's own historic sense of mission in expanding westward across the continent; it now chimed with a darker, more beleaguered perspective that the racial Other was within the gates. In the 1880s and 1890s America was being transformed by the so-called 'new immigration', which profoundly changed its ethnic make-up and caused widespread alarm. Indeed, it would not be an exaggeration to say that it traumatised many established Americans, especially the Anglo-Saxon social elite. WASPs had historically learned to live with Dutch and German Americans, fellow northern Europeans and also Protestants by and large, but they had been alarmed by the influx of the Catholic and Celtic Irish in the mid-nineteenth century, and now they had to contend with a much larger wave of immigration from Southern and Eastern Europe, which brought primarily Latins, Slavs and, of course, Jews, all of whom were concentrated mostly in the old north-eastern cities; and this on top of internal demographic shifts caused by the migration of southern blacks to northern cities following the abolition of slavery.[15] And the new immigration was fuelled economically by a new kind of rampant industrial capitalism and urbanisation, destabilising enough in itself, and seen by many as emblematic of the evils of the emerging modern world. All this, the old guard felt, was fatally compromising the hard-won identity of American society as a whole, and eroding its traditional bases of cultural and political power. It is hardly surprising that many, even those who had long retained a historic suspicion of Britain, began to feel the force of the 'old sweet Anglo-Saxon spell', as Henry James put it when lamenting the impact of these upheavals.[16] Many Anglo-Saxon Americans now felt they had a civilising mission within their own cities, bringing alien peoples to learn the ways of the United States.

[14] On the important racial dimension to Anglo-German relations see Paul M. Kennedy, *The Rise of the Anglo-German Antagonism, 1860–1914* (London and Boston: Allen and Unwin, 1980). Anglo-Saxonism stretched well beyond the United States and Britain, of course, as is exemplified in a figure such as Cecil Rhodes in Africa.

[15] MacDonald Smith Moore, *Yankee Blues*, is especially eloquent in conveying this trauma. It should be noted that although for Britain such threats were still viewed for the most part as external, increasing racial diversity in London, especially its growing population of eastern European Jews, was becoming a source of anxiety: see Jonathan Schneer, *London 1900: The Imperial Metropolis* (New Haven: Yale University Press, 1999), pp. 7–8.

[16] See Preface, 'Lady Barbarina', *The Art of the Novel: Critical Prefaces*, introduction by R. P. Blackmur (New York: Scribner's, 1934), pp. 208–9; quoted in Strout, *American Image*, p. 132. The Anglo-Saxon elite had for a long time felt a mission to elevate the taste of the lower orders; this class issue now intertwined with race, and was, as a number of writers have pointed out, crucial to the formation of American categorisations of high-, low-, and middlebrow culture: see in particular Jonathan Freedman, *The Temple of Culture: Assimilation and Anti-Semitism in Literary Anglo-America* (Oxford University Press, 2000), which devotes two chapters to Henry James, though many other authors are discussed.

They also eventually forced political action. Fuelled by influential polemicists such as Madison Grant and Lothrop Stoddard, racial and immigration debates in America intensified during the Great War and its aftermath, and eventually resulted in the newly restrictive Immigration Acts of 1921 and 1924, which established strict national, and in some cases racial, quotas.

VOICES FROM THE ANGLO-SAXON MUSICAL ESTABLISHMENT

What of music in this? With its potentially dangerous appeal to the senses and the emotions, music was especially vulnerable to such anxieties. In the English-speaking world music had only with great difficulty been assimilated to the stern moral imperatives of Victorian high culture, a feat achieved largely through the idealist cult of the symphony and absolute music; once accepted, however, it acquired enormous prestige and influence. Now, as the earlier quotation from Daniel Gregory Mason vividly suggests, it was in danger of capitulating once again to sensuality and other defilements, in this case racially imported. Of course, one of the reasons music had been suspect to Anglo-Saxons was that it had, by means of a vicious circle, traditionally been viewed as the preserve of the 'foreigner'; as the nineteenth century wore on, imported musicians were more and more often Jewish. In America this Jewish musical presence was massively augmented by the new immigration, and manifested itself not just in the more traditional domain of performance, but also increasingly in composition, posing a new kind of threat to Anglo-Saxon (or even Nordic) hegemony in controlling musical taste: America's fledgling creative independence was in danger of being hijacked by alien elements.[17] And Jews were deeply implicated in what in the 1920s came to pose a much more serious and broadly based racial and aesthetic threat: the increasing influence, even prestige, of popular styles that were dominated by black and Jewish musicians. Jazz was a particular lightning rod, its reception profoundly shaped by the combination of threat and primitivist allure which blacks typically represented to white Europeans and Americans.

---

[17] Jewish musical genius, in composition as well as performance, was a favourite theme of contemporary fiction, often linked to an ambivalent notion of sexual potency: see Freedman, *Temple of Culture*, especially chapter 3, which focuses on George du Maurier's enormously popular novel *Trilby* (1894). Matters were complicated by the highly feminised view of music typical of Anglo-Saxon culture during this period, and the anxieties which this created for male composers in particular: see, for instance, Judith Tick, 'Charles Ives and Gender Ideology', in Ruth A. Solie (ed.), *Musicology and Difference: Gender and Sexuality in Music Scholarship* (Berkeley: University of California Press, 1993), pp. 83–106. Issues of masculinity in the construction of Anglo-Saxon identity are beyond the scope of this chapter, but they have important implications for music. It is also not possible here to explore distinctions between different Jewish groups within the United States, or between different phases of immigration; it is clear, however, that differences in background and outlook between, for instance, mid-nineteenth-century immigrants from German-speaking countries, and later arrivals from Russia and Poland, were significant for music.

An Anglo-Saxon musical establishment, centred in East Coast universities, reacted vigorously, if ultimately unsuccessfully, to counter these multiple threats. Macdonald Smith Moore's 1985 book *Yankee Blues: Musical Culture and American Identity* is the most searching, if in certain respects limited, study so far of this ideological struggle.[18] Even Moore, however, while briefly noting a broader Anglo-Saxon ideological underpinning to writing on musical aesthetics,[19] fails to consider more direct connections between the American and British musical scenes: surprisingly, neither he nor any other writer raises the possibility – even if only to dismiss it – that anxious British-Americans in the field of music might have looked to the 'mother country' for inspiration or solace. Moore's omission is especially surprising because in some ways the chief protagonist of his book is Daniel Gregory Mason. Yet Mason was not the first prominent American musician to suggest that Anglo-Saxon blood might – or should – run thicker than dividing Atlantic water in matters of musical style. Around 1900 Horatio Parker, teacher of Charles Ives and professor at Yale, whose own works enjoyed considerable success in Britain around the turn of the century, wrote:

I have great hopes for English music … The Germans and French have made enormous strides in recent years, but I am not sure that they are in a direction in which [the] Anglo-Saxon need strive to follow. I hope for a powerful school of Anglo-Saxon music in time – less subjective and nerve-racking than that of Continental races, more broad, reserved and self-contained, with a larger respect for that economy of resource which characterizes all true artistry, and I hope that Americans may bear their part in the development of this school.[20]

And in his journal of a trip to Europe in 1902, reflecting on a meeting with Richard Strauss, he writes:

On the whole, I am inclined to think that music among the Anglo-Saxons is built upon a more solid foundation, one better calculated to sustain the weight of an imposing super-structure, than the music of the Germans. The music of the Germans is now so colored by externals that it has hardly a separate existence. That of the French seems not to come from deep enough, not to go deep enough – superficial. That of the Italians is opera – a form with such manifest limitations that one may almost regard it as outside the sphere of reasonable activity among Anglo-Saxons. For the present English and American music is surely as a whole more impersonal, more abstract than thin, and if it remains untainted by these seems sure to bring forth results of great beauty and value. German, French and Italians unite in one grand scramble to dodge the obvious ways of putting things.[21]

---

[18] See n. 1. [19] *Yankee Blues*, pp. 52–3.
[20] See Isabel Parker Semler and Pierson Underwood, *Horatio Parker: A Memoir for his Grandchildren, Compiled From Letters and Papers* (New York: Putnam, 1942), p. 110. The date and exact source of this passage are not made clear by Semler and Underwood, but from the context it seems likely that it was written in Parker's journal and refers to his 1899 trip to England.
[21] Ibid., pp. 164–5.

Two important assumptions stand out from these passages: first, that race, broadly construed, affects or even determines musical style; and, second, that 'American' is synonymous with 'Anglo-Saxon'. Mason's themes of healthy emotional restraint and sobriety, and of undemonstrative depth (popular stereotypes of the Anglo-Saxon character, of course) are here clearly prefigured. Evident also is an underlying confidence, typical of the era, that the Anglo-Saxon race, and America in particular, is poised to take on world leadership in every significant arena of human activity; and the implication that Britain and England may become custodians of a musical legacy created largely by other countries, Germany in particular, but now in danger of being squandered by them.

It was perhaps inevitable that in the xenophobic and racially confrontational climate of the years after the First World War the rather mild musical Anglo-Saxonism of Parker and others would take a more sinister turn. It was Daniel Gregory Mason who gave this trend perhaps its most eloquent and high-profile expression. As an extremely widely read writer whom Arthur Farwell, a pioneer of musical Americanism, dubbed the 'official voice' of music in America,[22] Mason wrote extensively and frequently about British music, and admired Elgar and Vaughan Williams in particular. He felt that their music epitomised the deeply passionate yet outwardly reticent English character, and by extension the same Anglo-Saxon racial traits that had determined the Yankee – and by extension American – temperament: here was an antidote to 'Oriental extravagance' for American composers and audiences. In all his writings Mason, following Matthew Arnold and other late-Victorian prophets of culture, stressed music's civilising mission, and its obligation to elevate, not alienate, the masses. His stature was such that in 1924 no fewer than five of his books were included in a list of just sixteen purportedly essential texts for music-lovers; as a writer he even numbered Charles Ives among his admirers, despite their very different approaches to composition.[23]

MUSIC AND MISCEGENATION

Mason's writings are worthy of much closer attention, but for now I will pass on quickly to another, now even less well-known figure, who makes Mason seem like a mere dilettante in the field of racism, and who connects musical Anglo-Saxonism to a different and ultimately more varied network of associations. Pianist and composer John Powell (1882–1963), a close friend of Mason's, is all but forgotten today, but he was one of the leading

---

[22] See Barbara Zuck, *A History of Musical Americanism* (Ann Arbor: UMI Research Press, 1980), p. 69.
[23] On Mason's widespread popularity as a writer, see Moore, *Yankee Blues*, p. 65; on Mason and Ives, pp. 54–5. To his credit, Ives does not seem to have shared Mason's racial prejudices. Although his music is virtually forgotten now, Mason also enjoyed considerable success as a composer during his lifetime.

American musicians of his time.²⁴ A pupil of Leschetizky, and a friend of Joseph Conrad (with whom he discussed a possible operatic collaboration) and Auguste Rodin, Powell had played at the White House for President Wilson in 1916, and was well known in Europe as well as the United States; his *Rhapsodie Nègre* for piano and orchestra (1918), prefaced by a quotation from Conrad's *The Heart of Darkness*, was enormously successful in the years after the First World War. He had had a long-standing interest in British folk music surviving in the US, but it was in the early 1920s that he began to preach in earnest the gospel of Anglo-American folk song, arguing both for its preservation as a living folk tradition, and for its incorporation into art music by American composers. (Mason, incidentally, was something of a sceptic concerning the value of folk music for his particular ethnic agenda.) By the late 1930s both these ideas would have become defining features of American musical life during the Depression, from Woody Guthrie to *Appalachian Spring*. But Powell was well in advance of these developments, and approached the issues from a radically different political perspective than the broadly populist and left-wing orientation with which we now – rather simplistically – associate the later movement. Powell did not emerge from a complete vacuum. In the decades before the First World War there had been intense, if narrow, interest in British folk-song traditions living on in the New World; this was dominated by literary scholars building on Child's famous ballad collections, and focused almost exclusively on text rather than music, but it did serve to highlight the historical continuity of cultural ties with the British Isles.²⁵ In this context it is instructive that when John Lomax published his pioneering volume of cowboy songs in 1910, which broke sharply with academic tradition through its inclusion of tunes, frankly popularising intent, disparate sources, and emphasis on the pioneering West, he still took pains in his preface

---

[24] For the fullest account of his life and work see Ronald David Ward, *The Life and Works of John Powell (1882–1963)*, unpublished Ph.D. thesis, Catholic University of America (1973). He is discussed briefly in Chase, *America's Music*, 1st ed., pp. 401–2 (this account was retained in the second edition but removed for the third, where there is no discussion of Powell) and in Charles Hamm, *Music in the New World* (New York: Norton, 1983), pp. 421–2. The only account to analyse some of his ideas in a broader cultural context is David E. Whisnant, *All That is Native and Fine: The Politics of Culture in an American Region* (Chapel Hill: University of North Carolina Press, 1983), especially chapter 3, which deals primarily with Powell's folk-music activities. Powell's profile as an internationally prominent concert pianist and composer interested in Anglo-American folk song and racial Anglo-Saxonism invites comparison with Percy Grainger. On at least one occasion Grainger played a work by John Powell (see John Bird, *Percy Grainger*, rev. 3rd ed. (Oxford University Press, 1999), p. 253), and Powell mentions in passing Grainger's folk-music compositions in the essay cited below, but it is unclear whether the two knew each other. Grainger was on very friendly terms, however, with Daniel Gregory Mason whose music Grainger championed: see in particular Grainger's letter to Mason in Malcolm Gillies and David Pear (eds.), *The All-Round Man: Selected Letters of Percy Grainger, 1914–1961* (Oxford University Press, 1994), pp. 204–8.

[25] For useful introductions to this phase of activity see D. K. Wilgus, *Anglo-American Folksong Scholarship Since 1898* (New Brunswick, NJ: Rutgers University Press, 1959), chapter 3; and, from a rather different perspective, Benjamin Filene, *Romancing the Folk: Public Memory & American Roots Music* (Chapel Hill: University of North Carolina Press, 2000), chapter 1.

to trace the links back to England, even drawing a romantic line of descent from the mead-halls of Beowulf to the cattle trails of Montana.[26] Such connections were given a further boost by the development of links with English folk-music scholars, most notably through Cecil Sharp's extended collecting visits to the Southern Appalachians during the First World War, and the establishment around the same time of American branches of the English Folk Dance Society.[27]

Sharp and others were clear that there was a positive racial agenda to their work: in preserving and fostering folk-music traditions, especially where social change and musical fashion threatened their extinction, Sharp believed that he and his co-workers were making sure that Anglo-Saxon Americans 'may as quickly as possible enter into their racial inheritance';[28] they and many others believed that in this mountain culture they were tapping into one of the few surviving pure springs of Anglo-Saxon racial stock anywhere in the world. Powell went a great deal further, in a more aggressive manner typical of the post-war period. He led another life beyond his musical career, one that has disappeared from view even more thoroughly than his musical activities. A well-connected native of Virginia, he combined music with racist political activism; in the 1920s he was a prime mover behind the formation of the Anglo-Saxon Clubs of America, and, more dramatically, lobbied successfully for a harsh tightening of his state's laws against inter-racial marriage, including a sharp reduction in the amount of African-American or Native-American blood required to categorise a person as non-white. Though the 1920s were the zenith of his engagement in this area, he continued to agitate on such issues throughout his life.[29] He set out his credo on race and music in an extended lecture entitled 'Music and the Nation', first given under the auspices of the Rice Institute (now Rice University) in Houston in April 1923, and subsequently repeated in many places around the country; he also published it in several different forms. (I shall refer here to the version published by the Rice Institute.[30]) Having first warned against unchecked immigration and miscegenation, which threaten the 'annihilation of white civilization' throughout the world, he argues here that 'Anglo-Saxon' folk song, as he calls

---

[26] *Cowboy Songs and Other Frontier Ballads* (New York: Macmillan, 1910), p. xxi.
[27] On Sharp's American collecting see Maud Karpeles, *Cecil Sharp: His Life and Work* (University of Chicago Press, 1967), chapters 11–13. Sharp established North American branches of the English Folk Dance Society in 1915.
[28] Olive Dame Campbell and Cecil J. Sharp, *English Folk Songs From the Southern Appalachians* (New York: Putnam and Sons, 1917), p. xx.
[29] Though explicitly critical of his ideas on music and race, none of the references to Powell in the standard literature cited in n. 22, or his entry in the *New Grove*, mentions his political activities, suggesting a lack of awareness of this aspect of his life; his racial activism is chronicled in detail, however, in Ward, *Life and Works of John Powell*, chapter 3.
[30] 'Music and the Nation', *The Rice Institute Pamphlet* 10/3 (1923), 127–63. An abbreviated version appeared several years later in the major journal *The Etude*: 'How America can Develop a National Music', *The Etude* 42 (May 1927), 349–50.

Anglo-American folk song, is the only viable basis for a true American music.[31] It not only provides a link to the Anglo-Saxon ideals that underpin the republic; it is also superior, he claims, to the folk music of other racial groups because it offers a subtly graduated range of emotions rather than polar extremes:

> [I]n general, folk-song has its serious limitations. Its phases of expression are usually confined to the more fundamental and primitive aspects of life experience; the most usual types are the grimly tragic and the unrestrainedly gay, with scanty intermediate gradations. Not so, however, with the Anglo-Saxon folk-song. Here the whole gamut of life is aptly and beautifully expressed ... Here, at last, we have a basic idiom thoroughly competent to express our national psychology.[32]

After this lofty and passionate claim for Anglo-Saxon folk song Powell continues with the even more radical, and highly topical, proposal that folk song could be used to help assimilate new immigrants: 'It would open the secrets of our psychology and emotional reactions, our traditions and our behavior, to those musically sensitive foreigners as could nothing else.'[33] Like Mason, he also finds Anglo-Saxon inspiration in contemporary British music, Vaughan Williams in particular. Powell is unswerving in his adherence to the general principle, embraced by Vaughan Williams and of course many other contemporaries, and deriving ultimately from Herder, that folk song must form the foundation, however far buried, of any national school of art music.

Not surprisingly, although Powell makes thinly veiled references to Jewish influences,[34] for him the greatest musical menace to America was the rising popularity of black musics, and especially their cross-breeding with white music.[35] Thus between them, Powell and Mason offer Anglo-Saxon responses to the two primary phobias of the old-stock musical elite. Obviously issues surrounding black music were bound to be more sharply polarised in the South than elsewhere in the US, but it would be wrong to marginalise Powell as a local peculiarity. He certainly achieved national recognition for many of his activities. He was a popular performer and lecturer all around the country, not just in the South, and high up in the Federation of Musical Clubs of America. In the early 1930s he was a key

---

[31] 'Music and the Nation', 135.
[32] Ibid., 160–1. We might compare here Mason's remarks on Jewish emotional extremism; both authors, of course, were invoking well-established tropes of the Anglo-Saxon character as being characterized by emotional moderation, in contrast to the perceived volatility of Latins, Slavs, Jews, and most other racial groups.
[33] Ibid., 163.
[34] He refers, for instance, to the taste for Tin Pan Alley song as 'artificially manufactured by the lowest and vulgarest type of foreign musical parasite' (p. 150), an anti-Semitic jibe which would have required no translation for an audience of the day.
[35] Powell believed black music had its own primitive appeal in the right context (as in his own *Rhapsodie Negre*, which is in any case tragic in tone), but that it should not cross-pollinate with the music of other races.

figure in founding the celebrated White Top folk festival, which rapidly achieved national fame – enough to receive a visit from Eleanor Roosevelt in 1933, who also provided introductory remarks to a series of programmes on folk music that Powell made for the National Broadcasting System in 1934[36] – and later in the decade he served on the National Advisory Committee of the Federal Music Project. He also had some success as a composer, producing a sizeable corpus of works based on Anglo-American folk song. He received invitations to talk about his ideas on music and race outside the South, such as on the West Coast and in the Midwest (and one should perhaps note here that the Ku Klux Klan was as strong, if not stronger, in Indiana and Ohio during this period as in the South). Powell's role in direct political activism must have been known to a good number of people outside Virginia; he certainly made no attempt to keep it a secret. Of course to accept Powell as a performer, or even invite him as lecturer, was not necessarily to endorse his views (his friend Mason for one thought his ideas on miscegenation a 'pet fanaticism'[37]). Yet there is good reason to believe that many of his ideas would have met with much tacit sympathy at least across the country, and they were anyway echoed by numerous other writers of the period.[38]

By the mid-1930s the Anglo-Saxonist rhetoric had been swept up by broader and often contradictory discourses, not least that surrounding the more heterogeneous and genuinely populist folk movements of the period. But swept up, not swept away. Indeed, in certain respects Mason's and Powell's views became more widespread, even if diffused into a less racially explicit rhetoric. The economic collapse of 1929 centred on the speculative financial markets of New York brought in its wake a widespread disillusionment with cosmopolitan, urban modern America, and an idealisation of rural life and of the past, situating America's national soul in a social and temporal matrix that was predominantly Anglo-Saxon, or at the very least Nordic.[39] The related celebration of America's democratic roots in the colonial era could not help but emphasise the British cultural heritage, even if Britain had at that time been the oppressor of freedom; and the onset of the Second World War, and the eventual Anglo-American alliance

---

[36] 'White Top' was the name of the mountain site of the festival, a rather extraordinary coincidence given the racial ideology underlying the event. Blacks and black music were almost entirely excluded, and despite its national prominence, the festival was deemed patronising and reactionary by Charles Seeger and other left-leaning folklorists (see, for instance, Whisnant, *All That is Native and Fine*, pp. 205–7) – though Seeger thought Powell's compositions based on Anglo-American folk song the most successful of their kind (see Zuck, *History of Musical Americanism*, p. 149).

[37] Ward, *Life and Works of John Powell*, p. 76.

[38] As has been widely discussed in the literature on American music, jazz was the source of the most intense concern, even panic, over race and music during this period; for numerous examples see Moore, *Yankee Blues*, pp. 82–92.

[39] For a synoptic view of this trend in a variety of different cultural arenas see Charles C. Alexander, *Here the Country Lies: Nationalism and the Arts in Twentieth-Century America* (Bloomington, IN: Indiana University Press, 1980), chapters 5 and 6.

cemented these sympathies into an unprecedented bond. Musically such interests fuelled the rediscovery of the colonial musical heritage, and the wider Anglo-American folk-song revival, and in the art music of the later 1930s and 1940s these sources largely displaced jazz and other popular styles, albeit temporarily, as the primary markers of Americanism in the concert hall.[40] The leading icon of musical Americanism during the 1930s was the Western farm-boy Roy Harris, and his reception contained a strong pro-Anglo-Saxon subtext (sometimes main text), and an implicit challenge to other races' ability to represent America.[41] Yet ironically, within a few years it would be Copland, a Brooklyn Jew, who would set the seal on a musical style that truly came to epitomise a musical American identity reflecting the heroic and democratic ideals of the era – but that is another story.

---

[40] See Zuck, *History of Musical Americanism*, pp. 146–53.
[41] See Moore, *Yankee Blues*, pp. 160–8, and Levy, *Frontier Figures*, chapter 2. Harris's pre-eminence as the leading icon of American music before the rise of Copland is often overlooked now.

CHAPTER 17

Rethinking the revue nègre: *black musical theatre in inter-war Paris*

Andy Fry

'KEEPIN' IT REAL': *BAMBOOZLED* IN PARIS

In Paris to conduct research on black musical theatre, I had an uncanny experience. As I thumbed through entertainment listings in the latest *Pariscope*, two men in blackface stared out at me (Fig. 17.1). They were presenting *The Very Black Show*, as Spike Lee's recent film *Bamboozled* was known in France. This polemic on the representation of African Americans portrays a black TV writer instructed to dig into his (supposed) roots for the glimmer of a hit show. Exasperated, he delivers exactly what seems to be expected of him: *The New Millennium Minstrel Show*, complete with chickens and watermelons, blackface and comic attire. Suddenly, it seemed, my subject had become *à la mode*.

Critics disagreed. While the response to *Bamboozled* in France was mixed, reviewers found its relevance to them limited if not lacking: they distanced the minstrel mask both geographically (a US phenomenon, ignoring the extent it had travelled) and historically (a nineteenth-century theatrical tradition, forgetting *Bamboozled*'s setting in contemporary TV). Race, critics seemed to argue, was an American problem; and at that, one of the past.

More egalitarian online discussion lists offered contrasting views – ones in which French attitudes were implicated. One writer thought *Bamboozled* the 'best film for all self-respecting blacks to see'; a 'lucid critique of the current position of blacks in the Western media', which was especially relevant 'in France ... where minorities must still caricature themselves to appear on TV'.[1] The fate of the movie with Parisian audiences, then, came as little surprise: released in a handful of mainstream houses, it was soon showing in only one, Images d'Ailleurs, 'premier espace cinéma *black* de Paris' – the cinematic equivalent of a ghetto.

My interest in *Bamboozled* is more than anecdotal. The film asks questions that resonate with my research. How is 'black culture' defined and who may access it? When does 'authenticity' become stereotype? Can people of African descent shape their representation on stage and screen? Or is their role always a figment of the white imagination? If the contemporary French

---

[1] 'The Very Black Show (Bamboozled)', *Allocine* online discussion forum, www.allocine.fr/film/fichefilm_gen_cfilm=27060.html (first consulted 1 May 2001).

Figure 17.1: 'Mantan' and 'Sleep'n' Eat' in Spike Lee's *Bamboozled* © MM, New Line Productions, Inc. All rights reserved. Photo by David Lee. Photo appears courtesy of New Line Productions.

media too is implicated, I wanted to recover a forgotten historical pedigree: African-American shows in Paris between the wars.

One moment at least should have been recalled: *La Revue nègre*, Josephine Baker's first Paris show, in 1925. Assembled in New York by white American Caroline Dudley, an all-black troupe famously performed putative scenes of African-American life – Mississippi Steam Boat Race, New York Skyscraper, Charleston Cabaret, etc. – on the stage of the Théâtre des Champs-Elysées. Most shocking was Baker and Joe Alex's 'Danse de sauvage', barely clad, in feathers – the definitive jungle scene. Certain descriptions – André Levinson's 'black Venus that haunted Baudelaire', Janet Flanner's 'unforgettable female ebony statue', even Robert de Flers' 'lamentable transatlantic exhibitionism which has us reverting to the ape' – are regularly cited to signify an almost apocalyptic moment.[2] No account of *les années folles* is complete without it.

La Revue nègre has thus come to represent both the apex of African-American entertainment in Paris and, paradoxically, the crux of a reaction against it. Karen Dalton and Henry Louis Gates, for example, consider the show a last flowering of racial tolerance: an expression, in their words, of 'the communal sigh of relief African Americans exhaled' in this 'color-blind land of tolerance' where 'they could savor the freedom of feeling like a human being for the very first time'. But then they invoke the so-called 'Call to Order' in French culture and society – and *Mein Kampf*! – to insist: 'This climate of openness would not last.'[3] Here both chronology and geography are distorted in order to locate an incipient conservatism, if not fascism. Other authors find support for this argument in contemporary statements now dismissing jazz by composers such as Darius Milhaud. In effect, they construct an end to cosmopolitan post-war ebullience and an anticipation of the cultural politics of Vichy.

But was *La Revue nègre* so unique? Less often cited, the most experienced music-hall critics, such as Gustave Fréjaville, were more measured in their praise: 'It's a small event, in the history of Parisian music hall ... To tell the truth, we had already seen just about all this in detail, either in variety acts, or in revues.'[4] He could trace a tradition of African-American music and dance in Paris right back to cakewalkers at the beginning of the century. Aside from jazz musicians (generally interval entertainment), recent examples multiplied: two of Baker's co-stars, Louis Douglas and Joe Alex, were already familiar; the year before, a whole troupe of 'Coloured Girls' had appeared at the Moulin Rouge.

---

[2] André Levinson, 'Paris ou New-York?: Douglas; La Vénus noire', *Comoedia*, 12 October 1925; Janet Flanner, *Paris Was Yesterday: 1925–1939* (New York: Viking, 1972), p. xx; Robert de Flers, 'La Semaine dramatique', *Le Figaro*, 16 December 1925.

[3] *Josephine Baker and* La Revue nègre: *Paul Colin's Lithographs of* Le Tumulte noir *in Paris, 1927*, with an Introduction by Henry Louis Gates, Jr and Karen C. C. Dalton (New York: Harry N. Abrams, 1998), pp. 4, 12.

[4] Gustave Fréjaville, 'Chronique de la semaine', *Comoedia*, 8 October 1925, in Paris, Bibliothèque Nationale, Département des Arts du Spectacle, Collection Rondel (henceforth, Rondel), Ro 16443(3).

Neither did they disappear soon thereafter. Even limiting the field to the larger black troupes – to *revues nègres* – African-American performers were a recurrent feature of Parisian music hall throughout the *entre-deux-guerres*, the Call to Order notwithstanding. Far from falling out of fashion, subsequent shows may have infiltrated French *popular* culture more deeply than the original. Sketching their history opens an illuminating window on race and representation in Paris, specifically a process of cultural negotiation between African Americans and the French.

WHITE-PRODUCED SHOWS: THE *BLACKBIRDS*

Two troupes of 'Blackbirds' are central to the story. Their manager-director was a white American, influential on black revues both at home and abroad: Lew Leslie, whose nickname 'Papa Plantation' gives a fair idea of his shows. The first, *Blackbirds of 1926*, was presented at the new 'théâtre-restaurant' Ambassadeurs (moving later to the Théâtre des Champs-Elysées). It was spare on skits but strong on song-and-dance acts, often with a comic element. Favourites were the opening plantation number, 'Down South', in which a homecoming Florence Mills (star of the show) burst out of a huge cake on her Mammy's birthday; a jungle dance for Mills and her 'Zulues'; and Johnny Hudgins' 'In Silence' in which, in blackface and white gloves, he mimed a song whose notes were supplied by the band (Fig. 17.2).

A few critics, particularly those in the right-wing press, took up the mantle of Robert de Flers to attack the whole enterprise. But this much was significant: *Blackbirds of 1926* was berated more as a sign of American modernity than as a descent into primitive barbarity; if *La Revue nègre* had still seemed to retain a whiff of the jungle, there was no doubting that this was New York chic. Even in the US (as *Dixie to Broadway*, in 1924), opinion had been divided as to how black – or rather 'black' – the Blackbirds were. Where one critic bemoaned a lack of 'the fundamental jokes of blackface comedy, and . . . but fleeting references to razors, craps and chicken stealing', another noted 'a passionate fidelity to the eternal verities of tempo not in the inheritance of Nordics'.[5] This conversation continued in Paris, where *La Revue nègre* was the primary reference point. Critics disagreed on their favourite show but not on the terms of the discussion: *La Revue nègre* had been 'wild and impromptu', 'barbaric and hot', 'so raw and of such a discordant savagery';[6]

---

[5] Percy Hammond, 'The Talented Colored Folks Make a Lively Show of "From Dixie to Broadway"', *Tribune*, New York, 30 October 1924; Heywoud Broun, 'The New Play: At the Broadhurst: "Dixie to Broadway"', *World*, New York, 30 October 1924, both in New York Public Library, Billy Rose Theatre Collection, 'Dixie to Broadway' file.

[6] Pierre Lazareff, 'Aux Ambassadeurs: Lew Leslie présente "Black Birds 1926"', *Le Soir*, 30 May 1926; Les Sept Dames du 3e rang [pseud.], 'Aux Ambassadeurs: Black-Birds 1926', *Minerva*, 13 June 1926; Gustave Fréjaville, 'Aux Ambassadeurs: "Black Birds 1926"', all in Rondel Ro 18740.

Figure 17.2: Newspaper cartoon of Florence Mills and Johnny Hudgins in *Blackbirds of 1926*[7]

Blackbirds was 'tempered', 'most civil and most civilised' – perhaps 'too civilised' – 'less fantastic [and] less eccentric'.[8]

The comparison extended, too, to the female stars: in the Blackbirds' Florence Mills, Josephine Baker (now 'exotic' idol of the Folies Bergère) faced her first serious competition. But while it was not unknown for Mills to don a wig and grass-skirt for a jungle number, her real appeal lay elsewhere. It was less her looks that attracted Europeans – 'a monkey-like profile', one critic put it; another called her a 'little bulldog' – as the dignity and force of personality she projected on stage.[9] There was a tragic side to Mills' comedy, one that her sudden death a year later, aged thirty-two, has done nothing to dispel. Even Mills' signature song, 'I'm a Little Blackbird Looking for a Blue Bird' was scarcely an obvious hit: she wanted not only for love but for a freedom denied her as a person of colour. In Paris, the song provided an opportunity for the French to boast of their racial tolerance compared to cruel Americans – a claim that millions in the French colonies would not readily have understood.

---

[7] In Gustave Fréjaville, 'Aux Ambassadeurs: "Black Birds 1926"', *Comoedia*, 30 May 1926, in Rondel Ro 18740.

[8] Les Sept Dames, 'Aux Ambassadeurs'; René Bizet, 'Ambassadeurs', *L'Intransigeant*, 31 May 1926; Fréjaville, 'Aux Ambassadeurs' (also Bizet, 'La Revue Black Birds'); Legrand-Chabrier, 'Sous les projecteurs: Cirques – music-hall', unidentified clipping, 6 June 1926, all in Rondel Ro 18740.

[9] Pierre Brisson, 'Chronique théatrale: Une Soirée aux Ambassadeurs', *Le Temps*, 31 May 1926, in Rondel Ro 18740; Paul Achard, 'Music-Hall: The Commanders Band, Black Birds', *Paris-Midi*, 21 July 1926, in Rondel Ro 15702(5).

One critic thought Mills a 'chaste and modest' 'black fairy' compared to the 'demon' Baker; with her 'deliberate sense of decency' (*volontaire décence*), he said, 'she could dance at the Vatican'.[10] Another put it more bluntly: 'In Josephine Baker, there is Africa. In Florence Mills, there is only America.'[11] Emigré Russian intellectual and dance critic André Levinson concurred that Mills' performance was a 'sweetened travesty' of Baker's 'carnal magnificence': 'It is no longer the tigress who stands before us but the marquise, who has rubbed a little burnt cork on her cheeks, instead of her customary rouge, before dancing a Court Charleston "ad usum Delphini".'[12] One might suppose that Levinson, a conservative (if eclectic) critic well known for his staunch opposition to the Russian Ballet's divergence from classical tradition, would have been delighted by black dancers' 'progress'; but he was more ambivalent. For him, the acculturation of black styles, as well as their adoption by white society, signalled a loss of purity, albeit of a pure savagery: cultural contact, Levinson seemed to fear, threatens traditions with extinction – and this was as true of the 'primitive' meeting 'civilisation' as it was of his precious classicism under attack from barbarian hordes.

For the first time, claims for *Blackbirds of 1929*'s authenticity were, in a limited sense, correct: the show was presented more or less as on Broadway where, the year before, it had been the most successful black show of all time (running for an extraordinary 518 performances, as *Blackbirds of 1928*).[13] It featured a rapid-fire alternation of singing and dancing around some familiar themes – a prologue 'Way Down South', a 'Scene in Jungle Land' – along with the occasional skit of no greater originality: a poker game, a boxing match, a spooky graveyard sketch (Fig. 17.3).

One scene above all fascinated the French critics: a gloss on DuBose Heyward's play *Porgy* (some years before Gershwin's *Porgy and Bess* of 1935). As far as it can be reconstructed, there were two main numbers: one a song for Bess, which I shall come to in a moment; the other a wake scene for Robbins (killed by Crown) turning into a celebration. Accompanying this in the programme (and slavishly reiterated in the press) was a quasi-ethnographic 'explanation' whose origins are obscure: seeking cash for a proper burial, the mourners 'create, by their songs, a sort of hysteria that pushes the men to steal and the women to sell themselves to whites'.[14]

An imperfect idea of the music can be gained from a recording made several years later in which Ethel Waters replaces Geneva Washington in the

---

[10] Pierre Varenne, 'Aux Ambassadeurs: Black Birds 1926', *Paris-Soir*, 1 June 1926, in Rondel Ro 18740.
[11] Legrand-Chabrier, 'Sous les projecteurs'.
[12] I.e. 'purified'. André Levinson, 'The Negro Dance: Under European Eyes', *Theatre Arts Monthly*, April 1927, repr. in Joan Acocella and Lynn Garafola, eds., *André Levinson on Dance: Writings from Paris in the Twenties* (Hanover, NH: Wesleyan University Press, 1991), pp. 74–5.
[13] Allen Woll, *Black Musical Theatre: From Coontown to Dreamgirls*, repr. (New York: Da Capo, 1991), p. 125.
[14] Programme located in Rondel Ro 15743.

Figure 17.3: Paul Colin's poster for *Blackbirds of 1929*

role of the mourning Serena but the Cecil Mack Choir is retained.[15] Into the brief duration of a '78' are squeezed three contrasting sections: a doleful call and response between leader and choir as the people of Catfish Row raise money for Crown's burial ('Sing, brother sing'); an up-tempo section in which the mortician demands swift action, the choir again responding in harmony ('What dat you say?'); and a variant on the St Louis Blues featuring Serena singing in impassioned counterpoint with her community ('Oh, Lordy, Lordy'), first lamenting Crown's death then gaining strength to go 'on her way'. The religio-sexual intoxication invoked by this scenario, as well as the huddled mourners on stage and the repetitive interlocutions of the music, acted very powerfully on the French imagination. According to one

[15] Cecil Mack Choir with Ethel Waters, 'St Louis Blues', 23 December 1932 [B12790–A, Brunswick 6521], reissued on *Lew Leslie's Blackbirds of 1928* LP [Columbia, Mono OL6770 (1968)].

critic, it was 'certainly the most beautiful thing that *art nègre* has yet sent us'; another had 'never seen anything more moving in the world'.[16]

Most extreme in his reaction was the 'surrealist-ethnographer' Michel Leiris, in the renegade journal *Documents*. Leiris took the show as a model for escaping the conventions that held the arts – and society – in an ever more suffocating grasp, a view widely shared among his iconoclastic circle. The break of *Document*'s editor Georges Bataille with the Surrealist movement's leader, André Breton, had turned on politics as well perhaps as on a definition of their project: Bataille, it is said, desired not a *sur*-realism (above or beyond reality) but a *sous*-realism (under or beneath it), to borrow Petrine Archer-Straw's apt term.[17] Instead of a free life of the mind, Bataille and company were concerned with the very real business of the body and its urges – sex, defecation, violence – which he summed up as *la bassesse* (baseness): a position that put them at odds with Breton's comparatively conservative notions and with his more orthodox communism.

For Leiris, even 'civilised' life offered flickers of existential clarity incited by moments of such rawness (often sexual) that they broke through to the savage inside: 'civilisation', he suggested, 'can be compared to the thin layer … that forms on the surface of calm waters … until an eddy comes along and unsettles everything'.[18] He found one such moment in his unexpected encounter, on a Montmartre street, with one of Blackbirds' troupe, wet roses in her hand – a sexual metaphor none too difficult to fathom.[19] Another, less complete, he found in 'Porgy', whose scenario was of a 'hysteria so intense that it should be capable of pushing the audience to the immediate realisation of sordid acts and extravagant debaucheries', but whose effect was partly lost on an audience who could not completely vanquish their 'spinelessness' (*veulerie*).[20]

As his diary shows, Leiris' attraction to African Americans, as later to Africans, was often of a frankly sexual nature; and his writings repeat in inversion tropes of primitive physicality and spirituality opposing western cerebralism – a more or less unhelpful form of 'positive racism', as he later came to realise.[21] As we have seen, then, French views can surprise us today: the most flagrant stereotypes may contain a nub of good

---

[16] Hanry-Jaunet, 'La Revue des Lew Leslie's Blackbirds', *La Presse*, 13 June 1929; Pierre Varenne, 'Au Moulin Rouge', *L'Oeuvre*, both in Rondel Ro 585, doc. 74b.
[17] Petrine Archer-Straw, *Negrophilia: Avant-Garde Paris and Black Culture in the 1920s* (London: Thames and Hudson, 2000), p. 143.
[18] Michel Leiris, 'Civilisation', *Documents: Archéologie, beaux-arts, ethnographie, variétés* 1/4 (July 1929), 221.
[19] Michel Leiris, 'Alberto Giacometti', *Documents* 1/4 (July 1929), 209.
[20] Leiris, 'Civilisation', 222.
[21] Michel Leiris, *Journal, 1922–1989*, ed. Jean Jamin (Paris: Gallimard, 1989), 196–7. For Leiris's mature reflections on his youthful obsessions, see 'Michel Leiris: "L'Autre qui apparaît chez vous"', *Jazz Magazine*, no. 325 (January 1984; special 'Jazz en France' issue, ed. Michael Haggerty), 36.

266   *Local contexts*

intention (albeit a naive one); but superficial resonance with familiar notions of cultural difference may, on the contrary, imply a belief in racial separatism.

COLONIAL DESIRE AND HYBRIDITY: THE FEMALE STARS

No longer content with one female star, *Blackbirds of 1929* had two: Aida Ward and Adelaide Hall. Very different artistes, their repertoire was carefully tailored to their stage personalities. Ward's understated distinction and delicate voice added to the charm of sentimental airs such as 'Porgy' (a love song for Bess from the scene already discussed). While Heyward's Bess was no angel, to be sure, there is scant sign of worldliness in Jimmy McHugh's song: Bess redeems herself through love for the crippled Porgy, her new respectability and contentment finding expression in music that is syllabic and lacks any hint of syncopation; whose typically stepwise movement and simple sequences form regular arch-like phrases (Ex. 17.1). Adelaide Hall, on the other hand, demanded satisfaction in the lusty 'I Must Have That Man'; and she revealed more than her soul in up-tempo song-and-dance numbers such as the jungle scene's 'Diga Diga Doo' (Ex. 17.2).

A 1932 Duke Ellington recording of the latter number gives an idea of the effect: a mysterious, vocalised 'clarinet' sails over a repeated bass figure

Example 17.1: 'Porgy' from *Blackbirds of 1928/9* (music, Jimmy McHugh; lyrics, Dorothy Fields), sung by Aida Ward, first eight bars of chorus

Example 17.2: 'Diga Diga Doo' from *Blackbirds of 1928/9* (music, Jimmy McHugh; lyrics, Dorothy Fields), sung by Adelaide Hall, first sixteen bars of chorus

answered by pleas from a muted trumpet in the brief introduction; the piano enters driving forward into a first statement, on the trumpet, complete with the glissandi and growls characteristic of the 'jungle' genre; colourful lyrics leave little to the imagination – 'I love you and you love me, and when you love it is natural to, Diga diga doo diga doo doo, Diga diga doo, diga doo'; rhythm section and singers jostle the beat impatiently, adding to the

Figure 17.4: Newspaper cartoon of *Blackbirds of 1929*[22]

music's edginess.[23] And all this before we recall the dancing of a troupe of semi-naked women performing wild, 'African' steps (Fig. 17.4). They were 'the most attractive tribe of little savages' one critic could imagine; another compared them to 'young wildcats in the bush'.[24]

The contrast between the two stars – which re-embodied on one stage, many noted, that between Mills and Baker – was baffling to the French critics. Where Ward had become 'perfectly civilised', Hall remained 'completely primitive'[25] (Fig. 17.5). In response to this difficulty, a formulation touched on before was developed at some length: that African Americans might represent neither a pure native culture nor a modern American one, but a mix of the two – a hybrid in other words. If theirs was a mixed race, the logic went, this could explain their lack of uniformity, in character as much as in skin tone. Much ink was spilled on the 'artificiality' of the race.

Replacing essentialised blackness with hybridity in this way, French writers begin to chime superficially with some of today's criticism. Before leaping to the assumption that their views were becoming more 'progressive', however, we need to rehearse a theoretical debate. While the term 'hybridity' is, of course, key to postcolonial writing, one of that discipline's foremost recent scholars, Robert Young, urges caution. By invoking it, he argues, critics risk aligning themselves with dubious historical precedents. In the past, hybridity tended to suppose that races were distinct species ('polygenism'). It thus often represented a more reactionary position than either 'monogenetic' view: the religious doctrine of races

---

[22] *Le Quotidien*, 16 June 1929, in Rondel Ro 585, doc. 74b.
[23] Mills Brothers with Duke Ellington and his Famous Orchestra, 22 December 1932 [B12781–A, Brunswick 6519], reissued on *Lew Leslie's Blackbirds of 1928* LP.
[24] Edouard Beaudu, 'Moulin-Rouge: La Revue des Lew Leslie's *Black Birds*', *Le Petit Journal*, 15 June 1929; 'D'où viennent les "Oiseaux noirs"', *L'Intransigeant*, 30 June 1929, both in Rondel Ro 585, doc. 74b.
[25] P. Loiselet, 'Les Black Birds au Moulin-Rouge', *Le Soir*, 12 June 1929, in Rondel Ro 585, doc. 74b.

LES BLACK-BIRDS AU MOULIN-ROUGE

Aïda WARD   Adelaïde HALL   Earl FUCKER

Figure 17.5: Newspaper cartoon of three stars of *Blackbirds of 1929*[26]

with a single origin that split; or the evolutionist argument that races mark points along a scale of civilisation. Hybrids, like mules, were infertile, it was argued, and thus would soon die out. If, as was often self-evident, they were able to procreate, then a process of degeneration would follow, commonly understood in cultural as well as biological terms. Theorisations of hybridity were also, Young maintains, marked by 'colonial desire': an obsessive rehearsing of the consequences of the guilty appetite for – and, often forced, union with – the other that was a feature of colonial movements the world over. They are thus ambivalent: 'contradictory, disruptive and already deconstructed' in his words.[27]

Even Count Gobineau's four-volume *Essai sur l'inégalité des races humaines* of 1853–5, which remained central to racial thinking as late as the Third Reich, can be considered a theory of hybridity. Civilisations (of which, he argued, there were few) were built by whites intermixing with other races; all great cultures were hybrid. But – here's the catch – located in their vitalising mix was an instability that would eventually lead to degeneration. The life and death of a society were bound up in its hybrid race. As has been common, Gobineau was misunderstood by Maurice Muret in his 1925 *Le Crépuscule des nations blanches* as a complete injunction on interbreeding. Instead, Muret restated another widespread theory most influentially made

---

[26] Unidentified clipping, in Rondel Ro 585, doc. 74b. Earl Tucker's hip-gyrating 'snaky' dancing, recognised as an antecedent of Elvis Presley's, is perhaps captured a little too well in the misspelling of his name.

[27] Robert J. C. Young, *Colonial Desire: Hybridity in Theory, Culture and Race* (London: Routledge, 1995), p. 27.

in the French context by Pierre Paul Broca in 1860: mixing between proximate races was beneficial; that between distant ones dangerous.[28]

This view increasingly found support among the French Eugenics Society. According to William Schneider, greater immigration in the 1920s encouraged a move from the 'positive eugenics' that had sought to promote the growth of a healthy population before the war toward a 'negative eugenics' based in part on racial selection. Georges Vacher de Lapouge, who in 1909 had controversially urged his countrymen to replace 'Liberty, Equality, Fraternity' with 'Determinism, Inequality, Selection', came back into fashion; in 1926, he arranged and wrote the preface for a French translation of the American eugenicist Madison Grant's *The Passing of the Great Race* (1916). René Martial adopted the biochemical indexes that had relocated race from anatomy to biology to propose a model of immigration based on tree grafting: the closer the match, the more chance the cutting would take (or the immigrant assimilate); flanking the French on the index were, conveniently enough, other non-threatening Western Europeans.[29]

Where race mixing was of most pressing concern, of course, was not in the metropolis but in overseas territories. French colonial ideology is as multifarious as the theorists and ministers who decided policies and, no less important, the governors who implemented – or ignored – them on the ground; but, broadly speaking, France moved away from its original notion of assimilation (in any case, realised in only small part) toward a looser, so-called 'association' of colonies that was theorised in the late nineteenth century and put into practice in the early twentieth.[30] One lens through which this shift can be viewed is the treatment of mixed-race children born in the colonies to white men and colonial women. As Owen White has recently shown, in the nineteenth century relationships with natives were not only accepted but often encouraged as a tool of assimilation ('making French' in a peculiarly biological manner).[31] This policy suffered from its own success: people of mixed race were soon of sufficient number to form a distinct ethnic identity and begin to claim greater rights. The worst fear of opponents of race mixing seemed to have been realised: the creation of a group of dangerous *déclassé* hybrids who contested the regime's power. Colonial administrators were henceforth encouraged to bring their wives.

---

[28] Pierre Paul Broca, *Recherches sur l'hybridité animale en général et sur l'hybridité humaine en particulier considérées dans leurs rapports avec la question de la pluralité des espèces humaines* (Paris: J. Claye, 1860).

[29] William H. Schneider, *Quality and Quantity: The Quest for Biological Regeneration in Twentieth-Century France* (Cambridge University Press, 1990), chapters 8 and 9, pp. 208–55.

[30] Raymond F. Betts, *Assimilation and Association in French Colonial Theory, 1890–1914* (New York: Columbia University Press, 1961); Alice L. Conklin, *A Mission to Civilize: The Republican Idea of Empire in France and West Africa, 1895–1930* (Stanford University Press, 1997).

[31] Owen White, *Children of the French Empire: Miscegenation and Colonial Society in French West Africa, 1895–1960*, Oxford Historical Monographs (Oxford University Press, 1999).

It is no surprise that traces of the scientific, moral and political debates about hybridity – in which barely disguised desire intermingled with apprehension about its consequences – are found in reactions to *Blackbirds of 1929*. Pierre Brisson, for example, described the troupe in the following terms:

> None of these human products is really black, and you have the most complete range of mulattos ... quarteroons, Caribbean Negroes or mongrels ... the unexpected crossbreeds of a crossroads-city ... The lightened girls are more beautiful and tempting; the men, muscular and vigorous ... And there is all the same the old tam-tam of the grandparents, the old smell of a bloody feast that racks their loins into a frenzy.[32]

André Levinson took Brisson's basically positive (if hardly flattering) exercise in the exoticisation of a vital hybridity – and in desire – and tacitly transmogrified it into a more disturbing phenomenon he called '*métissage au théâtre*'. As if précising Brisson, he argued:

> It's *métissage*, whimsical crossing of races, capriciously proportioned and grafted mixing, violent distortion, contamination, transfusion of sap, which multiplies, exasperates – and drains, as with this lovely Florence Mills, dead, sickly flower, at twenty-four – the vitality of America's coloured man.

Any lingering notion of this tradition's purity had to be dispelled:

> Among these Afro-Americans, we are in the presence not of an indigenous tribe in a state of heavenly savagery, but of ... as motley a mix as possible ... the supreme and final explosion of an ethnic singularity decomposing.[33]

Levinson inverted Brisson's concept of a vigorous hybridity to make African-American culture – people – an aberration about to implode (both possibilities, of course, could be found in Gobineau). But even Levinson was not immune to 'colonial desire' and its attendant anxiety. In the same article, he argued: 'We are in the hold of this hybrid art, bastard, but all the more intense'; it was an 'aphrodisiac love potion', 'which burns us as it wastes away'. Thus it was that the Blackbirds found themselves caught up in a debate about the French 'race' and its culture. More familiar now, African Americans had come to represent not only a source of a vitalising (or terrifying) primitiveness but as an example of racial mixing – just the issue with which the French were grappling both at home and in the colonies.

A HOME-GROWN ALTERNATIVE?: *BLACK FLOWERS* (1930)

While I have focused on French reaction, two articles on *Blackbirds of 1929* in the Baltimore *Afro-American* provide a rare opportunity to engage with conflicting opinion among the community itself. The activities of

---

[32] Pierre Brisson, 'Au music-hall', *Le Temps*, 17 June 1929, in Rondel Ro 585, doc. 74b.
[33] André Levinson, 'Le Métissage au théâtre', *Comoedia*, 21 July 1929, in Rondel Ro 9805(2); repr. in his *Les Visages de la danse* (Paris: Éditions Bernard Grasset, 1933), 270–1.

African-American artists at home and abroad were of great interest in the black press. Rarely, however, did writers diverge from a strict party line: the success of performers was celebrated as a sign of racial uplift; recognition in Europe, in particular, conferred legitimacy and suggested opportunities lacking in the States.

So much is clear in a report by the troupe's stage manager boasting that *Blackbirds* was 'the hit of Paris' and that Adelaide Hall was 'another Josephine Baker'.[34] On the same page, however, a member of the famous university choral group the Fisk Jubilee Singers, who were touring Europe at the time, gave an altogether different take: 'Watermelon eating on stage shocks American travelling abroad'; 'Razors, pistols, cops, dishonesty riles visitors'. Not altogether dismissive – he admires in particular the 'Porgy' scene and the men's dancing – this writer concludes that: 'All in all "Blackbirds" is probably doing more harm than good. It is giving to Paris the wrong idea of the typical American Negro.'[35] This response is characteristic, of course, of the sensibilities of the Harlem Renaissance – a period when the 'talented tenth' charged with uplifting the race were more commonly imagined as writers and composers than as tap dancers and jazz musicians. But it begs a question: how much scope did African-American performers have in this era to control their depiction on stage?

At once borrowing on the success of *Blackbirds of 1929* and, perhaps, proposing an alternative model came African-American director (and dancer) Louis Douglas's Black Flowers in their show *Liza* the following year. For the first time, one critic marvelled, this was 'a show entirely created and played by blacks without the slightest contribution from whites'.[36] Not that the issue of hybridity entirely disappeared. Pierre Brisson's position was ambivalent, located between evolutionism – 'their uncertain race is no longer black [but] it is not yet white'– and a process of intermixture that would have made some shudder: 'old blood renewed by animal sap'. Levinson was wrong, however, to suggest they were degenerate: 'Decadence is not among them, it is in us', Brisson maintained.[37] Another critic disagreed: the troupe had 'an imperfect structure and legs that are too fat or too spindly, as is the case among those of mixed blood'.[38] For most, however, the presence of Douglas as director indicated a cultural authenticity whatever the make-up of the race.

Several signs indicated that this was not an ordinary black show: *Liza*'s venue (the venerable Théâtre de la Porte Saint-Martin), billing (as '*Théâtre*

---

[34] 'S. H. Dudley Writes from Paris', *The Afro-American*, Baltimore, 24 August 1929.
[35] L. K. McMillan, 'McMillan in Paris Sees "Blackbirds"', *The Afro-American*, Baltimore, 24 August 1929.
[36] 'Avant-Première: À la Porte Saint-Martin: Le Spectacle nègre des Black Flower [*sic*]', *L'Oeuvre*, 31 May 1930, in Rondel Ro 585, doc. III.
[37] Pierre Brisson, *Le Temps*, 9 June 1930, in Rondel Ro 585, doc. III.
[38] A. de Montgon, 'Spectacle nègre à la Porte-Saint-Martin', *Le Petit Parisien*, 5 June 1930, in Rondel Ro 585, doc. III.

nègre') and compound genre ('*opérette-revue nègre à grand spectacle*'). Nor was it, although it drew liberally on their conventions. In effect, Douglas assembled stereotypically 'black' scenes – a boxing match, a crap game, a Negro cabaret – into a more or less coherent narrative: Liza (another dynamic female entertainer, Valaida Snow) forsakes her fiancé for a New York dandy; the two men fight and she returns to the cotton plantation. To be sure, this did not rewrite the book of black theatre, but its attempt to climb the ladder of genres was significant. What is more, it may have signified on stereotypes even as it reproduced them: the last two scenes juxtaposed two plantations, the first in a Harlem cabaret, the second down South, the one no more real than the other.

Liza broke other conventions, too. For one, the performers remained by and large conspicuously fully attired. Only in the cabaret scene was nudity tolerated, focusing fetishisation of the black body on this show-within-a-show. And while the two principal male characters might suggest rural and urban minstrel figures, Jim Crow and Zip Coon, Douglas played his character with such poignancy and melancholy that he brought to mind no demeaning stereotype but a *commedia dell'arte* character, '*un pierrot romantique*'.[39] While no music is available, the programme and press reviews suggest it leaned heavily on spiritual-type numbers featuring the Utica Jubilee Singers as well, of course, as fast-paced songs and dances led by Felix Winfeld and his Black Flowers Jazz. The variety was capable of representing, one critic thought, the different '*états d'âme*' of the American Negro: vitality matched with sadness.[40] In sum, *Liza* reveals an unexpected power for African Americans in this period to modify their representation on stage; but it also indicates, no less clearly, that they worked within an externally determined range of possibilities in order to ensure their success.

A TRADITION CONTINUED: THE 1930S

It would be wrong to suggest that black revues continued with such pace through the 1930s. The economic slowdown led by the Wall Street Crash made risky ventures such as European tours impossible. Even in France, where instability was slower to take effect, labour laws restricting the number of foreigners employed were increasingly cited (if rarely enforced) as French performers felt the pinch. To make matters worse, with the rise of cinema, many music halls were converted into movie theatres. All the same, the early 1930s saw the first visits of important jazz musicians (Louis Armstrong and Coleman Hawkins among them) and even bands (Cab Calloway's and Duke Ellington's, for example). What is more, black

---

[39] Hanry-Jaunet, 'À propos de: Spectacles nègres', *Le Soir*, 8 June 1930, in Rondel Ro 585, doc. III.
[40] Robert Le Bret, 'A la Porte Saint-Martin: Les "Black Flowers" dans une opérette nègre: "Liza"', *L'Ami du peuple du soir*, 5 June 1930, in Rondel Ro 585, doc. III.

entertainers continued to grace the French stage in the more modest variety shows, as they had done for at least a decade.

What comes as a surprise is a resurgence of black shows in the later 1930s: *Harlem Black Birds 36* at the Alcazar Theatre and *Le Cotton-Club* at the Moulin Rouge in 1937. The first, again produced and directed by Louis Douglas, bore a suspicious resemblance to *Liza*: a loose plot moved the performers between a mythical southern plantation and a no less mythical Harlem.[41] Critics agreed on a sense of *déjà vu* but typically enjoyed it. The second show was more completely successful.[42] Again black-directed, by Clarence Robinson, it featured Teddy Hill's Orchestra: one of 'the poorest bands to come out of Harlem in the Swing Era', in Gunther Schuller's opinion, but with the virtue, nevertheless, of a young trumpeter called John Birks ('Dizzy') Gillespie.[43] For some, the revue, which still included a jungle number among much high-paced dancing by the likes of Bill Bailey and the Berry Brothers, lacked somewhat in 'nostalgic laments' revealing the 'primitive soul'; but another, aware of society opinion, simply insisted: 'You must have seen these Negroes'.[44]

Most extraordinary, Hugues Panassié, France's foremost jazz critic in this period and tireless propagandist for 'jazz hot', reviewed the show in the extreme right-wing if not proto-fascist paper *Insurgé*: 'This current of fresh and vigorous blood', he said, 'ought to serve to drag Europeans away from the limp amusements in which they are more and more bogged down.'[45] An interesting compound, Panassié exploits the right's language of decadence but proposes a radical solution: not at all the recovery of national spirit through a revival of folklore that is associated with the closed nationalism of Vichy; rather a continued reference to outside cultures – African Americans of all people. His argument resonates most strongly of all with the surrealist-turning-anarchist Michel Leiris; hardly an obvious view to find, in late-1930s France, in a paper that vehemently opposed the Popular Front, demonised Russian Communism and maintained an ambivalent respect for German National Socialism. It was not just opportunism that found Panassié writing in such a venue: his own Catholic monarchism, which went as far as opposition to suffrage, was little less reactionary.

Panassié's comments explode several of the assumptions with which I have taken issue. African-American music theatre was not chased out of France in

---

[41] The programme is transcribed in Rainer E. Lotz, *Black People: Entertainers of African Descent in Europe, and Germany* (Bonn: Birgit Lotz, 1997), pp. 377–9.
[42] A programme is in Rondel, R. Supp. 655, 'Revues représentées en 1937'.
[43] Gunther Schuller, *The Swing Era: The Development of Jazz, 1930–1945* (Oxford University Press, 1989), p. 422.
[44] Pierre Varenne, 'Au Moulin Rouge: Le Cotton-Club', *L'Intransigeant*, 21 June 1937; 'Le Cotton-Club au Moulin-Rouge', *Le Temps*, 15 June 1937; and André Warnod, 'La Revue de Cotton-Club au Bal du Moulin-Rouge', *Le Figaro*, 17 June 1937, all in Paris, Bibliothèque Nationale, Département des Arts du Spectacle, 8° Sw 103(1), 'Cabarets: Bal du Moulin Rouge, 1937–1960'.
[45] Hugues Panassié, 'La Revue du Cotton-Club', *Insurgé: Politique et social* 1/23 (16 June 1937).

the mid-1920s, as the story of high culture's engagement with it has sometimes supposed. Interest did not even peak for another few years. Nor did cosmopolitanism cede to conservatism in discrete, successive moments, as the discourse of the Call to Order often seems to imply. A wider view – one interested in popular culture in and for itself – tells a different story: an ambivalent coexistence of liberal and reactionary tendencies (about race among other issues) throughout the inter-war period. In this we can, more even-handedly, locate the roots not just of Vichy ideology but of its discontents: the wartime hipsters called *zazous*, for example, among whom resistance may have been signified by the adoption of swing.

But French opinion on African Americans and their music was not – not yet at least – straightforwardly political: extremes of right and left sometimes met at the opposition they constructed between black and white musics, cultures and peoples. On all sides a pungent mix of half-absorbed racial theories (themselves equivocal) supported numerous partisan positions. To their enormous credit, performers from Florence Mills to Louis Douglas did not just perpetuate stereotypes, but used their strength and versatility to make a chink in the armour of race, racism and racialism. But if the challenges they embodied led hybridity to replace purity (i.e. savagery) as a paradigm, we must recognise that it too spanned the gamut from *re*generation to *de*generation.

As *Bamboozled* makes plain, this process of black negotiation with white expectation continues even today – a fact the mainstream media, in France as elsewhere, typically refuse to acknowledge. Although they date from long ago, these shows are closer to us than we are often prepared to admit. Recovering this forgotten history indicates yet again how deeply musical and theatrical representations have, for better and worse, engaged the racial imagination. It is not only naive but reckless to consider that they have ceased to do so.

Index

Numbers in bold refer to images

Adler, Guido, 11
A Star is Born (film), 45
Abrahamsen, David, 94
Adorno, Theodor W., 76
Africa: 50
   supposed cultural inferiority, 50
African-American Music: as label, 14
   as 'authentic' black culture, 26
   as constitutive of idea of race in American history, 29
   as modern construction of many racialist discourses, 29–30
   'black musics' as threat to American music, 255
   'jungle scene', 260–3, 266–8
   musicality as natural, 40
   relationship to modern African-American subjectivity, 30, 32
   relationship to modern identity, 47
   shows in Paris between the wars, 260–75
   See also: Revues nègres
African Americans: 'threat' as product of national construction, 41
   as 'artificial' race in French inter-war discourse, 268–71
Afro-modernism, 32, 36
Albania: new forms of racism, 8
Alex, Joe, 260
Alkan, Valentin, 127, 141
Ambros, August Wilhelm, 171
America, 115, 244
   American Nordicists, 115–24
   Anglo-American folk music, 253–5
   Midwest oral tradition, 4
   'new immigration' and race, 249
Anderson, Paul, 32–4
Anglo-Saxonism, 115, 245–57
   and 'special relationship', 245–50
   anti-Semitism in, 246
   as 'race', 248
   miscegenation and Powell's notion of Anglo-Saxon folk song, 254–5
Antiflamenquismo: *See Flamenco*
Anti-Semitism: *See Jews*
Appalachian Spring (Copland), 253
Aranzadi, Telesforo de, 217

Archer-Straw, Petrine, 265
Arendt, Hannah, 83, 104, 114
Ariadne auf Naxos (Strauss), 141, 173
Arias, Gino, 190
Armstrong, Louis, 32, 273
Arnold, Matthew, 252
Around Music (Sorabji), 125
Aryan race, 73, 109, 111, 147, 155–6, 181
   Bourgault-Ducoudray's concept of 'Aryan music', 155–6
Australia, 115
Austria and Austro-Hungarian Empire, 14
   musical repertories recording project, 14–15
Austro-Hungarian Imperial Academy of Science, 14–15

Bach, Johann Sebastian, 57, 59, 133, 134, 166, 219
Bailey, Bill, 274
Bainton, Edgar, 143
Baker, Josephine, 260, 268, 272, 279
   compared with Florence Mills, 262–3
Balakirev, Mily Alekseyevich, 105
Balbo, Italo, 190
Balibar, Etienne, 105
Ballets Russes, 232, 234, 263
Balmaseda, Manuel, 231
Bamboozled (film) 258, **259**, 275
Barenboim, Daniel: association with West-Eastern Divan Orchestra, 14
   performances of Wagner in Israel, 16
Baroja, Pio, 237, 238
Barthes, Roland, 66
Bartók, Béla, 6, 15, 58, 188
Barzizza, Pippo, 198
Bastian, Adolf, 56
Bataille, Georges, 265
Bayreuther Blätter, 51
Beethoven, Ludwig van, 51, 57, 60, 157, 173, 174, 179, 220
   import for Weininger's self-construction, 93–5
   Weininger's account of, 88
Bell, Alexander Graham, 119
Benigni, Umberto, 182
Benoit, Alexandre, 213
Berg, Alban, 79, 85

Bergery, Gaston, 211–12, 214
Berl, Heinrich, 169, 179–80
Berlin Sound Archive, 60
Berlioz, Hector, 133, 173
Bernstein, Michael André, 18
Bixio, Cesare Andrea, 198
Bizet, Georges, 136
Blackbirds: See Revues nègres
Blackface minstrelsy, 40–1, 44–5
   in inter-war Paris shows, 273
Blanc, Giuseppe, 192
Blavatsky, Madame, 139
Blei, Franz, 92, 93
Bloch, Ernst, 103–14
   'Man and Music', 104
Blume, Friedrich, 19, 181
Boccioni, Umberto, 186
Bodas de sangre (García Lorca), 224
Bohlman, Philip V., xiv, xix, 3–23, 143, 229
Bonaparte, Prince Roland, 151
Bordes, Charles, 167
Borghi, Giovanni Battista, 158
Börne, Ludwig, 51
Borodin, Alexander, 196
Bose, Fritz, 60
Boulez, Pierre, 76
Bourgault-Ducoudray, Louis: understanding of *chansons populaires*, 154–6, 157, 159, 160
Bovio, Livero, 192
Brachvogel, Albert E., 39
Brahms, Johannes, 38, 57, 173, 174
Brasillach, Robert, 210
Breton, André, 265
Brigham, Carl C., 121
Brisson, Pierre, 271, 272
Britain: 115, 244
   as mixed race in Grainger's view, 117
   British folk music in America, 253–5
   English Folk Dance Society, 254
   Imperial Britain as context for Sorabji's 'Oriental Orientalism', 142
   See also: Anglo-Saxonism
Broca, Pierre Paul, 270
Brown, Julie, xiv–xxii, 45, 84–101
Bruckner, Anton, 171, 173
Burrin, Philippe, 211
Burton, Richard, 130
Busoni, Ferruccio, 126, 134, 136, 141
Byron, Lord (George Gordon), 237

Caba, Carlos, 237
Caba, Pedro, 237
Calloway, Cab, 273
Canetti, Elias, 85
Cante jondo: musical styles, 234–6
   Cante Jondo Competition (Granada), 224, 234–40, 241
   Falla on racial origins of, 240–2
   See also: Flamenco
Carli, Mario, 188

Carpathian Mountains, 9–10
Cartography, musical, 16, 19 [Figure 1.5]
Casavola, Franco, 188
Casella, Alfredo, 186, 188, 221–2
Céline, Louis-Ferdinand, 201
Centro Sperimentale di Cinematografia, 193
Certeau, Michel de, 27
Cervantes, Miguel de, 243
Chailley, Jacques, 207
Chaleur (Sorabji) 133, 137–41, **138**
Chamberlain, Houston Stewart, 49, 51–2, 61, 91, 93, 97, 104, 115, 121
   Bloch's relationship with Chamberlain's view of Jews, 108–11
Chanson populaire (Weckerlin), 148, 160
Chansons populaires du Vivarais et du Vercors (D'Indy), 161
Chansons populaires: 148–54
   analysis of 'Chanson mexicaine', 148, **149**
   Bourgault-Ducoudray and Indo-European *chansons populaires* as 'Aryan music', 155–6
   Bourgault-Ducoudray on Breton chansons, 155
   Bourgault-Ducoudray on Greek connections of, 154
   monogenist view of, 152
   polygenist view of, 158–60
   Weckerlin on racial character of, 148
   See also: La Pernette
Chase, Gilbert, 246
Chateaubriand, François René, 231
Chisholm, Erik, 128, 130
Chopin, Frederic, 136, 158
Christophe Colombe (David), 148
Christoforidis, Michael, 230–43
Ciano, Costanzo, 194
Cilea, Francesco, 195
Cinecittà, 193
Clair, René, 204
Claudel, Paul, 207
Coeuroy, André, 212–13
Coningsby (Disraeli), 102
Conrad, Joseph, 253
Contributions to the Analysis of Sensations (Mach), 84
Contro il negrismo musicale (Marinetti), 188
Coomaraswamy, Ananda, 125, 132
Copland, Aaron, 257
Crawford, Richard, 246
Croce, Benedetto, 187, 189
Crosby, Bing, 45
Cruz, Jon, 24, 26, 28–9
Currid, Brian, 37–48

Dadaism, 186
Dahlhaus, Carl, 82
Dalton, Karen, 260
D'Ampezzo, Cortina, 194
D'Annunzio, Gabriele, 187, 206–7
Darwin, Charles, 50, 110, 152
Darwinism, 53, 248

Das Heimchen am Herd (Goldmark), 172
Das Judentum in der Musik (Berl), 179–80
Das Rassenproblem in der Musik (Blume), 19
Das Rheingold (Wagner), 98
Das Siegfried-Idyll oder Die Rückkehr zur Natur (Waltershausen), 175–6
Davenport, Charles B., 117
David, Félicien, 148
De Caro, Gaspare, 199
De Caro, Roberto, 199
De Coulanges, Fustel, 149
De Man, Paul, 201
De Quatrefages, Jean Louis Armand, 158, 167
De Schloezer, Boris, 213
Deathridge, John, 65–83
Debussy, Claude, 108, 132, 137, 175, 186
Declaration on Race, 191
Del Campo, Conrado, 216
Delage, Maurice, 132
Delius, Frederick, 121, 132
Denis, Maurice, 160
Denyer, Frank, 125
Der Dämon (Rubenstein), 172
Der Fliegende Holländer (Wagner), 90
Der Ring des Nibelungen (Wagner), 49, 72
  as referred to by Weininger, 89
Der Untergang des Abendlandes (Spengler), 179
Descent of Man, The (Darwin), 50
Diaghilev, Serge, 234
Diaspora: *See* Displacement
Dichiarazione sulla razza: *See* Declaration on Race
Die Deutsche Musik der Gegenwart (Louis), 171–3
Die deutsche Musik und unsere Feinde (Huschke), 175
Die Königin von Saba (Goldmark), 172
Die Meistersinger (Wagner), 90
Die Musik der Gegenwart (Storck), 177
Die Musik der Gegenwart und der letzten Vergangenheit (Niemann), 173
Die Musik seit Richard Wagner (Niemann), 173
Die Wibelungen (Wagner), 70, 72, 73
'Diga Diga Doo' (song by Jimmy McHugh from *Blackbirds of 1929*) 266–8, **267**
D'Indy, Vincent, 159–60, 161–6
  Symphonie, 164, 202, 210
Displacement: discourse of, 6–22
  songs bear history of, 8
Disraeli, Benjamin, 102–3, 114
Dixon, Roland, 115
'Djelem, Djelem' ('I've Traveled, I've Traveled'), 3, 4–5
Doegen, Wilhelm **16, 17, 18,** 55
Dolar, Mladen, 67
Doncieux, George, 164
Doriot, Jacques, 209
Douglas, Louis, 260, 272–3, 274, 275
Douglass, Frederick, 24
Downes, Olin, 107
Draeseke, Felix, 171
Dreyfus Affair, 103, 159

Drieu La Rochelle, Pierre, 210
Du Bois, W. E. B., 12, 32
Du cinéma sonore à la musique réelle (Honegger), 204
DuBois, Théodore, 156
Dudley, Caroline, 260

East-Western Divan Orchestra: *See* West-Eastern Divan Orchestra
Echos du temps passé (Weckerlin), 148
Eichenauer, Richard, 59–60, 61, 181, 227
El amor brujo (Falla), 224, 225, 232–3
El retablo de Maese Pedro (Falla), 243
El sentimiento nacional en la música española (Villar), 218
El sombrero de tres picos (Falla), 233
Elektra (Strauss), 173
Elgar, Edward, 252
Ellington, Duke, 32, 266, 273
Ellis, Alexander, 11
Enesco, Georges, 158
English Folk Dance Society, 254
English Folklore Society, 151
Entartete Musik: Decca recordings, 14
Ente Nazionale Industrie Cinematografiche (ENIC), 193
Erasure: racialised result of discourse of displacement, 6
Eschenbach, Wolfram von, 68
Essai sur l'inégalité des races humaines (Gobineau), 71, 75, 83, 109, 269
Eugenics, 52, 117
  French Eugenics Society, 270
  opponents to, 53
  'race hygiene', 53
  Second International Congress of (1921), 119–20
  See also: Race science
Europe, James Reese, 32
Europe: and 'governmentality', 48
  contemporary forms of nationalism, 10, 11
  East Central Europe oral traditions, 5
  European colonialism in musical representation, 12
  European uniqueness in modern conception of music, 28
  singing/song in eighteenth-century accounts of European history, 28
  Wagner's plans for cultural renewal, 69
Evans, Andrew, 56

Faccetta nera (Micheli/Ruccione), 196
Falla, Manuel de, 188, 219–21, 224, 226
  attempt to create a Spanish musical identity, 230–43
  Falla's invocations of race, 220
Fantaisie sur des thèmes populaires françaises (D'Indy), 160
Fantasia Baetica (Falla), 233
Fantasia Contrappuntistica (Busoni), 126

Farwell, Arthur, 252
'Fascinating Rhythm' (Gershwin), 44
Fascism: Fascist Italy, 182
    Fascism in France between the wars, 201, 209–10
    See also: Italy, France
Faure, Michel, 215
Ferrándiz, Manuel, Antón, 217
Fervaal (D'Indy), 159, 160
Fétis, François-Joseph, 50, 147
Film, 45, 46–7
    as tool of propaganda in Fascist Italy, 193–4
Firman, Sidney, 43
Fischer, Jens Malte, 169
Flamenco, 224, 230
    antiflamenquismo and racialised views of gypsies, 237–40
    See also: Cante jondo
Flanner, Janet, 260
Flaubert, Gustav, 130
Flers, Robert de, 261, 262
Forns, José, 217
Foucault, Michel, 47
Foundations of the Nineteenth Century, The (Chamberlain), 104
    French translation thereof, 108
    Godet's preface to French translation, 109
Fox-Strangways, Arthur, 132
France: anti-Semitism in, 202
    Celtic tradition and musical identity, 159
    chansons populaires and racial discourse, 148–54
    fascist circles between the wars, 201
    French fascism's use of music, 209–10
    See also: Chansons populaires
Franco, General Francisco, 226
Frantz, Constantin, 51
Franz Joseph, Emperor, 13
Freddi, Luigi, 193–4
Fréjaville, Gustave, 260
Freud, Siegmund, 85, 139
Friedemann Bach (Brachvogel), 39
Frogley, Alain, 244–57
Frontisme, 211–12
    Honegger's association with, 212
Fry, Andy, 258–75
Fulcher, Jane F., 201–15
Futurismo e fascismo (Marinetti), 189
Futurists: Italian Futurists and the idea of Nation, 186

Gance, Abel, 204, 206
García Lorca, Federico, 224, 234, 240, 243
Garland, Judy, 45
Gascue, Francisco, 223
Gates, Henry Louis, 260
Gatti, Guido, 113
Gautier, Judith, 233
Gautier, Théophile, 231, 237

Gerber, Arthur, 92
German Folklore Union: *Landschaftliche Volkslieder* project, 18
Germany, 41–4
    anti-Semitism in, 168
    concept of 'Germanic race', 57–8
    concept of race in German musical discourse, 49–62
    'degenerate music' exhibition, 49
    German *Sonderweg*, 50, 61
    National Socialism, 49, 168
    Pan-Germanism, 52
Gershwin, George, 44, 263
Geschichte der deutschen Musik (Moser), 178
Geschichte der Musik (Storck), 171, 177
Geschlecht und Charakter (*Sex and Character*) (Weininger), 84
    as psycho-biographical tract, 99
Ghuman, Nalini, 125–43
Gide, André, 211
Gillespie, John Birks ('Dizzy'), 274
Gillies, Malcolm, 115–24
Gilman, Sander, 96
Giménez Caballero, Ernesto, 225
Gimpera, Boch, 217
Giordano, Umberto, 195
Giuntini, Aldo, 189
Glasenapp, Carl, 72
Glinka, Mikhail, 156
Gluck, Christoph Willibald, 60
Gobineau, Joseph Arthur de, 51, 52, 71–3, 75, 76, 83, 109, 118, 147, 269, 271
    Gobineau revival in Germany, 51
    Todorov on, 83
    Wagner's meeting with, 71
Godet, Robert, 104, 108–12, 114
Goebbels, Joseph, 80–1
Goehr, Lydia, 18
Goethe, Johann, 11
Golden Cockerel, The (Rimsky-Korsakov), 141
Goldmark, Karl, 106, 171–2
Grainger, Percy Aldridge, 115–24
    Nordic ('blue-eyed') English, 123
    private views on race, 123–4
    understanding of Nordic music, 122
Granados, Enrique, 196
Grant, Madison, 118–22, 124, 250, 270
Gray, Cecil, 126–7
Grieg, Edvard, 188
Grunsky, Karl, 169, 170–1, 177
Guimet, Emile, 158
Gulistān, 133, 134, 141
Günther, Hans F. K., 59
Günther, Hans F. K., 181
Guthrie, Woody, 253
Gypsies: as stock character of operetta, 38
    explained in biological racist discourse, 39–40
    history in Europe, 37
    in Falla's attempts to represent Spain, 231–3
    See also: Romas

'Gypsy Laddie, The' (Child Ballad No. 200), 3, 4–5, 22–3
  music 22
Gypsy music: as cornerstone of Spanish musical identity, 230, 235
  as integral to *cante jondo* and flamenco, 235
  as overdetermining notions of personhood, 38
  in 'art' and salon music, 38–9
  link to jazz, 43, 44
  musician as transnational subject, 37, 41–3
  racist discourse as product of border control, 41
  relationship to modern identity, 47
  virtuosity/stardom, 38
  See also: Romas

Habermann, Michael, 127
Hajek, Leo, 15
Hall, Adelaide, 266, 268, **269**, 272
Hall, Stuart, 127
Handel, George Frideric, 60, 158
Handy, W. C., 32
Hankins, Frank H., 115
Hänsel und Gretel (Humperdinck), 172
Hanslick, Eduard, 68
Harlem Renaissance, 32, 272
Harris, Roy, 257
Harrowitz, Nancy A., 99
Hartman, Geoffrey H., 14
Hawkins, Coleman, 273
Haydn, Joseph, 60
Heinitz, Wilhelm, 59
Herder, Johann Gottfried von, 7, 50, 255
Heredity in Relation to Eugenics (Davenport), 117
Herf, Jeffrey, 11, 206
Heseltine, Philip, 129
Heyward, DuBose, 263, 266
Hill, Teddy, 274
Hindemith, Paul, 186
Histoire de la chanson populaire en France (Tiersot), 156, 160
Hitler, Adolf, 49, 61, 80–1
  as reader of Weininger, 100
Hoffmann, Stanley, 214
Hollywood, 45
Holocaust, 4, 16–19
Honegger, Arthur, 201–15
  and the journal *Plans*, 203–4
  appropriation by fascist circles in 1930s, 207
  association with Frontisme, 212
  career throughout Vichy France, 213–15
  involvement in French 'fascicising' circles, 201
  involvement in 'non-conformist' movement, 202–04
Hornbostel, Erich M. von, 11, 14, 54, 60
Hot Blood (film), 46–7
'Hot rhythm', 41, 44, 45
Hudgins, Johnny, **261**
Huebner, Steven, 159
Hughes, Langston, 33
Hugo, Victor, 231

Humperdinck, Engelbert, 168, 172
Hungary: in German imagination, 46–7
Hurston, Zora Neal, 30, 32, 33
Huschke, Konrad, 175
Hyams, Barbara, 99
Hybridity: in nineteenth-century French racial thinking, 268–9
  in Robert Young's postcolonial theory, 268–71
  Locke's view of African American culture, 33

Ibsen, Henrik, 88, 92, 95
Iceland: folk music, 57
Idelsohn, Abraham Zvi, 11, 14
Il delitto politico e le rivoluzioni (Lombroso), 185
Illiano, Roberto, 182–200
Imperio, Pastoria, 232, 239
Impressions from the Jungle Book (Scott), 139
Incantations aux fossiles (Honegger), 215
India: Sorabji's interest in Indian music, 133–41
  Sorabji's 'Indian' variations as 'Oriental Orientalist', 141–3
Indian Music (Coomaraswamy), 132
Inno a Roma (Pizzetti), 193–4
Inno a Roma (Puccini), 194
Israel Symphony (Bloch), 112
Istituto LUCE (L'Unione Cinematografica Educativa), 193, 195
Italy: Futurists and the idea of Nation, 186
  racism in Fascist Italy, 182
Ives, Charles, 251, 252

James, Henry, 249
Jāmī (Sorabji), 134, 141
Janik, Alan, 96
Janni, Mauro, 199
Jardin parfumé, Le (Sorabji), 130, 134, 136, 141
Jazz, 26, 250, 274
  as America's classical music, 26, 31
  changing views of for Italian Futurists, 188–9
  Contro il negrismo musicale (Marinetti), 188
  in Fascist Italy, 197–9
  link to racial figure of gypsy, 43, 44
  link to racial figure of Jew, 49
  link to Tin Pan Alley and Hollywood, 45
  studies, 31–2
Jean-Aubry, Georges, 220, 222
Jeanne d'Arc au bûcher (Honegger), 202, 206–8, 210
  enthusiastic reception in pro-fascist journals, 209, 212–14
Jefferson, Alan, 80
Jesus Christ, 65, 69
  as invoked by Weininger, 90
Jesus Christus unser Heiland (Bach), 166
Jewish self-hatred:*See Self-hatred*
Jews: 102, 257
  anti-Jewish laws in Fascist Italy, 199
  anti-Semitism, 49, 168, 182–3, 202, 211–12, 246
  as threat to emerging American creative independence, 250, 255

Berl on Mahler's and Schoenberg's ('Jewish') music rescuing European music, 180
Bloch's self-construction as authentic Jewish composer, 106–8
fate of music under the Nazis, xiv
Jews in Italy, 190–1
Kurt Weill's Jewish identity, 168–9
music of, 9
spirit reached via the 'barbaric', 112–14
Weininger's type Jew, 84–5
Jodl, Friedrich, 92
Johnson, James Weldon, 31, 32, 35
Jolson, Al, 45
Joyce, James, 85
Jung, Guido, 190
Jungle Book (Kipling), 139

Kafka, Franz, 85
Kaiser, Joachim, 82
Kalman, Emmerich, 38
Katz, Mark, 34–5
Kelley, Robin D. G., 26
Kindertotenlieder (Mahler), 179
Kipling, Rudyard, 116, 118, 139
Klinger, Max, 94
Kodály, Zoltán, 58, 188
Koechlin, Charles, 208
Köhler, Wolfgang, 60
Korngold, Erich Wolfgang, 177, 180
Kramer, Gorni, 198
Kraus, Karl, 85, 96–7, 169
Ku Klux Klan, 256

La musica futurista (Casavola), 188
La vida breve (Falla), 231
LaCapra, Dominik, 17
Lach, Robert, 54, 55, 58–9
Lachmann, Robert, 60
Lagarde, Paul, 51
Lagardelle, Hubert, 214
Lamour, Philippe, 203
Landschaftliche Volkslieder project, 18
Lapouge, Georges Vacher de, 270
Le Bon, Gustave, 104, 159
Le Corbusier (Charles-Edouard Jeanneret), 204, 206, 207
Le Crépuscule des nations blanches (Muret), 269
Le Rider, Jacques, 91, 97
Lee, Spike, 258
Léger, Fernand, 204
Lehár, Franz, 38
Leifs, Jón, 57
Leiris, Michel, 265–6, 274
Léry, Jean de, 7
Les Lois psychologiques de l'évolution (Le Bon), 159
Leschetizky, Theodor, 253
Leslie, Lew, 261
Lessing, Theodor, 96
Lessona, Alessandro, 196
Levi, Erik, 18, 100, 168–81

Levi, Hermann, 69
Levine, James, 82
Levinson, André, 263, 263, 271, 272
Lifar, Serge, 211
Liszt, Franz, 5, 38, 136, 141, 158
Liza: See *Revue nègres*
Locke, Alain, 26, 32–4
Lohengrin (Wagner), 90
Lomax, John, 253
Lombroso, Cesare: influence on PNF (Italy), 184–5
Lorenz, Alfred, 57
Lorenz, Ottokar, 57
Lott, Eric, 44
Louis, Rudolf, 169, 171–3, 176, 179
Lualdi, Adriano, 198
Lucka, Emil, 93, 94, 97
Ludwig II, King, 68–70, 74, 83
Lully, Jean-Baptiste, 148
L'uomo delinquente (Lombroso), 184

Macedonia: new forms of racism, 8
Mach, Ernst, 84
Machado y Álvarez, Antonio, 231, 236
Machines agricoles (Milhaud), 186
McHugh, Jimmy, 266
Maeztu, Ramiro de, 226
Magee, Bryan, 79–80
Mahler, Gustav, 79, 128, 133, 174, 175–80
negative critiques of Mahler's music as Jewish, 172–3, 177–9
positive critique of Mahler's music as Jewish, 180
Mairena, Antonio, 236
Malicious and Perverse Variation on Ase's Death by Grieg (Sorabji), 136
Manifesto futurista dell'aeromusica sintetica geometrica e curativa (Marinetti and Giuntini), 189
Manzanares, Vicente, 237
Manzano Pabanó, Francisco, 233
Marinetti, Filippo Tommaso, 186, 187, 188–9
Mario, E. A., 192
Martial, René, 270
Marx, Karl, 110
Mascagni, Pietro, 188, 192, 197
Mason, Daniel Gregory, 245–7, 250–6
Massenet, Jules, 195
Massin, Benoit, 52
Massine, Léonide, 234
Masters, Edgar Lee, 119
Maurras, Charles, 214
Mayakovsky, Vladimir, 187
Medtner, Nicolas, 125
Mélodies populaires des provinces de la France (Tiersot), 161
Mendelssohn, Felix, 106, 170–1, 178
Menéndez Pelayo, Marcelino, 217
Mérimée, Prosper, 237
Merlin (Goldmark), 172

Meyerbeer, Giacomo, 106, 170–1, 178
Mi Contra Fa (Sorabji), 125
Micheli, Renato, 196
Milhaud, Darius, 186, 260
Miller, H. J. W., 142
Mills, Florence, **261**, 268,
    271, 275
    compared with Josephine Baker, 263–3
Minstrelsy: *See Blackface minstrelsy*
Mistral, Frédéric, 151
Modernism/Modernity, 43–4, 46, 76
    American 'new immigration' as
        symptom, 249
    racialised attacks on modernism, 57
    represented in spirituals and jazz, 35
Montaigne, Michel de, 7
Moore, Macdonald Smith, 251
Morel, Bénédict August, 71
Móricz, Klára, 102–14
Moser, Hans-Joachim, 169, 178–9
Mozart, Wolfgang Amadeus, 58, 60,
    158, 171, 219
Mules and Men (Hurston), 30
Müller, Laurenz, 92
Muret, Maurice, 269
Murgía, Manuel, 217
Murray, Albert, 30
*Music and Some Highly Musical
    People* (Trotter), 27
Musik und Rasse (Eichenauer), 59
Musikgeschichte des 19. Jahrhunderts
    (Grunsky), 170–1
Mussolini, Benito, 183, 189–90, 193–4,
    199, 203, 205, 214
Mussorgsky, Modest Petrovich, 58, 108, 112

Naipaul, V. S., 131, 142
National Fascist Party (Italy): racialised thinking
    within, 184
Nationalism: Bloch's distinction from 'racial
    consciousness', 107
    contemporary forms of European, 10
    narratives of, 5
Nazi musicology, 18
Neue Ästhetik der musikalischen Impotenz
    (Pfitzner), 176
New Negro, The (Locke), 32
Newman, Ernest, 70
Nichols, Beverley, 134
Nicolodi, Fiamma, 186
Niemann, Walter, 169, 173–4, 179
Nietzsche, Friedrich, 11, 88
Noches en los jardines de España (Falla), 232
Noel, Eugenio, 238–40
Nordic race, 57, 248
    American Nordicists, 115–24
    Eichenauer on, 59–60
    Grainger's understanding of, 121–2
    Nordicism, 115
Núñez de Arce, Gaspar de, 237

Ocón, Eduardo, 231
Olóriz Aguilera, Federico, 217
Opus Clavicembalisticum (Sorabji), 126, 130,
    133–4, 136
    'Quasi tambura' variation, 134–9, **135**
Opuscules sur la chanson populaire
    (Weckerlin), 153
Orientalism: and Sorabji, 130–2
    Sorabji's music as 'Oriental Orientalist', 141–3
    Sorabji's notion of Orientalist music, 132
Ors, Eugenio d', 221
Ortega y Gasset, José, 218, 237
Osborn, Henry Fairfield, 119
Other: and ownership of music, 7
    expressed in music, 12
    racialised as result of being without place, 7

Pacific 231 (Honegger), 207
Palestrina (Pfitzner), 176
Palestrina, Giovanni Pierluigi da, 51
Panassié, Hugues, 274
Parade (Satie), 186
Paris, Gaston, 151
Parker, Horatio, 251, 252
Parsifal (Wagner), 65–83, 77, **78**, **79**, 172
    and Otto Weininger, 88, 91, 92, 98
    performances of during Second World
        War, 79
Partito Nationale Fascista (PNF): *See National
    Fascist Party*
Parzival (Eschenbach), 68
Pas d'acier (Prokofiev), 186
Pasler, Jann, 147–67
Passing of the Great Race, The (Grant), 118, 270
Paxton, Robert, 211
Pear, David, 115–124
Pedrell, Felipe, 219, 241
Peer Gynt (Ibsen): as referred to by
    Weininger, 88, 95
Pérez-Zalduondo, Gemma, 216–29
Pernette, La: analysis of several notated versions
    160–6, **162**, **165**, **166**
Peyton, Dave, 32
Pfitzner, Hans, 57, 62, 168, 171, 176–7, 180, 225
    as reader of Weininger, 85, 100–1
Phaedre (Honegger), 206
'Phurde, bajval, phurde' ('Blow, Wind, Blow',
    Nikolic-Lakatos), 19–21
Pizzetti, Ildebrando, 184, 193–4
Plans (journal), 203–4, 207, 208
    'planisme', 205–6, 214
PNF (Partito Nationale Fascista): *See National
    Fascist Party*
Por nuestra música (Pedrell), 219
Porgy (play by Heyward), 263
'Porgy' (song by Jimmy McHugh from
    Blackbirds of 1929) 266, **266**
Porter, Eric, 31–2
Pott, August Friedrich, 72, 83
Potter, Pamela M., 18, 49–62, 101, 169, 181, 227

Poulenc, Francis, 202
Pound, Ezra, 201
Powell, John, 252–6
   aggressive racism thereof, 254–6
   lecture on 'Music and the Nation', 254
Pratella, Francesco Balilla, 186, 187–8
Preziosi, Giovanni, 182
Probst, Ferdinand, 97
Prokofiev, Sergey, 186
Protocols of the Learned Elders of Sion, 182
Puccini, Giacomo, 175, 183, 194, 195

'Quasi rag indiana' (Sorabji), 133
'Quasi tambura' (Sorabji), 133

'Race music', 34
Race science: and gypsy music, 39–40
   and the science of music, 11–12, 14–19
   as appropriated by European scholarship, 10
   as product of 'governmentality', 47
   musical experiments in First World War prisoner-of-war camps, 15, 53–5
   relation between language and physical traits, 52–3, 147
   traces in contemporary music trade journals, 25
   See also: Eugenics
Race: as buzzword, 53, 56
   and characterology, 85
   association with biological difference, 25
   cultural race, 36
   miscegenation and Powell's notion of Anglo-Saxon folk song, 254
   monogenesis, 74, 268
   monogenesis and French *chansons populaires*, 151, 152
   'musical acclimatisation' in *chansons populaires*, 152, 157–8
   origins of concept in music, 50
   polygenesis, 74, 268
   polygenesis and French *chansons populaires*, 151, 158–60
   race spirit reached via the 'barbaric', 112–14
   racial consciousness versus nationalism, 107
   'racial soul', 59
   social race, 36
   theoretical race, 36
   See also: Hybridity
Rachmaninov, Sergei, 121
Racial Realities in Europe (Stoddard), 118
Radano, Ronald, xiv, xix, 24, 29–30, 44, 143, 229
Radio, 41–3
   as tool of propaganda in Fascist Italy, 194–6
Rameau, Jean-Philippe, 148
Ramsey, Guthrie P. Jr, 24–36
Rapoport, Paul, 136
Rappaport, Moritz, 92, 94, 96, 97
Ravel, Maurice, 132, 137, 225
Rebatet, Lucien, 212
Recording technology: *See Sound recordings*

Reger, Max, 134, 172, 173
Reinhardt, Max, 169
Renan, Ernest, 150, 151
Revelge (Mahler), 179
Revolt against Civilization: The Menace of the Under Man, The (Stoddard), 118
Revues nègres: La Revue nègre, 260
   Blackbirds, 261–72
   Blackbirds of 1926, 261, **261**
   Blackbirds of 1928, 263
   Blackbirds of 1929, 263, **264**, 266–8, **268**, **269**, 271, 272
   Liza, 272–3
   Black Flowers, 271
   Harlem Black Birds 36, 274
Rhapsodie Nègre (Powell), 253
Ribera, Julián, 242
Rimsky-Korsakov, Nikolay Andreyevich, 105, 141, 195
Ripley, William, 117–18, 120
Rising Tide of Color against White World-Supremacy, The (Stoddard), 118
Rite of Spring (Stravinsky), 112, 232
Robinson, Clarence, 274
Rodgers, Joel A., 32
Rodin, Auguste, 253
Rodlauer, Hannelore, 91
Rolland, Romain, 139, 156, 206
Romagna (Pratella), 187, 188
Romancero gitano (García Lorca), 224, 240
Romas, 4
   as subject of English-language songs, 10
   music of, 9–10, 19–22
   See also: Gypsies, Gypsy music
Roosevelt, Theodore, 120
Rosenberg, Alfred, 79–80
Rosenfeld, Paul, 105–7
Rousseau, Jean-Jacques, 50
Roussel, Albert, 132
Rubenstein, Ida, 206, 207, 213
Rubinstein, Anton, 106, 172
Ruccione, Mario, 196

Saami: repertories, 9
Sachs, Curt, 54, 60
Said, Edward, 127, 130
   association with West-Eastern Divan Orchestra, 14
Sainte-Hilaire, Isidore Geoffroy, 152, 156
Saint-Saëns, Camille, 158
Sáinz de la Maza, Regino, 225, 227
Sala, Massimiliano, 182–200
Salas Viu, Vincente, 222
Salazar, Adolfo, 220–1, 222, 224–5, 240, 241
Santarelli, Emilio, 188
Sarfatti, Margherita, 190
Satie, Erik, 186
Scandinavianism, 115
Schelomo (Bloch), 113
Schemann, Ludwig, 51, 71

Schering, Arnold, 57
Schneider, Marius, 60, 227
Schneider, William, 270
Schoenberg, Arnold, 85, 177, 180, 220, 221
 Berl on Schoenberg's ('Jewish') music rescuing European music, 180
Schola Cantorum, 167, 210
Schopenhauer, Arthur, 65, 68, 76, 81, 87, 97
Schreker, Franz, 85, 176, 177
Schubert, Franz, 60, 173, 219
Schuchardt, Hugo, 231
Schuller, Gunther, 274
Schultze-Naumburg, Paul, 59
Schumann, Robert, 60, 158, 171
Schünemann, Georg, 15, 16, 55
Schuré, Edouard, 159
Schwarzkopf, Elisabeth, 80
Science, race: See Race science
Scipione l'Africano (film), 193–4
Scott, Cyril, 139
Self and ownership of music, 7
'Self-hatred': Weininger's understanding of, 95–6
 'Jewish self-hatred', 96–100, 104
 'Misautisch', 96
 objections to concept of Jewish self-hatred, 96
Sengoopta, Chandak, 85
Serbia: new forms of racism, 8
Sex and Character (Weininger): See *Geschlecht und Charakter*
Sharp, Cecil, 254
 Anglo-Saxon racial agenda of, 254
Siegfried (Wagner), 74, 98
Silence: in scholarship, 16–19
 See also: Taboo; Trauma
Singin' in the Rain (film), 45
Sketch of a New Esthetic of Music (Busoni), 134
Skryabin, Aleksandr Nikolayevich, 127, 141
Société des traditions populaires, 151, 154
Society for Comparative Musicology, 60
Sonderweg, German: See Germany
Sorabji, Kaikhosru Shapurji (Leon Dudley), 125
 Indian, then Parsi racial self-identification, 129–30
 interest in Indian music, 133–41
 interest in Persian poets, 130
 victim of Orientalism, 130–2
Sorel, Georges, 205, 214
Souls of Black Folk, The (DuBois), 12
Sound recordings, 34–5, 55
 as privileging sound over printed score, 34
Spaeth, Siegmund, 106
Spain: concept of 'raza' as Spanish people, 217
 Falangism's fascination for German Nazism, 227
 Latinism, 222
 Mediterraneanism, 221, 225–6
 peripheral nationalisms and the race question, 223–5
 'raza' as soul of a regional group of people, 217
 'raza' as synonym for Catholicism, 218, 226–8
 'raza' with rare biological connotations, 217
 'Spanishness' (Hispanidad), 225–6
 See also: Falla; Flamenco; Cante jondo; Gypsies
Specht, Richard, 178
'Special relationship', 247. See also: Anglo-Saxonism
Spender, Stephen, 201
Spengler, Oswald, 85, 179–80
Spirituals and slave songs, African-American, 24, 26, 44
 aestheticised, 26
Spotts, Friedrich, 79–80
Spratt, Geoffrey, 215
Stein, Gerhard, 40
Steingress, Gerhard, 230, 235
Sternhell, Zeev, 209
Stoddard, Lothrop, 118–21, 250
Storck, Karl, 169, 171, 177–9
Strauss, Richard, 141, 168, 172, 173, 201, 220, 251
Stravinsky, Igor, 112, 188, 234
Ström, Ella, 115
Stumpf, Carl, 11, 15, 54, 55
Suite 1922 (Hindemith), 186
'Swanee' (Gershwin), 44
Swoboda, Hermann, 99
Symphonic Variations for Piano Solo (Sorabji), 139
 'Quasi rāg indiana', 139, 140
Symphonie sur un chant montagnard français (D'Indy), 160
Szymanowski, Karol, 132

Taboo, 16
 See also: Silence in scholarship
Taine, Hippolyte Adolphe, 104
Tantrik Symphony for Piano Alone (Sorabji), 133
Tchaikovsky, Pyotr Il'yich, 121
The Music of Hindostan (Fox-Strangways), 132
Thomas, Ambroise, 195
Three Jewish Poems (Bloch), 111–12
Tiersot, Julian, 154, 159, 160–7
Tin Pan Alley, 45
Tocqueville, Alexis de, 83
Todorov, Tzvetan, 66, 71, 83
Tomlinson, Gary, 18, 27–8, 34, 35
Traité des dégénérescences physiques, intellectuelles et morales de l'espèce humaine et de ses causes qui produisent ces variétés maladives (Morel), 71
Trakl, Georg, 85
Transcription, 28–9
 as transforming African Americans into 'subjects', 29
 as transforming music into modern scientific artefact, 26
 Gary Tomlinson on musical orality versus musical literacy, 27–8
Trauma: and historical representation, 16–19
Travellers in the United Kingdom and Ireland, 9
 repertories, 9

Tristan und Isolde (Wagner), 68, 88, 98
Trotter, James Monroe, 27
Turina, Joaquín, 228, 240

Über die letzten Dinge (*On Last Things*) (Weininger), 84
Unamuno, Miguel de, 222, 237, 239
United States: history of African Americans, 37
  and 'governmentality', 48

Valois, Georges, 205–6, 209
Van Dieren, Bernard, 132
Vaughan Williams, Ralph, 252, 255
Villar, Rogelio, 218, 219, 223
Virchow, Rudolf, 53
Völkerschauen, 54–5
Volkslieder (Herder), 7
Von Waltershausen, Hermann Wolfgang, 175–7
Voss, Egon, 76

Wagner, Cosima, 66, 73, 81
Wagner, Nike, 88, 91, 92, 93
Wagner, Richard: 61, 65–83, 97, 113, 121, 157, 159, 161, 201, 219–21
  anti-Semitism of, 14, 49–51, 58, 102–7
  Bloch's relationship with Wagner's view of Jews, 106–8
  influence on Otto Weininger, 84–101
  'Judaism in Music', 50, 70, 91, 100, 103, 169–81, 184
  own supposed racial make-up, 60, 90–1
  performances in Israel, 16–17
  positive attitude towards Jews, 69–70
  regarding Jews as incapable of miscegenation, 81
Wagner, Wieland, 81
Wagner, Wolfgang, 81

Wallaschek, Richard, 54
War, First World: experiments in First World War prisoner-of-war camps, 15
War, Second World: performances of *Parsifal* during, 79
Ward, Aida 266, 268, **269**
Warlock, Peter: *See Philip Heseltine*
Waters, Ethel, 263
Webern, Anton, 85, 221
Weckerlin, Jean-Baptiste, 148–67
Weill, Kurt, 168–9
Weimar Republic: gypsy bands, 43
  musicology, 18
Weininger, Otto, 84–101, 115, 169
Weismann, August, 118
Weissmann, Adolf, 58
Werfel, Franz, 169
Wertheimer, Max, 60
Wesendonck, Mathilde, 68
West-Eastern Divan Orchestra, 14
White, Owen, 270
Whitman, Walt, 116
Wilson, President Woodrow, 253
Winfeld, Felix, 273
Wittgenstein, Ludwig, 85
Wolf, Johannes, 55
Wolzogen, Hans von, 66
World music, 7

Young, Robert, 74, 268–9

Zandonai, Riccardo, 196
Zelinsky, Hartmut, 65, 81–2, 91
Zemlinsky, Alexander, 85
Zigeunerliebe (Lehár), 38
Zigeunerprímas, Der (Kalman), 38
Žižek, Slavoj, 67, 86
Zuberi, Tukufu, 24, 25, 29
Zweig, Stefan, 85